UNIVERSITY OF SAINT JOSEPH

3 2528 12656 0343

Culture and Crisis

D1522919

CULTURE AND CRISIS
The Case of Germany and Sweden

Edited by
Nina Witoszek and Lars Trägårdh

Berghahn Books
New York • Oxford

First published in 2002 by

Berghahn Books

www.berghahnbooks.com

First paperback edition printed in 2004

Copyright © 2002 Nina Witoszek and Lars Trägårdh

All rights reserved. Except for the quotation of short passages for the purpose of criticism and review, no part of this book may be reproduced in any form or by any means, electronic or mechanical, including photocopying, recording, or any information storage and retrieval system now known or to be invented, without written permission of the publisher.

Library of Congress Cataloguing-in-Publication Data

Culture and crisis : the case of Germany and Sweden / edited by Nina Witoszek and Lars Trägårdh.
    p. cm.
  "This volume was inspired by the seminars of the project Gemenskap at the European University in Florence, and in particular by the conference on 'Crisis in Germany and Scandinavia' that took place in Pratolino in September 1997"--Prelim. p.
  Includes bibliographical references and index.
  ISBN 1-57181-269-5 (cl: alk. paper) - ISBN 1-57181-270-9 (pbk.: alk. paper)
    1. Germany--Intellectual life. 2. Sweden--Intellectual life. 3. Germany--Historiography. 4. Sweden--Historiography. 5. Sweden--Social conditions. 6. Germany--Social conditions--20th century. 7. National socialism--Psychological aspects. I. Witoszek, Nina. II. Trägårdh, Lars.

DD61 .C85 2002
943--dc21   2002018401

British Library Cataloguing in Publication Data

A catalogue record for this book is available from the British Library.

Printed in United Kingdom by Biddles / IBT Global

Cover photos:

Sven Boberg: 'Sleep in Peace' (1910)
The Museum of Sketches, Lund, Sweden
Photo: Christina Knutsson

Friedrich August von Kaulbach: 'Germania' (1914)
© Deutsches Historisches Museum

Contents

Contributors

Piero Colla is currently completing a Ph.D. in Social Sciences at Ecole des Hautes Etudes en Sciences Sociales in Paris. His publications include numerous essays on the Swedish welfare state, eugenics, and national identity, including the book *Per la Nazione e per la Razza*.

Manfred Henningsen is Professor of Political Science at the University of Hawaii in Honolulu. He has published a study on European anti-Americanism (*Der Fall Amerika*) and *Erik Voegelin's Modernity Without Restraint* (1999). He is also a regular contributor to the German cultural journal *Merkur*.

Yvonne Hirdman is Professor of Gender History at the National Institute for Working Life and the History Department at Stockholm University. She has published extensively on contemporary Swedish history with a special focus on the Labor Movement and the Welfare State.

Reinhart Koselleck is Professor Emeritus at the University of Bielfeld and the author of the influential *Critique and Crisis: Enlightenment and the Pathogenesis of Modern Society* (1985), among many other works.

Benjamin Lapp is Associate Professor at the History Department of Montclaire State University. He is the author of *Revolution from the Right: Politics, Class, and the Rise of Nazism in Saxony, 1919–1933*.

Erik Ringmar is Associate Professor at the Department of Political Science, London School of Economics. His publications include *Identity, Interest and Action: A Cultural Explanation of Sweden's Intervention in the Thirty Years' War* (1996).

Göran Rosenberg is the founder and former editor of the major Swedish cultural journal *Moderna Tider*. He is the author of *Det förlorade landet, en personlig historia (Lost Land, a Personal History of Zionism, Messianism and the State* *of Israel,* published also in French, Dutch, Danish, Norwegian, and German). His TV documentaries ("The Black City and the White House" and "Goethe and Ghetto") won prizes at international festivals in Monte Carlo and Prague.

Lars Trägårdh is Assistant Professor at the History Department of Barnard College, Columbia University, New York. He has written extensively on the history of Swedish and German political culture, and he also publishes regularly in the leading Swedish newspaper *Dagens Nyheter.*

Robert Wokler is a professor at the History Department, University of Exeter and at Budapest University, and an editor of the Cambridge University Press Eighteenth Century History Series. His publications include *Rousseau* (1997) and *Diderot: Political Writings* (1996).

Nina Witoszek is Director of Research/Associate Professor at the Center for Development and the Environment, Oslo University and a Fellow at Mansfield College, Oxford University. Her publications include *Talking to the Dead: A Study in Irish Traditions* (1998) and *The Postmodern Challenge: Perspectives East and West* (1999), and *Norske naturmytologier: Fra Edda til Økofilosofi* (1998).

Acknowledgments

This volume was inspired by the seminars of the project *Gemenskap* at the European University in Florence, and in particular by the conference on "Crisis in Germany and Scandinavia" that took place in Pratolino in September 1997. The authors would like to thank the directors of the project, Professor Bo Stråth and Professor Bernd Henningsen, for their encouragement and patience. The completion of the book has been made possible by the financial support of the *Habitus* Project at the National University of Ireland in Galway, and by a grant from the Norwegian Research Council. Finally, we owe a debt of gratitude to Prof. Pat Sheeran and Dr. William O'Reilly, whose insights and advice were invaluable in revising the essays. We also wish to thank Helen Litton for her technical assistance in the work on the volume.

Introduction

NINA WITOSZEK AND LARS TRÄGÅRDH

Among the many ways to evaluate the achievements of different societies, two are especially striking. For the romantic poet William Blake (as later for Nietzsche) a civilization was to be assessed by the status accorded to genius; for the philosopher Locke by the tolerance extended to mediocrity. The twentieth century has witnessed two exemplary embodiments of these positions and their corresponding myths of the Superman and Everyman. For a long time in the European imagination, Germany was Blakean, Scandinavia was Lockean.

It is tempting to suggest that the first myth produced the Faustian *Übermensch*, the second the "gray heroism" of the middle way. In the first, self-realization was linked to hate and death (Hitler pronounced happiness to be the domain of cows and Englishmen), in the second, to communal wellbeing. One yielded authoritarian tyranny, the other the gentle despotism of an average Mr. Svensson. The first privileged *zaum* (an eloquent Russian word meaning "bypassing reason"); the second deified rationality. In one, what might be called the coral reef mentality was of paramount importance; in the other individual autonomy. One pursued revolution, the other rapprochement and consensus. One was Dionysian, the other Apollonian.

Today, of course, such hard and fast oppositions are more and more suspect. If there is such a thing as a "whore with a heart of gold," then Sweden increasingly reveals itself as an ex-virgin with the heart of a whore (cf. Myrdal, Jr's. "whores of reason"). Comparisons of the Swedish system to totalitarian regimes, once incidental and subdued, are now more pronounced, even in fashion. Recently a number of studies have revealed the basic "powerlessness" of the individual in what was once regarded as the most democratic society in the world. There is even talk about a Swedish *folkhem* variant of "fascism," a notion dramatically reinforced by the recent

Notes for this section begin on page 10.

debate on the very high rates of forced sterilization carried out in the name of national health during the heyday of Social Democracy.[1] In short, Sweden is no longer–perhaps never was–the moral summit of the Western world.

Much of the current critical deconstruction of the Swedish model is not only revealing in itself but also long overdue. At the same time a degree of caution is warranted: easy and uncritical labeling of everything from white male domination to the social-democratic welfare state as fascism and total-itarianism, obliterates that which makes cultures, institutions, and ideologies different from one another. True, even a cursory review of nineteenth- and early twentieth-century developments in Germany or Sweden reveals a number of affinities in the spheres of science, education, art, politics, and myth-making.[2] Yet, for all their mutual cross-fertilization, Sweden and Germany embraced two opposing self-images and followed two different trajec-tories of modernization.

One of the most fascinating areas of exploration and comparison is that of the opposing political strategies used by Sweden and Germany to tackle the economic crises of the 1920s and 1930s. In both countries the years of slump were marked by an intense glorification of national community. Both romanced, though in different ways, national socialism as a way out of their predicament. In both cases there followed an extraordinary identification of people, nation, and political leadership. Last but not least, in both countries Christianity was challenged by the quasi-religion of the state or, more accu-rately in the case of Sweden, by the *sacralization* of the social-democratic ethos. Yet one yielded an ecstatic Romantic cult of the *Übermensch*, whereas the other fetishized a rationalist-humanist vision of the "good state." In Nazi Germany it was the *Volk* as Race and *Ethnos* that became an object of idola-try. In Sweden, the Social Democrats managed to channel the need for *gemen-skap* into a kind of civil religion based on their dual perception of themselves as inheritors of the reassuring tradition of the absolutist state as well as the democratic voice of the people (folk as *Demos*). Here, the Social Democratic Party came to function simultaneously as both King and People.

Numerous questions present themselves. Why have the semiotic refer-ents of Swedish identity–based, as in Germany, on salient emblems of nature–never upset the balance of primordial and civic ingredients? Why, in this case, were blood-and-soil allegiances so elegantly tempered by doctrines of liberalism and individual autonomy? Why is it that the Swedish peasant came to personify the received wisdom that Swedes had democracy in the blood, while his German counterpart came to symbolize the fundamental incom-patibility of Germany and democracy? Is it simply differing sociopolitical structures and economic predicaments that explain the opposing responses to the challenge of modernization?

The aim of this volume is threefold. Firstly, it enquires into the ways in which cultural preconceptions inform, enable, and limit what is politically and economically possible in a world of ostensibly rational interest. Secondly, by focusing on the empowering traditions of two charismatic European cultures, it sets out to interrogate–and reevaluate–the conventional perceptions of the Enlightenment legacy. Thirdly, it aims to throw light on the much-neglected cultural dimension of European integration, especially on the ways in which varying cultural traditions support or conflict with the challenge of European citizenship.

The Concept of Crisis

We have decided that a useful starting point–and a lens through which to inspect the Swedish and German responses to modernization–is the notion of crisis. Reinhart Koselleck's opening piece provides us with an introduction to the conceptual history of "crisis," outlining the historical, semantic, and theological dimensions of the concept and illuminating the ways in which today the notion of crisis has become "an inalienable aspect of our everyday world." Building on his first major work, *Kritik und Krise,* Koselleck associates modernity with crisis. The very subtitle of that seminal book–"Enlightenment and the Pathogenesis of Modern Society"–suggests a rather bleak view of the Enlightenment legacy. Indeed, he declares, "Europe's history has broadened; it has become world history and will run its course as that, having allowed the whole world to drift into a state of permanent crisis."[3] This state of affairs is linked to the internal logic of a new political order in which "critique" inevitably produces a continuing crisis, but it is also a consequence of the acceleration of time, which, Koselleck argues, has meant that the "space of experience" has shrunk, leaving man with uncertain, utopian visions at "the horizon of expectation." Quoting Tocqueville, he laments that "as the past has ceased to throw its light upon the future, the mind of man wanders in obscurity." [4] Zygmunt Bauman shares this perception, and has suggested that "crisis, in as far as the notion refers to the invalidation of customary ways and means and the resulting lack of certainty as to how to go on, is the normal state of human society."[5]

Like many things postmodern, the crisis-as-normality approach is both new and old,[6] if only because the perception of crisis as happening at every moment is manifest already in the Gospel of St. John. More problematically, by treating crisis as a constant attribute of life, one deprives the term of any heuristic value. If crisis happens all the time, then there is no crisis. The ubiquity of crisis rhetoric obliterates the fact that for certain cultures–Ireland or Poland, to mention but two–the end of the millennium signals less another breakdown than a long-awaited exit out of enduring political, cultural, and economic impasses.

Our choice of the notion of crisis as the key analytical category has been prompted both by the strongly felt necessity to reevaluate the accepted *doxa*

on the apocalyptic side of modernity, and by the polarizing, clarifying function of crisis with regard to community's central values. Hence we have
chosen to draw on classical definitions of crisis: Tillich's *kairos,* Jasper's
"boundary situation," Rokkan's "critical junctures," and Habermas's theory
of crisis as the opposite of normality, a break with the past, a moment of
choice and decision. Unlike the more mundane "problem," which is a difficulty whose solution does not bring into question established fundamental
values and meanings, a crisis calls for momentous paradigm shifts and reeval-
uations. It is a moment of creativity when new modes of thinking and new
habits come into play. At the same time, for all the innovation, daring symbolic crusades, and new lifestyles that come in its train, a crisis tends to bring
the past, or at least an imagined past, back into the present. The examples of
Sweden and Germany demonstrate the extent to which successful solutions to
national trauma demand a sanction from tradition, however transmuted or
modified by current need. The past is mobilized, not just because it offers a
dizzying release from choice. Crisis is always a déjà vu experience; it invokes
the memory of past imbroglios, solutions, and failures and exhumes authoritative narratives that prompt a community what to feel and how to respond
to new challenges.

Community and Crisis: The Legacy of Culture and Identity

As a "drama of recollection," crisis inevitably forces communal identity to the
fore. Indeed, there is a sense in which national identity is crisis-bound, man-
ifesting itself with special force not in situations of equilibrium but in
moments of threat and insecurity. To invoke Karl Polanyi, it is during times
of "great transformation", when the very idea of community appears to be
under siege, that its explicit defense becomes a rallying cry.[7] At such
moments culture and identity, which have hitherto been as unnoticed and
ubiquitous as the air we breathe, suddenly become perceptible and significant, and the founding tradition of a community reveals its potency.

The cases of Sweden and Germany suggest that crises like those of the
1920s and 1930s, or more recent ones, can be thought of in radically different ways. On the one hand, the crisis may appear to be terminal, proof that
a certain way of life–say, that of the Weimar Republic–is fatally diseased. On
the other, crisis may be perceived as a temporary fever, possibly induced by
a foreign virus, something to be dealt with, whereupon health and "normality"–represented, say, by Swedish democracy–will be recovered.

The web of connections linking crisis, memory, identity, and social change
provides a useful context for identifying the magnetic cores or values around
which cultures are configured. It is important to ask at what point a social, economic, or cultural problem is redefined as a crisis. Who are its chief codifiers?

Are they mainly highly visible politicians and experts–Hitler, Himmler, Branting, Wigforss, Alva and Gunnar Myrdal–or are they also the less visible agents of national *Bildung*: writers, priests, and philosophers? What accounts of crisis filter down through the authorized and marginalized narratives of a community? What old and new myths sustain communities in peril? What exactly is remembered and what is forgotten? And what is the connection between narrativity and violence, between text and social performance? Can we talk about any enduring semiotic traditions or deeply ingrained "cultural scripts" that facilitate the emergence of paramilitary gangs in one case and inspire the pacifist ideals of study groups at Folk High Schools in the other?

Questions such as these are central to several of the contributions to this volume. Erik Ringmar's comparative study focuses on the crucial phases of the European passage to modernity in an attempt to identify the institutional mechanisms that brought about the crisis of political culture in Germany and prevented it in Sweden. In her analysis of the Social Democratic discourse of the 1930s in Sweden, Yvonne Hirdman demonstrates the ways in which the concept of crisis was "invented," codified and deployed by the Swedish political and scientific establishment with Alva and Gunnar Myrdal and other Social Democrats in the lead. Göran Rosenberg's essay draws attention to the merits–but also the hazards–of Swedish myths and rhetoric of consensus. In the past they informed enlightened solutions to social and political dilemmas, but today they exacerbate rather than assuage the crisis of political and social institutions in the country. Nina Witoszek asks in what way elements of the dominant ethos in Swedish and German society facilitated the acceptance of particular "rescue packages" put forward by political leaders at times of crisis. She compares the durable ethical patterns, role models, and scenarios of action that dominated school curricula, religious education, family values, community ethos, and national aspirations over an extended period of time. Crucial to this comparison is Hannah Arendt's distinction between the "voice of conscience" and public imperatives, between a "good man" and a "good citizen."[8] Similarly, Piero Colla's analysis of the notion of citizenship and the long repressed Swedish memory of World War II shows how the premises of civil behavior need not necessarily be destroyed only by totalitarian oppression but may be dismantled under democratic conditions. This is demonstrated by the sad Swedish record in the 1930s and 1940s with respect to forced sterilization of "unfit" Swedish citizens at home and the denial of entry of Jewish refugees from Nazi Germany.

Crisis and Modernity

Koselleck's linkage of modernity and crisis identifies Nazism as a distinctly modern pathology, part of a larger, endemic "crisis of the Western world." As

Ben Lapp's close reading of several accounts on the genesis and character of Nazism suggests, this is indeed one important line of interpretation of the German descent into Nazi dictatorship. Ranging from Adorno and Horkheimer's *The Dialectic of the Enlightenment* to Detlev Peukert's more recent but similarly influential analysis of National Socialism in Germany, these works tend to argue that, as Christopher Browning has put it, National Socialism is not an aberration of Western civilization but rather the "culmination of certain of its tendencies."[9] However, Lapp argues, an equally powerful model seeks to show that the roots of the Holocaust must be sought not in a general pathology of Enlightenment rationality but in a specific "German ideology" (George Mosse), in the "mind of Germany" (Hans Kohn), and most specifically in a deep-rooted culture of "eliminationist anti-Semitism" (Goldhagen).[10]

This focus on German peculiarity plays a crucial role outside Germany. Thus "Germany" is often transformed into an imagined space of pure evil in comparison with which "we" can be imagined as relatively "good," or as the victims of such evil. In this vein, Manfred Henningsen focuses on collective memory and the crisis of national identity in present-day Germany. Henningsen contends that the German catastrophe has become a central component of a globalized memory of World War II, with Germans linked to images of death and tyranny. In the process of this globalization of German public memory, as he points out, German historians could not keep control over German history in Germany. Instead, ownership of the Holocaust has become a contested matter, with German historians competing with American Jews for whom the Holocaust is a central site of collective memory.

The most fruitful approach may be the one that sees Nazism as both distinctly German and as quintessentially modern, as a particular, culturally determined inflection of a more general tendency. This position calls for a comparative approach, and as a number of the contributions in this volume demonstrate, a comparison between Germany and Sweden can indeed yield yet another perspective on the pathology of the Enlightenment legacy. On the one hand, a closer look at Scandinavia largely appears to corroborate Jeffrey Herf's argument that "it was the Enlightenment's weakness, not its strength, that made reactionary modernism a force of political significance in Germany" and that "Auschwitz remains a monument to the deficit and not to the excess of reason."[11] After all, it is the rational-minded social engineers of Sweden that came up with a "model" society that has been the envy of many progressive politicians and thinkers around the world. As Nina Witoszek, Lars Trägårdh, and Robert Wokler argue, it is Scandinavia, rather than Germany, that should be studied as the prime location of the maladies and contradictions of the Enlightenment legacy.

Take for example eugenics, which Peukert cites in his attempt to show that the origins of the German "Final Solution" are to be located in the "Spirit of Science."[12] It might be argued that his thesis is deeply problematic insofar as it is applied to the "irrational" racial policies of Nazi Germany. The Swedish case might, in fact, have served him far better. In Sweden, as Maciej Zaremba has argued, eugenics was firmly linked to both economic rationality and democratic politics.[13] The reason why the genetic and social engineering carried out in the name of Social Democracy is so troubling to us is precisely that the project is still with us today, at least in its fundamental imperative. Furthermore, it is now, as then, by and large thought of as essentially benign. As Colla argues, the dismal history of eugenics in Sweden has in fact been known for some time. But it is only recently, and even then most reluctantly, that concerted attempts have been made to air this dirty laundry, to bring into public consciousness this instance of "repressed memory."

Modernity and National Identity

The cases of Sweden and the Weimar Republic illustrate that modernization can be either facilitated or undermined by deep-seated values and belief systems. Indeed, most contributions demonstrate that the assumption that a democratization of attitudes, beliefs, and convictions would follow immediately in the footsteps of the establishment of democratic, parliamentary institutions is one of the more fantastic expressions of the ahistorical rationalism of the last century. Rather, modern life is like a hermit crab in the shell of a previous formation. According to this perspective, claims to the effect that the "Swedish model" based on rationality and science has managed to produce a new *homo scandinavicus* are problematic, to say the least. How are we to measure the "rationality" of social engineering if that planning leans heavily on earlier traditions with which the community identifies?

Remarkably, the very proclivity for "modernity" appears in the Swedish case to be part of a "tradition." Whereas in Germany modernization provoked nostalgia for the past, pitting visions of *Heimat* and *Gemeinschaft* against the specter of urbanization, industrialization, and *Gesellschaft*, the Swedes embraced with remarkable relish the prospect of becoming a modern nation. As Arne Ruth once noted, even Swedish right-wing nationalism of the era of national romanticism was progressive rather than backward-looking: "Compared to the Wagnerian cultural pessimism that accompanied the industrial breakthrough in Germany, it stood out as almost a champion of rationality."[14] The figure of the engineer came to embody this spirit of practical-minded, Swedish rationality. The Swedish Social Democrats were no less enthusiastic, and as Magnus Ryner has observed, they soon came to identify with "the unambivalent modernity of Americans, which contrasted with the ambivalence of inter-war Europe."[15] As the Germans were voting in greater and greater numbers against Weimar modernity and for a *Volksgemeinschaft* centered around the image of the ancient German peasant, the Swedes organized the Stockholm Exhibition of 1930, the great symbol of Sweden's love-affair with all things rational, utilitarian, and modern.[16]

Similarly, the Swedish preference for democracy was rooted less in a rational-minded *Verfassungspatriotismus* than in a rather more mystical notion that, as a Social Democratic poster from the 1930s had it, "the way of democracy is the Swedish way." This was no more reasonable than the corresponding idea in Germany that democracy was a "Western" and thus decidedly un-German notion. Indeed, the Swedish case further corroborates Rousseau's insistence that democracy would stand or fall on the basis of the successful indoctrination of the young in the mores of civil religion. Fundamentally, democracy is a cultural matter. Exposing the falsity of the common dichotomy between so-called "ethnic" and "civic" nationalism, the Swedish experience points to the centrality of sentiment and "unreason" at the heart of democratic patriotism.

The European Community and the Crisis of National Sovereignty

The intersection of culture and crisis also bears in an intriguing way on the future of national community in the new Europe of the EU. As Lars Trägårdh argues, it is a great historical irony that whereas during the crises of the inter-war period it was Sweden that found History to be on the side of the Future, while Germany's thousand years foundered in twelve years of murder and self-destruction, the roles are now partly reversed. In 1848 Marx spoke of "a specter" haunting Europe. Today that specter is no longer that of communism but of the very capitalism that Marx so presciently evoked, a force that has put "an end to all idyllic relations."[17] What Marx envisioned was not just the destruction of the "motley feudal ties that bound man to his natural superiors," but also the elimination of the most modern form of community: the nation. By rejecting the idea of a state-bound political revolution in favor of a global social revolution, Marx failed to appreciate the power of the nation-state to contain and assimilate capitalism to serve its own ends. However, as we enter the twenty-first century, his "globalization thesis" seems to have returned with a vengeance. In Europe, in particular, hardly a day goes by without some commentator heralding the coming of a post-national order of things.

This specter of a post-nation-statist Euroland awakens various degrees of anxiety. Again, the Germans appear to be far better placed than the Swedes to handle the looming threat to the utopia of national community. It is not simply that the EU from the outset was a project that was partly rooted in the desire to tame and contain Germany forever. This impulse was also mirrored in the wish among leading German politicians and intellectuals that Germany should merge with and dissolve into Europe, thus permanently solving the "German question." After all, with the Hitler state, German *völkisch* nationalism was discredited for all but a very few, and since 1945 a near-consensus around a pro-European, federalist vision has come to prevail. This transition was made all the more plausible by the fact that there already existed an "other" German national narrative, one that linked "Germany" to the federalist legacy of the Holy Roman Empire, the German Confederation, and the Second Empire. Indeed, the only time Germany was ever truly organized along nation-statist lines was during the twelve years of Nazi rule. Thus the contemporary discourse on subsidiarity and confederalism sits rather comfortably within the historical parameters of German political culture, Hitler's *völkisch* dystopia notwithstanding. In Sweden, by contrast, the very success of the grand nation-statist project, beginning with the 1933 "crisis agreements," has meant that Swedish national identity has become tightly linked to the welfare state. Swedes came to see themselves as the most modern of peoples, inhabiting the very model of the future. The deep-seated suspicion of Europe that is so characteristic of the Swedes can be viewed as a reversal of the German desire to become European. From the vantage point of the most democratic and equal nation in the world, Europe to the south of Denmark could only be imagined as a bastion of neo-feudalism, papism, patriarchy, hierarchy, disorder, and inequality. This attitude is reinforced by the extreme statism of the Swedish social contract, which involves a marked hostility towards continental notions like federalism, subsidiarity, or civil society.

If for German Chancellor Kohl and his heirs the break with the past—the national past—constituted an opportunity and the promise of future peace and freedom, a number of leading Swedish politicians on the left insist that giving up national sovereignty is a "tragedy," the abandonment of a unique and "most ancient tradition of popular rule."[18] For many Swedes at the beginning of the new century, the break with what Nina Witoszek has called the Swedish "Family Romance" is perceived not as liberation, but as a source of further decline. The modernists of yesterday have become the reactionaries of today. Even those leading Social Democrats who came to support Swedish membership in the EU did so not because a larger "European home" inspired a vision of a better future, but because they felt the heavy breathing of an all-powerful secular trend. The Swedish decision to join Europe has been largely an act of capitulation to a perceived teleology rather than a result of any collective enthusiasm for an innovative ideological or economic plan.

There is no doubt that in both cases the challenge of merging national identity with a larger, transcultural self-image will put enduring, deep-seated cultural patterns to a test. As Daniel Bell has argued, culture is not a site of growth but a process of gradual accretion of varying responses to the "core questions that confront humanity."[19] Cultural production grows out of the human predicament: the fact that men and women are thrown into the world and attempt to make sense of it through religious beliefs, moral codes, art, language, and custom. At points of crisis, a mobilization of significant cultural traditions may bring about a cultural *ricorso* that might well defy political and economic processes. Will the prospect of the new European lead to an imaginary paradigm shift at the end of history–or will the old "habits of the heart" resurface again in a new guise? Is there some validity, in the light of this, to Fernández-Armesto's claim that though "Communism and fascism have been dismissed as extinct dinosaurs ... they will come back, clawing at one another in the streets, like revivified clones out of Jurassic Park"?[20]

Notes

1. Roland Huntford's *The New Totalitarians* is a well-known, if questionable, source (London: Allen Lane, The Penguin Press, 1971). For an update on "Swedish fascism" see Ulf Nilsson, "Vet föräldrarna om det?" MS, 1997. For a review of the debate see the September and October 1999 issues of *Moderna Tider* (Stockholm, 1999). On the question of state vs. civil society and individual rights in the Swedish context, see Lars Trägårdh, *Bemäktiga individerna: Om domstolarna, lagen och de individuella rättigheterna i Sverige*, SOU 1998: 103 (Stockholm: Fritzes, 1999).

2. For comparative studies of the social construction of the community in both cultures see the work of "Project Gemenskap," 1996-1999 (dir. Bo Stråth and Bernd Henningsen, European University, Florence/Humboldt University, Berlin). See also Bo Stråth, *Language and the Construction of Class Identities: The Struggle for Discursive Power in Social Organisation: Scandinavia and Germany after 1800* (Gothenburg: Gothenburg University, 1990); Bernd Henningsen, Janine Klein et al. (eds.), *Tyskland og Skandinavia 1800-1914. Impulser og brytninger* (Deutsches Historische Museum, Nationalmuseum, Norsk Folkemuseum, 1998); Lars Trägårdh, "Varieties of Volkish Ideologies: Sweden and Germany 1843-1933" in Stråth (ed.), *Language and the Construction of Class Identities*; Lars Trägårdh, "The Concept of the People and the Construction of Popular Culture in Germany and Sweden 1848-1933," unpublished dissertation, University of California, Berkeley, 1993.

3. Reinhart Koselleck, *Critique and Crisis* (Cambridge, Mass.: MIT Press, 1988), 5.

4. Alexis de Tocqueville, *Democracy in America* (London, 1889) II, 303. Quoted by Koselleck in *Futures Past: On the Semantics of Historical Time* (Cambridge, Mass.: MIT Press, 1985), 27.

5. Zygmunt Bauman, "On Crisis, Culture and the Crisis of Culture," MS presented at the conference "Communities in Peril: The Memory and History of Crisis in Germany and Scandinavia," 2-5 October 1997, European University, Florence.

6. For a useful review see Frank Kermode, *The Sense of an Ending* (Oxford: Oxford University Press, 1967), 48-51; Stein Rokkan et al. (eds), *Citizens, Parties, Elections* (Oslo: Scandinavian University Press, 1970); Paul Tillich, *The Courage To Be* (New Haven: Yale University Press, 1952); Pitrim Sorokin, *The Crisis of Our Age* (Oxford: Oneworld, 1992); Karl Jaspers, *Man in the Modern Age* (London: Routledge, 1951). See also Krzysztof Michalski, *O kryzysie*, Rozmowy w Castle Gandolfo series, vol. II (Vienna: Instytut Nauk o Czlowieku, Warsaw: Respublica, 1985).

7. Karl Polanyi, *The Great Transformation: The Political and Economic Origins of Our Time* (Boston: Beacon Press, 1957).

8. Hannah Arendt, *Crises of the Republic* (New York: Harcourt and Brace, Harvest Book, 1962; reprt. 1979), especially the chapter on "Civil Disobedience," 49-102.

9. Theodor Adorno and Max Horkheimer, *Dialectic of Enlightenment* (London: Verso Classics, 1977); Detlev Peukert, *The Weimar Republic: The Crisis of Classical Modernity* (London: Allen Lane, 1991); Browning quote is from an interview with Ron Rosenbaum in Ron Rosen-

baum, *Explaining Hitler* (London: Macmillan, 1998), 365-366. See also Ben Lapp's chapter in this volume.

10. George L. Mosse, *The Crisis of German Ideology* (New York: Schocken, 1981); Hans Kohn, *The Mind of Germany* (New York: Harper & Row, 1960); Daniel Goldhagen, *Hitler's Willing Executioners: Ordinary Germans and the Holocaust* (New York: Knopf, 1996).

11. Jeffrey Herf, *Reactionary Modernism: Technology, Culture and Politics in Weimar and the Third Reich* (Cambridge: Cambridge University Press, 1984), 273.

12. Detlev Peukert, "The Genesis of the 'Final Solution' from the Spirit of Science," in David Crew (ed.), *Nazism and German Society, 1933-45* (New York: Routledge, 1994), 274-299.

13. Maciej Zaremba , *De rena och de andra* (Stockholm: Bokförlaget DN, 1999).

14. Arne Ruth, "The Second New Nation: The Mythology of Modern Sweden," *Dædalus*, vol. 113, no 1., 1984, 81.

15. Magnus Ryner, *Neoliberal Globalization and the Crisis of Swedish Social Democracy*, Working Paper SPS no. 98/4, Florence: European University Institute, 1998.

16. For a further discussion of the centrality of "modernity" to Swedish national identity, see Lars Trägårdh, "Welfare State Nationalism: Sweden and the Spectre of 'Europe,'" in Lene Hansen and Ole Wæver (eds.), *European Integration and National Identity: The Challenge of the Nordic States* (London and New York: Routledge, 2002).

17. Karl Marx and Friedrich Engels, *The Communist Manifesto* (New York: Appleton-Century-Crofts, 1955).

18. Quote from Rolf Karlbom, "Lång svensk folkstyrelsetradition" in *Kritiska Europafakta*, no. 26 (Göteborg: Nej till EG, 1993), cited in Trägårdh, "Welfare State Nationalism."

19. See Daniel Bell, *Winding Passage: Essays and Sociological Journeys 1960-80* (New York: University Press of America, 1984), 333.

20. Felipe Fernández-Armesto, *Millennium* (London: Bantam Press, 1995), 700.

2

Some Questions Concerning the Conceptual History of "Crisis"

Reinhart Koselleck

Today, anyone who opens a newspaper can find references to "crisis." The concept indicates uncertainty, suffering, an ordeal, and suggests an unknown future whose suppositions will not permit sufficient clarification. That much was established by a French dictionary in 1840, and the definition of crisis is no different today.[1] The inflated use of the term encompasses the scope of our activities–domestic and international politics, culture, economics, the church and religion, every branch of the humanities and social sciences, the natural sciences, technology and industry–inasmuch as these are conceived to be component parts of our political and social systems; in short, the term is an aspect of our everyday world. If the multiple usages of the word were a sufficient index of actual crisis, we would be living in a crisis of all-encompassing proportions. However, this illustrates a widespread manner of speech rather than contributing to the diagnosis of our plight.

In what follows I intend to pare from the history of the concept "crisis" some of its structural characteristics, hopefully contributing to the strengthening of my contentions and making them more precise. I begin with a broad characterization of the history of the concept. Then I sketch several semantic models of the concept to which its modern usage can be traced. Finally, I pose anew a few questions that follow from the liaison of modern conceptual speech with the Christian tradition.

Notes for this section begin on page 23.

A Historical Synopsis of the Concept

"Crisis" belongs among those fundamental concepts of the Greek language for which there are no substitutes. Derived from "krino"–to separate, select, decide, judge; to size up (e.g., opponents for competition), clash, fight–"crisis" tended to indicate a final, irrevocable decision. The concept implied alternatives that allowed for no further revision or elaboration: success or catastrophe, justice or injustice, life or death, ultimately salvation or damnation.

For example, in battle "krino" referred to those forces that would carry the day. With this usage Thucydides discreetly inserted the great battle of Thermopylae into the general scheme of things (as Montesquieu would do as well), thus making it possible for the battle to quietly decide the outcome of the war with Persia.

In the Hippocratic School, "krino" referred to the critical stage of an illness in which the struggle between life and death was played out, where a verdict was pending but had not yet arrived.

In the area of politics–as given in Aristotle–it referred both to the maintenance of the law and to its making, in which every citizen was called to participate; as in political decision-making, each man was granted the right to judge.

Within theology, at least after the New Testament, "crisis" and "judicium"–both adopted from the language of the law–acquired a new and, as it were, unsurpassable significance: that of the Judgement of God. "Crisis" was present in the life and times of the faithful, whether as the "crisis" of the Last Judgement at the end of time, or as the judgement thought to have already come with the worldly appearance of Christ and his everlasting light. Potentially, the concept comprehended each and every decisive moment in the inward and the outward lives of the individual and his community. "Crisis" dealt with definitive alternatives between which a choice or commensurate judgement had to be made; in each case to which crisis referred, the alternative outcome could also apply.

"Crisis" was therefore a concept that implied a temporal dimension, or in modern terms, if you will, implicitly expressed a theory of time. Whether order was to be generated through the maintenance or the creation of law, or whether it depended upon proper identification, as was the case, according to Galen, in medical judgement–the precise phase of an illness had to be diagnosed in order to risk a prognosis–it was always the case that a certain point in time had to be ripe for any action to succeed. "Crisis" in theological terms also had a temporal context, but one whose precise moments were unknown. Consider the case of St. John, who accepted God's message in order to escape damnation here and now, although the time of the last judgement remained hidden.

"Crisis" directs itself, as it were, toward the necessity of time to make itself comprehensible as a concept. In almost every discussion of "crisis" there is the awareness of uncertainty as well as the obligation to forecast the future so as to prevent a calamity or to find deliverance. In the course of these discussions, the respective point of termination becomes limited in different ways to the thematic conditions of everyday experience.

From antiquity to the early modern period, both the word and the concept sustained themselves in the Latin tongues, as "crisis" in medical parlance and as "judicium" or "judicium maximum" in theology. For example, in his *Compendium Theologiae* (Ch. 242), Thomas Aquinas distinguished three temporal phases in the judgement exercised by the Son of God: the judgement that the individual meets during his lifetime; the judgement at the hour of death; and finally, after Christ's return, the Last Judgement. During this period "crisis" evolved, so to speak, in the language of its trade, wedded to the institution of the church and thereby to each of the four faculties of Scholasticism.

After the adoption of the Greco-Roman word into the various European languages—that is, after the waning of the Middle Ages—the concept came to comprehend more and more realms of experience: daily politics, warfare, psychology, a self-developing economics, and finally a rediscovered history. One might even claim that the concept "crisis" contributed to the elaboration of these considerations into independent branches of learning. The medical usage of "crisis" stands above all the others as godfather to further applications. In advancing the concept "crisis," the medical usage advanced as well the concept of the nation-state as metaphorical corpus. It served that end by diagnosing the state's sickness or health, by pronouncing upon its prospects for life or death.

By the eighteenth century, however, the concept had become self-sustaining. Reference to the medical sense of "crisis" was now deliberately metaphorical, as can be seen in Rousseau. For instance, in Germany talk centered around the structural and administrative crisis within the Reich. In the course of these discussions the point arose that the internal laws and form of the federal constitution were no longer sufficient for the stabilization of the empire; therefore a supplementary federation of Princes was instituted, from which descended the wording of the Preamble of 1785.

During the eighteenth century "crisis" traversed a course similar to that of "revolution" and "progress," concepts that had become temporalized and self-reliant as their spatial or natural portent evaporated with the Enlightenment. This enabled them to gain the status of primary and historical concepts. During the Great Northern War, with the ascendancy of the Russian Empire, the first evidence of the temporalization of crisis appears with Leibniz, who saw rising up in his mind's eye a new constellation of world powers: "Momenta temporum pretiosissima sunt in transitu rerum" ("The moments of the times are most precious as things shift"). "Now Europe is in a state of flux and crisis the like of which it hasn't seen since Charlemagne."[2] Here the concept came into a historical-philosophical context; moreover, it entered this context in such a way that the course of the eighteenth century was increasingly obliged to fulfill its stipulations.

"Crisis" became a fundamental concept for the philosophy of history, which ushered in the claim to interpret the entire course of history from a particular point in time. Since then it has always been one's own point in time that is experienced as critical. And the reflection of one's own temporal circumstances not only arrays the entire past for judgement, but displays the future for prognosis as well.

Since the French Revolution, "crisis" has been the central interpretative factor for both political and social life. This is certainly true for the long, open-ended period of the Industrial Revolution, which was accompanied and influenced by scientifically differentiated theories of crisis and the business cycle.

Given the practice of interpreting the entire course of history from one standpoint, and in surprising contrast to the example of national economy, no explicit theory of crisis was developed during the nineteenth century. The work of Jacob Burckhardt is the only exception. Marx himself, who tried to connect his economic theory with a philosophy of history, came to a dead stop when elaborating a theory of crisis, as Schumpeter explicitly claimed. Even in the twentieth century, theories of crisis confine themselves to specific areas of inquiry such as psychiatry or political science. Global theories of crisis, like those implicitly behind the efforts of eighteenth- and nineteenth-century philosophers of history, are today quickly dismissed as unserious; they are thought to be insufficiently demonstrable empirically and thereby unworthy of defense.

With this historical synopsis behind us, we now turn to the semantics of crisis as a fundamental historical concept.

Three Semantic Models

While the original medical sense of "crisis" strongly influenced the political application of the term, a great many theological usages were also fed into the basic historical concept. This was already the case at the time of the English Civil War of 1640–1660, as its descriptions demonstrate. It was also the case with regard to the historical-philosophical and reflective use of the term prevalent from the last Enlightenment. The power of God's judgement and the dynamics of the apocalypse continually echoed in the use of "crisis," and doubts should arise regarding the theological derivation of this newly constituted formulation, although this derivation does not demonstrate itself by mere proclamation. This derivation can be seen in the fact that the historical-philosophical diagnosis of crisis readily functions with concrete, compulsory alternatives; these are detrimental to a differentiated diagnostic but nevertheless seem to be effective and plausible because of the prophetic language itself. Of course, in putting forth the following three semantic models of "crisis," I risk unduly simplifying the historically proper use of the concept.

Firstly, history can be interpreted as continual crisis. World history is world judgement; only world history passes judgement on the world. This model deals with one concept of progress.

Secondly, "crisis" can designate another, singular, accelerating type of process, in which conflicts burst open an existing system; following the crisis the system reconstitutes itself in a new set of circumstances. Here "crisis" indicates the passing of an epoch, a historical watershed, a process which, *mutatis mutandis,* can repeat itself. Although in terms of isolated cases history always remains unique, this concept engenders the possibility that change can take place in analogous forms. Therefore, I suggest that it be labeled as the concept of the iterative epoch or event.

Thirdly, "crisis" can suggest the last crisis within a prevailing historical moment; in this conception comparisons to the Last Judgement are only metaphorical. Measured against the present course of our history this model must be labeled utopian, but it cannot be ruled out. Considering the means that exist for our total destruction, it has every opportunity of realization. Nonetheless, this conception of crisis is purely future-oriented and, in contrast to the other models, points toward a final resolution of conflict.

These models actually never appear in the pure forms of my description. As encountered in the language of philosophical or theoretical history, they are mutually supporting. They overlap one another in their applications. They measure out differently in different contexts. What is common to all three models, despite their impregnation with theological connotation, is the fact that they offer historically immanent patterns of explanation which dispense, at least in theory, with references to the intervention of God.

Some further elucidation is required of the basic premises of the three models.

World History as Continual Crisis

"World history is world judgement" is an expression from Schiller, advanced as the motto of modernity. The passage appears by chance in a love poem where Schiller bemoans a situation come and gone, one that on its face is forever irretrievable. "What one declines at the appointed hour not even eternity can retrieve."[3] Formally speaking, the line secularizes the Last Judgement whose temporality it faithfully retains. In this sense it carries with it a pronounced anti-Christian element, since every transgression relentlessly enters the individual's biography, enters the moral and political history of the active community, indeed, enters world history itself. The model is compatible with that fate Herodotus lets shine upon all unique examples from history, which can always be read as the action of an immanent sense of justice. But Schiller's dictum raises a larger claim. Not only is an intrinsic sense of justice demanded for the unique historical event, which seems here to possess an almost magical air of appearance; it is also expected for world history as a whole. Logically, every act of injustice, every incommensurable action, every unpunished crime, every senseless and useless act, is necessarily pre-cluded. Consequently, the burden of proof as regards the meaning of history considered in this way increases enormously.

It is no longer the historian who, on the grounds of his superior knowl-edge of the past, believes himself capable *ex facto* of morally judging it. Now history itself is accorded the powers of an active subject. Now history becomes the judge of history. Now history equals justice itself. It was Hegel who took it upon himself to cushion the moral discrepancies and shortcom-ings that Schiller's dictum yields. Hegel's world history remains world judge-ment because the "world spirit" or "thought of God" must part with itself in history so as to find itself as judgement. Viewed theologically, his world his-tory deals with the last possible and last conceivable heresy for one who more or less intends to do justice to a Christian interpretation.

Schiller's dictum can be applied intact so long as history is interpreted as an immanent process. Liberals never tire of calling upon this position in order to deduct a moral legitimacy for their actions. Darwinian and imperi-alist philosophies of history can also be linked to this view, since such ends as the survival of the fittest are seen as redeeming the actions that produced them. Consider Hitler's sentimental renunciation of self-pity: whoever goes to ruin has justly earned his fate.

There are semantic options whose implications may not in any way be attributed to their linguistic origins. Whosoever undertakes to trace the derivation of Hitler back to Hegel or Schiller succumbs to a claim of histori-cal actuality, of cause and effect, which only proceeds selectively. World his-tory as world judgement asserts before all else that every situation is stamped with the same decisive earnestness, that everyone faces the consequences of his actions.

In this sense Schiller's dictum is also adaptable theologically. As Richard Rothe stated in 1837: "The entirety of Christian history is one great continu-ous crisis of the race."[4] Or as Karl Barth said, stripping this enduring crisis of all theological overtones in order to explicate it existentially, "So-called 'Sacred History' is merely the continuously running crisis of all history, not a history within or next to the history."[5] Here, as a concept, crisis forfeited finality, the transitional nature of its temporality pure and simple: crisis becomes a structural category within a Christian conception of history; escha-tology itself, so to speak, is assimilated into history.

The Concept of the Iterative Epoch: Crisis as Historical Watershed

"Crisis" is less exacting in terms of what I have called "the concept of the iter-ative epoch." This concept looks to the conditions of various possible courses of history to distinguish points of comparison and commonality as well as points of difference. This model does not raise the claim that it can interpret history in a lasting fashion or as a totality. Jacob Burckhardt understood anthropological constants in history as being available—within their respective historical articulations—as different courses of action for given crises. For example, he defined the period of the barbarian invasions during the decline of the Roman Empire as historically unique and significant, as a crisis that favored the rise of a church with claims to universality. In fact the only period that can be counted a lasting and open-ended crisis is the modern period in which he wrote. Behind every other example of historical crisis Burckhardt discovered more aspects of continuity than his startled colleagues cared to admit.

The economic concept of crisis also belongs under the aegis of the iterative model. Behind the example of economic crisis stands the weight of the metaphorical apparatus of the eighteenth-century understanding of equilibrium, which can never be empirically redeemed in its entirety. Roughly speaking, crisis appears when the equilibrium between supply and demand, between production and consumption, between the circulation of money and the circulation of goods, is disturbed; when this happens recession and the slide down the economic scale are said to become visible everywhere. Yet it is held as a law of experience that a general rise in productivity follows a recession induced by a crisis. The paradox of this doctrine seems to lie in the fact that equilibrium can only be maintained, or rather regained, if productivity rises continually and does not stagnate; otherwise decline appears to be inevitable. Inasmuch as this principle is dependent upon progress for its cogency, without progress it cannot be empirically redeemed. As Molinari, a nineteenth-century theoretician of business cycles, said: "Every advance, large or small, contains its crisis."[6]

That idea that crisis should be the engine of progress appears to be a semantic variant that has been redeemed only in the areas of the natural sciences, economics, technology, and industry. But there is a semantic parallel to this usage in the theological discourse of the Middle Ages: "In via vitael non progredi, retrogradi est" ("Not to progress on the path of life is to regress," Bernard of Clairvaux, 1090-1153). Put bluntly, "Whosoever does not gain, loses." This formulation hints at a possible common anthropological basis upon which the concept of iterative crisis might be founded. But it does not lead me to add theology to the list of the areas in which this principle has apparently triumphed.

This model could be described through any number of quotations, but a single, solitary example may stand for them all: "Out of every crisis mankind rises with some greater share of knowledge, higher decency, purer purpose."[7] These famous words are from Franklin Delano Roosevelt, spoken the day before his death.

Regarding this option, finally, the question must be asked: Is "progress" *the* lead concept for "crisis," or is rather the concept of the iterative event that guiding concept under which "progress" must be subsumed? If "crisis" as a conceptually iterative event lays claim to an enormous explicative potential, then progress, which crisis indisputably yields, can be accredited its relative claim to efficacy. Indeed, this type of progress is undoubtedly being called upon to solve our impending ecological crisis.

Crisis as the Final Resolution of Conflict

Crisis as the Final Resolution of Conflict: here the crisis in which one finds oneself bids to be the last, great, one-time resolution of conflict within one's life or within the life of the times. Following this, from a future standpoint, history itself will appear totally different. This semantic option is more frequently taken the less one believes in an absolute end to history via the Last Judgement of God. What is under consideration is the reshuffling, so to speak, of the theological grounds of belief, as demanded by the design of immanent history. There is no shortage of testimonials to this. Robespierre saw himself as wielding a moral justice that secured its ultimate success through the application of involuntary force; Thomas Paine believed, in view of the American and the French revolutions and the implication of crisis which they portended, that an absolute turn of events must lie in the not-too-distant future; and those original partisans of the French Revolution who became the embittered adversaries of the bonapartistic consequences of their actions can also bear witness to the character of this semantic option. For German examples one need only sound the names of Friedrich Schlegel, Johann Gottlieb Fichte, or Ernst Moritz Arndt.

The absolute nadir of history guarantees the sudden turn toward deliverance: in the case of France, the birth of sociology out of the spirit of the Revolution (not just that of the Restoration) can be offered as evidence. St. Simon and August Comte knew they were in the "Grande Crise Finale" which by scientific planning and rising industrial production could be driven to conquer the moment once and for all. Lorenz von Stein can also be mentioned in this context, for he perceived in the effort to arrange a compromise between capital and labor Europe's last best chance to forestall cultural recidivism and the fall into barbarism. Maintaining equilibrium meant producing progress through crisis. Although on its own terms this formula was successful only in limited areas of endeavor, it had consequences elsewhere.

Karl Marx was, so to speak, left dangling in an intermediate position. On the one hand he expected that the last crisis of capitalism would bring an end to class differences and yield a reign of freedom from oppression. On the other hand, however, he saw that the crisis, rather than preserving the *status quo* in a new order, had to be viewed as leading to the overthrow of the entire system by force. Marx worked both with a systematic, immanent concept of crisis in which the iterative structure of economic crisis was set forth, and with a concept of crisis that demanded the violent overthrow of that same iterative structure. Moreover, he deduced this latter conclusion from a set of circumstances which seemed to be driving world history toward a final great crisis; the supposed final struggle between the proletariat and bourgeoisie doubtless took place for Marx within the framework of a theological Last Judgement, which he was never able to ground purely economically.

Crisis as a Question for the Christian Tradition

In every case in which crisis is expected to utterly change the world, the expectation is easily exposed as an illusion of perspective. It is characteristic of the finitude of all human beings to regard their own situation as more important and more serious than all of the crises that have actually already taken place. But one should be careful–precisely in view of the teaching of the Last Judgement–not to dismiss the above self-fashioned evaluation of humanity as merely another error of perspective. For when it comes to the question of securing our survival, is it not the case that a great many acts of judgement are put forth as final? "Crisis" in the Greek sense of compelling sound judgement and prompt action under the commanding presence of some urgent necessity, remains an indispensable concept given the complex conditions of contemporary society. I want to illustrate this last point with a historical *Gedankenexperiment* (thought experiment).

It is part of Christian teaching that God will foreshorten time before the coming of the end of the world. Behind this doctrine is the cosmological idea that God, as the lord of time, can bring about the anticipated end of the world before it is foreseen, and that he will do so for the sake of the chosen people whose suffering is to be curtailed (Mark 13:20; Matthew 24:22). This mythological language of apocalyptic expectation can be subjected to psychologization or idealization. It is easy to see, in this faith in an immanent foreshortening of time, evidence of a wish on the part of the suffering and oppressed to exchange their misery for paradise as quickly as possible. Yet to observe the eschatological foreshortening of time among its many historical interpretations is to stand before the astonishing realization that since the first occurrence of this idea, which itself stands over and above historical time, there has been in fact a successive acceleration of history.

From a wholly different perspective, the history of scientific discoveries received an analogous interpretation. For Bacon it was a matter of hope and expectation that discoveries would occur in shorter and shorter intervals of time so that an even better mastery of nature would be possible. Such early moderns as Leibniz inferred from their data that historically immanent progress was getting faster and faster, accelerating so as to lead to a better worldly order. Now, although the acceleration of historical progress came out of the apocalyptic foreshortening of time, the contents of the interpretative model had changed completely. The attainment of paradise after the end of the world and the possibility of its attainment in this world became logically mutually exclusive conditions.

The cosmic foreshortening of time that was to precede the Last Judgement never fully incorporated the sense of the concept "crisis." Neither does the accelerating pace of modern history, the actuality of which cannot be disputed, allow itself to be properly conceived as "crisis." Scientifically or not, deliberately or not, sound judgement and prompt action are obviously required with regard to the question of whether and how human survival on this globe is to continue. The cosmic foreshortening of time, which, in the prior language of myth, was to precede the Last Judgement, can today be empirically verified as the accelerating sequence of historical events. In the words of Jacob Burckhardt: "All of a sudden the progression of the world transpires with frightening speed; developments which otherwise take centuries seem, like fleeting phantoms, to pass by in months and weeks and with their passing to be resolved."[8] The common generic term for the apocalyptic foreshortening of time that is to precede the Last Judgement, as well as for the phenomenon of historical acceleration, is "crisis." Should this be considered mere coincidence, as simply two distinct usages for the same figure of speech? In the Christian as well as the non-Christian sense of the term, in every instance, "crisis" indicates an increasingly urgent set of circumstances, the meaning of which mankind seems unable to escape.

In conclusion, therefore, a temporal hypothesis is called for that is not the least bit new. Consider the history of the genus "man." That history can be represented by three exponential time-curves. Measured by the five billion years since our planet was covered with a firm crust, the one billion years of organic life represents a relatively short span. But much shorter still are the ten million years of man's probable existence, the last two million years of which saw the employment of self-fabricated tools.

The second exponential time-curve can be plotted in the two million years since *homo erectus* distinguished himself with tools of his own making. The first document, so to speak, of genuine art is 30,000 years old, and the beginnings of agriculture and animal husbandry can be dated to about 10,000 years ago. The approximately 6,000 years of urban culture that have left traces of a written tradition are, in the context of the two million years of human productivity, a very short time-span indeed, and the achievement of poetic, philosophical, and historiographical reflection certainly takes place in its very latest moments.

The third exponential time-curve follows in outline the self-organization of urban culture, which began 6,000 years ago. Measured against this continuous history, modern industrial society based on science and technology unfolds over the last 300 years. The curve of the acceleration is indicated by three additional series of facts: the dissemination of information has accelerated to such a point that the identity of an event and the news corresponding to it are theoretically the same. Furthermore, the acceleration of travel has increased approximately tenfold since the replacement of natural travel aids (wind, water, animal) by the technological means of the steam engine, the electric motor, and the internal-combustion engine. The acceleration of the means of communication has enabled the world to shrink to the dimensions of a space-ship. The population explosion runs along an analogous exponential time-curve: from a half-billion people in the seventeenth century, the planet's population rose, despite mass exterminations, to two and a half billion at the middle of the twentieth century, heading in the direction of eight billion people by the century's end.

Although in some respects the three exponential time-curves might be dismissed as playing with figures, they openly delineate a limit beyond which further technical or scientific progress cannot take us. For it must always be remembered that the potential of autonomous humanity for self-destruction has multiplied many times over along these lines.

Thus the question arises whether our semantic model of crisis, as a kind of final resolution of conflict, has retained a better chance of realization than at any time previously. If this is the case, then everything depends upon directing our energies toward preventing extinction. It should be noted that the Catechism is similarly a theological response to crisis.

Of course, the three exponential time-curves can be read as intensifying the rate of acceleration, making it completely impossible to risk speculative accounts of the future. Perhaps the proper response to crisis consists in being on the lookout for those stabilizing factors that can be deduced from the long duration of the history of mankind. Then again, it could be that such questions can be formulated not only historically and politically, but also theologically. Whatever the case, from the historical point of view, we need to accommodate the acceleration in the special uniqueness of our time. Even this conclusion might prove an error in perspective, or better still, an error in judgement, if we discover in time the enduring conditions for our survival.

Notes

1. E. Duclerc et Pagnerre, *Dictionnaire Politique*, Paris 1868 (7th ed.), 'Crise', 298. For all succeeding examples and any further inquiry see my article "Crisis" in Otto Brunner et al. (eds.), *Geschichtlichte Grundbegriffe*, vol. 3 (Stuttgart, 1982), 617-650.
2. Gottfried Wilhelm von Leibniz, *Konzept eines Briefes an Schleiniz* (23 September 1712), Wladimir Iwanowitsch Guerrier (ed.), *Leibnez' Ru land betreffender Briefwechsel* (Petersburg/Leipzig 1873), T1, 2, 227f.; 1961, 39. "Et l'Europe est maintenant dans un état de changement et dans une crise ou elle n'a jamais ete depuis l'Empire de Charlemagne."
3. Friedrich Schiller, *Resignation: Eine Phantasie*, coll. Works, Sak-Ausg. ed. by Eduard von der Hellen i.a. (Stuttgart/Berlin o.J.), vol. 1, 199. "Die Weltgeschichte is das Weltgericht." "Was man von der Minute ausgeschlagen, gibt keine Ewigkeit zuruck."
4. Richard Rothe, *Die Anfange der christlichen Kirche und ihre Verfassung* (1837), quotation from Peter Meinhold, *Geschichte der kirchlichen Historiographie* (Munich/Freiburg 1967), vol. 2, 221. "Die ganze christliche Geschichte uberhaupt ist eine große kontinuierliche Krisis unseres Geschlechts."
5. Karl Barth, *Der Romerbrief* (1918), 9th ed., 1926; (Zollikon-Zurich 1954), 57, 32. "Die Sogenannte 'Heilsgeschichte' ist nur die fortlaufende Krisis aller Geschichte, nicht eine Geschichte in oder neben der Geschichte."
6. Gustave de Molinari, *L'Evolution economique du XIXe siecle Theorie du Progrès* (Paris 1880), 102f. "Jeder kleine oder große Fortschritt besitzt seine Krise."
7. Quotation from W. Besson, *Die politische Terminologie des Präsidenten F.D. Roosevelt* (Tubingen 1855), 20.
8. Jacob Burckhardt, *Weltgeschichtliche Betrachtungen*, ed. by Rudolf Stadelmann (Pfullingen 1949), S. 211. "Der Weltproze gerat plotzlich in furchtbare Schnelligkeit; Entwicklungen, die sonst Jahrhunderte brauchen, scheinen in Monaten und Wochen wie fluchtige Phantome voruberzugehen und damit erledigt zu sein."

3

The Institutionalization of Modernity
Shocks and Crises in Germany and Sweden

ERIK RINGMAR

The notion of crisis is one of the most common in our political vocabulary, yet it is rarely used with any degree of precision. In 1990s Sweden there were constant references to the "economic crisis," or simply, if more vaguely, "the crisis." What was meant by a crisis here was, it seems, the reduced ability of the state to tax the people, and the concomitant inability to maintain previous high levels of welfare provisions at a time of rising unemployment. Yet the word crisis is also often used in references to German history. Here the crisis that comes to everyone's mind is located in the 1920s and 1930s–the defeat in World War I, the economic collapse, and the subsequent rise of Hitler. To compare the Swedish crisis of the 1990s with the crisis of Germany after World War I would, however, seem inappropriate, even morally questionable. Comparing such disparate entities is like comparing the holes children dig in the sand at the beach with the holes made by bombs during a war.[1] The two are indeed holes, but they have nothing much in common apart from a verbal label. To look for a theory that explains the existence of all holes is surely madness! Similarly, we could argue, crises depend too much on historical contingencies–on a particular political leader, on a war that was lost or on an economy that was mismanaged. Swedish crises will for this reason always be different from German crises–or, for that matter, different from American, Portuguese, Peruvian, or Nigerian crises. There can be no theory of crisis that explains all cases.

Accepting this point, we could still argue that societies can be more or less *crisis-prone*. Whether we understand crisis in its etymological sense as a "decisive turning point," or in its more colloquial sense as a "social breakdown," it is obvious that some societies seem to go through endless series of crises whereas other societies seem to get away virtually crisis-free.[2] Societies, we could say, have a more or less robust constitution. Crisis proneness, as opposed to actual cases of crises, is a latent quality like, for example, the brittleness of glass. Latent qualities may or may not manifest themselves in actual events—glasses can be brittle without actually breaking, although their brittleness makes them more likely to break. The distinction between the latent and the manifest, between the potential and the actual, is interesting for our purposes. Even if we cannot explain why a certain glass broke on a particular occasion, we can nevertheless explain why it is brittle. The answer is that it consists of a certain material, was made with the help of a certain technical process, etc. If we add a bit of statistical analysis to this basic information, we can conclude that glasses of a certain type break with x percent probability within a y period of time. And although we rarely can predict the breaking of individual glasses, our prediction will be correct for the class of all glasses taken as a whole.

The same argument applies to the latent qualities of societies. Although we cannot have a theory of crises that allows us to predict individual cases, we can still explain why a particular society is crisis prone. Crisis proneness is a latent, not a manifest, quality. Just like the brittleness of a glass, the crisis proneness of a society depends on the basic elements that constitute it, but also on the process through which these elements were put together. That is to say, the crisis proneness of a society is a function of its institutional structure and its cultural and political traditions, but also a result of the historical process through which culture, politics, and institutions came to be wedded to each other. Adding a bit of statistical analysis to this basic information, we could, for example, draw the general conclusion that countries with a democratic government go through fewer crises than countries with dictatorships; or perhaps we could draw the more specific conclusion that countries with a censored press are more prone to experience cases of financial mismanagement and even famines.[3] Although such an analysis would rarely explain the actual crises of individual countries, it would nevertheless allow us to make predictions that would hold true for the body of all countries taken as a whole.

In addition to these constitutional properties, however, we need information regarding exposure. Exposure is a question of the positioning of something vis-à-vis a threat; the degree of exposure makes the latent quality more or less likely to manifest itself. Thus a glass is more exposed when located on the edge of a shelf than when located inside a cupboard, and a country may, for example, be more exposed if it has many heavily armed neighbors rather than one unarmed. Yet constitution and exposure are not by themselves enough to explain actual cases of crises. Even the most brittle of glasses placed at the edge of the highest shelf requires an event of some kind before it breaks. Societies too can have a weak constitution and high exposure and still, miraculously, survive. Before latent qualities become manifest, in other words, something has to happen that calls them into play. This something we could call a shock. Shocks are what push glasses off shelves or countries into crisis. Shocks can be of many different kinds. Some are a matter of good luck or bad; the competence or otherwise of political leaders; the sheer confluence of assorted events. But shocks can also be more systematic, results of processes rather than single events. In either case, shocks are difficult to predict. Shocks make history into the gradual unfolding of things, rather than the deduction of necessary conclusions from true premises.

In the end, the number of broken glasses, or societies, thus depends on the interplay of these three factors—constitution, exposure, and shocks. A constitution comes to matter as it is exposed, and becomes decisive through the shock. The stronger the constitution, the smaller the exposure, the bigger the shock must be before a crisis occurs; the weaker the constitution, the bigger the exposure, the less of a shock it takes to blow a society apart.

Although crises are difficult to compare, there can be no doubt that Germany has gone through more and worse crises than most countries—and more and worse crises, no doubt, than Sweden. This was certainly true of the twentieth century, but also of every other century since the Middle Ages. Why is this the case? The objective of this chapter is to try to answer this question; or, more modestly, to help us start thinking about ways in which this question could be answered. Based on our discussion thus far, there are three alternative hypotheses to consider. The first hypothesis is that Germany has experienced more and worse shocks than Sweden; the second hypothesis is that Germany's position has been more exposed than Sweden's; the third hypothesis is that Germany's constitution has been weaker than Sweden's. It is the last of these conclusions that I will try to defend. The crucial difference between Sweden and Germany, I will conclude, concerns the institutional structure of the two societies. As I will argue, the institutional structure helps a society achieve stability at times of crises, but institutions of the right kind can also make a society more flexible and thus better prepared to deal with whatever challenges it might confront.

Shocks of Modernity

Let us begin by dealing with the question of exposure. Located in the center of Europe, with few natural boundaries and divided politically, religiously, and economically, the Germans are sometimes said to have been particularly exposed to conflicts and war. Divided, they suffered constant internal conflicts, but when they sought to unite, their neighbors reacted with fear and hostility. As late modernizers, the Germans had to exert themselves to catch up with Great Britain, France, and the United States, and once they did, all export markets and colonies were already captured. Thus their efforts at catching up came to constitute threats to other, pre-existing great powers. More exposed to shock than most countries, Germany, unsurprisingly, has suffered more than its fair share of crises. Sweden, by contrast, would seem to be much better protected: safely tucked into a corner of northern Europe, united and at peace with itself and its neighbors. Yet even if this contrast might hold true for the twentieth century, the difference between the two countries largely disappears if we take a somewhat longer historical view. Sweden too was a continental power for much of its history, exposed to attacks from Danes, Poles, Austrians, and Russians; in fact, the animosity between Sweden and Denmark was not very different from that between Germany and France. In addition, Sweden certainly had its fair share of religious quarrels, problems of succession, violence and uprisings among peasants.[4] If we take a longer historical perspective, in other words, Sweden's exposure can certainly be compared to Germany's, yet, for some reason, in the Swedish case this exposure was rarely translated into crises.

Some shocks are purely contingent events, best described as coincidences or bad luck. For a historian, these are the Noses of Cleopatra which can never be entirely neglected, but which at the same time cannot be allowed to completely dominate an explanatory account.[5] Falling into the latter trap, historians have sometimes concluded that all German misfortunes are the consequences of megalomaniac rulers, incompetent generals, or animated preachers of the past. If Germany, the argument goes, only had been spared a particular war, or a particular peace treaty, everything would have been different. Sweden seems far less exposed to contingent events; the Swedes, for some reason, are luckier and their history is considerably calmer. But, again, this is largely a myopic view. Sweden too had its fair share of megalomaniacs, incompetents and preachers. In the seventeenth century, Sweden suffered a number of disastrous defeats on the battlefields of Europe; in the early eighteenth century, it lost its overseas empire; and in the early nineteenth century, it lost Finland, which until then had been considered an integral part of the country. These shocks can certainly be compared with the shocks suffered by Germany, yet for some reason in the Swedish case, in contrast to the German, they did not result in crises.

But there are also shocks administered not by individuals or contingent events, but by what we could identify as long-term processes. One such is the process of modernization to which all Western societies have been exposed since sometime around the year 1500. Modernization produces shocks because it constantly forces societies to change. Pre-modern societies were not static, to be sure, but in modern societies change is more frequent, more relentless, and more dramatic.[6] For a society, change poses a problem since it requires a high degree of flexibility on the part of individuals and groups. Modernity always forces us to reconsider our interests, our values, and our identities; in response to economic or social shocks, we have to change our occupation, place of residence, our passport, perhaps even our spouse and children. Many people will refuse to participate in such games; most people, after all, just want to go on being whoever they take themselves to be; some, especially those who stand to lose from any deviations from the status quo, will protest against all change. Yet such protests are often either futile, or cause new conflicts to arise. Change is required, yet at the same time it is unattainable. The result is a social breakdown. Modernity produces crises, in other words, either because the process of modernization is uneven, because its too quick, or because it is not fast enough.

Speaking more concretely, we could perhaps break the process of modernization down into three separate, but related, sub-processes. The first of these concerns the establishment of the state as a sovereign political actor in the late Renaissance; the second, the transformation of the state into a nation-state after the French Revolution; and the third, the transformation of the nation-state into a democratic state as a result of industrialization in the nineteenth century. All three sub-processes entailed tremendous changes; all three subjected societies to great and repeated shocks; and, as a result, societies everywhere were threatened by crises. What is particularly noteworthy for our purposes is that the process of modernization thus understood touched most European societies, and to roughly the same extent. There was, in the end, no escape from the problems of state formation, nationalism, or industrialization. For us, these similarities present an interesting possibility. Since the shocks of modernity were comparable in Sweden and in Germany, we would expect the social impact to be similar. To the extent that it was not, we have a discrepancy that requires an explanation.

Shocks of State-Building

State-building is the process whereby the state becomes established as a sovereign subject and recognized as such by audiences both at home and abroad. The process of state-building thus understood radically transformed European societies, creating new centers of power while depriving old elites of their rights. An administrative apparatus had to be put in place, taxes had to be collected, an army had to be established that could guarantee both domestic security and security against external threats. At each step along the way this process could be resisted, and each act of resistance dealt a shock to society. Farmers could refuse to pay the new taxes or to send their sons to the new wars; merchants could insist on independence for their towns and their commercial activities; the clergy could demand a continuation of the ties with Rome; the nobility could demand that their ancient privileges be preserved. In addition, foreign audiences–the body of princes, the Emperor or the Pope–could for whatever reason refuse to recognize the new state, and instead for whatever reason make war on it.[7]

First, consider the case of Germany. At the end of the Middle Ages, the eastern parts of the Carolingian empire, in contrast to the western, never united around one centralized entity. Instead, German-speaking lands continued to be divided into a multitude of different statelets.[8] This outcome no doubt avoided a number of conflicts. Local rulers did not have to be deprived of their privileges; it was not necessary to synchronize tax structures and legal codes. In fact, nothing much was imposed from above, except, for most of the territory, a vague allegiance to the Emperor. In practice, however, this decentralized structure did not always work very well. Fragmentation led to conflicts, and in the late fifteenth and early sixteenth centuries, a number of small wars were fought between different rulers.[9] In addition, decentralization made the constituent parts of the Empire into soft targets for attacks. While Germany as a whole was next to impossible to conquer, a few Protestant reformers or a foreign warlord could quite easily take over a principality or a bishopric or two. This division led to a series of crises, of which the Thirty Years War was the most devastating. This, the first modern, the first "total" war, was fought almost exclusively on German territory, and between 1618 and 1648 perhaps as much as a fifth of the German population perished.[10] In the eighteenth century Prussia and Austria, together with the many smaller German states, grew into sophisticated, fully functioning administrative units, but German division, and German wars, continued unabated until unification in 1871.

The Swedish process of state-building followed a more common European pattern, although it took place comparatively late.[11] It was only in 1521 that Sweden emerged as an independent political entity, and throughout the rest of the sixteenth century the Swedish kings fought to reaffirm their authority vis-à-vis the claims of both the aristocracy and the peasants. Complaints against taxes were the most common causes of revolt, but there were also those who took up arms in defense of their traditional faith; in addition, a protracted struggle over succession divided the royal house into a Catholic and a Protestant branch. Yet the Swedish kings always managed to reassert their authority and rally the country behind themselves and their particular version of Christianity. For Sweden, external threats were in the end more acute. From 1560 onwards, the country became embroiled in a series of foreign wars that only ended with the final collapse of the Swedish overseas empire in 1718. But since all these wars were fought on foreign soil and mainly with foreign resources, the impact on Sweden was limited, even at times of defeats on the battlefield.

Shocks of Nation-Formation

The process of nation-formation radically transformed the nature and role of the state. From the end of the eighteenth century onward, the state was no longer seen only as an impersonal political machine, but instead as the fore-

most embodiment of a new kind of entity—the nation.[12] The nation divided
people according to their similarities and differences; the nation was an imagined community of individuals who somehow saw themselves as belonging
together.[13] Understood as a political principle, nationalism required every
nation to have a state, and every state to have a nation. States without nations,
or nations that did not strive to capture states, were for this reason seen as ille-
gitimate.[14] Yet once legitimacy came to be interpreted in these terms, a tremendous amount of political, social, and geographical reshuffling was required.
Nations had to be created where none previously had existed; states had to be
recast in new molds, divided or amalgamated. All this cutting, pasting, copy-
ing, and deleting undermined the established political order and presented
new opportunities as well as new threats to both individuals and groups.

Again, let us begin with Germany. It is no exaggeration to identify
Napoleon and his armies as the most proximate causes of German nationalism.[15] Humiliation at the hands of the French was widely felt to require a
response but, lacking a unified state, the *rassemblement national* of the Germans
found a cultural rather than a political expression. German nationalism was
the nationalism of philosophers, poets and artists, not voters and statesmen;
Germany became a *Kulturnation* for the simple reason that it could not
become a *Nationalstaat*.[16] This fact alone had a profound impact on the nature
of German nationalism. Since no political or civic principles could bind people together, and since religion was a profoundly divisive issue, the emphasis
fell on more ephemeral bonds. Colored by the hues of the Romantic movement, the German nation was portrayed in emotional and explicitly anti-
rationalistic terms—rationalism, after all, was a French disease. Nationalists
emphasized the organic and the spiritual; Germans were somehow said to
form one body; they were of one blood and one will; they had, from the days
when Tacitus first described them to the day when Caspar David Friedrich
painted them, lived in the same primordial Teutonic forest.[17] In addition,
however, German nineteenth-century nationalism was also an urban and liberal movement which sought to unite the people against its autocratic and
cosmopolitan rulers; calls were made for democracy and a parliament,
human rights and a constitution.[18] Nationalism, in other words, was a popular revolutionary force, and the revolution, when it came in 1848, was for a
while very close to realizing these ideals. The *Nationalstaat* that eventually
appeared at the end of the nineteenth century, however, was more a *von oben*
creation of Bismarck's *Kulturkampf* than the genuine expression of a popular
mood. Lacking a firm connection to the state, German nationalism continued
to be a free-floating sentiment, ready to attach itself to any movement of
protest or discontent that happened to come along. As such it was easily
appropriated by the National Socialists in the 1920s and 1930s.

Swedish nationalism experienced a similar Romantic burst in the early
nineteenth century, and remnants of the movement lingered well into the

twentieth century. Yet the symbolism and the rhetoric of Swedish nationalism were entirely different from those in Germany. Swedish national identity had from the very beginning been profoundly identified with the state.[19] The kings of the seventeenth century had put serious efforts into the creation of a history and a culture befitting a major imperial power, and to a large extent these efforts were successful. A Swedish national identity has for this reason always been more or less synonymous with the identity of the Swedes as political subjects.[20] When *nationalromantiken* came into artistic and political fashion towards the end of the nineteenth century, the particular history of Sweden that was celebrated was to a large extent the history of its kings; there was simply no need to create mystical cultural bonds projected into a distant past since the real, and still existing, political ones sufficed. Swedish nationalism, in other words, was never a program that was meant to unite society in opposition to the state, but instead a program through which the state rallied society in its own support. Such state-directed movements are, strictly speaking, not nationalistic, but rather patriotic; Sweden, we could argue, has never known nationalism, but only, and only occasionally, patriotism.[21] In Sweden, society was never independent enough for a proper nationalism to develop; there never was a "civil society" or a "public sphere" independent of, and defined against, the "state." This, we could argue, is still the case today. It is striking, for example, that the term "civil society" is a neologism directly translated from English, with no true equivalent in contemporary Swedish. Indeed, the words "state" and "society" have, at least until very recently, been used interchangeably. The same is true for the term "public sphere." "Public" is usually translated as *det allmänna*, but *det allmänna* does not point us to a sphere independent of the government, but rather to synonyms such as "the state, the local community, the authorities."[22]

Shocks of Industrialization

The problems of industrialization concern not only how to bring it about, but also how to deal with its consequences once it happens. Somehow the preconditions for an industrial take-off have to be satisfied; resources have to be channeled away from traditional activities; people have to be moved and retrained; and markets have to be improved. Some of these activities can no doubt be carried out by individuals and companies, but much of the transition is likely to be the responsibility of the state.[23] Lobbying the government for a business-friendly agenda, industrialists put new pressures on the political system, clashing with traditional agrarian interests. For society as a whole, industrialization inevitably meant major social dislocations. For one thing, people had to leave their farms for new jobs in factories. Between the end of the eighteenth century and the outbreak of World War I, some 85 percent of Europe's population migrated—15 percent left for other continents, primarily North America, but some 70 percent moved from the countryside to cities

and towns.[24] With a seemingly inexhaustible reservoir of labor, factory work
was badly paid and the working conditions often deplorable. In this Dicken-
sian environment a working-class movement arose, translating the collective
weight of the workers into demands for shorter working hours, higher wages,
and the right to vote. The political problem was how to deal with these new,
and often competing, demands—from industrialists, on the one hand, and
from workers, on the other. The question was how to encourage industrialization while at the same time addressing what came to be known as "the
social question." This challenge was of course particularly acute at times of
depression and mass unemployment.

In both Sweden and Germany industrialization came late, associated with
the last couple of decades of the nineteenth century. In both countries industrialization was also rapid, resulting in a profound transformation of society in
a short period of time. In Germany, migration to the cities increased greatly
after 1850, as industrialization was stimulated by an extensive railway net-
work, the new German Customs Union, and an abundance of credit.[25] Major
conglomerates were soon formed in mining, steel production, chemicals, and
electronics as well as in weapons production. In parallel with the organizational strength of the industrialists, the trade union movement grew into the
greatest and most concentrated in the world, approaching nine million members in 1921. Throughout this period of accelerated growth, the German state
stimulated financial markets and provided business-friendly legislation, but,
starting in 1881, it also sought to address the social question through reforms
intended to meet the demands of the working class. During the Weimar
Republic, however, this model quickly disintegrated.[26] The working class was
radicalized as a result of the deprivations of the war and the postwar depression; the industrialists, for their part, were disgusted with concessions given to
the Left. Economic stagnation led to declining profits and unemployment,
and economics was translated into a zero-sum game where the gain of one
group was another group's loss. Predictably, politics soon became interpreted
in the same fashion. In the end, neither side of the political spectrum had
much faith in the regime and both started to pose their demands in extra-
political terms and in extra-political forums. The result was a quick and radical loss of legitimacy. The Republic had no way of accommodating the
conflicting demands, but neither had it the ability to reform itself.[27]

Sweden too was badly hit by the social dislocations brought on by industrialization, and just as in Germany, new pressures seemed for a while to
undermine the legitimacy of the state. There was a general strike in 1909 and
massive street demonstrations in 1914; Sweden was also affected by the post-
World War I recession and by the repercussions of the Wall Street Crash. In
contrast to Germany, however, the political center never folded. Instead,
through a series of bargains struck between Right and Left, workers and
industrialists, town and countryside, the state reasserted itself and regained

the initiative. The Social Democrats took a reformist rather than a revolutionary course when the party came to power in 1932. The public works programs and the social reforms initiated in the 1930s had a wide public appeal, and the Saltsjöbaden Accord, concluded between the employers and the major trade unions, guaranteed social peace. In the official rhetoric of the day, the Swedish state was a *folkhem*, a "home for the people." This Swedish consensus contrasted sharply with developments in Germany—1938, the year of the Saltsjöbaden agreement, was also the year of the *Kristallnacht.*

Institutional Responses in Sweden and Germany

Modernization, I argued, consists of three separate processes, and all three are likely to produce shocks. As we have seen, the shocks were quite comparable in Germany and Sweden, yet they produced very different results. In Germany, the process of state-building resulted in a weak, decentralized system of statelets, whereas in Sweden it led to a strong centralized state; in Germany, the process of nation-formation produced a popular nationalist ideology that lent its support to liberals and Nazis alike, whereas in Sweden, nationalist sentiments were the playthings only of the state; in Germany, industrialization broke up the Weimar Republic, whereas industrialization in Sweden, if anything, strengthened the social consensus and thereby also the state. The question is, of course, why was Sweden able to avoid the crises that Germany had to suffer? In the introduction to this chapter, I presented a model for how such a question could be answered. Crises, I claimed, are a combination of three kinds of factors: the basic constitution of a society, its exposure, and the shocks it receives. Taking a longer historical perspective, I argued that Sweden's exposure has been quite similar to Germany's, and, as we just concluded, the most important shocks—those associated with the process of modernization—have also been more or less similar. If these conclusions are accepted, it follows that any difference between Germany and Sweden has to be explained in terms of the constitution of the two societies. Let us briefly consider what this implies.

The most important part of the constitution of a society is its institutional structure. Institutions play a number of important roles. For one thing, they provide social interaction with stability, predictability and organization; institutions supply rules for behavior in given situations; they distribute punishments and rewards.[28] Responding to such incentives, we come to act and react in a predictable and increasingly unthinking manner. Imperceptibly, the institution takes care of things behind our backs, leaving us time to attend to more important matters; in this way houses of worship deal with religion and parliaments with politics, so that the rest of us do not have to.[29] Once actions and reactions are institutionalized in this fashion, they constitute a conservative force and a source of stability. A thoroughly institutionalized society is for this reason very resilient; its basic features remain intact even as its more superficial features are radically altered. This was Alexis de Tocqueville's insight when in *The Old Régime and the French Revolution* (1856) he looked back on the many violent shocks that France had suffered during the preceding century. The reason France survived the abuses of the *ancien régime*, the tyranny of the revolution, Napoleon and the wars was, he concluded, that the administrative system remained virtually intact, especially on a local and everyday level.

> Everyone kept to the rules and customs with which he was familiar in coping with the situations, trivial in themselves but of much personal import, which so frequently recur in the life of the ordinary citizen. He had to deal with and take orders from the same subaltern authorities as in the past and, oftener than not, the same officials. For though in each successive revolution the administration was, so to speak, decapitated, its body survived intact and active. The same duties were performed by the same civil servants, whose practical experience kept the nation on an even keel through the worst political storms. These men administered the country or rendered justice in the name of the King, then in the name of the Republic, thereafter in the Emperor's. [30]

It was an institution, in this case the public administration of the *ancien régime*, that provided France with a measure of continuity amidst the radical changes the country endured. The institution made France less crisis prone; it made it possible for people to avert, limit, or postpone crises.[31]

Although institutions often have the stabilizing influence that de Tocqueville pointed to, they can also serve to promote, even initiate, change. This may sound paradoxical given what we said about institutional stability, but the fact that institutions are difficult to change does not necessarily mean that their *effects* are conservative. Consider the example of a bank. Surely few institutions are more conservative than banks, yet their lending policies may at the same time be very progressive; the nature of what the bank does is, in short, quite different from the nature of what the bank is. In fact, we could talk about institutions as being more or less transformative, depending on the extent to which they facilitate social change. As it turns out, transformative institutions are crucial when it comes to dealing with shocks since they make a society more flexible; a society whose core consists of transformative institutions survives not because it always stays the same, but because it always changes.

Speaking more concretely, we could argue that transformative institutions play one or more of three separate roles. The first role concerns matters of deliberation and reflection. Institutions in charge of reflection–universities, for example, or the media–gather information and disseminate knowledge; they assemble as many different points of view as possible and establish procedures to arbitrate between them. The second role of a transformative institution is to guarantee the preconditions for entrepreneurship. Here we have institutions that provide legal frameworks for contracts and property rights, but also institutions that safeguard the operations of markets through which resources can be more efficiently used.[32] The third role of transformative institutions is that of dealing with questions of pluralism and conflict. The way they do this is typically to emphasize institutional procedures rather than substantial outcomes. That is, we need institutions like a rational bureaucracy, a fair electoral system, a constitution that protects human rights, and an independent judiciary. Such procedural institutions can command our loyalty even if we happen to disagree with the particular outcomes they produce. What matters, in other words, is not that we win every time we play, but rather that we know that the rules of the game are fair. People can, for example, pay allegiance to a political system even though they fundamentally disagree with a particular government, or trust in the justice system although they disagree with a particular judgement.

Together, these three kinds of institutions provide for a society that is always in a state of flux. Through reflection we discover new possibilities; through entrepreneurship these possibilities are acted upon; through the pluralism guaranteed by procedural institutions the outcomes of our actions are protected. Since they bring about change, transformative institutions are also crucial in dealing with shocks. Reflective institutions can help us come up with creative responses to military, natural or social disasters; entrepreneurial institutions can make sure that markets function well and that economic disasters are avoided; pluralistic institutions can create loyalty and thus reduce the impact of political disasters.

Returning to our historical material, what can we say about Germany and Sweden from this institutional perspective? What role did German and Swedish institutions play in the process of modernization, and what role did they play in avoiding, limiting, and postponing crises?

State-Building

In the Middle Ages, there were parliaments in both Germany and Sweden, as indeed there were all over Europe.[33] At the time, the parliament provided the only means by which the king could obtain information and advice from the people, and, most importantly of all, the only means by which the king could raise taxes.[34] Obviously, this provided the representatives of the people with considerable financial clout and thereby with considerable political power. In Germany, however, the estates were often too internally divided and too deferential to their rulers to use their power effectively.[35] When kings in the course of the seventeenth century increasingly managed to find their own, independent, sources of income, the power of the parliaments declined further, and in many cases the assemblies were completely disbanded.[36] From this time onward, the institutional basis for German state-building was not the parliament, but rather the bureaucracy and the army.[37] By the seventeenth century, public bureaucracies were increasingly influenced by the teachings of the new science of public administration, "police science," or cameralism.[38] The cameralists emphasised rational procedures, the functional separation of tasks, and the rule of law. In Germany, in contrast to France, there were no venal offices; instead the office-holder was, in fully Weberian fashion, separated from his bureaucratic position. The enlightened rulers of Prussia and Austria also codified their legal systems and rationalized them in accordance with the imperatives of natural law; in Prussia, widely recognized as the most efficient and well-governed country in Europe, it was even possible to sue the king.[39] The rationality of the bureaucracy extended also to the military. In fact, in Prussia the bureaucracy was officially subordinate to the army, and all state activities were undertaken in order to fulfill military needs. War became the organizing principle of society, and soon enough also an economic imperative. Prussia went to war to conquer more land to raise more taxes to go to more wars.

Sweden also was a rational, bureaucratic state, based on the latest administrative science. The reforms put in place by chancellor Axel Oxenstierna in the early seventeenth century provided the foundation for a bureaucracy that remains in place until this day.[40] In addition, Sweden was a country ruled by law, not by personal fiat; the Administrative Act of 1634 is sometimes considered the world's first written constitution. Just as in Germany, there was a Weberian separation between office holder and bureaucratic position, and an emphasis on matters of procedural justice and accountability. In addition, attempts were made to separate political and bureaucratic decision-making in order to guarantee impartial procedures; political ministries were separated from bureaucratic agencies; politicians were barred from intervening in individual cases; and the right to obtain official records made it possible to inspect the workings of the bureaucracy.[41] But Sweden was, of course, just like Prussia, a military state. Under King Gustav II Adolf in the early seventeenth century, the Swedes had what must have been the best fighting force in Europe. In contrast to Prussia, however, Sweden was never, except for a few decades at the tail end of the imperial adventure, a militarized state.[42] The Swedish empire was to a large extent a self-financing enterprise, and the army was used to terrorize foreigners, not Swedes. The crucial difference between Germany and Sweden, however, concerned the parliament. In contrast to his German colleagues, the Swedish king never managed to find his own independent sources of income, and for this reason he continued to be dependent on the cooperation of the parliament. The Swedish king was always too poor to run the country by force and from above; instead people had to be convinced of the adequacy of a policy before they would agree to new taxes. Sweden, therefore, was a *monarchia mixta*–a monarchy where sovereignty emanated jointly from the king and the people.[43]

Comparing these two models, we could perhaps say that the institutional structure of the Holy Roman Empire was ahead of its time in several respects.

It encouraged cultural, social, and political pluralism, if not within each constituent member, at least within the Empire as a whole. This was the institutional setting of a creative culture, of Germany as a land of *Dichter und Denker*.
Politically speaking, the Holy Roman Empire provided a potentially ingenious solution to the perpetual problem of competing sovereignties. The
Empire, we could say, was an EU *avant la lettre*, only with more subsidiarity.
Sweden, by contrast, may seem overly centralized and monolithic. In practice, however, German decentralization was a source of weakness rather than
strength, and although Sweden may have been dull, it was united. In their
emphasis on the bureaucracy and the military, the two models were quite
similar. Both bureaucracy and army no doubt functioned, in a Tocquevillean
fashion, as sources of stability at times of shock; as rational, efficient, and procedural, these institutions were also important conflict-resolving devices and
thus sources of legitimacy for the regimes.

The major difference between Sweden and Germany concerns parliament: its absence was a German liability and its presence was a great Swedish
asset. For one thing, parliament improved the quality of the decision- making
process. Parliamentary opposition from the peasants was, for example, an
important reason why Sweden fought its wars abroad rather than at home.[44]
The parliament, that is, provided an important financial check on the military
ventures of the regime. When foreign wars could no longer finance themselves, the Swedish empire collapsed.[45] In Prussia, by contrast, the lack of
resources led not to a reconsideration of policies, but instead to hardened
repression; when no more taxes could be raised, the king ran up debts, and
when the debts could no longer be serviced the entire regime was undermined.[46] When Napoleon's army swept across the border, the formidable
Prussian army revealed itself as quite incompetent. An important reason for
the precariousness of German states was also the personal nature of rule;
lacking an institutionalized political leadership, the regimes were never more
competent than their rulers. This was a problem if, for example, the ruler suddenly died, or if he was succeeded by an infant son. In Sweden, by contrast,
the sudden death of a king simply meant that the council and the parliament
took over the reins. Sweden, we could say, was ruled by institutions, not by
individuals. Thus, for example, the loss of the empire in 1718 did not lead to
a crisis, but instead to an extended period of parliamentary rule–the so-called
"Age of Liberty"–and when King Gustav III was assassinated in 1792, the
result was not, as in France, a Jacobin dictatorship, but instead an affirmation
of parliament's position and a return to constitutional government.

Nation-formation

The German nationalist revival of the early nineteenth century was, we said,
a movement of philosophers and poets rather than statesmen and voters. In
institutional terms, this meant that universities, academies, and also the press

came to play a pivotal role. It was in the universities that the ethnographic, historical and social facts of the Germans were gathered; it was here that the philosophical underpinnings of a German national identity were worked out by scholars like Johann Gottfried Herder, Johann Gottlieb Fichte, and others.[47] These ideas, dressed up in suitably Romantic garb, were then spread widely across Germany by newspapers and journals. After 1750, Germany experienced a virtual press boom, with several hundred new papers appearing each year.[48] In these pages, vigorous discussions were held on a wide range of topics—from contemporary affairs and history to morality and home economics. Uniting German readers throughout the many petty principalities, the press created, for the first time, a sense of a unified German culture and, as its carrier, a unified German nation. It was suddenly obvious what it meant to be a German—it was a person reading about the same events, at the same time, and in the same language.[49] Yet, as we saw, the nationalist movement ran into resistance as soon as it sought the establishment of other institutions; the revolution of 1848 never resulted in a parliament or in a constitution. The ephemeral being which was the collectivity of a German self never managed to translate itself into something more embodied.

In Sweden, the first notions of a national identity had already been formulated in the sixteenth century.[50] To be a Swede was, at the time, primarily a question of being a Protestant and a subject of the king. The church was also the institutional setting through which this sense of community was propagated. There was a church in every parish, all Swedes were required by law to attend services and, best of all, the clergy were all on the king's payroll. This institutional structure was particularly useful in times of war. From pulpits throughout the country, the people would be informed of the latest events on the battlefront, or reminded of the importance of obedience and unity. It was a problem, of course, that Sweden had so little to be proud of. As a major power, the country was expected to boast of a glorious past, but Swedish history contained lamentably few memorable occasions or individuals. What did not exist, however, could easily be invented, and for this invention the state relied heavily on the University of Uppsala.[51] Soon the professors had fabricated an illustrious history, complete with references to the Flood, the Trojans, assorted Biblical personalities, and to the ancient Goths, a tribe from whom, it turned out, the Swedes all descended.[52] When remnants of the fabled island of Atlantis—long thought to have sunk in the ocean—were discovered in Uppsala late in the seventeenth century, no one was particularly surprised.

As far as other institutions are concerned, the press played a role, albeit a minor one. In the latter half of the eighteenth century, there was something of a newspaper boom in Sweden, in particular after 1766 when the Freedom of the Press Act came to guarantee the free circulation of printed material. Yet, with a few notable exceptions, Swedish public debates were more muted than those in Germany.[53] The towns were never big enough and the bourgeoisie never numerous enough to form an independent public sphere. Instead it was the system of public primary education, established in 1842, that provided the best vehicle for Swedish nationalism in the nineteenth and twentieth centuries. Here, again, it was the history of the Swedish state that was taught.

As a way to deal with the crises of nation formation, the Swedish institutional setup was clearly the more successful. In essence, the Swedish nation was a creation of institutions completely controlled by the state—the Church, the universities, and the primary school system. The problems of nationalism were avoided, we could say, because a Swedish nation autonomous from the Swedish state never took shape. This was in part due to elite manipulation, but it was at the same time an expression of the fact that the state, while never "democratic" in any modern sense of the word, was still responsive enough to popular pressure. In Germany, by contrast, a national identity was formulated outside of, and in opposition to, the state. German nationalism was from the very beginning a revolutionary force—liberal in guise in 1848, racist in 1933. Revolutionary ideologies, as Alexis de Tocqueville noted, are irresponsible by virtue of the fact that they are dreamt up by people who are excluded from power and thereby from political experience; revolutionary ideas are always too abstract, too rational, and too idealistic.[54] This, we could argue, was exactly the problem with German nationalism both before and after 1848. The nationalist movement failed in obtaining its parliament and its constitution, and for this reason it never acquired the practical experiences, and thus the reality checks, that it so badly needed. The German nation could continue to be thought of in mystical and disembodied terms, since there were so few other ways in which to conceive it. German nationalism remained a free-floating sentiment looking for a body to inhabit; it was a specter haunting first Germany itself, then Europe.

Industrialization

Newly designed institutions need enthusiastic support if they are to become firmly established; there must be a consensus on the rules, or no one will play the game. For the new institutions of the Weimar Republic, there was never a consensus on the rules, and whatever support there was for its institutions cannot be described as enthusiastic. The Republic was constitutional, democratic, liberal, and procedural, yet it never managed to deal effectively with the problems of industrialization. In the end, the economic problems were too severe and the political polarization too extreme. The Weimar constitution was in many ways a very ambitious document, setting out the basic features of a democratic welfare state, yet it was continuously questioned by scholars, mistrusted by political actors, and undermined by judges.[55] The parliament was divided between a government of the left that continued to lose support, and an opposition of the right that was gaining in strength while fragmenting; often the government had no clear majority or was based on completely unviable party combinations. Corporatist arrangements provided for bargaining between employers and workers and for compulsory state arbitration, but instead of producing compromises, these institutions made conflicts more acute. In 1924, the system broke down as employers reacted to the intrusive meddling of the "trade union state." In the end, the economic and social problems of the time were completely overwhelming.[56] A stagnating economy led to reduced profits and wages, to business closures and mass unemployment; thus the situation was already bad when the effects of the Wall Street crash hit. There was no institutional cushion capable of absorbing these shocks. Instead the incipient welfare state was overburdened with new demands. Since what little prestige the Weimar Republic enjoyed was to a large extent based on its promise of welfare, the cuts in welfare provisions were directly translated into a loss of legitimacy for the regime.[57] With no faith in the established institutions, the forces of the far left and the far right decided to pursue politics by different and decidedly undemocratic means. By the early 1930s, these extremes of the political spectrum commanded the support of the majority of the German people.

The institutional setup in Sweden was similar in several respects. However, the Swedish constitution was not replaced, but instead it was flexibly adjusted to incorporate the features of a constitutional democracy. The franchise was, for example, expanded to include all adults. Similarly, while the Swedes also had to face political instability in the 1920s, with a rapid turnover of governments, as well as serious economic problems after 1929, the Swedish political institutions were not fatally undermined, and there was no radical polarization of the political spectrum. The parliament continued to be an important focal point for political struggles, and when the Social Democrats came to power in 1932, their policy was one of reform, not revolution.

The shocks of industrialization were similar in Germany and Sweden, I argued, and, as we have seen, the institutional setups were also roughly comparable. Fundamentally different, however, were the reactions of political parties and social groups. In Sweden, institutions continued to be seen as legitimate, while in Germany the legitimacy of the structure was rapidly undermined. These differences in perception are themselves best explained in institutional terms. Swedish institutions were ancient, the German were brand new; Swedish traditions were inclusive, the German were exclusive; Swedish culture was based on consensus, the German was based on absolutist rule. Not surprisingly, Swedes had entirely different expectations regarding their political system. Above all, Swedish political actors lacked viable alternatives. It was next to impossible to imagine a politics that was fought outside of the structures provided by the state. Thus, in Sweden, the political game remained the same. The prize was the right to form a government, and the way to win this prize was to maximize parliamentary seats. In Germany, however, the official political institutions were not the only options, and visions of alternative arrangements came easily—and not only to overheated minds. Memories of the Reich were still strong and many conservatives looked back on it with nostalgia; there was a Communist alternative, and still a very vibrant one, in the Soviet Union; and there was the nationalist dream of a *Volk* united under one all-powerful leader.

By way of summary, it is worth emphasizing the crucial role played by the institution of the parliament throughout the process of modernization. It was the parliament more than any other institution that saved Sweden from crises, and it was the lack of a parliament, or at least a viable parliament, that was the main factor behind Germany's continuous problems. Much of this importance is due to what we have identified as the Tocquevillean factor—the parliament provided an invaluable source of stability at times of shock. When the Swedes lost their king, for example, or their empire, or when they lost Finland, the parliament was there, ready to pick up the pieces. In Germany, by contrast, political rule was personal and thus always more precarious. Stability was provided by the army and the bureaucracy, which was fine, but only as long as these institutions could be paid for.

Parliaments are also extremely important because they are an almost perfect example of what we have called transformative institutions. That is, parliaments are a unique combination of the three institutional roles of reflection, entrepreneurship, and pluralism. In a parliament, the representatives of the people get together not only to make decisions, but also to deliberate.[58] The parliament, we could say, is a kind of double mirror; in its composition, it reflects the views of the people, but in its work it also reflects on, and transforms, those views. The better this deliberative function is carried out, the higher the quality of the final decisions. But parliaments are also places where rules are made, and an important set of such rules concerns the preconditions for effective entrepreneurship. Parliaments guarantee property rights and the sanctity of contracts; they provide the legal, social, and economic preconditions for properly functioning markets. Although enlightened kings could do as much, there are important reasons why parliaments are better at these tasks. Historically speaking, kings have always been tempted to confiscate people's property to raise taxes, to annul outstanding loans unilaterally, or to subvert markets by selling monopolies.[59] Parliaments may certainly be taken over by "special interests," but they are much more difficult to subvert in this way, while a king who is beholden to special interests is much more dangerous. Finally, parliaments are also procedural institutions and as such are well placed to deal with conflicts and to produce loyalty. There are rules that govern the process of being elected to parliament, making decisions in parliament, and forming and dismissing governments. As long as these rules are seen as fair, we will play the game even though we might not win every time.

We may not necessarily like a present government, but we can still feel a very strong allegiance to the system as such.

Parliaments are important, in other words, because they help us reflect on our options, since they help us implement decisions, and allow many different views to compete. A properly functioning parliament protects society against crises not by perpetuating a certain kind of society, but instead by always transforming it.

The November Tree Principle

Today, Sweden and Germany are of course similar in very many respects. Both countries are liberal and democratic, post-industrial, and affluent; both are sovereign, but also members of the EU. This outcome was the eventual result of a process of modernization that comprised the sub-processes of state-building, nation-formation, and industrialization. Although the end result of these three transformations is quite uniform, the routes that brought our respective countries to these outcomes have been remarkably different. Lacking the appropriate institutional structure, the German road to modernity was, as we have seen, considerably bumpier.

In a curious way, the differences we have found between Sweden and Germany remind us of the contrasts often drawn between Britain and France, usually understood in institutional terms. From Montesquieu onwards, authors have noted the power of the English parliament, the independence of the judiciary, and the vigorous debates in the English press.[60] In the eighteenth century, such institutional pluralism was often seen as a threat to the unity and peace of the state, and from the perspective of the French *ancien régime*, Britain's was "a government stormy and bizarre."[61] Yet Anglophiles at the time, and we today, are more likely to see Britain's institutional setup as a guarantee of its political liberties and economic dynamism.[62] Westminster is, at least in the rhetoric of after-dinner speeches, the "Mother of Parliaments."

At the heart of the contrast between Britain and France is the question of the appropriate relationship that ought to obtain between the state and society.[63] In France of the *ancien régime*, society played no role in politics and the king was the only public person; in Britain, by contrast, the king shared his power with the parliament both in theory and in practice. The long-term consequences of these institutional differences were profound. In Britain, in the course of the process of modernization, political demands were channeled through parliament and there moderated, further deliberated upon, and reconciled with other, initially contradictory, demands. The press added the voices of the politically under-represented to this process of public deliberation, thereby defusing revolutionary demands. In addition, the English judiciary was fair and independent, and legal guarantees of property rights made it possible to invest in manufacturing and in business ventures. In short, the constitution of Britain contained a number of examples of what I have called transformative institutions. The constitution of France, by contrast, guaranteed stability and unity, but only as long as its institutions remained viable. Lacking a way to transform itself, the institutional structure of the *ancien régime* eventually had to be replaced. The result was a revolution, and decades of internal chaos and external war.

As a sort of index of these differences between Britain and France, consider the longevity of the monarchy in England as opposed to its sudden death in France. In Britain, the monarchy survived not because it was powerful but, on the contrary, because it was powerless and posed no obstacles to change. In France, the monarchy had to be abolished before a real transformation could take place. In his essay *The English Constitution* (1867) the journalist Walter Bagehot made a similar point regarding the longevity of the House of Lords. "So long as many old leaves linger on the November trees," he says,

> you know that there has been little frost and no wind; just so while the House of Lords retains much power, you may know that there is no desperate discontent in the country, no wild agency likely to cause a great demolition.[64]

Perhaps we could call this the November Tree Principle, according to which the institutional structure of a society is all the more flexible and transformative, the more remnants of medieval institutions it contains. The older the institutions look, that is, the more modern they are.

Judging by the November Tree Principle, it is very interesting that the Swedish parliament retained its four estate format until as recently as 1866; that the Swedish constitution, together with the American, was the oldest in the world until it was finally changed in 1974; and that the Swedish monarchy still survives to this day. Throughout the process of modernization in Sweden, power was shared between king and parliament, and Swedish institutions allowed rather than blocked transformations. Just as in Britain, the kind of tension that could have resulted in a revolution never developed. In contrast to Britain, however, the lack of a Swedish revolution may be better explained by the absence of tension between state and society rather than by its defusing. In Britain, that is, the demands of society were channeled, moderated, and reconciled, but in Sweden, as we have seen, there were far fewer social demands that required channeling, moderation, and reconciliation. Instead the process of modernization was from the very beginning a state-led enterprise. Once the Swedish state was established, it, not society, was in charge of the process of nation formation, and once the Social Democrats had come to power, it was the state, not society, that dealt with the problems of industrialization. In Sweden, in short, there was less of an outside with which the state could be in tension; the corporatism of the medieval estates was in the twentieth century simply replaced by the corporatism of the welfare state. Yet it is unlikely that the relative consensus of Swedish political culture would have been maintained, had the political institutions failed to adjust so successfully to the challenges of modernization. Swedes are not docile, after all, and they are deferential to the state only as long as it makes sense to be so. As an agent of modernity, however, the Swedish state has, at least until recently, had the overwhelming confidence of the people.

As far as Germany is concerned, its emperors, kings, and *Kaisers* are today all but forgotten; its parliaments have come and gone; it has enacted and abolished countless constitutions. This was, just as in France, a consequence of the inability of the institutional structure to accommodate pressures from society. Since they could not be changed, the old authorities had to be replaced. Germany's constitution, in short, was never strong enough, and for this reason German history is the story of one crisis after another. In contrast to France, however, this weakness was more the result of the absence of a state rather than its overbearing presence. In the nineteenth century, there was no way to accommodate new nationalistic demands, for the simple reason that there was no German state that could do the accommodating. The demands of industrialism were indeed responded to by Bismarck—with both state-led industrialization and social programs—but during the Weimar period the state was once again seriously weakened. In contrast to Sweden there was, as we have seen, a strong, independent society in Germany that posed its demands both loudly and clearly, but since the appropriate institutions were not in place to channel these demands, the result was crisis.

We end up, consequently, with four paths to modernity. In Britain and Germany, society pushed for modernization, whereas in Sweden and France the state did so. In Britain and Sweden, tensions between society and the state were either defused or largely absent, whereas in Germany and France, social demands were impossible to accommodate due to the absence of an appropriate institutional structure. Judged by the November Tree Principle, in other words, England and Sweden have had the fairer weather; they were better able to survive the shocks that the process of modernization inevitably presents. Today all four countries are of course quite similar, and it is difficult to say that the institutional structure of Sweden or Britain is inherently superior to that of France or Germany. On the other hand, and as I have argued, the legacy of institutions matters, and a distinctly unmodern set of institutions should for this reason be not a source of embarrassment, but rather a source of confidence. Turning to questions of the EU, globalization, new technologies, and everything else that we can see coming up on the horizon, we do not have to be royalists to hope that our monarchies will continue to enjoy good health.

Notes

1. To invoke MacIntyre's image. See Alasdair MacIntyre,"Is a Science of Comparative Politics Possible?" in his *Against the Self-Images of the Age: Essays on Ideology and Philosophy* (Notre Dame: University of Notre Dame Press, 1971), 260.

2. On the etymology, see "Crise," *Dictionnaire historique de la langue française* (Paris: Robert, 1993); Reinhart Koselleck, *Critique and Crisis: Enlightenment and the Pathogenesis of Modern Society* (Oxford: Berg, 1988), 103–104.

3. Compare Amartya Sen, *Development as Freedom* (Oxford: Oxford University Press, 1999), 180–186.

4. See, for example, Eva Österberg, "Violence among Peasants: Comparative Perspectives on Sixteenth- and Seventeenth-Century Sweden," in her *Mentalities and Other Realities: Essays in Medieval and Early Modern Scandinavian History* (Lund: University of Lund Press, 1991), 89–112.

5. For a discussion, see Leszek Kolakowski, "*Fabula Mundi* and Cleopatra's Nose," in his *Modernity on Endless Trial* (Chicago: University of Chicago Press, 1990), 242–248.

6. "If there is such a thing as a modern tradition, it is a paradoxical tradition which always seeks to break with itself; by always breaking with itself, modernity constantly seeks to become different from what it is." Octavio Paz, "A Tradition against Itself," in his *The Children of Mire: The Charles Eliot Norton Lectures, 1971–1972*, translated by Rachel Phillips (Cambridge, Mass.: Harvard University Press, 1974), 1–18.

7. I discuss the problems of recognition in the context of Swedish state-formation in Erik Ringmar, *Identity, Interest & Action: A Cultural Explanation of Sweden's Intervention in the Thirty Years' War* (Cambridge: Cambridge University Press, 1996), 145–186.

8. For a short overview, see, for example, Thomas Ertman, *Birth of the Leviathan: Building States and Regimes in Medieval and Early Modern Europe* (Cambridge: Cambridge University Press, 1997), 224–63.

9. Ertman, *Birth of the Leviathan*, 238.

10. This represents a revision of earlier, much higher, figures. See Frank Tallett, *War and Society in Early-Modern Europe, 1495–1715* (London: Routledge, 1992), 161.

11. Ertman, *Birth of the Leviathan*, 311–314. See also Ringmar, *Identity, Interest & Action*, 95–103.

12. On the impersonality of the Absolutist state, see Koselleck, *Critique and Crisis*, especially 15–50.

13. Benedict Anderson, *Imagined Communities: Reflections on the Origin and Spread of Nationalism* (London: Verso, 1983). I discuss the nation as an expression of the modern definition of the concept of a person in Erik Ringmar, "Nationalism: The Idiocy of Intimacy," *British Journal of Sociology*, no. 4, 1998.

14. Ernest Gellner, *Nations and Nationalism* (Oxford: Basil Blackwell, 1983), 1.

15. For an overview of German nationalism, see, for example, Liah Greenfeld, *Nationalism: Five Roads to Modernity* (Cambridge, Mass.: Harvard University Press, 1992), 277–395.

16. Elie Kedourie, *Nationalism* (1960; reprt. London: Hutchinson, 1994).

17. For a brilliant discussion of this theme, see Simon Schama, "*Der Holzweg*: The Track through the Woods," in his *Landscape and Memory* (London: Fontana, 1995), 75–134.

18. Hagen Schulze, *The Course of German Nationalism: From Frederick the Great to Bismarck, 1773–1867* (Cambridge: Cambridge University Press, 1990), especially 56–63.

19. See, for example, Ringmar, *Identity, Interest & Action*, 156–164.

20. On the seventeenth-century mythology of "ancient Goths," see, for example, Axel Strindberg, *Bondenöd och stormaktsdröm: en historia om klasskamp i Sverige, 1630–1718* (1937; reprt. Stockholm: Gidlunds, 1971), 22–48.

21. Mary Dietz, "Patriotism," in Terence Hall, James Farr, and Russel L. Hanson (eds.), *Political Innovation and Conceptual Change* (Cambridge: Cambridge University Press, 1989), 177–193.

22. "Allmän," *Bonniers Svenska Ordbok* (Stockholm: Bonniers, 1981).

23. Compare Karl Polanyi, *The Great Transformation: The Political and Economic Origins of Our Time* (1944; reprt. Boston: Beacon Press, 1957) especially 111-129. See also Alexander Ger-

schenkron, "The Advantages of Backwardness," in his *Economic Backwardness in Historical Perspective* (Cambridge, Mass.: Harvard University Press, 1962).

24. Hagen Schulze, *States, Nations and Nationalism: From the Middle Ages to the Present*, translated by William E. Yuill (Oxford: Blackwell, 1998), 140–141.

25. Dudley Dillard, *Västeuropas och Förenta Staternas ekonomiska historia* (Lund: Liber, 1980), 260–261, 334–340, 366–369.

26. Detlev J. K. Peukert, *The Weimar Republic: The Crisis of Classical Modernity*, translated by Richard Deveson (Harmondsworth: Penguin, 1991), especially 222–282.

27. Peukert, *The Weimar Republic*, 6.

28. "Institutions," according to North, "are the rules of the game in a society or, more formally, are the humanly devised constraints that shape human interaction." Douglass C. North, *Institutions, Institutional Change and Economic Performance* (Cambridge: Cambridge University Press, 1990), 3.

29. This, at least, was Schumpeter's view of democracy. Joseph A. Schumpeter, *Capitalism, Socialism and Democracy* (New York: Harper Torchbooks, 1975), 269-302.

30. Alexis de Tocqueville, *The Old Regime and the French Revolution*, translated by Stuart Gilbert (1856; reprt. New York: Doubleday, 1955), 202.

31. On the stability of everyday life as a source of meaning and consolation, see the many examples given in George Orwell, *Nineteen Eighty-Four* (1949; reprt. Harmondsworth: Penguin, 1989), or, in a different voice, Milosz's poetry written in Warsaw, 1943. See Czeslaw Milosz, "Världen," in his *Samlade dikter. 1931–1987* (Stockholm: Brombergs, 1988), 50-69.

32. Compare Douglass C. North and Robert Paul Thomas, *The Rise of the Western World: A New Economic History* (Cambridge: Cambridge University Press, 1973), especially 9–18.

33. S. E. Finer, "Representative Assemblies," in his *The History of Government: II, The Intermediate Ages* (Oxford: Oxford University Press, 1999), 1024–1051.

34. J. C. Holt, "The Prehistory of Parliament," in R. G. Davies and J. H. Denton (eds.), *The English Parliament in the Middle Ages* (Manchester: Manchester University Press, 1981), 5–6, 19–24. On the "informing function" of medieval parliaments, see also Walter Bagehot, *The English Constitution* (1867; reprt. Brighton: Sussex Academic Press, 1997), 74, 151–152.

35. Ertman, *Birth of the Leviathan*, 236, 241.

36. H. W. Koch, "Brandenburg-Prussia," in *Absolutism in Seventeenth Century Europe*, edited by John Miller (Basingstoke: Macmillan, 1990), 123–155.

37. Ertman, *Birth of the Leviathan*, 224–225.

38. Marc Raeff, *The Well-Ordered Police State: Social and Institutional Change through Law in the Germanies and Russia, 1600–1800* (New Haven: Yale University Press, 1983), 43–179.

39. John M. Kelly, *A Short History of Western Legal Theory* (Oxford: Oxford University Press, 1992), 262–265, 283.

40. Discussed at length in Michael Roberts, *Gustavus Adolphus: A History of Sweden, 1611-1632* (London: Longmans, Green & Co, 1953–58), 67–245.

41. Michael Roberts, "Swedish Liberty: In Principle and in Practice," in his *The Age of Liberty: Sweden, 1719–1772* (Cambridge: Cambridge University Press, 1986), especially 106–107.

42. On the brief, failed, history of Swedish absolutism, see A. F. Upton, "Sweden," in John Miller (ed.), *Absolutism in Seventeenth Century Europe* (Houndsmills: Macmillan, 1990), 99–121.

43. Nils Runeby, *Monarchia Mixta: Maktfördelingsdebatt i Sverige under den tidigare stormaktstiden* (Uppsala: Studia Historica Upsaliensia, 1962).

44. See, for example, Meeting of the Parliament, June, 29, 1629, *Arkiv till upplysning om svenska krigens och krigsinrättningarnes historia* (Stockholm: Norstedt & söner, 1854), part I, 40. Or as the peasant estate more laconically put it: "it is better to tie the goat at the neighbor's gate than at one's own." Quoted in Nils Ahnlund, *Gustav Adolf den store* (Stockholm: Svenska kyrkans diakonistyrelses bokförlag, 1932), 46.

45. Bruce C. Carruthers, *City of Capital: Politics and Markets in the English Financial Revolution* (Princeton: Princeton University Press, 1996), 97.

46. Ertman, *Birth of the Leviathan*, 262.

47. Kedourie, *Nationalism*, 56–86. On the Counter-Enlightenment in Germany, see the work of Isaiah Berlin, for example *The Magus of the North: J.G. Hamann and the Origins of Modern Irrationalism*, edited by Henry Hardy (London: Fontana, 1993).
48. For an overview, see Hans Erich Bödeker, "Journals and Public Opinion: The Politicization of the German Enlightenment in the Second Half of the Eighteenth Century," in Eckhart Hellmuth (ed.), *The Transformation of Political Culture: England and Germany in the Late Eighteenth Century* (Oxford: Oxford University Press, 1990). See also Schulze, *States, Nations and Nationalism*, 43–47, 56–63.
49. Newspaper reading, according to Hegel, is a modern substitute for morning prayer. Quoted in Anderson, *Imagined Communities*, 39.
50. Ringmar, *Identity, Interest & Action*, 156–164.
51. Patrick Hall, *The Social Construction of Nationalism: Sweden as Example* (Lund: Lund University Press, 1998), 148–169.
52. Kurt Johannesson, *Gotisk renässans: Johannes och Olaus Magnus som politiker och historiker* (Stockholm: Almqvist & Wiksell, 1982), 95–190.
53. See, however, the contributions to Knut Johannesson, *Heroer på offentlighetens scen: politiker och publicister i Sverige, 1809–1914* (Stockholm: Tiden, 1987).
54. Tocqueville, *The Old Régime and the French Revolution*, 145–146.
55. Peukert, *The Weimar Republic*, 40–42. On the scholarly debates, see David Dyzenhaus, *Legality and Legitimacy* (Oxford: Oxford University Press, 1999).
56. Peukert, *The Weimar Republic*, 118–146.
57. Peukert, *The Weimar Republic*, 129.
58. In defense of parliaments as "talking shops," see John Stuart Mill, "Considerations on Representative Government," in *On Liberty and Other Essays* (1861; reprt. Oxford: Oxford University Press, 1991), 283. Compare also the contemporary discussion in Joseph M. Bessette, *The Mild Voice of Reason: Deliberative Democracy and American National Government* (Chicago: University of Chicago Press, 1994); Carlos Santiago Nino, *The Constitution of Deliberative Democracy* (New Haven: Yale University Press, 1996); Amy Gutmann and Dennis Thompson, *Democracy and Disagreement: Why Moral Conflict Cannot Be Avoided in Politics, and What Should Be Done about It* (Cambridge, Mass.: Harvard University Press, 1996).
59. On this general point, see Douglass C. North and Barry W. Weingast, "Constitutions and Commitment: The Evolution of Institutions Governing Public Choice in 17th Century England," *Journal of Economic History*, vol. 49, 1989, 803–832. Compare, for example, the arbitrariness of property rights in France during the *ancien régime*, discussed in Kathryn Norberg, "The French Fiscal Crisis of 1788 and the Financial Origins of the Revolution of 1789," in Kathryn Norberg and Philip T. Hoffman (eds.), *Fiscal Crises, Liberty, and Representative Government, 1450–1789* (Stanford: Stanford University Press, 1994), 253–298. On the breakdown of monopolies in England as a result of parliamentary control, see Robert B. Ekelund & Robert F. Hébert, "Mercantilism and the Dawn of Capitalism," in their *A History of Economic Theory and Method* (New York: McGraw-Hill, 1997), 39–65.
60. Baron de Montesquieu, "De la constitution d'Angleterre," chapter 6, book 11 of *De l'Ésprit des lois*, in *Œuvres complètes* (1748; reprt. Paris, Seuil, 1964, 586–590.
61. Compare the discussion in Keith Michael Baker, "'Public Opinion as Political Invention,'" in his *Inventing the French Revolution: Essays on French Political Culture in the Eighteenth Century* (Cambridge: Cambridge University Press, 1990), 178–185.
62. Compare R. C. van Caenegem, *An Historical Introduction to Western Constitutional Law* (Cambridge: Cambridge University Press, 1995), 123–125. For a contemporary discussion, see, for example, North and Weingast, "Constitutions and Commitment," 803–832.
63. Compare Koselleck, *Critique and Crisis*, 2–3, 22–50.
64. Bagehot, *The English Constitution*, 59.

4

Moral Community and the Crisis of the Enlightenment
Sweden and Germany in the 1920s and 1930s

NINA WITOSZEK

Communities of Interest vs. Moral Communities

Though Germany and Sweden share a common myth of origins and a history of *valfrändskap*, they have followed strikingly opposing strategies to come to grips with political-economic breakdown and disruption. Attention has been drawn to their contrasting attempts to tackle the crisis of the 30s: Sweden through political compromise and precursory Keynesianism, Germany through militarization and "reactionary modernism."[1] But the differing sociopolitical structures and economic predicaments that led to a savage Darwinist spectacle in one case and to a successful–if opportunist–Social Democracy in the other, are but one element of a complex aetiology of crisis. What remains less explored is the role of communal values in shaping these two opposing scenarios of response to political and economic traumas. What we know is that in Germany the mythology that accrued round the modernizing process was intertwined with an anti-individualist, "coral-reef" mentality and a story of Aryan superiority. In Scandinavia, on the other hand, it remained affiliated with narratives embodying, for the most part, an egalitarian and pragmatic ethos. We also know that just as there was a distinctive language of National Socialism with value-charged myths and mantras, so there was a language of Social Democracy with its own fetish words and fables. Admittedly, it is hazardous to make disembodied words, philosophies, and worldviews responsible for history rather than actual speaking, acting, and writing human beings. Yet there is a sense in which these very discourses and mythologies are like ancestral homes filled with memories in which communities feel and act.

Notes for this section begin on page 69.

Taking, then, as the point of departure the notion of culture as a "theater of memory" with its own spots of amnesia and areas of enhanced–Proustian?–remembrance in which the past never quite dies, I shall attempt to unfold and compare the moral visions sustaining the modernizing project in two cultures that stand today for opposite poles of the Enlightenment legacy. In what way did elements of the dominant interwar ethos in Swedish and German society facilitate the acceptance of particular "rescue packages" offered by political leaders? What were the main features of the national utopias promoted in the model of *Bildung/bildning* that formed several generations of Germans and Swedes prior to the Great Crisis? What was the relationship between the moral vision accepted by the majority in both societies and the totalitarian temptation? And how relevant is a comparative study of this relationship to the exploration of modern democracies in general?

The answers to these questions invite less an inspection of the "rhetorics of decline" manifest in, say, the media or in cultural fads and fashions of the time, and more a study of the *durable* ethical patterns, role models and scenarios of action that dominated school curricula, religious education, community ethos, and national aspirations in both countries. In what follows I shall attempt to carry out the comparison on the basis of the following premises:

1. Contrary to the Foucauldian argument, cultural continuity is not a *fata morgana*–it is inherent in the very fact that society creates and reproduces symbols and stories, which repeat themselves and mutate over many generations and are available for scrutiny.

2. Communities may be invented, constructed, or imagined by the national elite, but they are never passive objects of construction. Ultimately it is not intellectuals but people at large who are the arbiters of the "cultural fitness" of controlling stories and images. (By "cultural fitness" I mean an enduring ability to codify collective predicament, bring solace, or sustain grievance.)

3. Society is certainly ruled by interest but it is to an even greater extent ruled by emotional and moral imperatives that are encoded in its significant narratives and rituals. It is increasingly recognized that various cultures resort to different scenarios of action to resolve tensions or alleviate felt trauma. Such scenarios constitute the primary ethical environment of each member of the national community: they are marshaled by history lessons, recycled in national literature, taught by religious institutions, repeated *ad infinitum* by parents and peers. Again, they are less contingent stories or *ad hoc* inventions in Hobsbawm's sense than they are narrative and symbolic habits transmitted from generation to generation and attuned to the past. They provide ready vehicles for an emotional response to new challenges, they prompt a

community what to feel and how to behave in conflict situations, and mobilize or stifle social energies. They do so by invoking the memory of similar past crises, by quoting the words and deeds of the ancestors, by rehearsing past wrongs or triumphs. Hence, while it is futile to speak of a German or Swedish "national character," it is certainly possible to identify morally charged "master-stories" that have had an extraordinary reproductive potential in both cultures and that were repeatedly mobilized at times of crisis. As such they assisted or obstructed the accommodation of political and economic constraints.

4. It is certainly contestable whether, politically or economically, there exists a German *Sonderweg* or a separate path to modernity. But, following from the above, every culture–Germany and Sweden included–creates and pursues its own, narrative *Sonderweg.*

5. From the humanist perspective–a point of departure in this essay– not all significant master-narratives or rites lead to moral unity. They may result in an immoral unity.

6. Crisis does not necessarily yield social aberrations. On the contrary: it is often in extreme situations that the true image of a community is revealed (cf. Conrad's *Lord Jim*: the truth is wrung from us not in time of peace but by some cruel catastrophe). The common perception linking crisis to social anomaly is based on facile transfers from the animal to the human world. As I have indicated above, communities respond differently to traumas: from passivity and fatalism through aggression to romantic sacrifice.[2] Again, these responses have nothing to do with so-called "national character." Their sources lie, partially at any rate, in the semiotic environment in which several generations have been immersed: their models of cultural heroes, stories of past triumphs and defeats, and their informing ethos. As Dewey observed, even aesthetic systems may breed a disposition towards the world and have overt effects.[3] A totalizing view to the effect that "We are all potential Nazis" is too charitable with regard to those who supported a savage regime, and blatantly unjust to those who, in the face of torture and persecution, preserved their humanity and dignity to the very end. More, the trendy universalisation of guilt leads to the disturbing–and simplistic–conclusion that the humanities everywhere ultimately fail to humanize. Perhaps, as George Steiner has suggested, it is more relevant to search for those particular models of humanistic culture that contain "express solicitations of authoritarian rule and cruelty."[4]

7. In the ongoing assessment of modernity, "education towards citizenship" has been one of the key criteria. According to this

reading, German intellectuals abdicated from civic responsibility[5] while the Swedes managed to create a rich public realm. And yet, as I will try to show, there are problems with the Swedish–and indeed the current Western–model of citizenship. It struggles to reconcile what Hannah Arendt described as the opposition between a "good citizen" and "good man," or, alternatively, to bring together public imperatives and the "voice of conscience."[6] Such problems were anticipated by Machiavelli, who demonstrated the incompatibility of public morality, focused as it is on the welfare of the *patria*, and Christian precepts, which are apolitical and insist on a virtuous private life.[7]

Communities, Crises, and Elective Affinities

If Romantic Germany was founded on enthusiasm about its sublime Nordic soul, modernist Scandinavia was certainly taken by the superiority of German brains. For Sweden before World War I, Germany functioned as a "Great Good Place," a civilizational template, an example to follow. According to Ivar Harrie, a renowned chronicler of the times, the Swedish university was but a "branch of German research," the Swedish army "emulated a Prussian ideal," and Swedish newspapers quoted avidly from German dailies.[8] At the Great Baltic Exhibition in Malmö in 1914, the German pavilion–with its "imperial panache," "splendid industry," and "the Prussian spirit of unconditional devotion to state authority"–created the greatest stir.[9]

Some twenty years later German influence seems to have been equally pronounced. Both Swedish and German people shared a fetish about "community" (*Gemeinschaft/gemenskap*); both spoke obsessively about home (*Heimat/folkhem*); both displayed an extraordinary loyalty to their political leaders, not to mention the fact that "one could find a Prussian spirit in many a Swedish civil servant."[10] The parallels went further. The Swedish film director Ingmar Bergman states in his self-scathing autobiography that "Many of the teachers were National Socialists, Nazi-adherents, some from foolishness or bitterness, others from idealism and veneration of the old Germany, a 'nation of poets and thinkers.'… My brother was one of the founders and organizers of the Swedish National-Socialist party, and my father voted several times for them. Our history teacher worshipped 'the old Germany', our gymnastics teacher went to officers' meetings in Bavaria every summer; some of the pastors in the parish were crypto-Nazis and the family's closest friends expressed strong sympathies for the 'new Germany.'"[11]

For all the radical visions of the Social Democrats, Sweden followed its own principle of *festina lente*. It was slow both to embark on a social revolution and to recognize the Nazi threat. Stockholm of the 1930s was still class-

ridden, bathing in the afterglow of Oscarian ethics with its "norm-alized" citizens, distaste for emotional outbursts, and a bourgeois surveillance of the
unruly proletariat.[12] One of the best-sellers of the 1930s was *Lort-Sverige*
("Filthy Sweden"), whose author undertook a comprehensive "inventory of
the human material" in the country and remarked that Swedish villages were
infested with "idiots, imbeciles and psychically feeble individuals. ... As it is,"
he concluded, "the lack of planning implies an extremely serious danger not
only of the countryside being populated by inferior people but of the whole
Swedish race facing degeneration and decline."[13]

And yet, for all these analogies and inspirations, Sweden of the 1930s was
the ideological and cultural opposite of the community it tried to emulate. A
closer inspection of the "microcosm of crisis" of the Swedes and the Germans
reveals that, under siege, the two communities invoked different values, cultivated different heroes, dreamt different utopias. While the Germans were
blundering backwards into the future, the Swedes strolled forward, looking
back only so much, and certainly overlooking their imperial past.[14] What in
Sweden was the Middle Way, in Germany was the "rotten middle" (*faule
Mitte*).[15] While in Germany one marched, in Sweden one reasoned. When the
Weimar political elite and later Hitler attempted to transcend their difficulties
and mobilize the masses by the deployment of the dichotomous rhetorics of
Romanticism (highlighting racial and cultural difference, invoking Mother
Nature against degenerate civilization, dreaming of the superhuman and fum-
ing about encirclement and conspiracy), the Swedish Social Democrats followed what might be called a "harmonic imperative." The latter underplayed
conflict and tension and rested on the Enlightenment belief in the resolvabil-
ity of problems, not by blood and iron, but by rational analysis, compromise,
and consensus. Albin Hansson reiterated: "When people sometimes talk of
standing on the basis of class struggle that does not mean that one ... must
swear to a doctrine of hate and violence. ... It means quite simply that one
recognizes a fact and adapts one's actions with respect to it."[16]

As I will show, this "ecological" approach to crisis–ecological in the
sense of giving priority to adaptability and survival–was not just an ad hoc
strategy of political leaders but a "group-think" whose roots lay in the native
tradition. Similarly, the common vocabulary of modernity–*Heimat, Volk,
Gemeinschaft, Bildung,* freedom, socialism–was embedded in different pasts
and charged with different meanings. While the Germans dichotomized,
opposed, and contrasted, the Swedes fused, reconciled, and appeased. Thus
if the German *Heimat* opposed modernity (unreflectively identified with city
culture, exile, decadence, and Jewish domination) to an original home where
blood, race, and soil remained forever pure and devoid of politics, the Social
Democratic idea of *folkhem* (people's home) attempted to reconcile modernity
with *gemenskap,* the progressive with the conservative, the past with the future,
the public with the private. It drew heavily on an Enlightenment vocabulary

with its mantras of "equality," "freedom," "solidarity," and "responsibility." The uniquely Swedish concepts of co-worker (*medarbetare*), co-citizen (*medborgare*), and co-responsibility (*medansvar*) were the active components of the Nordic home mythology. They constituted what Harrie called *demosbildning*,[17] a creation of citizenship based on deletion of hierarchic distinctions and wide political participation.

As Fritz Ringer has persuasively demonstrated, in the German *Bildung* the cultivation of spirit, in accordance with the Romantic ideal of expressivity, was set in opposition to Enlightenment "civilization".[18] The Swedish *bildning* carried no such dichotomy; on the contrary, it encoded the ideas of modern rationality and pragmatic ethics. Whatever Alva Myrdal's views on the population question, she insisted that Swedish education was to be used as a basis for social and cultural amalgamation, not for segregation within a national community.[19] Sociologically, the values that the Social Democrats launched in school programs drew less from the bourgeois golden age–relatively short in duration–and more from the strength of peasant citizenship (after all, the decades after 1866 are known as the "age of peasantry"). Unlike the German *Bildungsbürgertum*, with its relentless search for a spiritual hegemony as a compensation for political impotence, the Swedish pursuit of knowledge was less the result of sublimation and more a preparation for participation in the political and economic life of the community. And unlike Germany, where ideas of the greatness and glory of the German nation ruled supreme, the key concept in the formulation of Swedish political and social ideals was not "greatness" but "goodness." Thus the Swedish state was a "good and beautiful state;" Swedish society was a "good society," the Swedish mother was a "good mother," etc.[20]

Four questions present themselves. Is there anything in the founding myths which were part of the German *Bildung* (in addition to, say, the political-economic predicament) that accounts for the national community's dramatic departure from the moral ideas of Spener or from Kant's vision of "the starry heaven above and the moral law within?" Secondly, how is it that the intensive moralization of politics under the Swedish Social Democrats and their humanitarian idea of citizenship failed to produce any significant acts of social protest against Swedish fraternal ties with the Nazi regime? What was the relationship between Swedish moral education and what might be described, after Sheldon Pollock, as acts of "active indifference" or "collaborative unknowing"[21] with regard to the Swedish policy vis-à-vis the Jews and other minorities before and during World War II? Here we may invert the question. In view of the well-documented elective affinities between Sweden and Germany prior to World War II and the tradition of statism in both countries, why was the Nazification of the Swedish community so low-key?

Triumph of the Will against the Family Romance:
The Moral Legacy of Founding Traditions

In his diaries Adolf Eichmann, the former salesman of electrical goods who became the chief technician of the Holocaust, explained his actions by pointing to "obedience" as a German trait. "Today, fifteen years after 8 May 1945," he concluded, "I know … that a life of obedience, led by orders, instructions, decrees and directives is a very comfortable one in which one's creative thinking is diminished."[22]

Eichmann's self-justification is striking, and not just because of his essentialist deployment of national stereotypes. What is intriguing is that Eichmann is more worried by the destructive effect of the code of obedience on creativity than by its dehumanizing potential.

There is yet another recapitulation of the disturbing effects of "doing one's duty" as demanded by *raison d'ètat*. In his diary of the Swedish elites' pliant stance towards the foreign policy of the Social Democrats, Herbert Tingsten suggests: "If we got a German or Nazi government in Sweden I presume that the majority of Swedish professors would support it, very much like the professors in Germany. … Swedish ingrained anti-Nazism did not guarantee courage or consistency in confused social circles."[23] According to Tingsten, the Swedish elites' compliance with the conciliatory politics of their government "was not exactly a betrayal of Sweden; it was … a moral betrayal, a betrayal of one's own belief."[24]

However limited and selective, both of those utterances illustrate a particular moral drama of Germany and Sweden, a drama that reaches its climax at the turning points of national history. In the first, the majority of the national community embraced a Machiavellian idea of citizenship. It was one in which a consistent vision of a strong, united, morally regenerated and victorious *patria* involved a rejection of Christian ethics in favor of a pagan (or, as some may wish to call it, aesthetic) morality. In the second case the Social Democrats struggled to resolve a conflict between the public and the private (Christian) realm and, consequently, were stuck with a confused morality based on incompatible value systems. As Machiavelli put it, "men take certain middle ways that are very injurious; indeed, they are unable to be altogether good or altogether bad."[25] As we shall see, this "injurious middle"–or rather muddle–has been an enduring motif in Swedish cultural texts, from the life of Gustavus Adolphus through Strindberg's drama to Myrdal's project of Sweden as the epitome of modern humanism.

In one of the numerous explanations of Germany's slide into Nazism, Wolfgang Mommsen concluded that it was a "product of the policy of crisis management that went disastrously wrong" due to the "weakness of the ruling elites and their inability to restrain ill defined emancipatory movements couching their demands in the language of nationalism."[26] This is certainly a plausible institutional explanation. To this we might add that neither of the two communities that revealed themselves in the crisis of the 1920s and 1930s was responding to new challenges in purely economic terms. Nor can the Germans and the Swedes be treated as mere end products of the manipulation of their rulers. I wish to suggest that both communities searched for guidance in two enduring, and radically opposing, myths and two contrasting types of ethics.

If myth tells us that what was once accomplished by our ancestors is holy and sacrosanct and can be repeated again, then a master-story that empowered and mobilized the Germans at the time of the post-Versailles tristesse–a narrative that was the imaginative engine of German greatness and its constant recharger, so to speak–was the mystique of Prussia. It was the memory of Prussia and its breathtaking rise from mediocrity and backwardness to the status of a major player in European politics that exerted a continuous blackmail on the rest of Germany. True, Prussia was detested by most Germans most of the time. But it was the kind of hatred–to borrow an image from W. B. Yeats–of the eunuchs for Don Juan riding through hell.[27] Prussia was emulated because it was a symbol of the triumph of will. It embodied a story of a kind beloved of all people all over the world: of the elevation of Cinderella, of the passage from rags to riches, of the phoenix rising from the ashes. The values it incarnated–discipline, obedience, and high respect for military valor–might not have been to everybody's liking, but they became popular by the mere fact that they were profitable and successful. As Emilio Williams argues, "three victorious wars and the glamor of the newly established empire made the overwhelming majority of the people lend ardent support to the expansion of the armed forces and to further diffusion of military patterns ... throughout German society. Liberal opposition to militarism in Prussia and the South gave way to ... almost unqualified support of the German states."[28]

Claims to the effect that the intoxication with the Prussian mystique was limited to the work of conservative historians such as Sibel, Droysen and Treitschke are problematic. Even acute critics of Germany's "mission impossible" fell under Prussia's spell. In 1914 Meinecke wrote: "[in recent times] ... the unfortunate tensions that existed between the conservative forces of Prussia and the liberal needs of a wider Germany have diminished. If our army succeeds in bringing about the full synthesis of the people's army and professional army, then in the life of our state the full synthesis of Prussian organism and Reich organism can also come about."[29] And Thomas Mann rhapsodized: "Our soldierliness has an intimate spiritual connection with our moralism; indeed, while other cultures have the tendency to assume civilian forms of cultural behavior into the most refined aspects of life, into art, German militarism is in truth the form and revelation of German morality."[30]

The conflation of German morality with militarism by leading German intellectuals had both a fertile and a fatal dimension. It was fertile in the sense that it permitted the recovery of national dignity through invoking the soldierly ethos of Prussia. It was fatal because, in the process of the mutation of the Prussian myth, the mixture of gold and dross that once made Prussia great was bound to thin out the "golden nuggets" (such as the Prussian tradition of tolerance and multiculturalism) and enhance the dross. Oswald Spengler, whose *Preussentum und Sozialismus* (1920) sold 650,000 copies, identified the central myth of Germany: "Prussianism is a life style, an instinct, a compulsion. ... The officer corps, the bureaucracy, the workers of August Bebel, 'the people' of 1813, 1870, 1914, feel, desire, act as a super personal whole. This is not herd instinct; it is something immensely strong and free, which no one who does not belong can understand."[31] Inherent in this claim was an aspiration to exclusivity and an idolatry of "compulsion" and "instinct" which the Germans had but to follow.

The crisis of the 1930s reinforced further the fascination with the Prussian ethos. (Bismarck understood as much when he said: "Great crises are the weather which Prussia's growth demands."[32]) Despite the loss of hegemony, Prussia blossomed in countless narratives and rituals. What was (mis)remembered—and hankered after—by the community at large was not the feeble achievement of liberal and federalist Germany but another "Prussian miracle." What was dreamt of was not a wishy-washy democratic leadership but a charismatic overreacher of the caliber of Frederick the Great or Bismarck. As Peter Gay argued, "By its very existence, the Republic was a calculated affront to the heroes and clichés that every German child knew, many German politicians invoked and, it turned out, most Germans cherished."[33]

Weimar-time was Germany's refusal to live in the here and now. It was the determination to remain in a mythical *illo tempore*: to attend to the great ancestral voices, which redeemed the national community from the futility of the tawdry present. In the competition of moral codes, the Prussian soldierly value system and the conflation of freedom and obedience were bound to overwhelm the German people's conception of nationhood in the first half of the nineteenth century.[34]

There is ample evidence to the effect that Hitler's spellbinding control of the masses was due less to his clever use of Nordic myths and icons than to his juggling the kernel elements of the Prussian myth (the Will, the leader, the army, duty, obedience, and destiny) to nourish the hope and hasten the restoration of the glorious past.[35] His inauguration as chancellor took place in Potsdam at the tomb of Frederick the Great. In *Mein Kampf* he spiritualized Prussia, turning it into a site of original purity and mastery that had been polluted by conspirators and Jews: "Prussia, the germ-cell of the empire, came into being through resplendent heroism and not through financial operations or commercial deals, and the Reich itself in turn was only the glorious reward of aggressive political leadership and the death defying courage of its soldiers."[36]

The most powerful evidence of the Prussia-inspired choreography of the German *Gemeinschaft* is to be found not in Wagnerian tableaus, but in Leni Riefenstahl's film documentation of Nazi rallies. It is here, in Riefenstahl's famous *cinéma de verité*, entitled, significantly, "The Triumph of Will", that the myth of Prussia was ultimately transfigured and debased. The film alternates between wide shots of multitudes of German troops saluting Hitler, and close-ups of worshipful faces caught in a rapture of submission. It is as if all of Germany arrived in uniform to pay homage to the heir of Frederick the Great before the last battle to unite the world under Germany. This is certainly something other than the original Prussia with its balance of *mythos* and *logos*. It is Prussianism at its most extreme, divorced from its original context and from its Christian foundations. Unlike England or America, where the *telos* of conquest and supremacy never really canceled out the myth of an autonomous individual, Germany, captured so powerfully by Riefenstahl's lens, opted for an ethics in which the difference between a person and a citizen, between a subject imbued with conscience and a subject of the state, was canceled by the Führer.

In the face of this spectacular Prussian-Teutonic extravaganza, Sweden of the 1920s and 1930s seems paltry and bargain-basement by comparison. It is sometimes claimed that Social-Democratic self-representations–free of large chunks of unwelcome national history (such as the imperial legacy) and saturated with ideas of egalitarian humanism, rationality, and science–were to produce a new *homo scandinavicus*. But rational planning does not necessarily mean social engineering, especially if–as in the case of Germany–it relies heavily on revamped past traditions with which the community identifies. As a matter of fact, the political leaders of Sweden drew on values, images, and myths that had been widely diffused and cherished by the people and that went back to the early nineteenth century.

As I have argued elsewhere, an extensive review of Swedish national literature and public discourse in the nineteenth century points to the codification of a new master-narrative about Sweden, one that could compete with the Sweden-as-Atlantis mythology fixated on imperial destiny.[37] The central images in this new story were home and family; their ideological thrust was the defense of privacy. Their moral message was the sanctity of Everyman in his home, that bastion against state intrusion. We might call it the "Swedish Family Romance."

Significantly, home here was less about roots and origins than about being at home and at peace in the universe. For most of the nineteenth century, Swedish *prästgårdar* (parsonages), coffeehouses, and salons resounded with the rhetorics of the "great family" where one could encounter "the feeling of home, goodwill and cordiality, happy kindness and understanding sympathy."[38] The great national poet, Gustaf Geijer, had boundless faith in the significance of home as the only environment to promote the ideal of the

Christian-liberal personality, which later came to imbue the dominant educational and ethical tradition of Sweden. Crucial to it was the notion of personal conscience: "We apprehend the voice of the fellow being or original being, which we all carry within us, in the law of conscience," he proclaimed. In Malla Silfverstolpe's famous salon, the "family was holy"—a boundless source of *gemenskap*. For the widely read Fredrika Bremer and later for Ellen Key, home was a "Fatherland in miniature" and a primary site of women's emancipation.[39] The grand national psychomachia, the battle between the private and the public, the individual and the state, was codified most powerfully by August Strindberg in his historical plays. Both *Gustaf Adolf* (1898) and *Erik XIV* (1899) are dramas of modern conscience: they show the divided self of a powerful, reckless ruler who, unlike his single-minded German counterparts, agonizes over his ethical choices and loses his home, family, friends, and sanity.[40]

The family romance was brought to a culmination by the doyenne of Swedish letters, Nobel Prize winner Selma Lagerlöf. In her masterpiece *Gösta Berlin's Saga* (1891) we find all the components of the home mythology on display. The story concerns multiple expulsions from and returns to home. The finale encapsulates all the central ideals of Swedish Family Romance: reconciliation, atonement, being at home, compassion, building bridges, canceling class boundaries, belief in the future—and labor.[41] Very much like her Romantic predecessors, Lagerlöf actively launched the values and mores of the home—especially of the preindustrial households managed by women—as a model for governing the state.[42]

And so it became. When in 1929 the Swedish Social Democrats proposed a "new"-old story that would consolidate and unify the nation at a time of social upheaval, they launched the *folkhem* (people's home) as their mantra.[43] The story was "new" in the sense of being politicized by the Social Democratic government; it was old in that it was a reformulation of the myth of nineteenth-century Sweden to which every child had been exposed through the school curriculum and family readings. It is customary to associate Social Democracy with an archetypally "masculine" set of values such as bureaucratic rationality, pragmatism, and scientific worldview. But, as Selma Lagerlöf proposed, the Swedish "household mythology" also cultivated values traditionally perceived as "feminine": compromise, adaptation, reconciliation, pacifism, survival. In his momentous speech Albin Hansson insisted that "The basis of home is togetherness and a sense of belonging. A good home doesn't make a difference between privilege, backwardness, between darlings and stepchildren. … In a good home equality, thoughtfulness, and cooperation rule."[44] If we further consider that many of the ideas running through this passage were already in the process of being institutionalized in powerful social projects such as *folkrörelse*, *folkupplysning*, and *folkhögskola*, then it is clear that the modern, foundational phase of the Swedish Family Romance had been accomplished.

Just as in the case of Hitler's invocation of the Prussian myth, the Social Democratic appropriation of the Family Romance was a semiotic coup, a repossession of a story and an image that had tremendous mobilizing potential in society at large. More importantly, it was the most effective way back to Swedish supremacy–this time not by military but by moral conquest.

Unlike the German Romantic *Heimat*, the Swedish rhetorics of home drew heavily on the Enlightenment ideals of "equality," "freedom," "solidarity," and "responsibility." And, unlike the German hometown legacy which represented the laws of social exclusion and gave primacy to communal membership,[45] the Swedish home, at least in theory, aspired to embrace all healthy and sane individuals irrespective of their class and origins. To put it in sociological terms, *Heimat* represented pure *Gemeinschaft*. *Folkhem* on the other hand, fused *Gemeinschaft* with *Gesellschaft*: a prime example of the Swedish tendency to reconcile opposites and obliterate distinctions.

What prewar Sweden and Germany shared were two ways in which, to invoke the words of Sir Samuel Ferguson, "the idea of erecting the bulwark of the state in the hearts of [the] inhabitants" was brilliantly executed.[46] One could say that it was done via the political establishment's skillful deployment of the founding myths of the community–but this is surely not the whole story. For we cannot forget that, in both cases, the existing democratic structures prior to the early 1930s allowed the people to be an active agent in choosing their myths and their heroes.

Heroes of the Community

Ian Kershaw, in his study of *The Hitler Myth*, claimed that the sources of the Führer's immense popularity "have to be sought in those who adored him rather than in the leader himself."[47] The Hero, a figure whose nature has been inspiringly illuminated by James Hillman, is less an independent entity than the creation of a community, an embodiment of its dreams and aspirations.[48] According to this reading, it is not so much that outstanding individuals give an example to be followed by lesser men: rather, they *follow* the ideal, which is already contained in the community's scenario of its better self. A hero resonates with what the community desires, and that is why he is a hero–not the other way round. "The hero does not so much found the city, as the city's collective acts invent him or her as a collective focus." In this sense he or she is "the idealized exteriorization of the community."[49]

When seen in this light, the idea of a national savior whose main features were later to be incarnated by the Führer had certainly been well established in national literature and wished for by generations of German intellectuals. From Goethe to Thomas Mann, the German intelligentsia was fascinated by ideas of genius and the superior individual. One does not need to probe very far or very deep to find the motifs of transcendence, of "going beyond," of defying the gods, as the central theme of German philosophy and literature. The obsession with a charismatic leader to whom laws of human morality did not apply characterized all *Stürmer und Dranger* (including Schiller); it was further developed by Klopstock and Fichte, theorized by Johan Georg Hamann and Schopenhauer, and taken to extremes by Nietzsche. [50] Julius Langbehn's *Rembrandt als Erzieher* (1890) linked the hero to ethnic purity by invoking an Aryan, German aristocrat, a "hidden emperor," and an "artist-dictator," "a Caesar-like, artistic individual, powerful and spiritually overwhelming." Such a demigod was celebrated both by Hegel, for whom ruthless leaders like Napoleon were the agents of spirit, and by Schmoller in his notion of "economic genius."[51] Exceptional individuals were no longer subject to Christian morality: they were entitled to a higher narcissism characteristic of the ancient pagan heroes. If we add to it the Hegelian morality, which insisted on external and historical laws rather than virtuous actions of individuals as moving history forward, then the concept of personal guilt and responsibility lost its relevance for the nation in pursuit of its historical mission.

What is certainly intriguing about the Nietzschean ideas of a superhuman "spiritual aristocracy" is that they were such an apt prefiguration of things to come. Christian Graf von Krokow observed the effects of this fixation before World War II: "Even at the university one stopped speaking about the 'republic of scholars' to talk instead about the 'aristocracy of spirit'".[52] Hitler did not relinquish the aristocratic principle; he inscribed it into nature and thus made it worthy of emulation: "By rejecting the authority of the individual and replacing it by that of the members of some momentary mob, the parliamentary principle of majority rule sins against the basic aristocratic principle of nature."[53]

While the German elite were increasingly captivated by a warrior code that defied Christian norms, the Swedes were trying to find a "viable position for civil self-assertion, a personal heroic ideal which would avoid militarization." The basis of heroism was to be "work, the ordinary, the daily, grey work."[54]

Again, this "grey heroism" had long roots. As I have argued elsewhere, the undisputed hero of the nineteenth century and the great emblem of Swedishness was not Gustavus Adolphus or Charles XII, and not a Viking chief, but a free peasant—*odalbonde*—whose values were glorified by the demiurge of Swedish Romanticism, Gustav Geijer. Very much as in the preceding centuries, Romantic Swedish literature reenacted the contest of two myths and two images of Sweden. One was aristocratic-imperial, the other—which we might call "eco-humanist"—linked images of nature to antiheroic values, peasant protagonists, and the ethos of survival. The received interpretations of Swedish Romanticism emphasize the first in the context of a resurgence of Nordic themes in the work of Götiska Forbundet. But the imperial Nordic fantasies entertained by the Gothic Society never really resonated with the public imagination (they lacked "cultural fitness," in other words). The acclaimed national icon was not a heroic overreacher, and not even a noble savage in touch with a mystical realm, but a freeholder with impeccable credentials as a citizen, a champion of democracy and a producer of national wealth. As such he hardly represented a romantic return to a golden age of primeval unity with nature. He stood not for a *via antiqua* but for a *via moderna.*

Contrary to the German glorification of aristocratic genius, the Swedes increasingly invoked *jämlikhet*: the egalitarian passion as a moral force.[55] The aristocratic ethos had to compete against the idea that "small is beautiful, poor is dutiful," reinforced in Swedish culture by the rise of liberal and socialist ideas. The liberal daily *Aftonbladet*–the "bible of Swedish people" (Tegner)–lampooned Swedish imperial fantasies. The scrutiny of national delusions was brought to a climax by August Strindberg in his *Svenska folket: I helg och söken* (1881-82), the first antiheroic account of the Swedish Age of Greatness.[56] It assaulted the wasteful–and murderous–virtues of glorious kings. By 1909, four years after the loss of Norway, the ancient heroes were such a liability that when a competition for a national monument was launched, Sven Bober's submission, entitled "Sleep in Peace," proposed a fat Mother Svea snoring on the throne flanked by Gustavus Adolphus and Charles XII squeezed into gaiters. That Bober succeeded in ridiculing the project owes much to the then concurrent general strike, one of the largest in European history. As a result no national monument was ever erected.[57]

Thus, if in the 1930s the German utopia was a restoration of the Teutonic Empire under the leadership of the Führer, the Swedish promised land pictured a "world without glitter or greatness, its inhabitants secure and happy as well-fed pigs."[58] The two corresponding sets of values represented two kinds of morality. One advanced a model of "Machiavellian citizenship," where the ideal of a strong, splendid, and victorious *patria* justified all sacrifices and suppressed all personal qualms about drastic solutions. The other, "Hamletic," vacillated between the demands of citizenship and the old Christian voice of personal conscience.

Moral Community and *Bildung*

In the late 1920s a certain Mrs. Emilie Fogelklon-Norlind embarked on an intriguing project. In view of the increasing secularization around her, she set out to map the Swedish "universe of the mind" by studying what books the Swedes read, what they thought of sex, politics, and religion and how they imagined their future. The evidence was collected from *folkhögskolarna*, Social Democratic youth clubs and study circles, agrarian associations, and

Free Church movements. Apparently, a "Swedish home with average ambitions" read Selma Lagerlöf, Tegner, Runeberg, Strindberg and Fröding–all of
whom wrote about the struggle for man's liberation from systems of power.
One of the most popular foreign books was *Im Vesten nich Neues*, next to the
works of Jack London and Thomas Paine. Though puritanism and asceticism
had certainly lost their appeal, the Christian precepts–diffused via parents,
folkskolan, and "moral training" before confirmation–maintained their validity for most Swedes.[59] It seems, morally speaking, that Sweden of the 1930s
did not shift very far from the nineteenth-century ideals of pacifism, democracy, and social reform propagated by Rydberg, Geijer, Almqvist, Tegner,
and Bremer.

And yet there was an Orwellian side to the Family Romance as adapted
by the Social Democrats. Although the education program professed to look
after "the need of all children to enjoy equal opportunities, the need to feel
safe and wanted in school,"[60] some children were clearly more wanted than
others. Apart from Selma Lagerlöf, the book successes of the 1930s included
Myrdal's *Kris i befolkningsfrågan* and Ludvig Nordström's *Lort-Sverige*, which
struck an alarmist note on the question of racial homogeneity and mental
hierarchy. The relatively compassionate dominion of the Christian Enlightenment was slowly replaced by the rule of experts preaching rationality,
progress, and science, attempting to justify the improvement of the race by
limiting the reproduction of the unproductive and the unfit.[61]

It has been suggested that in the late twenties, Swedish education was at
a crossroads: it could have gone to the radical left or to the reactionary
right.[62] Characteristically, it sought the middle way. Its nationalism was
"banal" rather than virulent, its history lessons downplayed Swedish imperial excesses, and–unlike its German counterpart–it cultivated individual
conscience. What it shared with the German model was the inculcation of
raison d'état as a superior ideal.[63] As Lars Trägårdh noted, in Sweden, as in
France, the notions of the rights of man stemming from the natural law tradition never properly took root, but were immediately overwhelmed by a
figure of the Citizen, above whom hovered the specter of Nation, Democracy, the General Will. All three were hostile to the notion of individual
rights, whose source of moral authority transcends the nation itself. Needless
to say, this provided a weak moral basis from which to criticize the state.[64]
There were two additional supporting factors: a strong tradition of identification of the people with their rulers[65] and the fact that the Social Democratic master-myth of a perfect, peaceful home was identical to the enduring
dreams of the community.

Just here lay the problem. First of all, social cooperation, loyalty, and solidarity do not necessarily presuppose a shared faith. They presuppose, as
Ernest Gellner argued, a shared doubt.[66] As the crisis was progressively
resolved, this doubt got less and less evident. The state itself was turned into

a gigantic household in which therapy, negotiation, and persuasion replaced political repression and thereby assuaged moral scruples. True, the idea of *folkhem* was spawned by thinkers and writers who certainly did not desire absolute power in the sense that Hitler did; much of its creativity accorded with Hamlet's "by indirections find directions out." Intrusive and ambitious governments, however, leave no indirection undirected. Even the idyllic wedlock of the Social Democrats and the people might become oppressive when too regulated. And even "third way ethics" has its liabilities when pushed to extremes.

It may well be that Swedish tradeoffs at times of crisis—an ecumenical alliance of the workers and industry, a mixture of humanism and utilitarianism that reconciled the demands of citizenship with those of private conscience—were the terrain upon which complicity with the Nazis was founded. There is thus a contradiction in Tingsten's argument that "the curtailing of all opposition [to the government's foreign policy] was so hard and efficient that the majority in a very short time gave up the thought of resistance or criticism."[67] Was quenching the opposition really so tyrannical, or even necessary? Tingsten himself notes that the general tendency to exculpate the Nazis and to soft-pedal their crimes "was strong even in those circles which distanced themselves from the regime and despised it."[68] Throughout his account of Swedish moral dilemmas during World War II, Tingsten makes a clear distinction between Swedes as *citizens* and as *persons,* between conscience and duty, betrayal and complicity, resistance and "bowing to circumstances like 'Pascal's reeds.'" [69]

It is almost impossible to recapitulate the vast mosaic of intellectual and moral strains in German culture before the Great Crisis. The time of trauma, however, distilled the dominant leitmotifs in the moral education of the German nation. As multiple studies have shown, the great majority of stories that the Germans told about themselves, whether in school textbooks, popular manifestos, or national best-sellers, rehearsed the familiar nationalist history of Germany: the myth of Prussian greatness, Reich, Führer, *Kulturmission,* imperial appetites, the military ethic, and the superiority of the German race.[70]

By comparison with Sweden, where the values of pacifism and pragmatism ruled supreme in the 1920s and 1930s, teaching in German schools was increasingly conducted in the spirit of the cult of the military. Initially, vulgar forms of nationalism and militarism in Prussian boarding schools contrasted with the democratic education of Hamburg, Saxony, Thuringia; after 1933 the creed of the National Socialist Teachers' League, founded in 1929, superseded that of all existing teachers'organizations.[71] As has been shown, from Kahnmeyer and Schulze's *Realienbuch,* published for elementary schools at Bielefeld before 1933, through the series *Geschichtliches Unterrichtswerk* (printed by Teubner) and the much-used geography textbook by Fischer-Geisterveck and E. von Sydltiz (edited by Rohrmann and published in Bres-

lau), to the popular Giese's civic textbook, large portions of the German educational ideal were permeated with the motifs of the master race, Germany's
encirclement in a hostile Europe, and the legend of the stab in the back. The
majority of history books eulogized Prussian militarism, condemned pacifism, contained illustrations and songs that glorified war, exculpated Germany from any responsibility for World War I, and proclaimed that "We
must have back the colonies of which we were robbed under empty pre-
texts."[72] As Walter Laqueur argued, "other societies had their Lagardes and
Langbehns but they never acquired such a mass following and sales of hun-
dreds of thousands."[73]

The available historical research shows that the institutions of higher education did little to oppose this trend. Meinecke's calls for *Bildung* towards good
citizenship (1926) did not have any serious follow-up. The majority of professors as well as the members of the Youth Movement were averse or indifferent to change, cherished expansionist ambitions, and did little to develop the
ethos of individual political responsibility.[74] But how little was little?

There are two ways of looking at the question. Both demand a prob-
lematization of the idea of citizenship. The Prussian educational model, supported by a set of enduring narratives and rituals, merged conceptions of
Bildung and *Besitz,* affirming the established order and the ideal of a strong
state.[75] That is not to say that the morality behind the German idea of citizenship did away with the concept of responsibility vis-à-vis the state; rather,
it was based on the condemnation of liberal decadence, the repudiation of
Christian "weakness," and a conviction that success creates more devotion
than an amiable character. From the vantage point of this essentially pagan
morality—and from the perspective of the great social objectives in the name
of which wicked acts had to be performed—such acts were no longer seen as
abhorrent but as rational and justified insofar as they contributed to the regen-
eration of the Fatherland. As such, only those who could not and would not
see a larger logical, theological, or metaphysical pattern in Germany's extermination policy condemned it. Brannimir Anzulovic has suggested that prolonged genocide is neither a question of the psychological mechanism that
makes large numbers of basically normal citizens engage in collective crimes,
nor of an eliminationalist trait in the national character (*pace* Goldhagen).[76]
Genocide is most reinforced by the threat of standing out of the group and by
its communal sanction and glorification as a long entrenched value. We might
add that it is further facilitated by the certainty of belonging to a new victorious world that assuages reservations about lawlessness and frees one from
moral responsibility. By drawing attention to the narrative-symbolic environment of genocide, Anzulovic has implicitly pointed to a paradox of citizenship: people committing crimes in the name of the *patria* like to think that
they are following their conscience. In fact, they confuse conscience with a
public duty inculcated in them by the authoritative stories of their community.

There is yet another dimension to the mutated "Prussian" idea of citizenship. While analyzing the legacy of Bismarck, Max Weber spoke about "a nation ... without any political will, accustomed to submit under the label of constitutional monarchy to anything that was decided for it."[77] This diagnosis would chime with the charge leveled at Bismarck by the Austrian poet Franz Grillparzer: "You claim that you have founded the Reich but all you have done is to destroy the *Volk*."[78] The destruction of the *Volk* meant, of course, its total disempowerment. If it is true that absolute power corrupts absolutely, it is also true that absolute powerlessness corrupts absolutely. Without the ability to make decisions there can be no choice to act morally. Powerlessness corrupts by eroding the sense of personal, not public, responsibility that is central to ethical conduct.

There were, then, two interesting developments here. In spite of one of the most eloquent nationalist vocabularies in Europe, what was going on in post-Bismarck Germany was, in fact, the destruction of the nation, a deprivation of will despite all the ranting about the Will. Secondly, there was a national sanction given to Hitler's project which stemmed not so much from a community of interest but from a particular "moral community" with its unique set of values. True, not all German "mandarins" withdrew into the ivory tower and washed their hands of civic responsibility. Many supported the Machiavellian idea of citizenship, putting the state before everything else, after the analogy of Periclean Athens, Sparta, or the Roman Republic (one need only recall that the whole energy of Ranke's historical thinking moved away from criticism towards the keen acceptance of power). As has been shown, if the Gestapo succeeded in becoming a fearsome institution, it was not because of its efficiency (it was actually understaffed) but through the wide cooperation of German citizens who enthusiastically performed their civic duty and denounced all suspect elements.[79]

An interesting moral contrast is provided by Norway, where in 1942 Quisling launched his plans to Nazify national education. Demanding obligatory membership in *Norges Læresamband*, he acted in the belief that the Norwegian teachers would bow down, just as the German teachers had. Yet in spite of massive arrests and deportations to Kirkenes, the teachers withstood the pressure, forcing Quisling to give in and re-open the schools. Upon their return to work they reiterated their vows: "The teacher's duty is not just to impart knowledge to the pupils. He shall teach them what is true and right. *Therefore he cannot, without betraying his vocation, teach anything that is against his conscience.*"[80]

The Norwegian teachers' civil disobedience illustrates very well the enduring conflict between the concept of an individual based on Christian conscience and the concept of the citizen rooted in a person's relation to the law. "Conscience is unpolitical," Hannah Arendt writes, "it does not tremble for the world or for my country, it trembles for the individual self and its integrity."[81] It is this conflict between a good man and a good citizen, between morality and politics, between the individual self and the member of a community, that the prewar generation of the Germans seemed to have resolved. The Swedish community—compromising, vacillating, falling between two stools, lying to themselves about themselves—became the stage of an emblematic drama of the Western secular conscience, a drama that has further intensified in postwar Europe.

Conclusions

I have tried to compare some aspects of the mythical and ethical biographies of two modern Western European cultures that supported their nation-building process with strikingly similar myths of origins, and displayed corresponding attitudes to the State and parallel social concepts, but that nonetheless ideologically diverged from one another. It is a hazardous comparison. One has to take into consideration the radically different environments involved. In one case we deal with a relatively homogenous society—both religiously and ethnically—which, by comparison with Germany, has been largely spared the trepidations and devastations of wars and revolutions. In the other case we are confronted with a multicultural, multireligious mosaic of communities that were continuously traumatized in the course of history and hence were naturally more prone to reach for consolatory narratives and ideological salvage kits. In one tradition individual rights had been brutally quenched by authoritarian rulers, in the other, the rights of the subject were basically respected, even under absolutist kings such as Charles XII.[82] One of the objectives of this essay, however, has been to focus less on institutional differences (highlighted by Erik Ringmar's contribution), and to draw attention to the powerful ways in which social memory was repossessed and appropriated by the Social Democrats in one case and by the Reich in the other, and used to blend the values of the community into those of the state. Three characteristics of this project become especially striking and require further study.

Firstly, what the examples of Sweden and Germany clearly demonstrate is that the so-called "invention of the nation" and its orientation it towards the achievement of particular goals was far from a mere conjuring trick. The extraordinary ability of the Nazis and the first Social Democratic governments to harness their communities into a project of political or moral conquest was not merely a function of institutional arrangements and socioeconomic conditions. Both the Swedish "Family Romance" and the Prussian "Triumph of Will" played a significant role in this process as symbolic structures cherished by generations, rehearsed by the national *Bildung*, and reenacted by popular rituals.

Secondly, the preliminary glance at Sweden and Germany as "moral communities" points to the necessity of revising some accepted notions of the Enlightenment legacy and its intrinsic connection with genocide. It may be that those who have examined the Enlightenment's "pathography" have misidentified the true sources of the Holocaust. As I have tried to show, a study of the communally sanctioned morality that underlay the Nazi projects of racial extermination indicates that it had little to do with the ideals of the Enlightenment. Rather, it was part of the revival of an old, Machiavellian, "pagan" idea of citizenship, which put the interest of the state above the demands of individual conscience and human rights.

Scandinavia, and Sweden in particular, point to a different Enlightenment: one marked less by Faustian aspirations and more by the ideas of egalitarianism, public discussion, justice, and social reform. This legacy is not without liabilities. It is stamped by a split between the Christian idea of a person and individual rights on the one hand, and the pragmatic principles of modern citizenship on the other. It accounts not just for a moral inconsistency in Swedish attitudes to oppression, but for dilemmas inherent in the politics of dialogue and appeasement that characterize postwar international politics in the West.

One conclusion of this essay is that it is Sweden rather than Germany that should be studied as the locus of the contradictions central to the Enlightenment project.[83] It is Sweden—with its triumph of Enlightenment reason and liberal democracy—that presents us with a precursory version of Fukuyama's "end of history," as it were. Between the 1930s and the 1960s Sweden was not utopian as it is sometimes claimed; it was a place where economic calculation and the solution of technical problems took precedence over creativity and where the general acquiescence suggested the end of ideology.[84] Even Sweden's attitudes to World War II, where the values of heroism were replaced by rational analysis and technology, and where a mildly tormented "spectator's stance" vis-à-vis the world's tragedies replaced intervention or participation, presaged the postmodern predicament of the Western world. No country has exposed so well the vulnerability of Habermas's *bürgerliche Offentlichkeit*, a public sphere comprised of citizens committed to the pursuit of social progress through self-emancipation and ideals of rational and critical discourse.[85] Sweden confounds the Habermasian ideal because, as the perfect opposite of a totalitarian state, it clearly illustrates that the much-celebrated "third way" may at any moment invite a wrong, totalitarian computation.[86] Unlike the situation in most authoritarian states, Sweden's project of perfection has not been imposed but has emerged, as it were, from the people themselves. For a very long time now the Swedes have aspired to be a community in which spontaneous goodness will replace civil coercion, and in which the ideas of "the rational pursuit of progress" will be equally shared by civil society and the government. And yet, as shown in this volume, it is precisely the rhetorics of consensus, the "pact mentality" shared by the citizens with the state, and the ubiquitous presence of the facilitative activities of the government (i.e. intense provision of education, health, medical service) that have gradually turned against themselves and contribute to the present crisis. At the end of the twentieth century, in a paradoxical tour de force, the Swedes realized that they have become "gratefully oppressed" victims of their own civil society: as Michele Micheletti has shown, "People have become trapped in interest organizations and need to be liberated from them."[87]

This again presents Sweden as a prototype of the contradictions inherent in the most benign, democratic system. In the contemporary prosperous world it is governments that increasingly spend on "moral" projects such as justice, welfare, and public education, while individuals, able to enjoy national provision of these necessities, are left free from any obligation to do other than to indulge themselves. As a direct consequence of the state's accretion of both morality and wisdom, the private realm–including private conscience–has steadily been absorbed into a regulated society. Further, the postmodern extension of the political to almost all spheres of life leads to confusion: political issues become defined as ethical and vice versa. Perhaps Mandeville's famous parable of the hive requires an inversion? Here every part may be full of virtue, yet the whole is far from being a paradise.

Tingsten summed it up succinctly: "The War was the test of Social Democracy which showed itself weaker and more flexible than we thought!" It is ultimately freedom outside the economic sphere that has to be attended to. If it is not observed, "it will be destroyed by a desert storm inherent in the very project of planning the future of the national household." [88]

Notes

1. For the general context see Marquis Child, *Sweden: The Middle Way* (New Haven: Yale University Press, 1936); Child, *Sweden: The Middle Way on Trial* (New Haven: Yale University Press, 1980); Steven Koblik, *Sweden's Development from Poverty to Affluence 1750-1970* (Minneapolis: University of Minnesota Press, 1975); Richard F. Thomasson, *Sweden: Prototype of Modern Society* (New York: Random House, 1970); Tim Tilton, *The Political Theory of Swedish Social Democracy* (Oxford: Clarendon Press, 1991); Jeffrey Herf, *Reactionary Modernism* (Cambridge: Cambridge University Press, 1984); Geoff Eley, *Reshaping the German Right: Radical Nationalism and Political Change after Bismarck* (New Haven: Yale University Press, 1980); Geoff Eley, *From Unification to Nazism: Reinterpreting the German Past* (London: Routledge, 1986); Richard Evans, *Rereading German History 1800-1996* (London: Routledge, 1997). For comparative studies of the social construction of the community in both cultures see Bo Stråth (ed.), *Language and the Construction of Class Identities: The Struggle for Discursive Power in Social Organisation: Scandinavia and Germany after 1800* (Gothenburg: Gothenburg University, 1990); Lars Trägårdh, *The Concept of the People and the Construction of Popular Culture in Germany and Sweden 1848-1933*, unpublished dissertation, University of California, Berkeley, 1993. See also the work of "Project Gemenskap," 1996-1999 (dir. Bo Stråth and Bernd Henningsen, European University, Florence/Humboldt University, Berlin); Bernd Henningsen, Janine Klein et al., *Tyskland og Skandinavia 1800-1914. Impulser og brytninger* (Deutsches Historische Museum, Nationalmuseum, Norsk Folkemuseum, 1998).
2. For an interesting comment on the role of culture as a contributing factor with regard to these responses, especially in the aftermath of the disintegration of the Soviet Empire, see Anatol Lieven, "Qu'est-ce qui une Nation," The *National Interest* no. 49, Fall 1997, 10-23. See also George Mead, *Mind, Self and Society: From the Standpoint of a Social Behaviourist* (1932, reprt. Chicago: Chicago University Press, 1964). For a case study see Erik Ringmar, *Identity, Interest & Action* (Cambridge: Cambridge University Press, 1996).
3. Quoted in Frank Kermode, *The Sense of an Ending* (Oxford: Oxford University Press, 1967), 108.
4. The problem has been discussed by George Steiner in *In Blackbeard's Castle: Some Notes Towards the Redefinition of Culture* (New Haven: Yale University Press, 1971), 11.
5. For the study of German intellectuals vis-à-vis Nazism see especially Fritz Ringer, *The Decline of the German Mandarins* (Cambridge, Mass: Harvard University Press, 1969); Alice Gallin, *Midwives to Nazism: University Professors in Weimar Germany 1925-1933* (Georgia: Macon Mercier University Press, 1986). See also Kurt Sontheimer, *Thomas Mann und die Deutschen* (München: Nymphenburger, 1961).
6. Hannah Arendt, *Crises of the Republic* (New York: Harcourt and Brace, Harvest Book, 1962; reprt. 1979), especially the chapter on "Civil Disobedience," 49-102.
7. See *The Discourses of Niccolo Machiavelli*, ed., transl., intr., notes by Leslie J. Walker, (1950; reprt. London: Routledge and Kegan Paul, 1975), vol. I, 26. See also Isaiah Berlin's chapter on "The Originality of Machiavelli" in his *Against the Current* (Oxford: Clarendon, 1991), 25-79; Giuseppe Prezzolini, *Machiavelli anticristo* (Rome, 1954), transl. into English as *Machiavelli* (New York, 1968).
8. Ivar Harrie, *Tjugotalet in memoriam* (Stockholm: Hugo Gebers Förlag, 1938), 11. For the German inspiration in Swedish culture see also Christina Stael von Holsten Bogoslovskiy, *The Educational Crisis in Sweden in the Light of American Experience* (New York: Columbia University Press, 1932); See also Henningsen, Klein et al., *Tyskland og Skandinavia 1800-1914.*
9. Ivar Harrie, *Tjugotalet in memoriam*, 12.
10. Herbert Tingsten, *Mitt liv. Mellan trettio och femtio* (Stockholm: Norstedt, 1962), 195.
11. Ingmar Bergman, *The Magic Lantern: An Autobiography by Ingmar Bergman* (London: Hamish Hamilton, 1987), 123.
12. See Allan Pred, *Recognizing European Modernities: A Montage of the Present* (London: Routledge, 1995), 25-7.
13. Ludvig Nordström, *Lort-Sverige* (Stockholm: Kooperativa förbundets bokförlag, 1938), 215-216.

14. Margaret Cole observed in 1938: "The Swedes are far less dominated by their own national history than most of the other countries of Europe." See M. Cole and Charles Smith (eds.), *Democratic Sweden: A Volume of Studies Prepared by Members of the New Fabian Research Bureau* (London: George Routledge & Sons 1938), 2. Gradually the Social Democratic "amnesia" deepened to the extent that at the celebration of the birth of Gustavus Adolphus, the great king was presented as the founder of the city of Gothenburg, not as one of the conquerors in European history. See Gudrun Dahl, "Wildflowers, Nationalism and the Swedish Land" in Andrew Brennan and Nina Witoszek (eds.), *Worldviews: Community, Identity and the Natural World* (Cambridge: White Horse Press, 1998). It seems that the social-democratic suppression of history was not entirely without precedent. There is evidence to the effect that in 1825 a committee of the greatest Swedish writers and luminaries such as Geijer, Tegner, Barzelius, and Fryxell (the so-called *snillekommitéen*), recommended that history had nothing to teach a child. Since history of the Middle Ages was found "ignorant and barbarous," and classical history as dangerous and encouraging rebellion, it was decided that sagas and fairy tales would be a better entry into the world of good and evil. See Orvar Löfgren, *Myter om svensken* (Stockholm: Liber, 1984), 113.

15. Cf. Moeller van den Bruck's "faule Mitte" in *Das Dritte Reich* (1922; reprt. Hamburg: Hanseatische Verlagsanstalt, 1931), 231.

16. Tilton, *The Political Theory of Swedish Social Democracy.* See especially Branting's speech "Klasskampens form kunna och bör humaniseras" (1905) in *Bilden av Branting, en antologi under redaktion av Jan Lindhagen* (Stockholm: Tiden, 1975), 350.

17. Harrie, *Tjugotalet in memoriam*, 233.

18. Fritz Ringer, *The Decline of the German Mandarins*, 5. On the pervasiveness of a dichotomous lexicon in the German sciences see Anne Harrington, "Metaphoric Connections: Holistic Science in the Shadow of the Third Reich," *Social Research*, vol. 62, no. 2 Summer 1995, 357-383.

19. Alva Myrdal, *Nation and Family: The Swedish Experiment in Democratic Family and Population Policy* (1941; reprt. London: Kegan Paul, 1945), 171. The threatening example of Nazi Germany provoked the discussion and reevaluation of the Prussian influence on the Swedish model of education, especially with regard to its elitist and authoritarian profile. See, for example, "Demokratiens skola och demokratiems ungdom", Socialdemokratiska Ungdomsförbundet, *Skolan och folket* series, 1941, 30-40. I will come back to this question.

20. "We are a beautiful country and a good country," declared Albin Hansson. " [Sweden] is a land with people's freedom and people's self government, with democracy planted in the Constitution, in people's traditions and attitudes." See Per Albin Hansson, "Tal till Sveriges flagga," (1934) in *Från Fram till folkhemmet. Per Albin Hansson som tidningsman och talare,* selected and edited by Anna Lisa Berkling, forword by Tage Erlander (Stockholm: Metodica Press, 1982), 147.

21. Sheldon Pollock, "Deep Orientalism?" MS (Collegium Budapest, 1998), 112.

22. Cited by Imre Karacs in "Memoirs of an accidental mass murderer," *The Independent*, 13 August 1999, Review section, 1.

23. Herbert Tingsten, *Mitt liv.*, 191.

24. Ibid., 313-315.

25. Machiavelli, *Discourses*, I, 26.

26. Wolfgang Mommsen, *Imperial Germany 1867-1918: Politics, Culture and Society in an Authoritarian State*, transl. Richard Deveson (London: Arnold, 1995), 171.

27. By analogy, whatever we think of the arrogance of the dollar or multinationals, it is American culture that, the world over, fascinates those very people who suffer most at its hands. See Jean Baudrillard, *America*, transl. Chris Turner (London: Verso, 1986; reprt. 1988), 77.

28. Emilio Williams, *A Way of Life and Death: Three Centuries of Prussian-German Militarism. An Anthropological Approach* (Nashville: Vanderbilt University Press 1986), 70; H. W. Koch, *A History of Prussia* (London: Longman, 1978), 139. On the influence of the Prussian myth see also Helmut Bohme, *The Foundations of the German Empire. Selected Documents*, transl. Agatha Ramm (Oxford: Oxford University Press, 1971); E. J. Feuchtwanger in *Prussia: Myth and Reality* (London: Oswald Wolff, 1970); Sebastian Hafner, *The Rise and Fall of Prussia*, transl.

Ewald Osres (1980; reprt. London: Orion Books, Phoenix Giant, 1988); Giles MacDonogh, *Prussia: The Perversion of an Idea* (London: Mandarin, 1994).

29. Quoted by Peter Pulzer, *Germany 1870-194: Politics, State Formation and War* (Oxford: Oxford University Press, 1997), 81.

30. Thomas Mann, *Thoughts in Wartime*, 1914. Cited in English by Pulzer, *Germany 1870-1945*, 79.

31. Spengler, *Preussentum und Socialismus* (1919), quoted by Feuchtwanger, *Prussia: Myth and Reality*, 7.

32. Otto Von Bismarck, *Gesammelte Werke* (Berlin, 1984) vol. I, 473.

33. See Peter Gay, *Weimar Culture* (New York: Harper and Row, 1968), 72. On the spread of symbols, rituals, and discourse embedded in the Prussian master-story, see especially Norbert Elias, *The Germans* (New York: Columbia University Press, 1996); George Mosse, *The Nationalization of the Masses: Political Symbolism and Mass Movements in Germany from the Napoleonic Wars Through to the Third Reich* (New York: Meridian Books, 1977); Walter Z. Laqueur, *Young Germany: A History of the German Youth Movement* (New York: Basic Books, 1962); Liah Greenfeld, *Nationalism: Five Roads to Modernity* (Cambridge, Mass.: Harvard University Press, 1992); Ritchie Robertson, "From Naturalism to National Socialism" in Helen Watanbe-O'Kelly (ed.), *The Cambridge History of German Literature* (Cambridge: Cambridge University Press, 1997).

34. Many shared the perception of liberalism as un-German, after Paul de Lagarde, who accused Bismarck of "kneading liberalism and despotism into one dough." See Golo Mann, *The History of Germany since 1789*, transl. Martin Jackson (1966; reprt. Pimlico: Random House, 1996), 236.

35. Hitler's relation to Rosenberg, the official Nazi mythographer and a great enthusiast of the North, shows that the Führer remained largely skeptical about the extravagant use and abuse of Nordic images in the creation of German *Gemeinschaft*. See Robert A. Pois, *German Fascism and the Religion of Nature* (London: Croom Helm, 1986), 17.

36. Adolf Hitler, *Mein Kampf*, transl. R. Manheim (London: Pimlico, Random House, 1992), 141.

37. Nina Witoszek, "The Fugitives from Utopia: Scandinavian Enlightenment Reconsidered," in Øystein Sørensen and Bo Stråth (eds.), *The Cultural Construction of Norden* (Oslo: Scandinavian University Press, 1997). As Michael Roberts has argued, "the Swedish kings' imperial ambitions never really captured the imagination of the Swedes. The policy of expansion faced a strong opposition both from the taxpayers and from the nobility. The conquest was the king's, not the people's fantasia." See Michael Roberts, *Essays in Swedish History* (London: Weidenfeld and Nicholson, 1967); Michael Roberts, *The Swedish Imperial Experience* (Cambridge: Cambridge University Press, 1979). On the Swedish nobles ready to sacrifice gains in Prussia to obtain peace see *Handlingar röranda Skandinaviens historia* XXXII (Uppsala, 1851). See also Georg Wittrock, "Gustaf Bondes politiska program," *Historisk Tidskrift*, 1913; Axel Strindberg, *Bondenöd och stormaksdröm* (1937; reprt. Stockholm: Gidlund, 1971).

38. See Arne Melberg, *Realitet och utopi* (Stockholm: Rabén & Sjögren, 1978), 56. See Fredrika Bremer, *Syskonliv* (Stockholm, 1848), 201. See also Bremer, *Hemmen i den nya världen* ("Home in the New World)," (Stockholm: Norstedt, 1866).

39. See Erik Gustaf Geijer, *Samlade Skrifter* (Stockholm, 1849-1855), I, part I, xxxii-xxxiii; Fredrika Bremer, *The H---Family* (London, 1845); Birgit Gerhardsson (ed.), *Ellen Key: 1849-1999: en minnesbok* (Linköping: Futurum, 1999); Ellen Key, *Kärleken och äktenskapet: Livslinjer* (Stockholm: Albert Bonniers, 1911-1914).

40. One of the most poignant scenes in *Gustaf Adolf* takes place in Stettin, where a tranquil idyll of a borger home is profaned by a violent intrusion of the agents of state power that take over the house as the royal quarters. The final words of a trumpeter who dies in the presence of the king are: "I want to go home." August Strindberg, *Gustaf Adolf* (1889; reprt. Stockholm: Gernandt, 1900), 61.

41. When the protagonist, the Major's Wife, lies on her deathbed, Gösta Berling, a colorful villain who dispossessed her, makes his peace with her while invoking a vision of a happy home: "Don't you hear what the hammer says? ... Your work shall continue. That farm

shall always be a home for great and true labour." I quote from a rather poor English translation: Selma Lagerlöf, *The Story of Gösta Berling*, transl. Robert Bly (Karlstad: Karlstad
Press, 1982), 308.

42. See especially one of Selma Lagerlöf's speeches, "Hem och stat," 1911. Selma Lagerlöf,
Skrifter (Stockholm: Bonniers, 1933-1966), vol. 3, p. 47.

43. It is claimed that the image of *folkhem* was first used by a conservative thinker, Prof. Kjellén, who declared: "At last on our own ground Sweden can be built into a happy home."
But there is another angle to the origins of the story. The idea of the people's home was
actually first launched in a Norwegian schoolbook by P. A. Jensen (*Laesebog for Folkskolen
og Folkhjemmet*, (1863; reprt. Kristiania: Cappelen, 1874). Rune Slagstad argues that "In
Norway *folkehjem* could not become a national symbol because of two spellings, the Southern *hjem* and the Northern *heim*." See Rune Slagstad, *De Nasjonale strateger* (Oslo: Pax,
1999), 202.

44. "Folkhemmet, medborgarhemmet" (1928) in Per Albin Hansson, *Från Fram till folkhemmet*
(Stockholm: Metodica Press, 1982), 124. Transl. mine.

45. Mack Walker, *German Home Towns. Community, State and General Estate 1648-1871* (Ithaca:
Cornell University Press, 1971), 417. Walker argues that "some visible or tacit traditional
communal limits have remained noticeably strong in German small-town life even until
now" (418).

46. Quoted by David Lloyd, *Nationalism and Minor Literatures* (Berkeley: University of California Press, 1987), 57.

47. Ian Kershaw, *The Hitler Myth: Image and Reality in the Third Reich* (Oxford: Clarendon Press,
1987), 2. See also Kershaw, *Hitler 1936-45: Nemesis* (London: Allan Lane, The Penguin
Press, 2000).

48. James Hillman, "Psychology, Self and Community," *Resurgence*, September/October 1994,
20.

49. Ibid.

50. The post-Romantic literature German proposed various combinations and permutations of
Hamman's definition: "Genius is that individual who rises above the mass of humanity
through the possession of divine mystical endowment." See *Schriften*, ed. F. Roth (Berlin,
1823-43), vol. II, 38.

51. G. W. F. Hegel, *Philosophy of History*, transl. J. Siberee, vol. 32 (London, 1878); G. Schmoller,
Grundriss der allgemeinen Volkswirtschaftslehre, 2 vol (Leipzig: Duncker & Humblot, 1900),
675.

52. See Graf von Krokow, *Preussen. Eine Bilanz* (Stuttgart: Deutsche Verlag-Anstaltl, 1992), 69.
On "Junkerization" of the German middle classes and student fraternities see also Elias, *The
Germans*, 95-97. On the pursuit of "aristocratic Prussianism" see Roger Chickering, *"We Men
Who Feel Most German": A Cultural Study of the Pan-German League* (Boston: Allen & Unwin,
1984), 112-118.

53. Hitler, *Mein Kampf*, transl. R. Manheim (London: Random House, Pimlico, 1992), 81.

54. Harrie quotes the ethos of American Constitution as a betrayed Swedish ideal: "We hold
these truths to be self-evident, that all men are created equal; that they are endowed by
their Creator with certain inalienable rights, that among these are life, liberty and the pursuit of happiness among men, deriving their just powers from the consent of the governed."
Harrie, *Tjugotalet in memoriam*, 230.

55. See Arne Ruth, "The Second Nation: The Mythology of Modern Sweden," *Daedalus*, vol.
113, no. 1, 1984, 56.

56. August Strindberg, *Svenska folket: i helg och söken, i krig och fred, hemma och ute eller Ett tusen år
av svenska bildningens och sedernas historia* (1882; reprt. Stockholm: Gidlunds förlag, 1974).

57. See Orvar Löfgren, "Materializing the Nation in Sweden and America," *Ethnos*, no. 3/4,
1993, 177.

58. See Tingsten, *Mitt liv*, 244.

59. Emilie Fogelklou-Norlind, "Vad man tror och tänker i svenska folkrörelse," 1920. Cited by
Harrie, *Tjugotalet in memoriam*, 115-125.

60. On the rationale of *folkhemmet* in Swedish education, see Rolland G. Paulston, *Educational Change in Sweden* (New York: Columbia University, Teachers College Press, 1968), 144.
61. Maciej Zaremba has convincingly argued that the moral sanction given to sterilization in most countries owed as much to the prevailing scientism and the rule of "experts" as to the worldview of the protestant Church. See Maciej Zaremba, "Skötesynden," *Moderna Tider*, May 1999, 42-43.
62. This was the policy pursued under the guidance of the then Minister of Education, Jon Almquist. See N. Bergstrand, *Analys av läroverkens målsättning 1898–1927* (Avhandling: University of Lund, 1972).
63. See Michael Millog, *Banal Nationalism* (London: Sage 1995).
64. See Lars Trägårdh, *Bemäktiga individerna: Om domstolerna, lagen och de individuella rättigheterna i Sverige*, SOU 1998:103, (Stockholm: Fritzes, 1999).
65. As Michael Roberts has convincingly demonstrated, the Vasas were successful in establishing an image of "good" Swedish monarchs against a "nasty" aristocracy and bureaucracy. "The monarchy was 'folkish', the kings were all accessible to their people—most of them excellent demagogues, finding easily the language in which to communicate with common men." See Roberts, *The Swedish Imperial Experience 1560-1716*, 82. The people's enduring intimacy with the king is perhaps best captured by a poster that hung in many Swedish houses in the 1930s as a souvenir of *bondetåget* in 1914. It represented the Nordic winterscape and a peasant on his way to the king to present his worries about the state's welfare.
66. Ernest Gellner, *Conditions of Liberty, Civil Society and its Rivals* (London: Hamish Hamilton, 1994), 96.
67. Tingsten, *Mitt liv*, 273.
68. Ibid., 274.
69. Ibid., 317.
70. See especially Gallin, *Midwives to Nazism*; Ringer, *The Decline of the German Mandarins*; David Abraham, *The Collapse of the Weimar Republic: Political Economy and Crisis* (Princeton: Princeton University Press, 1981); Fritz Stern, "The Political Consequences of the Unpolitical German," *History: A Meridian Periodical*, no. 3, 1960, 129; Christoph Weisz, *Geschichtsauffassung und politisches Denken. Münchener Historiker der Weimar Zeit* (Berlin: Duncker und Humblot, 1979), 210-267. Sheldon Pollock, especially, provides ample evidence of a huge investment on the part of the German state in Indological studies throughout the nineteenth and the first half of the twentieth century that "surpassed all the rest of Europe and America combined." The German Orientalism provided "software" for the tropes and ideology of totalitarianism and racism. See Pollock, "Deep Orientalism?," 82. See also Philippe Lacoue-Labarthe and Jean-Luc Nancy, "The Nazi Myth," *Critical Inquiry*, 1990, vol. 16, no. 2, 1990, 291-312; Raymond Schwab, *La Renaissance orientale* (Paris: Payot, 1950); Leslie A. Wilson, *A Mythical Image: the Idea of India in German Romanticism* (Durham, N. C.: Duke University Press, 1964); Ruth Römer, *Sprachwissenschaft und Rassenideologie im Deutschland* (Munich: Fink, 1985).
71. After Carl Heinrich Becker succeeded Boelits as Prussian Minister of Education from 1925 to 1930, the Prussian directives became more pronounced (cf. Becker's credo in *The Politico-Cultural Tasks of the Nation*, 1919). See R. H. Samuel and R. Hinton Thomas, *Education and Society in Modern Germany* (London: Routledge and Kegan Paul, 1949).
72. Giese's textbook proclaimed the law of the stronger as "the only just judgment, the natural selection, through which healthy and sound nations defeat the weak and inferior ones and provide space and prosperity for themselves." By 1927, fourteen editions of the book had been printed and 74,000 copies distributed. See Samuel and Thomas, *Education and Society in Modern Germany*, 75, 78-79.
73. Laqueur, *Young Germany*.
74. See Gallin, *Midwives to Nazism*, 20; Laqueur, *Young Germany*, 4-5.
75. Samuel and Thomas, *Education and Society in Modern Germany*, 4.
76. Brannimir Anzulovic, *Heavenly Serbia: From Myth to Genocide* (London: Hurst and Company, 1999).

77. Quoted in J. P. Mayer, *Max Weber and German Politics* (London: Faber and Faber, 1944), 59.

78. Evans, *Rereading German History*, 9.

79. Ibid., 79.

80. Slagstad, *De nasjonale strateger*, 107-108. Emphasis mine.

81. Arendt, *Crises of the Republic*, 60-61.

82. Roberts, *Essays in Swedish History*, passim.

83. See Nina Witoszek, "Stamsamhällets slut," *Moderna Tider*, no. 108, October 1999, 16-20.

84. In the early 1960s Martin Lipset declared: "Politics is now boring. The only issues are whether the metal workers should get the nickel more an hour, the price of milk should be raised, the old-age pension extended." This, we might suggest, was less a description of a general situation in Europe or America at the time and more a characterization of Sweden. See Martin Lipset, *Political Man* (1960; reprt. London: Heinemann, 1983), 9.

85. See Theodor Adorno and Max Horkheimer, *Dialektik der Aufklärung* (Amsterdam: Queido, 1947); Zygmunt Bauman, *Modernity and Holocaust* (Cambridge: Polity, 1989).

86. This perhaps explains Roland Huntford's tendentious and oversimplified study of Sweden as a "totalitarian" country. See Huntford, *The New Totalitarians* (London: Allen Lane, The Penguin Press, 1971).

87. See Michele Micheletti, *Civil Society and State Relations in Sweden* (Aldershot: Avebury, 1995), 85. For an analysis of the disempowering of Swedish society, see Trägårdh, *Bemäktiga individerna*.

88. Tingsten, *Mitt liv*, 342.

5

Crisis and the
Politics of National Community
Germany and Sweden, 1933/1994*

LARS TRÄGÅRDH

Introduction

To claim that the figure of the nation looms large in German history is something of a commonplace given the centrality of National Socialism and the Holocaust to German, European, even world history. When it comes to Sweden, a country many associate with the internationalism of men like Dag Hammarskjöld and Olof Palme, the assertion may seem less meaningful. Indeed, insofar as nationalism primarily conjures up images of racist and fascist utopianism, it might seem counterintuitive to associate the proverbially progressive, peaceful, and democratic Swedes with an ideology that gives primacy to nation and race. Yet, as I will argue, nationalism is not the sole property of the forces of the racist radical right, nor is the place of the nation and the *folk*–the people–to be discounted if we are to understand the social contract that lies at the heart of the modern Swedish welfare state.

In this chapter I will seek to show how the idea and ideal of national community has been central to the political imagination of Swedes and Germans alike. In particular I will focus on two distinct moments of crisis: first the political and economic crises of the 1930s, which in both cases were "resolved" by a turn towards "national socialism," and secondly the crises linked to the challenges to national sovereignty associated with the ascendancy of the European Union project after the passage of the Maastricht Treaty in 1991. I will furthermore argue that the legacies of the crisis resolutions of the 1930s came to inform the later debates about "the Nation vs.

Europe" in paradoxical ways. In Germany the disastrous experience with Nazi-inflected nationalism under the banner of *Volksgemeinschaft*–"people's community"–served to ready Germans from across the political board for the transnational, even postnational ideas inherent in the vision of European Union. In Sweden, on the other hand, the far more positive memory of the Social Democratic concept of *folkhem*–"the people's home"–has translated into deep skepticism regarding the merits of handing over sovereignty from a dependable, democratic nation-state to a European-wide federal political regime associated, correctly or not, with a so-called "democratic deficit" and a less solidaristic welfare policy.

Germany and the Promise of Europe; Sweden and the Specter of Europe

Germany was, of course, one of the founding partners of what is now known as the EU. Its original membership was tied to the allied effort to reconstruct Germany in the image of the democratic, capitalist West after the war. Within a larger vision of European peace and prosperity there existed a desire to tame and contain Germany. Indeed, whereas we are today used to thinking about the EU, and especially its historical predecessor, the European Economic Community (EEC), as a market community, a giant *Zollverein,* the original moves towards integration, anchored in the postwar Franco-German alliance, were grounded in security-driven arguments. This impulse from without was mirrored in a wish among leading German politicians and public intellectuals that Germany should "lose itself" (the Nazi past)–and/or "find itself" (the humanist, cosmopolitan Germany of Goethe)–by merging with and dissolving into "Europe" and "the West," while at the same time being allowed to play a major role within the common European political and, particularly, economic structures, including NATO as well as the EEC.

Thus Adenauer, a West-oriented Rhinelander, explicitly rejected Germany's "Prussian" past as well as the utopian longing for *Volksgemeinschaft*, an idea that had become too closely identified with the Hitlerite regime. Instead he sought to promote a vision of a Christian-Democratic Europe within which Germany could find its place. The disappearance of Prussia–the engine of German unification–as well as the choice of Bonn as the new capital, were aspects of this fundamental shift in German identity, as was the division of Germany which effectively further "de-Prussianized" (West) Germany.[1] But the pro-European stance of Adenauer, one that was also embraced by his fellow Christian Democrat and architect of the German reunification in 1990, Helmut Kohl, was shared, if in a somewhat different form, by the German left. Not only was there the legacy of the Austro-Marxist ideal of what they called "World-Switzerland," a politically and economically united

Europe within which the now stateless nations would still enjoy rights to cultural autonomy, but, as we shall see, the Greens as well as many Social Democrats over time also emerged as staunch supporters of a neo-Kantian or Habermasian vision of postnational citizenship and a United States of Europe.

Sweden, on the other hand, joined "Europe" only as a late-comer (January of 1995), and then only with a slim majority of the population voting "yes" after a heated and divisive debate.[2] Significantly, the opposition to Europe can be understood in terms of a reversal of the German desire to become Europeans: because Swedish national identity has been organized around the idea that Swedes are more, not less, "democratic," "progressive," and "egalitarian" than other nations, the discourse on Europe was–and is–far more likely to express anxiety over the "specter of Europe" than confidence in the "promise of Europe." More specifically, the idea of European integration poses a deep threat to the way in which many Swedes have come to understand the proper relationship between "state," "society," "nation," and "people."

Most crucially, Swedish national identity has come to be tightly linked to the welfare state, understood not simply as a set of institutions but as the realization of *folkhemmet*, the "people's home," the central organizing slogan of the Social Democrats, the party that has dominated Swedish politics since 1933. The extraordinary and lasting potency of this concept derives from the seamless way in which the two concepts of "the people"–those of *demos* and *ethnos*–have been fused into one coherent whole. That is, it is not simply that in Sweden the civic-democratic notion of the people has won out over the ethnic-cultural reading associated with, most infamously, the German experience, but rather that the Swedish concepts of *folk, folklighet*, and *folkhem* are part and parcel of a national narrative that has cast the Swedes as intrinsically democratic and freedom-loving, as having "democracy in the blood."[3] Thus, since to be a Swedish nationalist meant perforce to embrace democratic values, it was possible in the 1930s for the Social Democrats successfully to harness the power of national feeling, to become "national socialists," and fight off the challenge from domestic would-be Nazis.

Furthermore, and just as importantly, the "Swedish Model," as it came to be known, was characterized by an extreme form of statism, built on a social contract between a strong and good state, on the one hand, and the emancipated and autonomous individual, on the other. Through the institutions of the state the individual, so it was thought, was liberated from the institutions of civil society–the family, the neighborhood, the churches, the charity organizations. The inequalities and dependencies associated with these institutions were to be replaced by an egalitarian social order. In this scheme the state and the people were conceived of as intrinsically linked; the *state* was imagined as the institutional hard shell of the homely domain of *national* community, the context in which the ideal of solidarity could be joined to that of equality. The "people's home" was, in other words, also a *folkstat*, a "people's state."[4]

From this point of view, the left-wing supporters of the nation-statist Swedish welfare state could only imagine Europe to the south of Denmark as a backward bastion of neofeudalism, patriarchy, hierarchy, disorder, corruption, and inequality. Continental notions such as federalism, subsidiarity, and civil society were perceived as insidious, neoliberal, or "papist" ideas, fundamentally antithetical to the founding principles of the welfare state. Conversely, the political parties to the right have tended to see in Europe a chance to accomplish through the back door what they have consistently failed to achieve at the national level: the dismantling of the oppressive welfare state and the revitalization of the atrophied civil society. Liberals came to see the EU as a project promoting the freedom of the market from state regulation, and the freedom of the individual from the narrow confines of Swedish egalitarianism. Social conservatives and Christian Democrats, on the other hand, imagined the restoration of the "natural" social structures of civil society they felt had been undermined by the unholy alliance between big government and big business.

I will first outline the central national narratives, tropes and concepts that came to full fruition during the political storms of the 1930s, and which continue to enable and delimit the political debate in Germany and Sweden today. Next I will analyze the post-war debate over European integration from this discursive perspective in order to engage the questions posed at the outset of the chapter: Why is it that Germany, in spite of its traumatic and tragic history of obsession with the utopian figures of *Volk* and *Nation*, today seems poised to forgo the trappings of national sovereignty with relative ease? Why, conversely, is it that the victory of left-wing nationalism in Sweden, so crucial in warding off the lure of right-wing nationalism in the 1930s, has paradoxically resulted in a vaguely xenophobic and isolationist welfare state nationalism?

The Freedom of the Swedes: From Erik Gustav Geijer to Per Albin Hansson

At first glance nationalism does not appear to have played a major role in nineteenth- and twentieth-century Swedish politics. Many would agree with Gustav Sundbärg, who concluded in his classic work on Swedish "national character," *Det svenska folklynnet* (1911), that

> The small amount of patriotism that we can observe among the Swedish people has been of the old type, from the 17th century: national pride. Our people has, however, had no experience of what one during the 19th century has meant by national awakening. This, a people's instinctual drive to give expression to its innermost essence in every vital matter, has been completely unknown to us.[5]

In an influential essay from 1984, the leading Swedish public intellectual Arne Ruth also argued for such an absence of romantic nationalism, citing several other writers who "comment on the lack of a traditional sense of national heritage in modern Sweden."[6] And, Ruth adds, to the extent that there was such a thing as a modern Swedish nationalism, it was—in sharp contrast to development in the other Nordic countries—"almost exclusively an upper-class ideology."[7]

As we shall see, this is a view that requires modification, since it is not true that nationalism was absent, nor is it the case that it was primarily a right-wing, upper-class phenomenon. In fact, while it is true that national feeling was not mobilized in Sweden in the same overt and dramatic way as it was in Germany, a rather well-defined notion of Swedish peculiarity nonetheless developed during the nineteenth century. Indeed, a conception of Swedish national identity emerged during the first few decades of that century that proved both enduring and politically pregnant.

The primary locus for this "national awakening" was a loosely organized, numerically small, and relatively short-lived association called *Götiska Förbundet* (The Gothic Society), which was created in 1811 in the wake of the loss of Finland to Russia in 1809.[8] According to its leader, a minor government bureaucrat by the name of Jacob Adlerbeth, it was the "regrettable truth that the majority of Swedes of our time have deteriorated relative to our great ancestors," abandoning the "seriousness and power of the North" for "the wantonness of Southern Europe." What to do, asked Adlerbeth: "By what means can a people that throws itself upon ruin be saved?" Only, he answered, "by recovering its original national character." Thus, "we have found that our highest purpose is to revive the old Goths' spirit of liberty, manliness, and common sense."[9]

While Adlerbeth's high ambitions for the Gothic Society were not to be fully realized, the writings of its members—many of whom became leading members of the Swedish cultural elite—would come to have considerable impact within the literary, folkloric, and historical circles of nineteenth-century Sweden. They published translations of old Icelandic sagas and Nordic mythology; they produced a series of folksong collections; they wrote romantic poetry. However, for our purpose the most important body of work was that of the poet and historian Erik Gustaf Geijer, a man whose influence on Swedish self-understanding has been compared to that of Arndt in Germany. In his poetry, published in *Iduna*, the journal of the Gothic Society, and above all in his monumental histories of the Swedish people, Geijer established an enduring narrative on Swedish national character and the historical drama through which this character was forged.

The main protagonists around whom this "myth" was organized were the free Swedish yeoman peasant—*odalbonden*—and the King. Together they fought the good fight for personal and national freedom, against the foreign powers and domestic lords who were bent on enslaving the uniquely free Swedish peasant, on the one hand, and on submitting the nation to foreign rule, on the other.[10] In particular the partly historical, partly mythical figure of Engelbrekt came to figure prominently in this account. According to legend, Engelbrekt led the peasants out of the province of *Dalarna* (Dalecarlia) in a successful revolt against the Danes during the time of the Kalmar Union[11] in the fifteenth century and he subsequently—so the legend—organized the first Swedish parliament in 1435. In this schema, patriotism coincided with a love of personal freedom. The political and social rights of the peasants came to be associated with the "soul of the people." The "national" and "democratic" imperatives came to be inextricably fused, and with this followed the idea that the state and the people were joined in a common endeavor to safeguard the two freedoms, that of the nation and that of the individual.

The influence of Geijer on the way in which Swedes have imagined themselves and their "national character" has been enormous. His foundational myth of the Swedish nation was reproduced in textbooks that by the beginning of the twentieth century were used by most, if not all, Swedish students, and his conception of Swedish history and Swedish national identity found expression in the writings of political figures spanning the entire ideological spectrum. I have elsewhere traced the reception of this myth into nineteenth- and twentiety-century historical literature and history textbooks;[12] let me here confine myself to one example, namely the classic, standard school text on Swedish history by Odhner (first published in 1899, and reprinted many times thereafter). Having dramatically retold the story of Engelbrekt, Odhner concludes that

> He gave back to Sweden's *allmoge*[13] its freedom and independence, he called the towns-men and the peasants to national assemblies, he awoke the slumbering national feeling by uniting the various separate groups in order to save the nation. From his time one can talk of not simply different provinces, estates and classes in Sweden, but also of a Swedish Nation.[14]

The Swedish Social Democrats and the Turn towards a National Socialism

This essentialist view of Swedishness, derived from Geijer's conception of Swedish history and national character, was also common at the outset among leading figures within the fledgling workers' movement as it began to gain strength at the turn of the century. Take, for example, the Social Democrat Bengt Lidforss, who, during the great general strike of 1909, lost himself in a particularly romantic-heroic vision of the Swedish working-class movement, one tinged with xenophobia to boot.[15] The working-class, he wrote, is the marrow and core of the Swedish people, the blood inherited from the parents through innumerable Swedish generations. It is *folket* that stands up to all the managers, bosses, stockholders with mostly exotic names and of foreign descent, like the Swedish *allmogen* under Engelbrekt ... did against the Danish lords of the past.[16]

However, it was only after the collapse of the Second International and the introduction in 1920 of general suffrage (and thus a sense of the inclusion of the working class in the nation) that the Social Democrats began to move aggressively to mobilize the national theme at the expense of the old socialist internationalism. Soon after World War I a series of books and articles appeared that signaled this new attitude on the part of the Swedish Social Democrats.

A first phase in the process of appropriating "the national" was characterized by the influence of the Austro-Marxists and their affirmation of the national idea as such. Younger Social Democrats like Nils Karleby and Rickard Lindström wrote a number of articles and books in the mid 1920s that were directly influenced by Otto Bauer's great work on the nationality question, *Die Nationalitätenfrage und die Sozialdemokratie.* Citing Bauer, Lindström asserted that "socialism must be built on a national basis" and that "we must accept the nation as a given ... to deny the nation is to deny life itself."[17] He agreed with Bauer that each nation has its own national character and its own peculiar "spirit." This represented, of course, a major revision of Marx's own view of the nation which was that it was destined for the dustbin of history, first to be fatally undermined by global capitalism and then to be swept away by world revolution.

During a second phase–culminating in the 1930s–the empty category of "national character" was increasingly filled with a positive and concrete content that linked the notion of what Lindström at one point called a Swedish "national socialism," to pro-statist and pro-democratic attitudes, themes that then were developed into a full-fledged national-democratic doctrine according to which the Swedish-Nordic democratic tradition was an expression of the peculiar Swedish *folksjäl* ("soul of the people").[18] In doing this, the Social Democrats explicitly attached themselves to the historical discourse associated with Geijer.

Thus Per Albin Hansson, the leader of the Social Democrats and a long-term prime minister of Sweden, recalled the legacy of Engelbrekt–"the man we from our childhood years have learned to see and honor as a man of the people"–the founding of the parliament, and the popular fight for national and personal freedom:

> It is a long time ago that the old peasant chief answered the calling of the *herrar* ["the lords"] with a stern reminder that "the workers are flesh of our flesh and bone from our bone." But the same is still true. The best of democratic tradition can be found among peasants and workers. Just like the peasant-class during its

struggle for influence protected the *folk*-freedom, so has the working-class. Here there is a common inheritance to administer.[19]

Thus, "Engelbrekt and Gustav Vasa—the two great liberators of the nation and the people—became for us in school the ideals, the mighty freedom-fighters to whom we looked up and whom we wanted to follow."[20] This was the tradition of freedom in which the Social Democratic workers' movement was merely the last link, Hansson argued:

> The concept of freedom has over time been extended, lordship and oppression has been broken down in new areas, new *folk*-groups and classes have successfully fought their own freedom-fight, won equal citizenship-rights, liberated themselves from slavery and slave-mentalities. Figures have been added to our gallery of heroes, a few older ones have perhaps been pushed aside, but others remain. It is warranted to speak of a tradition of freedom in our country, independent of the changes in society.[21]

Thus, he concluded, "our Swedish people is essentially democratic. It loves freedom and hates oppression."[22] That is, democracy in Sweden was not simply a matter of ideology or of dry constitutional arrangements; it was no "mere" *Verfassungspatriotismus.* Rather, it was rooted in the very soul of the people:

> It is with every reason that we Swedes are proud of our country. It is a country of *folk*-freedom and *folkligt* self-government, where democracy is rooted not merely in the constitution, but also in our traditions and in the disposition of the *folk*.[23]

These words were spoken during the early 1930s, just as the Social Democrats and the Peasant Party formed a lasting popular/populist alliance under the banner of *folkhemmet,* and it is with the peasant-worker alliance of 1933 that the Social Democratic deployment of the Geijerian trope reaches its fullest form. The old pitting of a nationally-minded King and patriotic and freedom-loving Peasant against the treacherous and faithless Lord is reinvented: the aristocrats of old become the industrialists and capitalists of today, and the peasants are joined by the workers as the true representatives of the *folk* and the nation. As in the German right-wing nationalist imagination the Jew is equated with cosmopolitan capitalism, so for Swedish left-wing nationalists the capitalist elite is viewed with enduring suspicion as not sufficiently national or patriotic, a trope that we will be able to pursue well into the contemporary debate over the EU in Sweden.

Central to this nationalist turn of the Swedish Social Democrats was a general shift after 1929 from *klass* (class) to *folk* as the key, organizing concept.[24] That year Hansson wrote an important essay in the leading Social Democratic journal *Tiden,* entitled "Folk och klass" ("*Folk* and class"), in which he explicitly embraced the notion that the party must project itself as a party of the people, so as not to be trapped within the exclusionary and adversarial language of class and class-struggle. Showing a fine understanding of the power of words, Hansson wrote that "the class-struggle might be an ever so horrible fact," a fact that must not, however, blind us to the superiority of the *folk* concept as a propaganda tool:

> There is something much more exciting about the thought that we are fighting for the *folk*. To such an appeal everybody will listen; in the coming together of the *folk* most of us want to be a part.[25]

Indeed, such sentiments led Hansson further and further towards a truly all-embracing national(ist) position. If the initial move was to include both peasants and workers as bona fide members of the *folk*, joined in a common struggle against *herrarna*, by 1935 even this residual notion of class conflict was eliminated. In yet another speech featuring Engelbrekt, given on the occasion of the "Day of the Peasant," he declared that "it was *gemenskapen* (community/unity) among the Swedes that Engelbrekt wanted to bring about. Today it is also true that popular-national (*folkligt nationella*) aspirations can have no other goal."[26] Although there is much that separates us into groups and classes, "in the midst of all that, *gemenskapen* still spills forth; the nation is one and the people is one, we live together and are dependant on each other."[27]

The list of all the different people whose efforts add to the common good of the national community is telling–and utterly unlike any a Social Democrat would have produced ten years earlier: the peasant, the worker, the teacher, the thinker and the leader, the fisherman, the shopkeeper, the housewife. Of course, this rather high-flown nationalist rhetoric must be read against the developments in Germany, where just a few years earlier the Protestant peasants and many other sections of the *Volk* had overwhelmingly voted for Hitler, making the failure on the part of the German Social Democrats to harness and appropriate the national feeling only too apparent.

Still, Hansson's tone and language is striking as he plays with the deep ambivalence of the *folk*-concept; one moment the *folk* is fighting *fogdar* and *herrar*, the next moment the great *folkhem* is invoked. Together these references form a "Geijerish" discourse, part mythical, part historical, on the founding of Sweden and the essence of Swedishness, a grand historical process culminating in the accession to power of the Swedish working class, the Social Democratic Party, and Hansson himself. In this conception *folkhemmet*, the historically rooted identification of the national with the democratic, came together with singular power; *ethnos* and *demos* merging in what came to be the central metaphor of the national-socialist Swedish welfare state. The Social Democrats were in the process transformed from a marginal party of the unpatriotic, internationalist left into the dominant and eminently national party, and it was their version of Swedish national identity that came to be the hegemonic one: from 1933 until the present, with only short periods out of power, the party has ruled Sweden and has therefore been in a position to shape the construction of modern Sweden, its institutions as well as its national myths.

What about nationalism of the right during this period? To be sure, both traditional conservatives and members of the radical right made attempts to mold Swedish nationalism on their own terms. In general the turn of the nineteenth century was characterized by an outburst of national Romantic feeling.[28] Decades of emigration to America were followed by the loss of the last vestige of Sweden's Great Power legacy when Norway broke away from the union with Sweden in 1905. This prompted concerned patriotic Swedes to organize a public commission exploring what had gone wrong with the Swedish national character, and conservative intellectuals and poets wrote a number of literary and political tracts calling for national rejuvenation.[29]

While the conservatives also relied on the tradition of national-romantic history associated with Geijer, they tended to focus more on the glory of the Swedish kings, especially the Vasa kings–from Gustav Vasa, through Gustav II Adolf, to Charles XII–than on the power of the proto-democratic peasants' estate. Similarly, in the case of Engelbrekt, they would emphasize his role as the savior of the nation rather than focus on him as the protector of the liberty of the peasants. However, they never could fully escape the rather narrow confines of the Geijerian trope, with its dual celebration of king and peasant, which tended to undermine the conservative and authoritarian political agenda of the Conservatives.

The central concept of *folkhemmet* was also contested. In fact, it was originally coined and used by conservative intellectuals and political figures some twenty years before Per Albin Hansson and the Social Democrats successfully appropriated it. The earliest citation dates to 1896, but the more well-known coinage is that of the influential conservative political scientist Rudolf Kjellén, who in 1912 deployed the word as a distinct political concept in an article called "Nationalism and Socialism." False prophets who divided the nation needed to be unmasked, he wrote; "only on the basis of its own traditions can Sweden be made into that happy *folkhem* that it is meant to be."[30]

Kjellén linked the idea of a *folkhem* to another new term that he had coined two years previously, that of *national-socialism*. Anticipating the national socialism of the German Nazis and echoing similar arguments by contemporary German conservatives who promoted what they called a "German socialism"–i.e., a socialism of national unity devoid of class struggle–he spoke positively about the workers' movement and the collectivism that he saw as a valuable aspect of socialism. However, he opposed the ideas of "class" and "class-struggle," which he felt weakened the nation:

> Thus the Socialism of the Socialist Party reduces this idea [of solidarity] to the working-class. Extend this idea to embrace the whole of the *folk*–think of a

national-socialism [his emphasis] instead of a class-socialism–and what is dangerous to society becomes a wonderful societal power.[31]

Throughout the 1920s and 30s further unsuccessful attempts were made
by conservatives to establish a right-wing reading of the *folkhem* slogan, as well
as its close relative, *folkgemenskap*, a direct translation of the German *Volksgemeinschaft*.[32] In particular the youth wing of the Conservative Party, *Svensk
Nationell Ungdom* (SNU), was active in debating the Social Democrats over
who was the rightful voice of the people and the nation. Eventually, SNU
turned down the road of Nazi-inflected nationalism and was finally cut loose
from the Conservative Party itself. Subsequently, neither it nor the various
official Nazi parties in Sweden met with significant success. The problem
faced by the would-be architects of Swedish right-wing nationalism was that
the very moment they raised the nationalist banner, they were also forced to
contend with the already existing Geijerian myth of Swedish national character. And this was a myth that in its *concrete substance* proved hard to reconcile
with the basic thrust of radical right-wing, antidemocratic nationalism along
the lines familiar elsewhere in Europe (outside of Scandinavia), since the story
of the Swedish nation was at heart a celebration of democracy and freedom.[33]
    If, then, the nationalist road was foreclosed, what we see developing in
Sweden instead, starting in the 1930s, is the beginnings of a Right that is an
advocate of the free market, the rule of law, and individual (first and foremost
property) rights. This division between a national-socialist left and an anti-
socialist, free market right has, in fact, endured to the present day, even though
the *nationalism* of the left is complicated and partly hidden by a simultaneous
enthusiasm for *internationalism* in the (limited) form of development aid and
high-profile involvement in the UN and other international organizations.

Germany after Napoleon: Völkisch Nationalism vs. Prussian Patriotism

Compared to its counterpart in Sweden, the national myth-symbol complex
of "Germany" is richer, or at least more complex. This is hardly surprising
given the bewildering political history of Germany. Still, German nationalism
too is grounded and concretized in certain identifiable narratives that, taken
together, form a coherent discursive field. The central fact, which serves as
the point of departure for all German nationalisms, is the absence of political
unity in the form of the modern nation-state, or even the pre-modern territo-
rial state. (This is, of course, in stark and significant contrast to the Swedish
case.) This, in turn, is the legacy of the Westphalian settlement of the Thirty
Years' War, which left in place the Holy Roman Empire of the German
Nation, a political entity whose confederal constitution provided for a rela-

tively weak emperor and a great deal of power devolved down to a plethora of small kingdoms, duchies, free cities, and other quasi-sovereign units.

This lack of a unified, centralized state came over time to be experienced increasingly as a kind of absence. "Germany? But where is it? I don't know how to find such a country?" Goethe and Schiller famously wrote, and they were but two among many bewildered and concerned German thinkers and poets.[34] In terms of nationalism, the simultaneous presence of a sophisticated German *Kultur* and absence of a (coherent and unified) German *Staat* provoked a variety of responses. One, which we can trace back to Herder, was the "invention" of the idea of nation-as-culture. In the case of Herder himself, this took the form of a radical antistatism, and a celebration of what we today would call cultural "difference," a grand vision of a universal *Völkergemeinschaft* ("community of peoples") living in peace in what could best be described as a universal civil society, i.e. a nonstatist order held together somewhat mysteriously by a kind of organic social glue that Herder named *Zusammenwirken*. He contrasted this organic conception of the nation as a *Volk*, with an individualized collective "soul" and an "authentic" culture, with the *Volk*-deadening "Machine-State" of the then emerging, modern, "French," nation-statist Europe.[35]

Another, and opposite, reaction was to seek a solution to the spectacle of political fragmentation associated with the Holy Roman Empire and its successor, the German Confederation, by way of mimicry of France. This utopia of a single, politically unified Germany emerged during the Napoleonic Wars, when "Germany" became the plaything of Napoleon; he not only dissolved the Holy Roman Empire, but also defeated Prussia. This embrace of the nation-state as the ideal political formation in turn found a variety of expressions. Fichte, for one, accepted the Herderian celebration of the *Volk* as the true, organic core of the nation, but in contrast to Herder, Fichte accepted the necessity of the State as the protector of the vulnerable *Volk*, thus prefiguring the conceptual bifurcation of the nation-state into the hard, masculine idea of the *Vaterland* and the soft, feminine idea of *Heimat*.

Fichte's conception of a close linkage of nation and state was one that, unlike Rousseau's idea of the nation-state as the object of civil religion, did not per se assume a democratic social contract that placed the citizen and the nation-as-a-civic-state at its center. Quite the opposite: one could imagine a rather Prussian-looking state, whose main virtue was its ability to project military power abroad and ensure social order at home.[36] Of course, this was a conception of the relationship between people, nation, and state that would reappear in both its Bismarckian and, even more, Hitlerian guise. But, in general, early nineteenth-century *völkisch* nation-statism was associated more with the democratic left, which cast the idea of a national-democratic Germany against the existing *Kleinstaaterei*, the loose system of authoritarian, petty states, associated with both national division and political backwardness. In one form or another—in an economic liberal nationalist form as in the case of List, or in a more cultural-romantic shape as in the case of Jahn, or with an eye to the Swedish political system as in the case of Arndt–this liberal-*völkisch* nationalism was to dominate until 1848.

The failure of the liberal Revolution/Unification of 1848 was, as historians have noted, a major watershed. Disgusted leftists, among them Marx, declared the German national character to be essentially and hopelessly "philistine," petty-bourgeois, and unfit for political self-emancipation (in contrast to the French, with their tradition of political revolution). The liberals turned from liberal nationalism to national liberalism–shifting the emphasis from the (German) nation to the (Prussian) state, culminating after the 1871 unification in their support of Bismarck.[37] The victory of Prussia and the Bismarckian unification of Germany also resulted in the rise to predominance of an alternative story about Germany, its roots, its character, and its *telos*, namely the Prussian narrative of Germany.[38]

At the core of the Prussian narrative was the *state*-building enterprise celebrated most famously by the prominent historian Treitschke. According to this national myth, one that focused on Prussian-German virtues and the teleology of "iron and blood," Germany's destiny was to be built, through war, under Prussian leadership, from Frederick the Great to Bismarck. Associated with this conception of German national character were the German soldierly virtues that have become synonymous with Prussian Germanness: piety, honesty, duty, obedience, orderliness, flair for organization, will to discipline, and so forth. With rapid and highly successful industrialization, these virtues were "civilianized", mutated into a modernized version of the Prussian character, casting Germany as an economic great power, and the German as the efficient and obedient worker bee.

However, the making of Germany was in the end a far more subtle process than one of simply Prussianizing Germany. While it is true that Bismarck and his national-liberal allies at first did attempt something like that, these efforts led to failure in the *Kulturkampf* directed against Catholic Germany. Rather, the ultimate solution to the German question under Bismarck was in the end essentially to build on the pluralist, federal tradition associated constitutionally with the Holy Roman Empire and culturally with Herder, albeit under strong Prussian imperial leadership. Thus Second Empire Germany was never "nationalized" in the sense that France was during the First and Third Republics, with its systematic destruction of the traditional pattern of provinces and local traditions, and the turning of "peasants into Frenchmen." Instead, the individual *Länder* not only continued to exist (if consolidated into larger and, according to then current liberal theory, more viable units) but retained far-reaching powers, while, all things said, the jurisdiction and power of the central, federal government remained limited.

Indeed, as historians have shown, the magical, organizing concept for German nationbuilding during this period was not, in fact, the *Nation* or the

Volk, but rather the *Heimat.* The latter idea–roughly translated as "home-land"–allowed for a concentrically expanding process of identity formation, from local *Heimat,* through the *Land* as *Heimat,* to *Heimat Deutschland,* expressed constitutionally in that "unified" Germany remained a federal political order, rather than being reconstituted as a unitary state.[39] Conversely, from the point of view of *völkisch* nationalists of either the liberal-democratic bent or of the anti-Semitic racist variety, if 1848 was a tragic moment in that it represented the failure of the long-hoped for and antici-pated *völkisch* revolution, 1871 constituted a kind of betrayal of this ideal since it excluded German Austrians while including Poles and Danes within the framework of a "little-German," Prussia-centered unification.

Both the Prussian-German and *völkisch* national narratives presented the left with a dilemma similar to the one faced by the Swedish right, that is, with conceptions of national identity that would prove a dubious source for a nationalism compatible with their own leftist political agenda. At best German national character came to be seen as "unpolitical," rooted in notions of the virtues of deep German *Kultur,* which were opposed to the superficial and far more overtly political *civilisation* of the French, embedded in the legacy of Enlightenment and Revolution.[40] But worse than this, after the Prussian seizure of Germany, Germanness increasingly came to be associated not with Goethe and Schiller, but with Prussian military virtues, and as such funda-mentally lacking in democratic essence and potential.

This boiled down to a context in which an inspiring left-nationalism was to prove difficult to construct. "History" itself suggested, on the contrary, that the German story was–from the leftist point of view–an essentially tragic one, providing precious little prospect for a heroic reversal of fortune. Not only was there Treitschke's Prussian story to deal with, but there was also the momentous Peasants' War of 1525. The place of 1525 in the German histor-ical imagination can fruitfully be compared to that of the Swedish peasants' uprising led by Engelbrekt in 1434. Both allow for a deep historical reading of national character and destiny, both link the peasants of yesterday to the workers of today, but while in the Swedish case the story is a happy and heroic one, and one that serves to romantically ally peasants and workers, the opposite is true in the German case. Instead, the tragedy of 1525 fed a rather different narrative on the character and fate of the German peasant. The Ger-man peasant was painted in Herderian hues as the purest of Germans, but also as an eternal loser, first a victim of serfdom and feudal tyranny, then the hapless dupe to the heinous machinations and schemes set in place by the Jews. The latter were in turn cast as the ultimate embodiment of all that was evil and degenerate about urban, capitalist, and cosmopolitan modernity.[41]

It is not surprising that Engels, in his book on the Peasants' War, linked the failure of the revolutions of 1848 to the lost Peasants' War of 1525.[42] Engels castigated the German peasants for their "provincial narrow-minded-ness" and concluded by noting that "he who, after the two German revolutions of 1525 and 1848, and their results, still dreams of a federated republic, belongs in a house for the insane."[43] The "sane"–Marx and Engels–turned from the agenda of national and political revolution to that of international, social revolution; from emancipation as national citizenship to emancipation as universal manhood in the post-revolutionary, post-statist, and post-national, universal civil society of socialism.

But the classical Marxist solution to the problem of "German misery"[44] was not the only one proposed by German and German-Austrian Social Democrats. In a return to an updated, Herderian conception of *Völkergemeinschaft,* the Austro-Marxists–Otto Bauer and Karl Renner in particular–elaborated a theory of nationality in which the "national question" (ever pressing in Austria-Hungary) was resolved by decoupling state and nation. They envisioned an order in which the European nations would be united politically and economically, on the one hand, while granted full rights to cultural and linguistic autonomy, on the other. This idea was encapsulated in the notion of the so-called "World-Switzerland," effectively a utopian prefiguring of the EU.[45] These Social Democrats embraced the nation, including very much the German one, yet looked for a larger political and economic structure that could defuse the dangerous thrust of German nationalism and also allow for the legacy of confederalism in Germany. While this scheme spectacularly failed to stir the imagination of the Germans during the 1920s and 30s, it was to reappear with renewed force after World War II, to be realized, at least partially, in the guise of the EU.

Central to current predominance of the neo-Herderian, federalist trope was the collapse of its potent historical alternative: unitary, *völkisch* nationalism. Conversely, the rise and momentary victory of *völkisch* nationalism was made possible by the demise of its historical rival, Prussian legitimist patriotism. As we noted earlier, *völkisch* nationalism was during the Second Empire largely overshadowed by Prussian patriotism, on the one hand, and by the federalist tradition, on the other. However, this did not mean that *völkisch* nationalism disappeared entirely. True, *völkisch* nationalism of the democratic variety was largely finished with the failures of 1848. Instead, building on the narrative of the victimized German peasant I summarized above, the idea of the nation came increasingly to be understood primarily in ethnic and racial terms. While retaining the original emphasis on a unitary (rather than federalist) conception of the ideal German state formation, the concepts of *Volk* and *völkisch* were after 1848 redefined and purged of their democratic elements–privileging *ethnos* at the expense of *demos*, if you will–and invested with distinctively racist, anti-Semitic connotations after 1870. In politics the post-1870 variety of *völkisch* nationalism came to virulent, if limited, expression in various radical right parties, and perhaps most importantly as an idiom central to the successful agrarian interest group, the Agrarian League

(*Bund der Landwirte*), which was responsible for the political mobilization of many German peasants, especially in the Protestant north and west.[46]

The political potential of the *völkisch* movement came fully to the fore after the German defeat in World War I. With the collapse of the Prussian-led German Empire and the flight of the emperor himself, Prussian legitimism ceased to be a conservative force and, if anything, began to feed a more radical, revanchist style of politics, later termed the "Conservative Revolution."[47] Thus, in the vacuum on the right that followed the reconstitution of the political field and the founding of the Weimar Republic, revolutionary *völkisch* nationalism came to flourish in a climate of nationalist resentment over Versailles, distrust of the new Republic, and continual political and economic crisis. Without a viable left-wing nationalism rooted in an alternative and resonant reading of the German national narrative, the "national" idea was, as Reinhart Koselleck has pointed out, monopolized by the right after World War I.[48] The consensus around the *Volksstaats*-conception that had come together in the war experience was replaced by a bitter polarization and a general breakdown of the German political community into what has been referred to as *Teilkulturen*, i.e., mutually hostile political cultures.[49] The adjective "national" was used to exclude from the *Volk* the "non-national" elements, above all the "internationalist" Marxist parties. A "civil-war rhetoric" was developed in which *Nationalismus* stood—in the words of Hitler—for the "nationalization of the consciously anti-national mass."[50]

For the German Social Democrats, on the other hand, the discourse on "nationality" remained bound up with "inter-nationalism." The objective was—pace Bauer and Renner—to create a European community in which the various nationalities could "disappear" as political entities and instead find expression as cultural-ethnic communities within the larger economic-political structure. This utopia of a European community was written into the 1925 Heidelberg Party Program of the German Social Democrats. However, it could not compete with the more narrow, sharper-focused, more concrete nationalism that was rooted in national myths expressed in and constructed through the medium of literature and history books. And behind this evasive, if theoretically sophisticated, way of relating to the national issue, there lurked a fear of the people, an *Angst vor dem Volk*, a worry about the meaning of the German "national character" for the possibility of a popularly supported, national-minded, democratic socialism in Germany. Was it perhaps the case, German and Austrian Social Democrats would repeatedly come to lament, that the two concepts "democracy" and "Germany" were in fact irreconcilable?

In a characteristic turn of phrase, one such Social Democrat, Friedrich Austerlitz, expressed deep doubts that the Germans were "capable of democracy."[51] Writing towards the end of World War I in an essay entitled "Deutsche Demokratie," he echoed the Swedish Social Democrats that we have cited above in asserting that democracy is less a set of rational ideas than a *Gesinnung–*

a deeply rooted way of thinking: "There can exist in a country a wealth of democratic institutions, and a genuine democracy might still be missing; a country can, conversely, carry democracy in its blood even when its institutions do not fully embody the democratic ideal."[52] In Germany, Austerlitz felt, the "Prussian spirit" ruled, the devotion to monarchic rule and the *Obrigkeitsstaat* was a German *Eigentümlichkeit* (peculiarity), and the population was infused with a will to be subjects, towards an *Unterordnung mit Freude* ("joyful submission"), translated into positive German terms as "loyalty," "dependability," and "discipline." These dispositions towards obedience constituted for Austerlitz a profound expression of *das deutsche Wesen* (the German "being," "character," "essence"). The German people, he felt, had no will and no taste for power, only for duty.

The failure of the German Social Democrats to play the national card was mirrored negatively in the success of Hitler's vision of *Volksgemeinschaft* and national socialism, which were built on a fusion of the *völkisch* and Prussian national narratives. Paradoxically, however, the success of right-wing nationalism would soon prove fatal to the idea of German nationalism. With the collapse of the Hitler state, German *völkisch* nationalism was discredited in all but a few eyes (those of the intransigent radical right): a near consensus was eventually formed around the "World-Switzerland" position, a conception that continues to constitute the basis for the pro-Europe position in Germany. However, as we shall see, this pro-European, federalist vision comes in a conservative as well as a leftist variant. It is also a consensus which has been challenged by a post-1989 so-called "new democratic right" that seeks to reassert the legitimacy of German national sovereignty and reject the Adenauer-to-Kohl commitment to a United States of Europe.

Sweden after 1945: The People's Home versus Europe

Swedes and foreign observers were quick to juxtapose the economic and political success of post-1933, Social Democratic Sweden with the contemporary collapse or crisis of democracy elsewhere. As early as 1935 Per Albin Hansson could be heard declaring that "Democratic *Norden* can serve as a model for people in other parts of the world,"[53] and one year later Marquis Childs mythologized the notion of a "peculiarly" democratic Sweden in one of the most internationally influential books ever published about Sweden, namely, *Sweden—the Middle Way*, a work that came to define Sweden for a generation of Americans.[54]

However, while the fundamental perception of Sweden as the home of democracy and equality remained central, the rise of the "Swedish Model" during the post-1945 period entailed something more than the idea that the Swedes were exceptionally gifted when it came to the business of making democracy work. The nationalism of the Social Democrats became less overt as nationalism in general was increasingly discredited in the context of World War II and the Holocaust. While retaining the notion of democratic exceptionalism, the Social Democrats modernized the national narrative; the emphasis on the historical link to the free peasant receded in favor of an emphasis on Sweden's development from "poverty to affluence" into the prototypical modern society–Engelbrekt found competition in Volvo as the premier symbol of Swedish national prowess. Utopian social engineering and a hard-headed emphasis on the role of the state as the guarantor of equality, welfare, and individual autonomy at times overwhelmed the romantic celebration of national democracy.[55] Having said that, it is also clear that these shifts, while important in understanding the character of the Swedish welfare state and the design of its social welfare policies, did not alter the fundamental perception of Sweden as the premier home of freedom, democracy, and equality.

The European question was rather marginal to the Swedish debate until 1961, when Harold Macmillan decided to hand in a British application for EEC membership. Since the Swedish economy was dominated by industrial firms who depended on their access to an international market, the Social Democrats had for a long time favored free trade even as they rejected the closer political, military, or even economic integration that would pose a threat to "neutrality," thus joining the looser EFTA free trade area rather than the protofederalist EEC. Since a British departure from EFTA would have affected Sweden directly, an intense discussion ensued in Sweden, especially and most importantly within the Social Democratic party, which totally dominated the political scene, remaining in power continuously from 1933 until 1976.

In this debate Sweden was continually cast in the trope of democracy, equality, and social solidarity. "Europe," by contrast, was pictured by the Social Democrats, and the left at large, in terms of the so-called "four Ks": *konservatism, kapitalism, katolicism, kolonialism* (conservatism, capitalism, Catholicism, colonialism). That is, "Europe" was conceived of as the conceptual opposite of "Sweden." It was the realm of untamed capitalism, it suffered from the legacy of colonialism, its social policies were informed by backward notions rooted in Catholic social thought, and politically it was dominated not by Social Democratic parties but by Christian conservatives of different shades. Indeed, the specter of Catholicism and papism has long been and continues to be a source of worry for Swedish Social Democrats and secular leftists in general. As one Swedish historian has dryly noted, commentaries on the "continent" written by leading Social Democrats often read as though they were written during the Thirty Years' War.[56]

A particularly influential book in the debate of the early 1960s was *We and Western Europe*, co-authored by the famous economist Gunnar Myrdal, in which the Swedish welfare state was compared with the EC. Symptomatically, Myrdal described the EC as a collection of states "with a more primitive form of social organization than ours,"[57] arguing that

> it is above all the securely Protestant countries that have progressed economically and all other ways. ... In so far as political democracy can be thought of as part of "European culture," then we must remind ourselves of its weakness in the countries south of Scandinavia on the European continent with the possible exception of Holland (although the division between Catholics and Protestants is problematic and among other things is expressed in the fact that the country for long periods of time lacks a government). That democracy is far more self-evident, unshakable and efficient in the Anglo-Saxon immigrant countries and in Scandinavia we all know.[58]

Another typical contribution from the left at this time was that of Enn Kokk, a central figure within the Social Democratic Party. Kokk emphasized the "undemocratic" character of both the EC member states and the structure of the EC itself. Painting a portrait of a conservative Western Europe, where even nominal socialists and social democrats were found wanting, Kokk recounted the details of how the unholy alliance of capital and papism ruled in West Germany, Italy, and France. He concluded that the picture of contemporary political life in Western Europe was *dyster* (gloomy) indeed:

> Today's Franco-German combination, an alliance between General de Gaulle and Dr Adenauer at the forefront of a Catholic, conservative and capitalist western Europe is a disquieting creation. Today Western Europe is, in spite of the "dynamic" EEC, a politically dead landscape.[59]

In the event, the debate of 1961-62 was a bit of a false alarm since de Gaulle eventually cast a French veto against British EEC membership. The case was reopened, however, when de Gaulle departed from the scene in 1969 in the wake of the upheavals of May 68. This time, the stakes were higher since both Britain and Denmark (and Norway, it seemed for a moment) resolutely made their move from EFTA to the EEC. The Euro-federalist forces found themselves at a relative low point, and Olof Palme, prime minister at the time, initially seemed to have toyed with the idea of a closer association, perhaps even membership. Nonetheless, the anti-European front soon mobilized and raised objections, most of which followed the pattern set during the debate of 1961-62, and the upshot of the debates of 1970-71 was yet another rejection of the membership option, announced by Palme in March of 1971.

However, with changing economic and political conditions in Europe and the world after 1989–particularly with the sense that Sweden had reached an economic dead end and now suffered from a deepening crisis–a decision to apply for membership in the EU was made by the Social Democratic government on 26 October 1990. With this followed an intense political battle leading up to the referendum on EU membership in November of

1994, a debate characterized by a dramatic resurgence of the left-nationalist narrative. As one author put it in a 1992 book title, the lines were drawn in a struggle that pitted "the People's Home against Europe."[60]

During the campaign preceding the referendum over EU membership, the left-wing "No!" side argued vehemently against giving up national sovereignty, and conjured up vivid images of the political, social, and cultural differences between Sweden (and *Norden*) on the one hand, and Europe on the other. The left-leaning organization *Nej till EG* ("No to the EC") delighted in linking the EU with prostitution, drug liberalism, sexism, elitism, and the "democratic deficit." As the titles and images of the pamphlets distributed during the 1993 campaign suggest, "Europe" was equated with a "bordello" or "a women's trap," and "Brussels-power" (i.e., the power of a bureaucratic elite) is contrasted with "*folkstyre*" ("rule of the people").

This vision of "Europe" was contrasted with the democratic, solidaristic, and national welfare state. As Göran Greider, a leading voice of the anti-EU forces within the Social Democratic party, declared: "I believe in the nation-state," because "democracy assumes a sense of community." By contrast, he claimed, to create a so-called "European human being" would amount to nothing "but the setting loose upon the world yet again the unruly beast" associated with the predemocratic times before the French Revolution and the construction of the modern, democratic nation-state.[61] In "Europe," the message went, the market would rule, and the weak would be left to fend for themselves as the *Gemeinschaft* of the nation-state gave way to the *Gesellschaft* of a cosmopolitan federation.

A similar note was struck in the pamphlets distributed by the Left Party. Thus the nation-state, it was argued, "is in Sweden intimately associated with democracy," and "Swedish membership in the supra-national and undemocratic European Union would mean for us a considerably inferior form of democracy."[62] The EU was a neoliberal project that had "developed in an artificial manner without popular/national (*folklig*) support":[63]

> The EU is inextricably interwoven with Western European Big Capital. The history, structure and future development of the EU, as detailed in the Maastricht Treaty, speaks its own, clear language. To vote No to Swedish membership in the EU is part of the struggle against the growing power of international capital.[64]

The Left Party also attacked the principle of subsidiarity. The concept, they informed the readers in one of their election campaign broadsides, is "coined by a Catholic pope"[65] and "derived from the authoritarian Catholic social doctrine, meaning 'submission' or 'secondary.'"[66] Furthermore, it is a principle central to the continental welfare system, one that places a very un-Swedish emphasis on the family and instead serves to throw women, children, and the elderly back into the hands of the patriarchal family. Whereas in Sweden the individual is the basic unit, in the EU-countries legislation takes the family as its point of departure. This is what is called "familism." It is in this perspective that we must understand the so-called subsidiarity principle.[67]

Responding to critics who branded them as nationalists, Göran Greider and other anti-EU campaigners emphasized that nationalism comes in "good" as well as sinister forms. Thus Rolf Karlbom, a historian at the University of Gothenburg, wrote in an anti-EU periodical that those who accuse the No side of narrow nationalism miss the point that Swedish national identity—and thus Swedish nationalism—is historically linked to democracy, solidarity, and humanity. "There is no reason," he notes, "to be ashamed of Swedish history. It is not a matter of national romanticism or of chauvinistic patriotism to point out that next to Switzerland, Sweden has the most ancient tradition of popular rule." Quoting approvingly from a pamphlet from the 1930s, Karlbom suggested that this propensity for "people power" amounted to a "deeply rooted spirit of the people."[68]

Indeed, a few years after the referendum, the still active "No to EU" organization organized a series of demonstrations, during which the struggle of Engelbrekt and Gustav Vasa against foreign rule and feudal oppression of the "little people" was reenacted in a modernized version. Conjuring up a vision of a EU as a latter-day version of the Kalmar Union, the Brussels bureaucrats and the bosses of the multinational firms were identified with the foreign bailiffs and lords against whom the brave Swedish peasants had revolted in the name of national independence and personal freedom. The message was clear: it was time for the people to rise up once more and defeat yet another infernal attempt to deprive them of their ancient rights in the name of a union that would only serve the interest of the privileged "Euro-class."

Another important element in the iconography of the No side was the figure of *Norden.*[69] Jörgen Bengtsson, a founder of the organization *Alternativ till EG,* argued that *Norden*—as opposed to the EU—was a "natural" *gemenskap,* with a common history, culture, religion, linguistic affinities, and economic development. *Norden,* he claimed, "constitutes a *folklig* community and is relatively speaking ethnically homogeneous," where people "think more or less the same, have the same lifestyle and temperament, have a sense of belonging together, and have a similar view of important human and social questions."[70] Specifically, Bengtsson argued, "*Norden* stands for a unique social model," one that involves a taxation-financed, universal welfare state, a high level of general education, a tradition of egalitarianism, a strong position for women and minorities, active labor market policies, and a well developed tradition of *folkstyre* (rule of the people).[71] By contrast, the EU was viewed, in the words of Greider, as a "club for the executives of the multinational corporations" and a fundamental threat to the welfare state and the Nordic social contract.

The notion that Swedish women had achieved a greater degree of gender equality became another central argument, one that was intimately linked with the defense of the strong state threatened, as we have already seen in the Left Party pamphlets cited above, by the Catholic principle of subsidiarity. Only the state, it was argued, could deliver women from the oppressive conditions that characterized "civil society," with its hierarchical and patriarchal structures. The EU was described as "women's trap," where women had little access to state-financed day-care, were thus unable to work, and became, as a consequence, dependent on men.[72]

For the No side, then, social justice, equality, solidarity, individual autonomy, gender equality, and freedom to show solidarity with the poorer countries of the world all depended on the continued existence of the nation-state. Solidarity could develop only within the imagined community of the nation; only a democratic state could guarantee the survival of the nation; without a people's home the individuals would exist only as atoms in the heartless world of the market and the so-called civil society. Additionally, this emphasis on the democratic and sovereign nation-state expressed itself in a policy that placed neutrality and solidarity with the struggling nations of the third world at the center. Swedish left-wing nationalism thus envisioned a global order of sovereign nation-states, linked internationally in a way that did not threaten the fundamental principle of national sovereignty. This position found expression in Swedish support of the UN and other intergovernmental organizations.[73]

The nationalism of the left is not simply rooted in essentialist notions of a democratic Swedish "soul-of-the-people"; rather, this conception, often assumed rather than overtly stated, is fused with a leftist *statist* position that links social equality, national solidarity, and individual autonomy to the presence of a strong state. That is, in sharp contrast to Germany, the social contract on which the welfare state is built is one between individual and state at the expense of the intermediary institutions of "civil society," such as the family, and private and voluntary organizations. The latter are associated with demeaning private charity, unequal patriarchal relations, informal (ab)uses of power, etc., i.e., the "usual suspects," the "Catholic" vices. In other words, what is significant about Swedish left-nationalism is what we may call its Rousseauian moment, the dual emphasis on the good power of the democratic state and the virtues of individual autonomy, a social contract that I have elsewhere termed "statist individualism."[74] Indeed, a central paragraph from the *Social Contract* could well serve as the template for the Swedish welfare state:

> The second relation is that of the members of the body politic among themselves, or of each with the entire body: their relations among themselves should be as limited, and relations with the entire body as extensive, as possible, in order that each citizen shall be at the same time perfectly independent of all his fellow citizens and excessively dependent on the republic–this result is always achieved by

the same means, since it is the power of the state alone which makes the freedom of its members.[75]

While this position tends to alarm readers of a more liberal (in the classical sense) bent, it is for many Swedes part and parcel of an outlook that holds that ties of personal servitude and dependency–being subject to the capricious power of families, churches, charities–are a much greater evil than the formal, distant, impersonal, politically controllable power of the state.[76]

This is far from the assumption automatically made by German leftists, who are not only suspicious of any talk of "healthy" German nationalism, but also tend to view statism–the "colonization" by the state of civil society–with a critical eye. Thus both Jürgen Habermas and Claus Offe, to name two, have used the idiom of "new social movements" and "civil society" to construct a critique of the (welfare) state.[77] In Sweden, on the other hand, it has been the "bourgeois" parties on the right–the Conservatives under Bildt, the tiny Christian Democratic Party, some Liberals, and particularly the writers associated with the conservative-libertarian think-tank *Timbro*–who have tried to mobilize the rhetoric of "civil society," with its origins in pre-1989 oppositional movements in the former Communist world of Eastern Europe, to associate the Swedish welfare state with the totalitarian regimes to the East and the dangers of excessive state power and Big Government. These politicians also see the EU as one way of dismantling the Social Democratic welfare state through the European back door, in contrast to the pro-EU Social Democrats, who harbor fantasies of being able to refashion Europe at large in the image of Social Democratic Sweden.

Germany Our Fatherland, United Europe Our Future: From Adenauer to Kohl

In contrast to this enduring Swedish legacy of nation-statism, the collapse of German *völkisch* nationalism led to a revival of both federalism and the idea of the stateless, cultural nation that would come to inform both notions of "Germany's" proper place within the larger European context and the question of how to organize Germany internally. In fact, the twelve-year period of Nazi rule was the only time Germany has ever been organized as a centralized state,[78] and in the aftermath of the Nazi experience a consensus formed that mixed elements of the Conservative, Catholic "subsidiarity principle" with leftist internationalism in the spirit of "World-Switzerland." Indeed, understandably mesmerized by the enormity of the Nazi rule of horror, postwar historians have paid relatively little attention to the federalist tradition. However, given the centrality of this tradition to the future of Europe, it may well be time for historians and political theorists to turn their gaze to this legacy, in the spirit of Mack Walker's important and in many ways singular book, *German Home Towns*.[79] As Geoff Eley has pointed out, writing German history in terms of its failure to be like England or France is problematic,[80] and so is an exclusionary obsession with the past roots and future specters of the Nazi period at the expense of other aspects of the German past.

To be sure, minor currents of both left-nationalism[81] and extreme-right nationalism of the ethnic, *völkisch* variety have continued to exist even after 1945. While the former has hardly mattered at all, the latter has served more to galvanize the antinationalist left, the liberal middle, and the moderate right than it has presented a real threat to the stability of German democracy. In spite of the shrill accounts of surging neo-Nazism in the German and international press or, possibly more ominous, recent attempts by a "New Democratic Right" to elaborate a pro-national sovereignty, "healthy" German identity alternative to the CDU (Christian Democratic) tradition of *Westbindung* and Europeanization, Kohl's and Adenauer's pro-European vision still rules. On the other hand, it is also clear that within the broad postwar consensus, it is this Conservative, Christian Democratic conception, founded on the twin pillars of subsidiarity and federalism, that has come to dominate over its leftist double, rooted in rather more fuzzy notions of Kantian internationalism and neo-Herderian multiculturalism.

In the immediate postwar period, however, the emergence of such a consensus across the SPD-CDU spectrum around a federalist solution was by no means a foregone conclusion. On the contrary, the Prussian Kurt Schumacher and the Rheinlander Konrad Adenauer embodied the split between the federal and unitary state options whose histories are sketched out above. Schumacher favored a democratic-socialist variation on the nation-statist theme, a kind of return to the pre-1848 position of the liberal and democratic nationalists. He viewed with suspicion the CDU embrace of the principles of subsidiarity and federalism and worried that a strong position of the *Länder* would in fact make the reconstruction of Germany more difficult. Thus he promoted an *Einheitsstaat* (unitary state), albeit with far-reaching decentralization and self-government at the local level.[82] Adenauer, on the other hand, happily broke with the Prussian mold and decisively moved to Westernize Germany within a broader vision of a Western Christian Europe based on the principles of subsidiarity and federalism and the firm anchoring of Germany in an alliance with France and, ultimately, as a member of a United States of Europe.

Part of Schumacher's alleged "nationalism" was rooted in his clearly stated dislike of a Westernization/Europeanization that was inextricably linked to what he felt was a Faustian deal with (American) capitalism. Indeed, it is hard to separate Schumacher's anticapitalism from his purported "nationalism." Certainly his oft-quoted reference to Adenauer as "*Bundeskanzlers der Allierten*" must be seen in this perspective, since the SPD (the Social Democrats) and Schumacher incessantly emphasized their West-orientation. As Schumacher said in the Bundestag in 1949, "We Social Democrats have always unambiguously decided for the human and cultural style of the West."[83] Indeed, the representatives of the capitalist-bourgeois interest were in fact mere "nationalists from yesterday" posing as "*Neo-Europäer*" in the interest of profit, in the future to be unmasked as "the nationalists of tomorrow." By contrast, what the SPD wanted was a "true" internationalization of Europe, and by way of reference to the position of the 1925 Heidelberger Program, the SPD explicitly called for a "*Vereinigten Staaten von Europa.*" As was the case for the Austro-Marxists and the Weimar SPD, such a solution would also solve the "national" problem of divided Germany, especially poignant for a Prussian like Schumacher who in fact wanted a reunification according to the 1937 borders, or at least as close to these as possible.

At any rate, the success of Adenauer's *Westbindung*-politik grounded in Ludwig Erhard's *Soziale Markwirtschaft* policy, along with the SPD's definitive turn to centrist reformism after the Bad Godesberg Party Congress in 1959, effectively created a broad consensus around the European solution to the German question. One might, perhaps, see Willy Brandt's *Ostpolitik* as a kind of afterglow of Schumacher's insistence that the unification process should not be sacrificed on the altar of *Westbindung* and Capitalism, and certainly Brandt's stirring speech on the eve of unification in 1990 leaves little doubt about his German patriotism. Still, this was not a nationalism that in any way stood in opposition to his Europeanism, and if Schumacher had earned his right to embrace the German nation through his many years in Nazi prison camps during the war, so Brandt's exile during the war, and particularly his act of reconciliation in Poland when he knelt at the grave of the unknown soldier, gave him particular leeway to express national(ist) sentiment.

On the other hand, the anticapitalist, anti-Western rhetoric of the early Schumacher era found new expression among the '68ers and the Greens, for whom American capitalism, NATO, and the EC blended into one major force to be combated. At the same time, in spite of attempts by figures like Herbert Ammon, Peter Brandt, Wolfgang Venohr, and Martin Walser to foster a debate over "left-nationalism" in the late 1970s and early 1980s, these were marginal forces. A minority among leftist writers bemoaned such a missing leftist national identity, asking why the leftists "never show the national colors at their meetings" nor put down flowers at the Hermanns-Denkmal; but their complaints were largely passed over in silence by most other leftists whose transnational anticapitalism resolved into an equally universalist embrace of world-revolution[84]. Insofar as we can speak of a left-liberal nationalism among mainstream thinkers, it would be the Habermasian *Verfassungspatriotismus.* However, given its connotations of an explicit rejection of the Romantic sensibility associated with nationalism and the lack of any developed notion of a special German national narrative to incite even a

modest amount of passion, *Verfassungspatriotismus* tends–to paraphrase Delors–
to rate right up there with the internal free market as a symbol unlikely to stir
much collective popular enthusiasm.

With the fall of the wall and the ensuing unification, the context for
national and European politics changed dramatically, and we will now turn
to the most recent debates on the left and right in reunified Germany. There
is a certain dynamic that on the one hand opens up space for a new, national
right to emerge and on the other hand pushes the left, and most spectacularly
the Greens under Joschka Fischer, to embrace an unambiguously pro-European position and shed the cold-war rhetoric that had cast the West and the
East as more or less equally bad.

The founding moment of this dynamic can be seen to be the famous shift
in the chanting of the Leipzig crowds during the heyday of the *Wende*, when
the democratic slogan *Wir sind das Volk* was transformed into the national slogan *Wir sind ein Volk*. This touched a sensitive spot among those always on the
ready to pick up on any *völkisch* tendencies at the popular level; fears that
soon were to be confirmed by beatings and burnings of foreign workers.
Thus the names of Rostock, Mölln, and Solingen came to signify the revival
of German ethnic nationalism and in turn to stimulate a whole genre of rather
alarmist writings from the left, the liberal middle, and the "European" wing
of the CDU.

Margarita Mathiopoulos' influential book, *Das Ende der Bonner Republik*,
dramatized the sense of loss and anxiety over the new *Berliner Republik*
already obvious in the debate over where the new all-German capital was to
be located.[85] In this work Mathiopoulos gave voice to a common fear on the
left that the dreaded "German nation was awakening" yet again[86] and that the
Verfassungspatrioten were now wantonly abused by an emerging nationalist
right. Among the many writers that struck a similar note were Dieter
Oberndörfer,[87] Günter Grass,[88] and many others.[89] Even the CDU politician
Friedbert Pflüger, in his 1994 book *Deutschland driftet* (Germany adrift), took
the "end of the Bonn republic" theme and connected it to what he refers to
as "eine neue *Konservative Revolution*," a revival of the Conservative Revolution of the Weimar period, the body of writing and political mobilization on
the right that is thought to have created the legitimating climate in which
National Socialism could incubate and grow. Pflüger worried about what he
calls the "virus" of nationalism that must be checked before it spread through
the body politic.

Pflüger's book was dedicated to the memory of Adenauer, and he meant
by this to place himself squarely within the Christian-European tradition that
he identifies with Adenauer and Kohl. By contrast, he directed the readers'
attention to the dangers of the "new right" that he associated with a new "conservative revolution." Who were the new right-wingers? In fact they were
quite identifiable as a group, associated on the one hand with Ernst Nolte and

the conservative side of the *Historikerstreit* and, on the other, with the publisher Ullstein. A few articles, debates, and books in particular have been associated with this new group and its attempt to legitimize a new national-democratic position in the German mainstream political debate. Thus the 1992 anthology by a trio of Nolte disciples–Rainer Zittelmann, Karlheinz Weißmann and Michael Großheim–entitled *Westbindung,* along with the 1994 volume by Heimo Schwilk and Ulrich Schacht, *Die Selbstbewusste Nation*–signaled the serious arrival of the new right.[90]

The writers in these volumes attacked not just the antinationalist left, but more importantly the CDU "modernizers," including Pflüger as well as Kohl's main ally, Heiner Geißler, who until 1989 was the general secretary of the CDU. Geißler in particular was accused of being a "systematic social-democratizer of the CDU" out of touch with hardcore Christians, patriots, small business people, and *Vertriebene* (refugees). Symptomatically, their volume on the "self-confident nation" was–in sharp contrast to Pflüger's memorialization of Adenauer–dedicated to the patriots of 20 July 1944 *and* 17 June 1953, suggesting both the national orientation and the Nolte-inspired equalization of Nazi and Soviet responsibilities in the general totalitarian assault on civilized Europe, and implicitly granting (their conception of) Germany a place among the victims of such totalitarianism.

The new rightists argued that it was time for Germany to become more like a "normal" European nation-state, loosen its self-denying, self-loathing ties to the West, reassert its lost national sovereignty, and reject the Maastricht Treaty and the idea of the European Union. This position was an explicit challenge to the policy of the moderate center of the CDU, led by Kohl, whose view was that the national identity is properly balanced by regional ones, on the one side, and a European one on the other. Indeed, the latter theme was played masterfully by Kohl, who managed both to enthuse the East Germans with his instrumentalized nationalism–his promise to turn the new states "within a few years into flourishing areas"–and to calm the fears of anxious Europeans to the west and the east. Thus he ended his speech on the eve of the day of Germany unity, 2 October 1990:

> I ask all Germans: Let us prove ourselves worthy of our common freedom. ... The young generation in Germany–unlike any previous generation–now has every opportunity for a whole life in freedom and peace. We know that our joy is shared by many people in the world. They ought to know what moves us in this moment: Germany is our fatherland, united Europe is our future.[91]

Similarly, Geißler emphasized that his German identity was but one aspect of a broader identity whose even more important components were those of being a Christian and a democrat. Pflüger too, as we already noted, made his allegiance to the Adenauer/Kohl position perfectly evident. However, even as Kohl remained steadfastly committed to the European Union, there were signs of change. Geißler lost his position in 1989, and Wolfgang Schäuble, Kohl's eventual successor, made what some interpreted as tentative gestures in the "new right" direction, moving in, according to some observers (like the Social Democrat Glotz) to fill the national-conservative space left open by the death of Franz-Joseph Strauss and the retirement of Alfred Dregger. This was picked up by Weißman during a key debate over the new right in *Frankfurter Allgemeine Zeitung* in the spring of 1994, and even though Schäuble made a point of distancing himself from Weißman, the affinity was obviously there, if in a more moderate form.[92]

This new climate pushed the Greens firmly into the European camp, symbolized by Joschka Fischer's 1994 book *Risiko Deutschland,* in which he dramatically posed the two alternatives of "*Westbindung* or a return to the national, great power politics and striving for German hegemony."[93] At the same time—looking at this from a Swedish point of view—it is remarkable just how oblivious the German Greens and Social Democrats seem to be to the role played by a deep sense of national solidarity in the continued survival and vitality of really existing democratic states, not to mention its role in legitimating high-tax welfare state regimes.

Indeed, it is ironic to read the analyses of the German new rightists as they echo Swedish leftists' insistence on the centrality of national sovereignty in the promotion and defense of democracy and national solidarity. To be sure, the German new right is more interested in a strong state that will keep law and order internally and shut the immigrants out, whereas the Swedish leftists emphasize the emancipatory character of the Swedish welfare state. Yet, one is struck by the lacuna at the heart of German leftist democratic theory, which still has to answer the crucial question of whether democracy really can exist without some form of nationalism, some type of civil religion. The surge of right-wing nationalist discourse that followed the reunification only further reinforced the naive internationalist rhetoric of the European *Verfassungpatrioten,* if anything playing into the hands of the new "democratic" right of Pflüger's neoconservative revolution. Lambasting, on the one hand, what Peter Glotz in a book from 1990 referred to as *Der Irrweg des National-staats,*[94] and celebrating, on the other, an anticipated Kantian *Weltbürgerschaft* via an intermediary European citizenship, as Habermas does, is all fine and well in the abstract, but begs the question of how to create and sustain an emotive sense of solidarity and community in such a utopian world of communicative rationality. Habermas, for one, put great faith in "the new electronic massmedia," which he felt would finally realize the *Weltöffentlichkeit* (global public sphere) that Kant had projected at the time of the French Revolution; "der weltbürgerliche Zustand," Habermas concludes, "ist keine bloßes Phantom mehr."[95]

This flight of fancy should, on the other hand, hardly come as a surprise, since it is difficult for German leftists to conceive of a positive national identity rooted in a suitable and resonating national narrative. Given the history of German nationalism and the construction of narratives on German national identity, it is perhaps not so astounding that they would confuse nationalism at large with the racist, *völkisch* nationalism that in fact is a particular variation of German national discourse. Still, the hysterical tone in much of the writing of the holier-than-thou German left in the years after 1990 suggests an inability either to see the pre-1848 German nationalism in a clearer light, or to appreciate the power of the federal tradition, which, thankfully, has been put to good use by Adenauer and Kohl.

Conclusion

The construction of postwar, federal Germany has in many respects continued in the Bismarckian tradition of supporting traditional, conservative, patriarchal structures within a hierarchical order, from Family to *Heimat* to State, and, finally, the Federal Republic. Indeed, the Catholic notion of subsidiarity has not just come to dominate thinking within Germany, but has become the central organizing principle for the EU at large. The beauty of German federalism, with its sensitivity (at least theoretically) to the autonomy of the individual *Länder*, is that it is extendible to the EU as a whole without reducing the entire project to a mere customs union (as the British would want) or attempting to impose a politically suicidal form of centralism along French lines.

Thus, in facing the coming of what many see as a new political order characterized by a splitting of national sovereignty along "neo-medieval," or "post-sovereign" lines in an era of "fractal politics,"[96] there are good reasons to suspect that the German political culture is far better equipped than the Swedish one to deal with the prospect of "European citizenship," on the one hand, and a national identity construed in strictly cultural terms, on the other. Because this split, though problematic, is a long-standing and familiar one, one can well imagine Germans of both the left and the right being comfortable in some version of a European federation based on the principles of subsidiarity and/or "World-Switzerland." Indeed, as we have seen, prominent figures on the German left, like Jürgen Habermas, are actively pushing for a European-wide republic, on the one hand, and a decentralized democracy at the level of "civil society," on the other. Thus, European integration is perceived not as a threat to national identity but rather as a complement or extension. Indeed, far from constituting a new trauma, it seems to release Germany from the legacy of the real trauma, the disastrous attempt to realize the utopia of *völkisch* nationalism under Hitler.

If, therefore, the European question is unlikely to become very divisive in Germany, it is far more likely to continue to be so in Sweden, at least for some time to come. For the Swedish right, European integration implies the denationalization of Sweden and thus promises an escape from the narrow confines of Swedish egalitarianism. For Swedes located to the left, on the other hand, the EU represents a profound threat. For them Swedish national identity is tightly linked to the legacy of "national democracy," from Engelbrekt and Vasa to the Social Democratic welfare state.

In general, a decoupling of nation and state would appear to be wholly foreign to the Swedish political tradition; indeed, it would be hard even to formulate in intelligible terms. As critics of Swedish "statism" like to point out, in the Swedish language the terms people, nation, state and society are virtually synonymous. Additionally, the rhetorics of national community–*folkhemmet*–is invested with a positive memory of the successful resolution of the crisis of the 1930s, that is, the very reverse of the German historical experience. If for the Germans the break with the past–the national past–constituted an opportunity and the promise of future peace and freedom, a number of leading Swedish politicians on the left insist that giving up national sovereignty is a "tragedy," the abandonment of a unique and "most ancient tradition of popular rule."

Even those leading Social Democrats who came to support Swedish membership in the EU did so not because a larger "European home" inspired a positive vision of a better, post-nation-statist future, but because they had to do so for economic reasons. As I have argued elsewhere, if resistance to the EU was founded on the first leg of modern Swedish national identity–the idea of national democracy and social equality–the Social Democratic Yes-voters were motivated by the second leg, namely the emphasis on economic prowess, individual prosperity, and technological and cultural modernity as quintessential Swedish national character traits. It is too early to tell whether the Social Democrats–and the Swedes at large–will be able to refashion their sense of national identity solely along such technological and materialistic lines.

Notes

*   An early version of this chapter was funded through and presented to the Convenor Group on Challenges to Sovereignty at the Center of German and European Studies and the Center of Slavic and East European Studies, both at University of California, Berkeley. In addition, I would like to appreciatively acknowledge grants given by the American-Scandinavian Foundation and Barnard College, as well as additional assistance provided by the Copenhagen Peace Research Institute. I would also like to thank those who at various points have read and critiqued all or parts of the manuscript: the members of the Convenor Group at Berkeley, the members of the Willen seminar at Barnard College, Roland Anrup, Henrik Berggren, Erik Berglöf, Lene Hansen, Steven Koblik, Pascale Montadert, and Lisa Tiersten. A substantially different and longer version of the Swedish sections has been published as "Welfare State Nationalism: Sweden and the Spectre of 'Europe'" in Lene Hansen and Ole Wæver (editors), *European Integration and National Identity: The Challenge of the Nordic States* (London and New York: Routledge, 2002).

1.   The unification of 1990 upset this balance, and I will analyze the subsequent shifts in the National Sovereignty vs. Europe debate later in this chapter. However, although the territory of the old GDR was reconstructed along seemingly traditional lines as *Länder*, it is notable that Prussia was not revived as a *Land*.
2.   *Eurobarometer* polls consistently indicate that the Swedes rate among the most EU-negative of all EU member state nationals.
3.   See, for example, the popular and widespread manual on "civics" (*medborgarkunskap*) authored by the Social Democrat Värner Rydén. "In no part of the world, aside from in England, has the idea that only a constitution that gives the people the decisive power to influence the fate of the country come to root itself in the very blood of the people." Värner Rydén, *Medborgarkunskap* (Stockholm: Nordstedt, 1923), 10.
4.   The concept *folkstat* was used by leading Social Democrats in Sweden, influenced by the German *Volksstaat*, although it eventually all but disappeared in favor of the "warmer," more communitarian notion of *folkhem*. See, for example, Arthur Engberg, "Fosterlandskärleken" in his *Tal och skrifter* (Stockholm: Tiden, 1945), 307.
5.   Gustav Sundbärg, *Det svenska folklynnet* (Stockholm, 1911), 3.
6.   Arne Ruth, "The Second New Nation: The Mythology of Modern Sweden," *Dædalus* vol. 113, no 1., 1984, 68.
7.   Ibid., 81.
8.   The Goths were one of the nomadic tribes that invaded Europe when the Roman Empire was going into terminal decline. Swedish writers, beginning with Johannes Magnus in his *Historia de omnibus gothorum sveonumque* (1554), constructed a rather fantastic tale to the effect that the Goths originally came from Sweden (along with much else that was great and good ...).
9.   Jacob Adlerbeth, "Stiftelseurkunden jemte stadgarna för det göthiska förbundet," *Iduna*, vol. 11, 1845, 2-3.
10.   As with many other national myths, this is a story that contains a measure of truth. The Swedish peasants were indeed unique in that they not only retained the land and escaped feudalism and serfdom, but even retained political representation, both at the national level—as the fourth estate—and at the local, village level—in the form of self-government. As Michael Roberts has put it: "It may well be true that the idealization of the yeoman peasant by such writers as E. G. Geijer has been proved to have but a shaky historical basis," yet in the final analysis "it is still safe to say that the peasant in mediaeval Sweden retained his social and political freedom to a greater degree, played a greater part in the politics of the country, and was altogether a more considerable person, than in any other western European country." Michael Roberts, *Essays in Swedish History* (Minneapolis: University of Minnesota Press, 1967), 4-5.

11. The Kalmar Union, against which Engelbrekt led a successful rebellion in 1434, was the union of Denmark, Norway, and Sweden formed in 1397 under the Danish Crown.

12. See Lars Trägårdh, "The Concept of the People and the Construction of Popular Political Culture in Sweden and Germany, 1848-1933," unpublished dissertation, University of California at Berkeley, 1993, and Lars Trägårdh, "Welfare State Nationalism: Sweden and the Spectre of 'Europe'" in Lene Hansen and Ole Wæver (eds.), *European Integration and National Identity: The Challenge of the Nordic States* (London and New York: Routledge, 2002).

13. *Allmoge, allmogen* refers to the peasants, the "little" people.

14. C. T. Odhner, *Lärobok i fädnerslandets historia* (Stockholm: Nya tiden, 1902), 97.

15. Lidforss is well-known for his anti-Semitic views.

16. The quote from Lidforss is taken from Staffan Björck, *Heidenstam och sekelskiftets Sverige* (Stockholm: Natur och Kultur, 1946), 292. Björck notes in the same footnote in reference to this early period around 1900 that "Socialdemocratic propaganda often made use of Engelbrekt," suggesting the deep roots of this leftist, nationalist discourse.

17. Rickard Lindström, *Socialism, nation och stat* (Eskilstuna, 1928), 11.

18. Rickard Lindström, *Socialism, nation och stat* (Eskilstuna, 1928), 12. The use of the term "national-socialism" is, of course, eye-catching. Since it pre-dates the prominence of German National-Socialism in the public awareness of Swedes, it is likely that Lindström used it quite innocently. While Swedish socialism indeed did became more and more national-minded through the 1930s and 40s, the term never caught on as central to Social Democratic discourse since it soon became firmly identified with Hitler's political movement and ideology, and with Hitler's imitators in Sweden itself.

19. Per Albin Hansson, "Land skall med lag byggas," *Demokrati* (Stockholm: Tiden, 1935), 112.

20. From a speech given in 1933. Per Albin Hansson, "Frihet och Självtukt" in *Demokrati* (Stockholm, 1935), 132.

21. Ibid., 132-133.

22. Per Albin Hansson, "Demokrati eller diktatur," *Demokrati* (Stockholm, 1935), 131.

23. Per Albin Hansson, "Tal till Sveriges flagga," *Demokrati* (Stockholm, 1935), 137.

24. This shift has, in fact, a longer history. For a more detailed analysis see Lars Trägårdh, "Varieties of Volkish Ideologies," in Bo Stråth (ed), *Language and the Construction of Class Identities* (Gothenburg; Gothenburg University, 1990), especially 42-45.

25. Per Albin Hansson, "Folk och klass," *Tiden* (Stockholm 1929), 80.

26. Per Albin Hansson, "På bondens dag," *Demokrati* (Stockholm, 1935), 264.

27. Ibid., 265.

28. Björck, *Heidenstam och sekelskiftets Sverige* .

29. For example, Sundbärg, *Det svenska folklynnet.*

30. Rudolf Kjellén, *Politiska essayer*, vol. 2 (Stockholm, 1915), 56. The article was first published 28 December 1912.

31. Ibid., 22.

32. The conservative genealogy and connotations of the *folkhem* concept in fact disturbed some leading Social Democrats. Thus Arthur Engberg, a future minister, wrote a series of articles in 1929 criticizing Per Albin Hansson for his usage of the "new" concept, and he specifically referred to Kjellén's earlier and, in Engberg's view, highly suspect use of that same term (Arthur Engberg, "Folkhemmet," *Social-Demokraten,* 15 September 1929, 4. Also see other articles published on 11-14 September that same year.)

33. For a more detailed discussion of this point, see Lars Trägårdh, "Welfare State Nationalism."

34. Quoted in James Sheehan, "What is German History? Reflections on the Role of the *Nation* in German History and Historiography," *Journal of Modern History*, vol. 53, March 1981, 1.

35. Johan Gottfried Herder, *Reflections on the Philosophy of the History of Mankind* (Chicago: University of Chicago Press, 1968); Isaiah Berlin, *Vico and Herder: Two Studies in the History of Ideas* (London: Hogarth, 1976).

36. Johann Gottlieb Fichte, *Addresses to the German Nation* (La Salle, Ill.: Open Court Publishing Company, 1922).

37. James Sheehan, *German Liberalism in the Nineteenth Century* (Chicago: University of Chicago Press, 1978).

38. Georg Iggers, *The German Conception of History: The National Tradition of Historical Thought from Herder to the Present* (Middletown, Conn: Wesleyan University Press, 1968).

39. See, for example, Celia Applegate, *A Nation of Provincials: The German Idea of Heimat* (Berkeley: University of California Press, 1990) and Alon Confino, "The Nation as a Local Metaphor: Heimat, National Memory and the German Empire, 1871-1918," *History and Memory*, vol. 5, no. 1, 1993, and Alon Confino, *The Nation as a Local Metaphor: Württemberg, Imperial Germany, and National Memory, 1871-1918* (Chapel Hill: University of North Carolina Press, 1997).

40. Fritz Stern, "The Political Consequences of the Unpolitical German" in his *The Failure of Illiberalism: Essays on the Political Culture of Modern Germany* (New York: Columbia University Press, 1992); Leonard Krieger, *The German Idea of Freedom: History of a Political Tradition* (Chicago: University of Chicago Press, 1972).

41. George Mosse, *The Crisis of German Ideology: Intellectual Origins of the Third Reich* (New York: Schocken, 1981); John Gagliardo, *From Pariah to Patriot: The Changing Image of the German Peasant, 1770-1840* (Lexington: University Press of Kentucky, 1969); Fritz Stern, *The Politics of Cultural Despair: A Study of the Rise of the "Germanic" Ideology* (Berkeley: University of California Press, 1961).

42. Interestingly, the national myth-makers of the GDR returned to the Peasants' War, the Wars of Liberation, and the 1848 Revolution as key moments for the writing of a "good" German history, one that culminated in the GDR. This has been admirably documented in a Spring 1997 exhibition in Berlin on the making of the GDR ("Parteiauftrag: Ein neues Deutschland").

43. Friedrich Engels, *The Peasant War in Germany* (New York: International Publishers, 1966).

44. Warren Breckman, "Diagnosing the 'German Misery': Radicalism and the Problem of National Character, 1830 to 1848," in David Barclay and E.D. Weitz (eds.), *Between Reform and Revolution: Studies in the History of German Socialism and Communism from 1840-1990* (Oxford: Berghahn, 1998).

45. The key text is Otto Bauer's *Nationalitätenfrage und Sozialdemokratie* (Vienna, 1907), but Renner and Bauer also wrote frequently in the major journals of the German and Austrian Social Democratic parties, such as *Der Kampf* and *Die Gesellschaft*. A selection of English language translations is available in Tom Bottomore and Patrick Goode, *Austro-Marxism* (Oxford: Clarendon Press: 1978).

46. Hans-Jurgen Puhle, *Agrarische Interessenpolitik und preussischer Konservatismus im wilhelminischen Reich 1893-1914: Ein Beitrag zur Analyse des Nationalismus in Deutschland am Beispiel des Bundes der Landwirte und der Deutsch-Konservativen Partei* (Hanover: Verlag für Literatur und Zeitgeschehen, 1967).

47. See Hermann Rauschning, *The Conservative Revolution*, (New York: G. P. Putnam's sons, 1941), Armin Mohler, *Die Konservative Revolution* (Darmstadt: Wissenschaftliche Buchgesellschaft, 1989), Roger Woods, *The Conservative Revolution in the Weimar Republic* (New York: St. Martin's Press, 1996),

48. Koselleck, "Volk," in Otto Brunner, Werner Conze, and Reinhardt Koselleck (eds.), *Geschichtliche Grundbegriffe*, vol. 7 (Stuttgart: Klett-Cotta, 1992), 398.

49. *Teilkultur* means "part-culture" and is deliberately used in opposition to the notion "sub-culture" that implies at least the possibility of the peaceful coexistence of a variety of different cultures. The ideal type is the U.S. experience of ethnic communities that form parts of a larger civil society held together by a common minimal commitment to the U.S. political system. See Detlef Lehnert and Klaus Meyerle (eds.), *Politische Teilkulturen zwischen Integration und Polarisierung: zur politischen Kultur der Weimaren Republik* (Opladen: Westdeutscher, 1990).

50. Quoted in Koselleck, "Volk," 401.

51. Friedrich Austerlitz, "Deutsche Demokratie," *Der Kampf*, August 1917, 16.

52. Ibid., 16.

53. Per Albin Hansson, "Nordisk demokrati," *Demokrati* (Stockholm, 1935), 220.

54. Marquis Childs, *Sweden: The Middle Way* (New Haven: Yale University Press, 1936).

55. Steven Koblik (ed.), *Sweden's Development from Poverty to Affluence, 1750-1970* (Minneapolis: University of Minnesota Press, 1975); David Jenkins, *Sweden: The Progress Machine* (London:

Robert Hale, 1969); Richard Thomasson, *Sweden: Prototype of Modern Society* (New York: Random House, 1970); Arne Ruth, "The Second New Nation."

56. Bo Stråth, *Folkhemmet mot Europa* (Stockholm: Tiden, 1992), 209.

57. Tord Ekström, Gunnar Myrdal, and Roland Pålsson, *Vi och Västeuropa* (Stockholm: Rabén & Sjögren, 1962), 33.

58. Ibid., 33.

59. Enn Kokk, "Världen, vi och Västeuropa," Föreningen Laboremus, *Förändringens vind* (Stockholm: Rabén & Sjögren, 1962), 135.

60. Stråth, *Folkhemmet mot Europa.*

61. Göran Greider, "Jag tror på nationalstaten," *Kritiska Europafakta*, no. 26, 1993, 16. A pamphlet published by "Nej till EG."

62. Vänsterpartiet, *Alternativ till EU-medlemskap* (Stockholm, 1994), 4.

63. From the official program of the Left Party with respect to EU: Vänsterpartiet, *Program för en alternativ europapolitik* (Stockholm, 1994), 6-7.

64. Vänsterpartiet, *Europeiska Unionen: Socialistiskt eller nyliberalt projekt?* (Stockholm, 1994), 23. Written by Stellan Hermansson, campaign secretary in the Left Party.

65. Yes, popes are usually Catholic: the double emphasis may well be taken as yet another proof of Swedish left-wing abhorrence of papism. Vänsterpartiet, *Frågor och svar om EU nr 2: Kvinnorna och EU* (Stockholm, 1994), 6.

66. Vänsterpartiet, *Program för en alternativ europapolitik*, 23.

67. Vänsterpartiet, *Frågor och svar om EU* no. 2, 6.

68. Rolf Karlbom, "Lång svensk folkstyrelsetradition" in *Kritiska Europafakta*, no. 26, 1993, 14.

69. *Norden* includes all the Nordic countries.

70. Jörgen Bengtsson, *Ge Norden en chans!* (Give Norden a Chance!), Alternativ till EG skriftserie, no. 1, 1993, 12-13.

71. Ibid., 13-14.

72. Marianne Eriksson, *Är EG en kvinnofälla?* Nej till EG Skriftserie, no. 10 (1993).

73. For a more detailed discussion of the historical importance of neutrality and intergovernmental internationalism in Sweden, see Lars Trägårdh, "Welfare State Nationalism."

74. This is a notion that I have coined and elaborated upon in a separate essay, "Statist Individualism: On the Culturality of the Nordic Welfare State," Bo Stråth and Øystein Sørensen (eds.), *The Cultural Construction of Norden* (Oslo: University of Oslo Press, 1997).

75. Jean-Jacques Rousseau, *The Social Contract* (New York: Penguin, 1968), 99.

76. For a sustained analysis along these lines see my essay on "Statist Individualism. "

77. See, for example, Jürgen Habermas, "New Social Movements," *Telos*, vol. 49, 1981, and Claus Offe, "New Social Movements: Challenging the Boundaries of Institutional Politics," *Social Research*, vol. 52, no. 2, 1984.

78. Disregarding the experience in the GDR.

79. Mack Walker, *German Home Towns: Community, State, and General Estate, 1648-1871* (Ithaca: Cornell University Press, 1971).

80. David Blackbourn and Geoff Eley, *The Peculiarities of German History: Bourgeois Society and Politics in Nineteenth Century Germany* (Oxford: Oxford University Press, 1984).

81. See Peter Brandt and Herbert Ammon, eds., *Die Linke und die nationale Frage* (Hamburg: Rowohlt, 1981) and also a brief discussion of this phenomenon in Hans Mommsen, "History and National Identity: The Case of Germany," *German Studies Review*, vol. 6, no. 1 (1983).

82. For an analysis of Schumacher's view on the new German nation-state, see Dieter Groh and Peter Brandt, *"Vaterlandslose Gesellen": Sozialdemokratie und Nation* (Munich: C.H. Beck, 1992), 233ff.

83. Ibid., 249.

84. Quote from an article written by Hermann Peter Piwitt, discussed by Friedbert Pflüger in *Deutschland driftet* (Düsseldorf: Econ, 1994), 115.

85. Margarita Mathiopoulos, *Das Ende der Bonner Republik* (Stuttgart: Deutsche Verlags-Anstalt, 1993).

86. "Die deutsche Nation erwacht" is the title of one of the chapters of Mathiopoulos's book, and it alludes, of course, to the famous Nazi slogan of the Weimar Republic.

87. Dieter Oberndörfer, *Der Wahn des Nationalen* (Freiburg: Herder, 1993).

88. Günter Grass, *Rede vom Verlust* (Göttingen: Steidl, 1992).

89. Also see Hajo Funke, *"Jetzt sind wir dran"*: *Nationalismus im geeinten Deutschland* (Berlin: Aktion Sühnezeichen, 1991).

90. Rainer Zittelmann, Karlheinz Weißmann, and Michael Großheim (eds.), *Westbindung: Chancen und Risiken für Deutschland* (Frankfurt/M and Berlin: Ullstein, 1992); Heimo Schwilk and Ulrich Schacht (eds.), *Die Selbstbewusste Nation* (Frankfurt/M and Berlin: Ullstein, 1994).

91. From a television address on the "Eve of the Day of German Unity"–2 October 1990– reprinted in Richard T. Gray and Sabine Wilke (eds.), *German Unification and Its Discontents: Documents from the Peaceful Revolution* (Seattle: University of Washington Press, 1996), 261.

92. For a discussion of the *FAZ* debate of 1994 and more generally the emergence of the New Right critique of the CDU middle, see Franz Oswald, "Integral and Instrumental Nationalism: National-Conservative Elite Discourse: The 'What's Right' Debate of 1994," in *Debatte*, no. 2, 1995, 24ff.

93. Joschka Fischer, *Risiko Deutschland: Krise und Zukunft der deutschen Politik* (Cologne: Kiepenheuer & Witsch, 1994).

94. Peter Glotz, *Der Irrweg des nationalstaats* (Stuttgart, 1990).

95. Jürgen Habermas, "Staatsbürgerschaft und nationale Identität: Überlegungen zur europäischen Zukunft," Nicole Dewandre and Jacques Lenoble (eds.), *Projekt Europa. Postnationale Identität: Grundlage für eine europäische Demokratie* (Berlin: Schelsky & Jeep, 1994).

96. For examples of such thinking among international relations scholars, see Ole Wæver, "Identity, Integration and Security: Solving the Sovereignty Puzzle in EU Studies," *Journal of International Affairs,* vol. 48, no. 2 (1995) and John Ruggie, "Territoriality and Beyond: Problematizing Modernity in International Relations," *International Organization,* vol. 47, no. 1 (1993).

6

Interpreting the Holocaust
Crisis of Modernity or Crisis of German Ideology?[*]

BENJAMIN LAPP

In an interview with Ron Rosenbaum, the eminent Holocaust historian Christopher Browning suggested that the mainstream popularity of Goldhagen's book *Hitler's Willing Executioners* stems from a widespread reaction against a current trend in Holocaust scholarship. This trend is characterized, Browning suggests, by an understanding of National Socialism not as an aberration of Western civilization but as a "culmination of certain of its tendencies." By contrast, Goldhagen's notion of a German culture dominated by "eliminationist anti-Semitism" focuses–argues Browning–on the narrow relationship of German and Jews, and thereby avoids the disturbing implications of the radical critique of Western civilization suggested by recent Holocaust scholarship.[1]

Browning raises an important point. There are, indeed, two dominant "paradigms" underlying the interpretation of Nazism. Broadly speaking, one locates Nazism in a peculiarly German pathology, whereas the second focuses on broader "Western" tendencies and relates Nazism to "modernity" in general and to a particular type of modernization process more specifically. Browning's implication that this conflict is a recent one needs, however, to be qualified: the two contrasting perspectives have older roots, and both have been represented in the work of German refugee scholars who fled Nazism in the 1930s. It is also important to emphasize that neither of the two perspectives represent camps that can be said to be homogenous in any way: there is a world of difference between Jürgen Kocka's highly complex and nuanced analysis of contemporary German history and Goldhagen's rather monocausal one, though both emphasize the "peculiarity" of the German experience. In this chapter, I will attempt to contextualize the current debate in the postwar historical literature on Nazism and the Holocaust.

During World War II, an early version of the *Sonderweg* (special path) thesis—a perspective that explicitly contrasted German political and historical
development with that of the Western European and American democracies—was represented by scholars such as William Montgomery McGovern,
who sought to locate the roots of Nazism in German intellectual traditions
dating back to Luther.[2] The influence of such simplistic and sweeping
overviews of German culture and history remained limited, however. Other,
more sophisticated, versions of the *Sonderweg* thesis could be found in the
work of George Mosse, Fritz Stern, and Leonard Krieger, all of whom
emphasized the strength of illiberal traditions such as *völkisch* thought, adula-
tion of the state, and political Romanticism, arguing that this legacy then
came to fruition in the context of the economic and political crises of the
Weimar Republic and the rise of National Socialism.[3]

Perhaps the most influential version of the *Sonderweg* thesis was developed by Hans-Ulrich Wehler and the Bielefeld school. Broadly defined, the
Bielefeld school argued that the lateness and rapidity of German industrialization, in conjunction with the inherited structures of the dynastic state—
Junkderdom, militarism, the dominance of old elites—prevented liberal
principles from taking root in German society. Economic modernization in
Germany was not accompanied by modern social values and political institutions—Germany had never experienced, they argued, a successful bourgeois revolution—and this had ominous implications: the lack of a liberal
tradition created the preconditions for the inherent instability of the Weimar
Republic and the Nazi seizure of power. Thus, the "crisis" of the 1930s was
rooted in the undemocratic structures of imperial Germany. Clearly rejecting
earlier apologetic versions of German history, the Bielefeld school provided
a new and refreshingly critical perspective on German historical development. It drew extensively on social theory (particularly modernization theory
and Max Weber's historical sociology), as well as on the work of refugee historians such as Ekhart Kehr and Hans Rosenberg. By the 1970s, the Bielefeld
school had articulated the most influential treatment of German history and
the most compelling explanation of the coming to power of the Nazis.[4]

The rather overdetermined Bielefeld model was, however, subject to criticism, and in the early 1980s a group of young British historians—notably
Geoff Eley and David Blackbourn —offered a scathing critique of the theory of
the *Sonderweg*. Influenced by such Marxist theoreticians as Poulantzas and
Gramsci, Eley and Blackbourn explicitly challenged the notions of German
peculiarity, a specifically German illiberalism, and German political backwardness. Eley and Blackbourn attacked the idea—central to the *Sonderweg*
thesis—that economic modernization in Germany was not accompanied
by "modern social values and political institutions."[5] The Bielefelders had
argued that the lack of a successful bourgeois revolution and the strength of
pre-industrial elites distinguished Germany from Western Europe and the

United States; in this basic difference lay the roots of the Nazi success. Black-bourn and Eley suggested, firstly, that the theory of the *Sonderweg* lay in a highly problematic and confused concept of bourgeois revolution. The historical concept of bourgeois revolution was, they suggested, dependent on an incompatible synthesis of Marxism and modernization theory; it presupposed that the bourgeoisie could be conceptualized as a "corporate political actor, with a collective class interest traceable through particular events and in ideas in a directly expressive way";[6] finally, it rested on a reductionist and historically inaccurate identification of the bourgeoisie with political liberalism. Thus, they argued, the view of the bourgeois revolution, "where the insurgent bourgeoisie triumphantly realizes its class interests in a programme of heroic liberal democracy is a myth." They also rejected the standard whereby Germany was compared to the British model—viewed in terms of a "harmonious synchrony" of industrialization, liberalization and democratization—and found wanting. This comparison, Eley wrote, rested on a highly idealized conception of the extent of political participation in mid-Victorian Britain.[7]

Eley and Blackbourn themselves did not entirely abandon the concept of a bourgeois revolution; rather, they redefined it. They associated the bourgeois revolution with a "larger complex of change (…) which cumulatively established the conditions of possibility for the development of industrial capitalism." By this standard, German unification had successfully secured the interests of the bourgeoisie. Given the growth of the labor movement, it was a "rational calculation of political interest" for the "leading fractions of the bourgeoisie" to enter into an alliance with the agrarians and resist any extension of democracy; the "authoritarianism of the Imperial Constitution was less a sign of pathology than of rational fittedness to historically specific circumstances."[8] While Eley and Blackbourn did not deal directly with the phenomenon of National Socialism, it is clear that they rejected the importance of "pre-industrial traditions"; instead, Eley pointed to the particular forms of German capitalist development and the "new structures of politics they helped to determine."[9] Likewise, Blackbourn stressed that Germany's "dynamic capitalism" constituted a heightened version of what occurred elsewhere, and that its consequences produced "Germany's exceptionally radical form of fascism."[10] The attack on the *Sonderweg* theory had major implications for the writing of German history, and a number of historians, Hans-Ulrich Wehler among them, have modified many of their positions. As Jürgen Kocka has pointed out, such old orthodoxies as the "feudalization" of the German bourgeoisie are no longer seriously considered; nevertheless, Kocka suggests, the *Sonderweg* theory still is useful for an analysis of Germany's bureaucratic traditions and the notably weak nature of German parliamentarianism.[11] Eley and Blackbourn never really addressed the tradition of "revolution from above" in Germany and the implications of that tradition for German political culture.[12]

Nevertheless, Eley and Blackbourn's challenge to the notion of German particularity, which instead viewed German political development in terms of a variant of capitalist modernization, opened the door for alternative historical explanations of Nazism. Increasingly historians of Germany (both in the USA and Germany) began to turn away from the rather uncritical modernization theory that had informed the Bielefeld school and seek other frameworks of interpretation. The analysis offered by the philosophers of the Frankfurt school, particularly Adorno and Horkheimer's *Dialectic of the Enlightenment*, proved particularly influential.[13] Written during the war and published in 1947, the book at first received little notice, and certainly had little influence on historians until it was rediscovered by the student movement in the 1960s and consequently translated into English.

In radical contrast to the *Sonderweg* theory, Adorno and Horkheimer saw the roots of Nazism not in a divergence from a Western norm, but rather in the Western tradition itself, specifically in the domination of nature emerging out of a peculiarly western instrumental rationality. In particular, the eighteenth century Enlightenment was called into question. Structures of domination and exploitation, Adorno and Horkheimer argued, were inherent in the Enlightenment itself and were directly responsible for the Fascist politics of the twentieth century. Reason, so highly valued in the West, had turned into barbarism. For Horkheimer and Adorno, the Nazi regime represented not a perverse aberration, a divergence from Western modernity, but the culminating crisis of a dialectic inherent in the Western tradition; nor did, according to the same logic, the defeat of that regime end the destructive potential of that tradition. On the contrary, the possibility of fascism remained in Western capitalist democracies; this possibility was particularly apparent in the "culture industry" typical of late capitalism. As Steven Aschheim has pointed out, while it is clearly dominated by the problem of Nazism, *The Dialectic of the Enlightenment* "collapses distinctive developments into ahistorical generalizations," making it "difficult to separate the phenomenon of National Socialism from a far wider and ongoing barbarism," "held to be characteristic of the entire capitalist west."[14]

Adorno and Horkheimer were not historians, to be sure; nevertheless their notion of a pathology peculiar to modernity and deeply rooted in Enlightenment concepts of reason proved particularly suggestive for historians seeking alternatives to the *Sonderweg* theory. There is, I would argue, a direct connection between the Frankfurt school analysis and that of the highly influential post-*Sonderweg* German historian Detlev Peukert. The crisis of the Weimar Republic that preceded the Nazi seizure of power was, according to his view, a "crisis of the classical modern," not a specific crisis of "German Ideology" or otherwise an expression of a German *Sonderweg*.[15] This crisis culminated in the National Socialist dictatorship, which represents, for Peukert, "modernity's most fatal developmental possibility.[16] "The challenge of Nazism," wrote Peukert, "shows that the evolution of modernity is not a one-way trip to freedom."[17]

More specifically, and in ways that clearly reveal his debt to the Frankfurt School, Peukert argued that the origins of the "Final Solution" can be located in the "Spirit of Science," that is, in eugenic attempts to regulate the human species. Examining the eugenics movement in an international and comparative framework, Peukert argued that Science, having failed to transcend the mortality of individuals, switched its concern to the racial gene pool, ultimately abandoning the utopian project of collective well-being in favor of the more easily attainable goal of the mass extermination of undesirable species.[18] Thus, Peukert wrote that the "specifically modern character of the 'Final Solution' derives from the swing to racial hygiene in the human and social sciences."[19] In other works, Peukert investigates the rise of social welfare and forms of social control and how these policies became implicated in Nazi racialism. In Saul Friedländer's words, Peukert's position defines the historical background of Nazism "in terms of a general crisis of modernity, the rise of racial science and a belief in a social engineering of sorts."[20]

Peukert's appropriation of the Frankfurt school critique of the Enlightenment and of instrumental rationality proved extraordinarily influential. At the same time it set the stage for a reaction along the lines of Goldhagen's neo-*Sonderweg* theory that has yet again focused attention on German peculiarity. As Omer Bartov has pointed out, Peukert's emphasis on Nazi biological politics "underplays the role of antisemitism and specifically of anti-Jewish policies in the Third Reich and generalizes biological politics to include much of the West, and thereby minimizes Germany's centrality in the development and implementation of this concept." [21]

A still more pronounced linkage between modernity and Nazism (and specifically Nazi anti-Semitism) is to be found in the work of the sociologist Zygmunt Bauman. Avoiding the sometimes facile characterizations of science that characterize Peukert's, Bauman puts racial anti-Semitism at the center of his analysis. At the same time, he sees the particularity of the Nazi Holocaust in its "modern" rather than specifically German traits. Thus, he argues, the Holocaust was "born and executed in our modern rational society, at the high stage of our civilization and at the peak of human cultural achievement, and for this reason it is a problem of that society, civilization and culture." The Holocaust was a peculiarly modern genocide since it was unthinkable without modern scientific organization and bureaucracy. Drawing on the Frankfurt school's critique of instrumental reason and Hannah Arendt's discussion of the "banality of evil", Bauman analyzes the bureaucratic mindset that was a precondition of Nazi mass murder and the way it interacted with a "scientific" racial anti-Semitism: "the choice of physical extermination as the right means to the task of *Entfernung* was a product of routine bureaucratic procedures: means-ends calculus, budget balancing, universal rule application."[22] Nazi racism was a modern form of social engineering, a practice that combined strategies of architecture, gardening, and medicine "in the service of the construction of an artificial social order, through cutting out the elements of the present reality that neither fit the visualized perfect reality, nor can be changed so that they do."[23] Most Germans, Bauman argues, were not rabid anti-Semites. Nevertheless, they felt it was not in their rational self-interest to speak out against the racist and genocidal policies of the regime. While he locates the choice of victim in the history of European/German anti-Semitism, he is quick to condemn those who would focus on the "Germanness" of the crime: "The more 'they' are to blame, the more the rest of 'us' are safe, and the less we have to do to defend this safety."[24]

Bauman's work foregrounded the role of the bureaucrat and social engineer in the Final Solution. This issue has also been further emphasized in the important and controversial work of the German historian Götz Aly. In a series of articles and books, Aly has documented the extent to which Nazi genocide was dependent on highly trained technocrats, many with advanced degrees, who were integral to the policies of occupation, enslavement, and extermination.[25] Moreover, the Holocaust was not simply the result of an age-old irrational anti-Semitic prejudice; rather, it was part of a "rational" plan to reorganize the demographic structure of Eastern Europe and to create living space for German settlers. Like Bauman, Aly sees it as a product of instrumental rationality linked to utopian social engineering. The "planning intelligentsia"–demographers, sociologists, economists, historians–advocated extermination as a means of socioeconomic modernization. Genocide, however, was not an end in itself, but rather an attempt to "boost social productivity" and ensure a "new ordering of the entire complex of class relations."[26] Thus Aly and his co-writer Heim conclude that "accepting insanity or hatred of the Jews going back to Martin Luther as grounds for the Holocaust is less disturbing than the discovery of such a coolly thought-out justification for genocide."[27]

Historians, while acknowledging Aly's contribution to our knowledge of the "Final Solution," have also been quick to criticize some of his central theses. As Michael Burleigh has pointed out, it is the irrelevance of economic criteria to the Final Solution which is striking: "Precisely what economic logic impelled the Nazis in June 1944 to transport 2,200 Jews in Rhodes a couple of thousand miles to Auschwitz, regardless of the loss of military materiel or more pressing transport priorities?"[28] Likewise, Yehuda Bauer writes that "if the problem of German resettlement in the eastern marches of the Reich was the motive for the murder of the Jews, why did the Germans deport to their death the Jews of Corfu and Rhodes, or those from Narvik in Norway and Bayonne in France?"[29] In his emphasis on technocracy and planning, Aly has been criticized for downplaying the role of radical anti-Semitism. Racism–an "irrationalist" ideology–does not find a central place in Aly's work, according to this critique. Furthermore, the Heim-Aly thesis suggests another potential problem with the Nazism-as-a-"crisis of modernity" model. Wolfgang Wipperman and Michael Burleigh have angrily criticized those who relate Nazism to modernity as allowing the "unique horrors of the Third Reich to disappear within a fog of relativising, sociological rhetoric. The fact of Nazi Germany's murder of millions of Jews, Sinti and Roma, and others at a specific point in time is obscured by talk of general genocidal impulses allegedly latent beneath the thin civilized crust of all 'modern' societies."[30]

Objections such as these have fed a reaction against "structuralist" theories of Nazism that downplay the "personal" aspects of Nazi mass murder in favor of an analysis of bureaucracy and regime-structure, questioning the position taken by (structuralist) historians such as Hans Mommsen, who in a typical formulation has argued that it was the "political-bureaucratic mechanisms that allowed the idea of mass extermination to become reality" that are significant for the historian.[31] The emphasis on impersonal structures has in itself come to be seen as highly problematic. Where, in this view, are the murderers? Are they simply nameless bureaucrats who could have appeared in any "modern" system? Certainly, the enormously positive reception of Daniel Goldhagen's book—a study which in great detail describes the killing process and argues that the executioners (ordinary Germans) derived great pleasure from the act of killing Jews, and that this pleasure can be attributed to the peculiar nature of German anti-Semitism—can be related to the ways in which structural theories about "modernity" on some basic level avoid the horror of the Final Solution and the specificity of the extermination of the Jews.[32]

Goldhagen's book received little support from the historical community, partly since it appeared to revive the *Sonderweg* theory of Nazism in a particularly crude form, reminiscent of the early "from Luther to Hitler school," and thus to challenge in fundamental ways the cherished theories of many established historians.[33] There is no doubt, however, that Goldhagen raised important points about popular anti-Semitism in Germany that historians, particularly those of the "pathology of modernity" camp, had avoided. At the same time, Goldhagen's refusal to consider the role of modern institutions in the Holocaust ultimately reduces the final solution to a massive pogrom, one more outrage in a long history of anti-Semitism. As Omer Bartov has pointed out, "to legitimize themselves in a modern world, antisemitism, Nazism and genocide all needed two crucial elements: a scientific stamp and a legalistic sanction." In other words, science and law—two of the foundations of modernity—were indispensable to the implementation of the Final Solution.[34] Furthermore, Goldhagen's notion of a peculiarly German "eliminationist anti-Semitism," which supposedly dominated German culture in the modern era, has been rejected by leading Bielefeld historians such as Wehler and Kocka[35].

Have we then reached an impasse? Must we choose between the "modernity-centered" and "Germany-centered" theories, between a structuralist and a narrative approach? If not, then clearly future research on Nazism and the Holocaust will have to locate the "crisis of modernity" in the particular context of German anti-Semitism and it will have to show that such a crisis expressed itself in a specific German inflection. And, indeed, promising strides in this direction have been made in recent research. In particular, by bringing together approaches that emphasize the peculiarly German elements and those that focus on the "modernity" of Nazism and the technocratic features of the Holocaust, Saul Friedländer has shown that the two perspectives are not necessarily incompatible. Friedländer argues that these two modes of interpretation are, in fact "dealing with two contrary but coexisting aspects of Nazism." For instance, *völkisch* and racist theories, widespread in Germany, increasingly legitimized themselves in quasi-scientific terms. Thus, Friedländer argues, "with regard to the Nazi myth of the Jew, archaic religious themes and so-called modern scientific theories were interwoven in a multifaceted representation of the archenemy of the Volk."[36] From this perspective, then, the Holocaust was *both* an outgrowth of modernity *and* the result of particular circumstances in Germany, suggesting that perhaps the opposition that Browning suggests between an approach which emphasizes German peculiarities and one that highlights modernity is a false opposition after all.

In the context of a volume comparing Sweden and Germany, one might, by way of conclusion, raise the question of why in Sweden, where neither anti-Semitism, nor the spirit of scientific modernity was by any means absent, the two were not joined in the lethal way they were in Germany. The question becomes all the more compelling given the gruesome history of eugenics and forced sterilizations in democratic Sweden, with a record second only to that of the Germans under Hitler.[37] As we have noted, Peukert's notion that the origins of the German "Final Solution" must be sought in the "Spirit of Science" has been viewed as deeply problematic given the economically "irrational" racial policies of Nazi Germany. Here the Swedish case might have served him better. In Sweden, as Maciej Zaremba has argued, eugenics was firmly linked to economic rationality, on the one hand, and democratic politics, on the other. [38] While it is possible to misread the Holocaust as a unique expression of evil, as Goldhagen does, such a misreading is difficult to make in the Swedish case. Therefore, insofar as we want to investigate the crisis and pathology of Western modernity, the obvious case of Germany might ultimately benefit from a comparison with that of Sweden.

Notes

* I would like to thank to my editors, Lars Trägårdh and Nina Witoszek, for their thoughtful comments and suggestions.

1. Ron Rosenbaum, *Explaining Hitler* (New York: Random House and London: Macmillan, 1998), 365–36. For an absolutely outstanding discussion of some of the general issues facing the historiography of the Holocaust in particular, see Steven Aschheim, "Small Forays, Grand Theories and Deep Origins: Current Trends in the Historiography of the Holocaust" in Steven Aschheim (ed.), *Culture and Catastrophe: German and Jewish Confrontations with National Socialism and Other Crises* (London: Macmillan, 1996), 115–135.

2. William Montgomery McGovern, *From Luther to Hitler. The History of Nazi-Fascist Philosophy* (London: Harras & Co., 1946). Such views were popularized in William Shirer's *The Rise and Fall of the Nazi Third Reich* (New York: Simon and Schuster, 1960).

3. Fritz Stern, *The Politics of Cultural Despair* (Berkeley: University of California Press, 1961); George L. Mosse, *The Crisis of German Ideology* (New York: Schocken, 1981); Leonard Krieger, *The German Idea of Freedom: The History of a Political Tradition* (Chicago: University of Chicago Press, 1972).

4. The Bielefelders have produced a huge body of literature. For a systematic presentation, see Hans-Ulrich Wehler, *The German Empire, 1871–1918* (Leamington Spa and Dover, N.H., 1985).

5. David Blackbourn and Geoff Eley, *The Peculiarities of German History: Bourgeois Society and Politics in Nineteenth-century Germany* (Oxford: Oxford University Press, 1984), 7.

6. Ibid., 56.

7. Ibid., 79.

8. Ibid., 124–26.

9. Ibid., 142.

10. Ibid., 292.

11. Jürgen Kocka, "German History before Hitler: The Debate about the German *Sonderweg*," *Journal of Contemporary History,* vol. 23, 1988, 3–16. More recently, see Jürgen Kocka, "Asymmetrical Historical Comparison: The Case of the German *Sonderweg*" in *History and Theory*, vol. 38, February 1999, 40–50.

12. An interesting critique of Eley and Blackbourn can be found in Steven Aschheim's "Nazism, Normalcy and the German *Sonderweg*," in Ascheim (ed.), *In Times of Crisis: Essays on European Culture, Germans and Jews* (Madison: University of Wisconsin Press, 2001), 105–121. Aschheim focuses on their neglect of the cultural and intellectual traditions that characterized the German variant of "modernity."

13. Theodor Adorno and Max Horkheimer, *Dialectic of Enlightenment* (London: Verso Classics, 1977).

14. Aschheim, *Culture and Catastrophe*, 6–7. For a discussion of the Frankfurt School and the *Dialectic of Enlightenment*, see Martin Jay, *The Dialectical Imagination* (Boston: Little, Brown and Co., 1973), 253–280.

15. Detlev Peukert, *The Weimar Republic: The Crisis of Classical Modernity* (London: Allen Lane, 1991), 274–282.

16. Detlev Peukert, *Max Weber's Diagnose der Moderne* (Göttingen: Vanderhoeck & Ruprecht, 1989), 82. Quoted in David Crew, ed. *Nazism and German Society, 1933-1945* (New York: Routledge, 1994), 25.

17. Detlev Peukert, *Inside Nazi Germany: Conformity, Opposition and Racism in Everyday Life* (New Haven: Yale University Press, 1987), 249.

18. See his essay "The Genesis of the 'Final Solution' from the Spirit of Science" in Crew, *Nazism and German Society*, 274–299.

19. Ibid., 290.

20. Saul Friedländer, "The Extermination of the Jews in Historiography: Fifty Years Later" in Omer Bartov (ed.), *The Holocaust: Origins, Implementation, Aftermath* (London: Routledge, 2000), 81.

21. Omer Bartov, *Murder in our Midst: The Holocaust Industrial Killing and Representation* (New York: Oxford University Press, 1996), 208.

22. Zygmunt Bauman, *Modernity and the Holocaust* (Cambridge: Polity, 1989), 17.

23. Ibid., 65.

24. Ibid, xii. For an intelligent critique of Bauman, see Yehuda Bauer, *Rethinking the Holocaust* (New Haven: Yale University Press, 2001), 68–83.

25. See especially Götz Aly, *'Final Solution': Nazi Population Policy and the Murder of the European Jews* (New York: Oxford University Press, 1999) and Götz Aly and Susanne Heim, *Vordenker der Vernichtung. Auschwitz und die Pläne für eine neue europäische Ordnung* (Hamburg: Hoffman und Campe, 1991).

26. See the discussion by Dan Diner in his *Beyond the Conceivable: Studies on Germany, Nazism and the Holocaust* (Berkeley: University of California Press, 2000), 139.

27. Quoted in Michael Burleigh, *Ethics and Extermination: Reflections on Nazi Genocide* (Cambridge: Cambridge University Press, 1997), 172.

28. Ibid., 176.

29. Bauer, *Rethinking the Holocaust*, 89.

30. Michael Burleigh and Wolfgang Wipperman, *The Racial State: Germany, 1933–45* (Cambridge: Cambridge University Press, 1991), 2.

31. Hans Mommsen, "Die Realisierung des Utopischen: Die 'Endlösung der Judenfrage' im Dritten Reich," in Wolfgang Wipperman, *Kontroversen um Hitler* (Frankfurt/M: Suhrkamp, 1986), 277. A critical discussion of Mommsen can be found in Wolfgang Wipperman, *Wessen Schuld: Vom Historikerstreit zur Goldhagen-Kontroverse* (Berlin: Elefanten, 1997), 103–105.

32. Daniel Goldhagen, *Hitler's Willing Executioners: Ordinary Germans and the Holocaust* (New York: Knopf, 1996).

33. For a selection of responses, see Julius H. Schoeps, ed., *Ein Volk von Mördern: die Dokumentation zur Goldhagen-kontroverse an die Rolle der Deutschen in Holocaust?* (Hamburg: Hoffman und Campe, 1996).

34. Bartov, *Murder in our Midst*, 68.

35. See Wehler in Schoeps, *Ein Volk von Mördern*, 193–209.

36. Friedländer, "The Extermination of the European Jews in Historiography: Fifty years later," 79–91. See also Saul Friedländer, *Nazi Germany and the Jews: The Years of Persecution, 1933–39* (London: Weidenfeld & Nicholson, 1997).

37. Gunnar Broberg and Mattias Tydén, "Eugenics in Sweden: Efficient Care" in Gunnar Broberg and Nils Roll-Hansen (eds.), *Eugenics and the Welfare State* (East Lansing: Michigan State University Press, 1996); Gunnar Broberg and Mattias Tydén, *Oönskade i folkhemmet: rashygien och sterilisering i Sverige* (Stockholm: Gidlund, 1991); Maija Runcis, *Steriliseringar i folkhemmet* (Stockholm: Ordfront, 1998).

38. Maciej Zaremba, *De rena och de andra* (Stockholm: Bokförlaget DN, 1999).

7

Politics and Catastrophe
Why Is the World So Obsessed with German History?

MANFRED HENNINGSEN

The year 1945 has lingered in German public and private memory as the year of the catastrophe. Yet the German experiences of catastrophe do not always, if at all, match the images that have become ingrained in the global memory of that year. For the world, Germany 1945 is forever connected with the pictures of corpses and survivors in concentration camps. Since 1945 Germans have been linked with apocalyptic images of death and persecution. Seemingly they have lost all control over the recorded public memory of their past.

The German memory of 1945 can easily be recovered by talking randomly to Germans who were alive at that time. I was then a seven-year-old boy living in a relatively remote and peaceful corner of the Nazi empire near the Danish border, in the small town of Glücksburg. The town is famous for a water castle and for its princely family, to which some of the ruling royal houses in Scandinavia are still connected. In May 1945, after the unconditional surrender of Germany, the castle became a prison for famous members of the Nazi elite, among them Albert Speer. These people were arrested by British troops in that part of Germany because the nearby city of Flensburg had become in late April 1945 the last capital of the Third Reich. On 1 May, the last leader of the Nazi empire, Admiral Dönitz, announced over Radio Flensburg the death of Hitler in Berlin. As a boy I witnessed the arrival of trucks with East Prussian and Pomeranian refugees who came either overland in horse-drawn wagons, or by sea from the coast of East Prussia to the Flensburg Fjord. I saw the German armies retreating from Norway and Denmark and disappearing into the surrounding forests. I heard stories about Russian and Allied prisoners of war breaking out of their camps and about the forced laborers from Eastern Europe threatening their German bosses. The arrival of British occupation troops contributed to the exhilarating sense of being present at a great adventure.

This boyish perspective was not shared by the adults, for whom 1945 meant the collapse and disintegration of German authority, the takeover of all governmental functions by the British, the requisition of houses by the occupiers, the enforced placement of refugees in already crowded houses and apartments, and the worsening of all kinds of shortages, including the rationing of electric power. And it meant the beginning of the formal de-Nazification process. Yet compared with other regions, 1945 in that part of Germany was almost idyllic.

In 1996 Dagmar Barnouw, a professor of German and comparative literature at the University of Southern California, published *Germany 1945.*[1] In this study she juxtaposed the German with the British and American experiences of Germany in that year. Her book challenges the photographic record of 1945 and the kinds of interpretation that usually accompany such illustrations. Photos and interpretations have frozen the experiences of Germany in a way that Barnouw wishes to confront. Her provocative work has not received many reviews. If we compare the reception of her book with the publicity that surrounded Goldhagen's bestseller of the same year, *Hitler's Willing Executioners*, the different responses become easy to understand. Goldhagen appeals to a universally shared disgust and anger directed at the perpetrators of the Holocaust. The sensational aesthetics employed in his book convince the readers that "the" Germans are anti-Semites of a terminal kind. Although none of the Allied powers fought World War II to prevent or even stop the Holocaust, the author manages to make us want to believe otherwise. In that sense, he has contributed to a growing Hollywood version of the war that has remade American understanding of itself as the only righteous and truly moral superpower at the threshold of the twenty-first century. The emotional impact of the book, however, was so overwhelming that even, or especially, Goldhagen's young German readers were totally persuaded by his reconstruction. What German intellectual debate had not quite accomplished, the publication of Goldhagen's book brought about.[2] The remnants of Nazi evil have been exorcised from German society. Indeed, according to Goldhagen, Germany has become a "model" for the world. As he explained in his speech in Bonn on the occasion of receiving the "Democracy Award" from a journal on international politics: "Germans have succeeded best at constructing an accurate national history because, drawing on both domestic and international sources, they have succeeded best at counteracting the prettifying, mythologizing, and self-deluding tendencies of national history writing."[3]

After perusing first Goldhagen's indictment of "the" historical Germans and then the praise of their paradigmatic contemporary behavior, Barnouw's account of American and British attitudes in 1945 serves to restore a sense of the initial response of the Western Allies to Germany. The catastrophe the Germans experienced in that year was seen by American and British photographers differently. "With few exceptions, most of them British," Barnouw writes, "allied photographers showed little interest in the German experience of total war." The wholesale destruction of German cities by British and American bombs, the flight of millions of people from the East, tens of thousands of German POWs in overcrowded camps–most of these images became recorded, if at all, from a detached and morally aloof distance. "After all," as Barnouw summarizes the Allied attitude, "Germans had 'asked for it', they had 'brought it on themselves', it was more important to show as clearly as possible that Germany had excluded itself from the community of civilized nations."[4] The photographic record of the concentration camps that was published in magazines like *Life* was the most self-evident justification for the elision of German suffering from global awareness. The monstrosity of German behavior toward Jews and other victims meant that Germans, at least for the time being, did not deserve to be treated as human equals. The global historical memory of 1945 Germany is still almost exclusively focused on the photographic record from the concentration camps.

Dagmar Barnouw is not an historical revisionist. She does not want to rewrite the history of the Holocaust. She wants an historical recognition of the German experiences of catastrophe, and she wants to overcome the privileging of the Holocaust as a unique historical experience. She questions the motives of the Allied military who forced German civilians, including children, to view the corpses of camp inmates, and she finds the photographic focus on German faces during these visits voyeuristic and obscene. Her blunt comments on the atrocity committed by strategic carpet bombing of German cities are unusual, though they had been made in the U.S. before in a similarly forceful way, albeit without much critical recognition.[5] (One influential exception may be Kurt Vonnegut's *Slaughterhouse Five* (1969), a novel that describes the author's experiences as an American POW in Dresden on 13 and 14 February, when the city was being leveled by British and American bombs and when 135,000 people died for no obvious military reasons. Yet the baroque title page of the book and its absurdist genre may have contributed to a blunting of any radical revaluation of the factual events.)[6]

Barnouw's arguments, however, go beyond a suggestion of genocidal actions. She considers, for example, that the alleged "abstract vastness of German collective guilt relieved the Allies of responsibility for a civilian population made homeless by the Allied endorsement of mass deportations."[7] Her harshest comments are reserved for contemporary Holocaust scholars who want to impose "the controlling perspective of an unquestioned centrality and uniqueness of Jewish persecution."[8] Her particular ire is directed against Saul Friedländer "who has never been interested in understanding others' pasts".[9] Whatever personal or intellectual biases may color Barnouw's remarks, she has touched upon the intriguing question of which of the experiences of catastrophe have actually shaped and transformed German political consciousness since 1945. Was German reconstruction driven by guilt and shame, or by self-pity and defiance? Which experience of catastrophe moved Germans in the direction of a new understanding of politics?

The long occupation of Germany by the victors of World War II saved Germans early on from having to debate the comparable importance of the catastrophe experiences. The occupation may actually have helped to prevent the country from plunging into civil war. Postwar Germany was deeply divided over the issue of the past. This division did not run just between the left and the conservatives; it split political camps internally. Anti-Western resentments, were, for all kinds of historical and contemporary reasons, rife among both Christian Democrats and Social Democrats. Yet the occupation of Germany and the beginning of the Cold War made it impossible to force the issue in public. With the emergence of the Holocaust literature in the early 1960s, the arrival of a self-confident and dissident student generation in the late 1960s, and the election of a political refugee from Nazi Germany, Willy Brandt, to the West German chancellorship in 1969, the cultural climate in West Germany changed.

The Federal Republic Westernized German political thinking, overcoming a division in German culture that had existed since the American and French revolutions at the end of the eighteenth century. This was a split between a Western republican model of politics and an authoritarian model that had emerged from the Prussian state and had been reinforced by Hegel's state-centered political philosophy. The privileged position of the state as the monopoly owner of politics came to an end. In addition, a convergence of perspectives on the Nazi empire took place. This convergence solidified in the 1970s and 1980s, despite the temporary scare created by left-wing terrorism in the 1970s, and the cultural uneasiness provoked by conservative historians in the *Historikerstreit* of 1986. The fall of the Berlin Wall in 1989 and the subsequent reunification of Germany prepared the way for a new debate on German history. Participants in this debate do not just come, like Goldhagen and Barnouw, from outside Germany. [10] The new German identity is a subject of intense discussion by German intellectuals from both former East and West Germany. Conservative writers in the old Western states and socialist writers in the new Eastern states, in particular, question the prevalent Western orientation. A peculiar mix of national and socialist ideas with pronounced anti-American and anti-Western overtones is being promoted. Weimar thought patterns that developed along the speculative dichotomy indicated by Ferdinand Tönnies in 1887, in his thoroughly reactionary and anti-Western book, *Gemeinschaft und Gesellschaft*, have resurfaced[11]. Does the world, fifty-plus years after World War II, have reason to become nervous again?

According to an article by Adam Gopnik in *The New Yorker* (1997), the world should feel reassured. In a report on the Venice Biennale, Gopnik had some interesting comments to make on the artist Anselm Kiefer and his huge canvases, sculptures, and environments on mythic, cultural, and historical themes:

> With the fall of the Berlin Wall, the mystique of German memory seems a lot less imposing as a theme. Germany is, for good or ill, a much more normal country now, and the insistence on locating a romantic landscape, rather than a Mercedes factory, at its core suggests a ... wishful thinking. We wanted the Germans to be exotic, grim, "Teutonic", even in repentance. Now Kiefer's subjects look like tourist traps, bearing the same relation to real German experience that a singing gondola ride bears to actual Italian life.[12]

Reassuring as Gopnik sounds about a "normal" Germany, he raises some disturbing questions about the intellectual interests of American intellectuals. Does the memory of Germany that has haunted and obsessed the world since World War II have anything to do with historical reality? Or is it a fantasy of American intellectuals conceived in order to scare–and entertain–the world?

Gopnik's glib comments on the importance of Kiefer's art after German reunification shed more light on the agenda of contemporary American culture critics than on the Western obsession with German history. After all, Germany was not only envisioned as a "romantic landscape" populated with "exotic, grim and 'Teutonic'" creatures and other "splendid blond beasts"; it was the birthplace of many of the philosophical, cultural, and scientific initiatives that fed the meta-narratives of modernity and energized the counter-narratives of post-modernity as well. The Jews of Europe, drawn thence in greater numbers than to any other European country in the eighteenth and nineteenth centuries, were attracted by the liberating and empowering promises of German culture. Gershom Scholem, the German-Jewish historian of religion who in 1970 in a famous letter to a young German writer argued "against the myth of the German-Jewish dialogue," described in a speech at the 1966 Jewish World Congress in Brussels how European Jews actually encountered German culture at the end of the eighteenth century and in the nineteenth.[13] Germany was admired as the mediator of modernity for a still predominantly medieval Jewry. The encounter took place at one of the most creative turning points in the history of German culture, namely the culmination of the bourgeois period. "One can say," Scholem declared to the predominantly Jewish gathering, "that it was a happy hour when the newly awakening productivity of the Jews which was going to take on such important forms after 1750 occurred just at a high point of great productivity of the German people. This amalgamation of a great historical hour," he continued, "has in terms of intensity and breadth no parallel in the encounters of Jews with other European peoples."[14]

The historian George Mosse traced this unique amalgamation from the eighteenth to the twentieth century. "Jews were emancipated not only in the bourgeois world of *Bildung* and the Enlightenment," he argued, "but also into the German wars of liberation against Napoleon. Jews were patriots attempting to document their emancipation and new citizenship by enlisting in these wars."[15] Like Scholem, Mosse emphasizes the role played by the two most important writers of the German classical period, Schiller and Goethe. Both represented the cosmopolitan transcendence of all political, religious, cultural. and ethnic closure. Schiller was read–in German, Hebrew and Yiddish–as the "prophet of freedom and equality–a poet who touched the emotion." Mosse elaborates the even more important function of Goethe: "Goethe's emphasis on individual freedom, his ambivalence toward all forms of nationalism, and, finally, his belief in *Bildung* seemed to foster Jewish *Bildungsbürger* of the period of Jewish emancipation."[16] Mosse pursued the theme of the assimilated German Jewish intellectual for whom the promise of humanity would come when the "final victory of the working class, and the abolition of existing property relationships would issue in the triumph of humanity, but such victory would be meaningless unless it was based upon *Bildung* and the Enlightenment."[17]

The Weimar chapter of the almost exclusively Jewish Frankfurt School represents this left formation of assimilated German Jewry. Its impact on the children of the middle classes from the 1950s to the 1980s in West Germany, the U.S., France, and other Western societies, is a testimony to the depth of cultural assimilation that the historical watershed of the Holocaust did not change. Hannah Arendt's struggle with the various cultural backgrounds that shaped her is another manifestation of continuities that receive no attention in the post-Holocaust literature.

When Hannah Arendt finally gave in to Karl Jaspers' insistent attempts to make her accept her German identity, she answered him (19 February, 1953) in a way that all Jewish members of the Frankfurt School would have endorsed:

> I think I can promise you that I will never cease to be a German in your sense of the word; that is, that I will not deny anything, not your Germany and Heinrich's [her husband Heinrich Blücher, M.H.], not the tradition I grew up in or the language in which I think and in which the poems I love best were written. I won't lay false claim to either a Jewish or an American past.[18]

She had written to him already in January 1933 from Berlin, answering questions about her Jewish identity: "Germany in its old glory is your past. What my Germany is can hardly be expressed in one phrase, for any oversimplification ... only serves to obscure the true problem of the situation."[19] She wrote this in response to an essay on Max Weber that Jaspers had sent to her. Jaspers characterized Weber as representing "German essence." Arendt commented: "I have the same difficulties with that as I do with Max Weber's imposing patriotism itself. You will understand that I as a Jew can say neither yes nor no." For her it was acceptable to speak about a "German mission" in relation to a culture of the future. She could identify with this mission, but she wrote:

> Germany means my mother tongue, philosophy, and literature. I can and must stand by all that. But I am obliged to keep my distance, I can neither be for nor against when I read Max Weber's wonderful sentence where he says that to put Germany back on her feet he would form an alliance with the devil himself. And it is this sentence which seems to me to reveal the critical point here.[20]

How critical the intended meaning of that comment on Weber really was became clear just twenty-nine days after Hannah Arendt had written her letter, i.e., on 30 January, when Hitler came to power.

Though it is highly speculative to ask whether Max Weber (who died in 1920) would have made the same choice as Martin Heidegger and supported Hitler as savior-"devil" of the German mission, his occasional indulgence in grandiose nationalist rhetoric also connects this occidental master thinker with the German national formation. The German origins of an exceptionally large group of master thinkers, writers, composers, artists and scientists, on the one hand, and the historical phenomenon of the Nazi empire, on the other, define the core of the obsession with German history. The Israeli historian, Steven E. Aschheim, has articulated this global puzzle succinctly in his book on *Culture and Catastrophe*:

> Whether one approached National Socialism as in some way an outgrowth of, or standing in dialectical relation to, 'history' and 'culture', or, indeed, utterly denied such connections, all these theories were occasioned by essentially the same sense of outrage, the shock that such events could issue from within a modern, civilized society, and in particular be perpetrated by *the* most Enlightened *Kulturnation*. The enduring fascination with (and deep need to account for) National Socialism and the atrocities it committed –the rich multiplicity of ruminations it has produced and its accumulative imprint on our political and intellectual discourse (as well as the accompanying, ubiquitous attempts to relativize or neutralize or elide and displace its significance and impact)–resides precisely in this, rather ethnocentric, sense of scandal and riddle, *the abiding astonishment that a modern allegedly cultured society could thus comport itself.*

Aschheim is quite aware that this question about the exceptional quality of the German configuration will be read outside the Western world as a reflection of Eurocentrism. Yet he justifies this Western obsession anyway when he writes:

> It is precisely the enduring outrage, and the ongoing fascination, generated by the penetration of the barbarous within the allegedly cultured, the transgression of basic taboos within the framework of advanced civilization, that has endowed Nazism with its distinctive status within Western sensibility.[21]

Aschheim's comments on the relationship between the cultural meta-narratives of meaning and the Nazi practices of mass killing throw light on the Western obsession. Yet they explain neither the ideological legitimation nor the acts of genocide. The Nazi genocide cannot be understood in terms of German culture. To see the Holocaust as a Jewish tragedy brought about by German culture turns this historical event into an exclusive German-Jewish confrontation whose relevance for the rest of the world will become more and more questionable. Some authors who emphasize the cultural origins of the Holocaust want to single out the Jews as the ancient people of the Bible and the Germans as the representatives of modernity. As persuasive as this reading of the putative tension between the ancients and the moderns within Western civilization may be for the interpreters of culture, it does not make us understand why *Jews* were the victims and *Germans* the perpetrators. After all, why would Jews be attracted by a culture whose historical essence was to kill them? Unless we accept a civilizational death-wish at the center of Jewish culture, the death connection between these two peoples remains unexplained.

The only way to break out of this cultural circle is to recognize the primacy of the Nazi regime as the agency of destruction. It is Nazi politics that promotes, legitimates, and actualizes the scenarios of catastrophe in Europe; thus we must look more to politics and less to culture. This focus also makes the Nazi regime comparable to other killing regimes in the twentieth century in other parts of the world. From this comparative angle, we recognize that there is nothing unusual, exceptional, or unique about the regime that orchestrated the Holocaust. The claims of uniqueness make no sense on the level of killing and suffering. On the contrary, *all* killing regimes in the twentieth century are comparable. The cultural specificity provides the legitimating environment in which the killing regimes operate. The more this specific legitimating environment becomes emphasized, the less comparable and the more parochial the particular killing regime will seem. The dangers of the uniqueness thesis of the Holocaust lie not only or primarily in the exclusive claim to suffering, thereby reaching for an exalted position in a hierarchy of victimized peoples. Far more dangerous is the possibility that the uniqueness claim will lead to a German-Jewish and, finally, a solely Jewish ownership of the memory of the Holocaust. The intended uniqueness will result, sooner rather than later, in unintended global obliviousness.

Certainly, American Jews try very hard to transfer the site of memory to the U.S. and link it to the civil religion of the American nation. Yet it is doubtful that this transfer will succeed in the long run. Apart from the fact that the Holocaust was a European event, the U.S., like Britain, did not pay much attention to the destruction of European Jews by Nazi Germany. Whether they were abandoned by the U.S. as David Wyman suggests,[22] or treated with "bureaucratic indifference" as Tony Kushner alleges in the case of Great Britain,[23] does not make much difference when it comes to the truth that the

Western Allies–not to mention the Soviets–did not go to war to save the
Jews. More importantly, in the case of the U.S. there are a few candidates
with a prior and greater right to be included in the symbolic record of American memory, e.g., Native Americans and African-Americans. That their
Memorial Museums are still missing from the Mall in Washington, D.C., long
after the tragic end of Indian removal and Black slavery, is reminiscent of the
German debate on how to remember the Holocaust. The shadows of the
original catastrophes loom large over contemporary politics.

Does the fact that German society has some difficulties in coming to
terms with the shadows of German history mean that one should abandon
the symbolic labor? Public amnesia is no answer, yet to ritualize the Holocaust memory as a sacred Jewish experience is no answer either. After all, the
Holocaust was not a Jewish but a Nazi project. For that reason, the growing
essentialization of the Holocaust as endowed with a unique Jewish meaning
makes the understanding of its origins even more difficult. What is the place
of the other 15 million victims of Nazi terror in this unique Jewish story of
meaning? Finally, do Jews need the experience of German terror for their
spiritual sense of being in the world? If they do, they exhibit a syndrome Eric
Voegelin described in his famous critique of Hannah Arendt's *The Origins of
Totalitarianism*: "The spiritual disease of agnosticism is the peculiar problem
of modern masses, and the man-made paradises and man-made hells are its
symptoms; and the masses have the disease whether they are in their paradise or their hell."[24] It's fair to say that both Voegelin and Arendt, who were
much closer in their understanding of totalitarianism than the apostles of the
current Arendt revival allow, would be harsh critics of the present trend of
letting the Holocaust memory take on the features of a substitute religion.[25]

Arendt was right when she emphasized in her reply to Voegelin that "the
success of totalitarianism is identical with a much more radical liquidation of
freedom as a political and as a human reality than anything we have ever witnessed before."[26] This political focus on twentieth-century catastrophes is at
the center of Tzvetan Todorov's book *Facing the Extreme* (1991). For him the
camps–not only the Nazi camps but the communist camps as well–are the
"extreme manifestation of the totalitarian regime, itself the extreme form of
modern life." The camps are the totalitarian regime's "quintessence."[27] Well
aware of postmodern and postcolonial tendencies to regard all power as ille-
gitimate, usurped, and unjustifiable, Todorov insists that the "world is not a
ghetto; nor is it one vast concentration camp. Nor is Auschwitz ... the
ineluctable ... outcome of modernity."[28] Speaking about the macro-crimes of
the regimes, he writes:

> Totalitarian crimes are crimes of a new species altogether and we must recognize
> their specificity. There is nothing either extrahuman or subhuman about these
> crimes, and yet something historically unprecedented has clearly occurred. Their
> cause resides neither in individuals nor in nations but in the political regime

under which they are committed. Once the totalitarian system is in place, the vast majority of the population ... are at risk of becoming accomplices in its crimes; that is all it takes.[29]

And finally, coming to the specific global focus on the Holocaust:

> The historian or political scientist must examine—and even dwell on—those aspects of the Nazi camps and Soviet Gulags that make these institutions unique and distinct from each other. But if the moral behavior of the individual is our subject, then unity must take precedence over uniqueness.[30]

I would phrase Todorov's conclusion somewhat differently. The universal understanding of human politics has to prevail over the uniqueness claims of any specific macro-killing. The memory of German history in the twentieth century will contribute to such an understanding if the specific characteristics of the German regime of terror make us see why it came to power and managed to perform its evil deeds. The failure of the Weimar Republic to defend itself against the enemies from within, and the failure of all organized German resistance from 1933 to 1945 against the Nazis in power, make us see why communities in peril may sometimes move towards the edge of hell. The collapse of sane politics will have these consequences. Hell will reproduce itself under all national, not only German, circumstances. The obsession with German history blinds the world to the eternal possibility of such returns, those that have already happened since 1945 and those that will occur in the future.

Notes

1. Dagmar Barnouw, *Germany 1945: Views of War and Violence* (Bloomington and Indianapolis: Indiana University Press, 1996).
2. See the articles in the German psychoanalytical journal *Psyche*, no. 6 (Stuttgart, 1997), on "Goldhagen und die Deutschen."
3. Daniel J. Goldhagen, "Modell Bundesrepublik", in K.D. Bredthauer and A. Heinrich (eds.), *Aus der Geschichte lernen/How to Learn from History* (Bonn: edition Blätter 2, Verleihung des Blätter-Demokratiepreises, 1997), 67.
4. Barnouw, *Germany 1945*, xi.
5. See Eric Markusen and David Kopf, *The Holocaust and Strategic Bombing. Genocide and Total War in the Twentieth Century* (Boulder: Westview, 1995).
6. The title page reads: "Slaughterhouse-Five or The Children's Crusade/A Duty-Dance with Death/by Kurt Vonnegut, Jr./A Fourth-Generation German American/Now Living in Easy Circumstances/on Cape Cod/[And smoking too much]/Who, as an American Infantry Scout/Hors de Combat/As a Prisoner of War/Witnessed the Fire-Bombing/of Dresden, Germany,/"The Florence of the Elbe"/A Long Time Ago/And Survived to Tell the

Tale/This is a Novel/Somewhat in the Telegraphic Schizophrenic/Manner of Tales/Of the Planet Tralfamadore/Where the Flying Saucers/Come From/Peace".

7. Barnouw, *Germany 1945*, 187.
8. Ibid., 21.
9. Ibid, 213.
10. For the non-German perspective see also Mark Fisher, *After the Wall: Germany, the Germans and the Burdens of History* (New York: Simon & Schuster 1995); Ian Buruma, *The Wages of Guilt: Memories of War in Germany and Japan* (New York: Farrar Strauss and Giroux 1994); Jane Kramer, *The Politics of Memory: Looking for Germany in the New Germany* (New York: Random House 1996).
11. See Christoph H. Werth, *Sozialismus und Nation. Die deutsche Ideologiediskussion zwischen 1918 und 1945* (Opladen: Westdeutscher Verlag, 1996).
12. Adam Gopnik, "The Repressionists," in *The New Yorker,* 14 July, 1997, 86f.
13. Gershom Scholem, "Against the Myth of the German-Jewish Dialogue," in his *On Jews and Judaism in Crisis: Selected Essays,* ed. Werner Dannhauser (New York: Schocken, 1976), 61-64.
14. Scholem, ibid., 78f.
15. George L. Mosse, *German Jews Beyond Judaism* (Bloomington: Indiana University Press, 1985), 8.
16. Ibid., 44.
17. Ibid., 56.
18. *Hannah Arendt–Karl Jaspers Correspondence, 1926–1969,* ed. L. Kohler and H. Saner (New York: Harcourt Brace Jovanovich, 1992), 207 (letter No.140).
19. Ibid., 19 (letter No. 24).
20. Ibid., 16 (letter No. 22).
21. Steven Aschheim, *Culture and Catastrophe: German and Jewish Confrontations with National Socialism and Other Crises* (New York: New York University Press, 1996), 9.
22. See David Wyman, *The Abandonment of the Jews: America and the Holocaust, 1941–1945* (New York: Pantheon Books, 1984).
23. See Tony Kushner, *The Holocaust and the Liberal Imagination. A Social and Cultural History* (Oxford/ Cambridge, Mass.: Blackwell, 1994).
24. Eric Voegelin, "The Origins of Totalitarianism," in *The Review of Politics,* vol.15, 1953, 73.
25. See, e.g., Lisa Jane Dish's comments in *Hannah Arendt and the Limits of Philosophy* (Ithaca, N.Y.: Cornell University Press, 1996), 124–126. Dish claims that Voegelin misunderstood Arendt completely and that "Voegelin and Arendt assess totalitarianism from utterly incompatible perspectives."
26. Hannah Arendt, " A Reply," in *The Review of Politics,* vol. 15, 1953, 83.
27. Tzvetan Todorov, *Facing the Extreme: Moral Life in the Concentration Camps* (New York: Henry Holt, 1996), 28.
28. Ibid., 29.
29. Ibid., 131.
30. Ibid., 135.

8

Race, Nation, and Folk

*On the Repressed Memory of World War II in Sweden
and its Hidden Categories*

PIERO COLLA

In the decades since the cessation of world war in 1945, specters have returned to haunt Sweden's collective conscience. Much recent historiography reflects this anxiety and the unsolved questions that plague the popular imagination of Sweden domestically and abroad.

There have been heated debates in other countries that were neutral during World War II, including Switzerland, over the question of "Nazi gold." But in Sweden, memories of that period are interlinked with another "dark spot" on the collective conscience: the eugenic project associated with the rise of Social Democratic social reformism.[1] The debate revolves around questioning the coherence of official memory, or rather the myth that has grown up in its place. This myth turned the values of solidarity and humanism into something of a national vocation. The fact that the current *querelle* is based on events that occurred a long time ago hardly makes it dated. After all, it involves a revision of a whole cultural experience that still bears on the present as both a social project–the building of the welfare state–and, above all, as a form of self-representation.

The fact that the controversy around the war period exposes the darker side of Sweden's historical conscience is no simple coincidence. Both in its foreign policy (where it has so often symbolized the West's "bad conscience") and in its social politics (famous for "experimental voluntarism"), the "Swedish model" of the postwar era has been looked upon as if its values were a given, divorced from any actual collective experience. Myth and historical consciousness tend to be mutually exclusive as approaches to reality.

Notes for this section begin on page 151.

The internationalist credentials of modern Sweden have been so impeccable that the national culture's hesitation about critically questioning its own past has often been read as further proof of its antiprovincial mission.

In order to shed light on the selective nature of collective memory and its "repressed" areas, we must ask what this dissociation from concrete historical experience was designed to safeguard. It is difficult in a short space to sum up all the positive connotations associated with the idea of *folkhem* (literally, "the people''s home"), a metaphor which, from the very start of the Social Democratic governmental project,[2] marked both its utopian aspirations as well as the reality of social welfare and well-being. In brief, we can say the metaphor indicates a relationship where individual morality blends into a public sphere that is credited with a state of perpetual innocence. For many years *folkhem* has created an illusion of national community strengthened, on the one hand, by the reputation that the "Swedish Model" enjoyed abroad, and on the other by the evocative ties it claimed with rural and community-based traditions of self-government.

It is intriguing that the fetish of *folkhem*, which came to symbolize the project of modern Sweden, is also a residue of an older worldview. Coined at the beginning of this century by a conservative politician as a symbol for the organic solidarity between people and nation, it was later adopted by the Social Democratic leader Per Albin Hansson to characterize the countercyclical program of his party during the Great Crisis. Later, the threat of war and the risks of invasion helped to consolidate the *folkhem* mythology by charging it with concrete, affective connotations. The reasons for the regenerative capacity of the "folk" myth may well lie precisely in the semantic ambivalence of the word itself, a word that conjures up both the idea of "fidelity" to a national ethos, and the quest for individual liberation. Above all, *folkhem* endowed institutions with a moral identity, integrating them into a democratic version of the theory of "general will."

For over forty years, public attempts to query the silences and compromises of the war years were held in check by internal resistance, if not by open attempts at dissuasion.[3] In many cases the establishment commissioned research in this field with a tacit call for caution and "prudence." As a consequence the resulting studies were often informed by a desire to play down the embarrassing records of the past.[4] The contrast with the tone of more recent historiography, even that penned by the same authors, is striking.[5] The fact that it has become possible to speak of an embarrassing period in irreverent tones can be attributed to the end of the Social Democratic hegemony around which the sense of collective belonging had consolidated.[6] Resistance can, however, still be glimpsed. It is interesting to note that (in the case of eugenics, for example) it was journalists, rather than professional historians, who pointed up how the official version of the experience of neutrality sought to camouflage historical embarrassments.

Oblivion as Foundation? National Identity and the Experience of Neutrality

The substantially passive, antiheroic dimension of Swedish diplomacy during the war is well documented and known. The compliance of the ruling class with Third Reich demands is reflected in the concessions granted to the Wehrmacht by the government of Per Albin Hansson for military transport across Sweden to and from Norway and Finland.[7] At the level of trade, Sweden moved, between 1939 and 1940, from loose ties with Great Britain to dependence on the more aggressive neighbor: for the entire duration of the war, binding political-commercial agreements were signed with Germany to supply top quality iron, wood, coal, and semifinished goods. Studies carried out by the Allies in the first year of intervention demonstrate that this arrangement was vital to the upkeep of the German war machine. The official values embodied in the Swedish "model"–championed in the 1930s as the answer to the crisis of European democracy–are not easy to reconcile with a clampdown on civil rights at home and with a foreign policy that was so given to compromise. In obvious contradiction to the myth claiming that Swedish neutrality was intended to safeguard democracy,[8] laws were passed to control and repress the free flow of information from the very beginning of the war.[9] Through the steady introduction of new legislation, the coalition government, in office since December 1939, placed all suspected anti-German activity under the control of the secret services (including not only idealistic movements struggling against fascism but also humanitarian initiatives striving to help war victims). Private citizens were subjected to widespread surveillance: after the war it was revealed that over 11 million telephone calls and 47 million letters and packets had been intercepted and inspected by the authorities between 1940 and 1944. Tougher control of the media was aimed at stifling all criticism considered dangerous to state security. Views likely to trouble public opinion or annoy the Reich were suppressed through the creation of a new, vaguely defined category of offenses punishable by detention.[10]

Until recently, scholarly analysis on this subject has focused almost exclusively on the ruling classes. There has been a conspicuous absence of studies on the general effects of the war on national culture. With regard to the issue of neutrality, the penchant of researchers to concentrate on the political and diplomatic management of the war and the home front has meant that the attention paid in Sweden to the sirens of pan-Germanism and totalitarianism has received short shrift. It has certainly been accepted that the threat of German occupation of the remainder of the Scandinavian peninsula in the spring of 1940 entailed certain concessions and "sacrifices" with regard to morals and national dignity. On the whole, the good faith of the institutional actors and their basic loyalty to democratic principles have not been doubted. It is true that the negligible political clout of national socialist style movements (even if they were relatively strong among youth and student organizations) meant that they never succeeded in getting a single representative elected to the *Riksdag*. This, however, hardly explains why the Nazis working in the country and their sympathizers present at all levels of society (the higher clergy, the magistracy, and the military hierarchy) were described, *a posteriori*, as an insignificant phenomenon.

It is not just concrete examples of surrender to German demands on the "home front" that have been suppressed in the common consciousness; the contradictions in the actions of the political elite have also been glossed over by historians. Such an attitude has been based on the assumption that all concessions made to the "new order" were the direct consequence of a tactical choice taken by the top echelons of the establishment. As such they never actually touched Swedish society as a whole. In order to fully understand this perspective, it is necessary to bear in mind a specific aspect of Swedish self-representations that may not be immediately evident to a foreigner: the idea that democracy has been a perennial presence throughout Swedish history, if not in reality then at least in spirit. It has been taken for granted that Swedish official institutions could be nothing other than democratic. The decision, during the period when the Social Democratic welfare state came to the fore, to ground the new political project in the rhetoric of the "popular community" served to further enhance this myth. The democratic values of the "folk," drawing on ancient feelings of ethnicity and belonging, traditional socialist solidarity, and the practical imperatives of modernism, were purposefully involved to obscure any potential associations with totalitarianism.

The difficulty in judging the history of totalitarianism from a moral point of view does not arise from any wish to deny the extreme character of totalitarianism itself. School curricula devote a good deal of space to the horrors of modern racism, even if most of the material is couched in the anodyne style of "scientific" pedagogy. It may well be that the reasons for this are to be found in the collective unconscious, shaped not only by shared historical experience but by an educational environment where national taboos coexist with ritual reiterations of the ethical referents that have helped to cement national unity. The relegation of racism to a distant past is supplemented by the educational effort to make every Swede identify with a noble and praiseworthy democratic tradition. The mission of opinion-building public institutions, such as the Swedish Institute,[11] is to propagate this identity abroad. One side effect is a distrust of the process of European integration, which is sometimes seen as undermining the cherished national self-image.

Another factor hindering debate has been the discomfort the political class has long felt in broaching the subject. They only set out to correct the matter when the effect of a lack of reflection on past history was demonstrated empirically (in a survey carried out in 1997, 25 percent of Swedish secondary school students doubted the historical truth of the Holocaust).

"Understanding History" has become a slogan of the moment. On 12 June 1997, in a debate between party leaders closing the parliamentary session of the year, Prime Minister Göran Persson introduced a campaign of reeducation entitled "Living History" (*Levande Historia*).[12] The aim was to compensate for a historical "cultural deficit" in the educational system caused by the slow erosion of humanist culture in the name of efficiency.[13] The immediate response has been to promote antiracism by means of "socially useful" messages. Eight hundred thousand copies of an enlightening pamphlet (a number equaled only by the copies of the Bible distributed previously) were printed by the government and sent to every parent whose children were of school-going age.[14] To promote the initiative further, information seminars were organized at schools, as well as guided tours, television broadcasts, and the opening of a new documentation center at the University of Uppsala. Rather than undermining the social consensus, however, the resulting discussion seems to have functioned as a way of restating it. The mechanisms that help to mold group identities by moderating the impact of new ideas through creating new channels of opinion-building are facilitated by the well-established Swedish tradition of study circles and popular universities. Much the same response has been elicited by a barrage of newspaper articles about the victims of sterilization, leading in 1997 to the establishment of a state commission to assess damages. These attempts to accelerate the process of "enlightening" the general public are as elevating as they are misleading. In many respects they prevent controversies coming to light by keeping them under the control of the institutions. Whatever the tensions in collective memory, they are promptly neutralized by the creation of a "new" charismatic official history.

In plotting the scope of the present chapter I analyze not so much the current debate as the "silences" that appear to be an inseparable part of it. While public discussion has long sought to marginalize the most embarrassing episodes from the past, some of the collective reflexes it reveals can help us to understand the values that were really at stake during the wartime period—a period not without tensions between alternative perspectives and social reactions. As late as 1969, a university monograph on the history of the daily paper *Svenska Dagbladet* blamed Torgny Segerstedt[15] (a journalist and intellectual who showed courage during the war by criticizing both the Nazi regime and the demoralizing action of the Swedish "fifth column") for both his "irresponsibility" and his "anti-Swedish" stance. The use of the "anti-Swedish" tag is symptomatic, as ideological conformity was expected as a token of patriotism.[16] The fact that even today critics who have exposed darker episodes in the collective consciousness are objects of similar recrimination may be taken as a sign of a certain unacknowledged continuity. Nor is it merely a coincidence that most of the commentators who have dared reopen the debate have been scholars and journalists of foreign origin. The controversy sur-

rounding the period of neutrality was so intense at a certain stage that xenophobia began to reemerge in the traditionally fair play arena of Swedish public discourse. Some went so far as to question the loyalty of critics, or to
dismiss their arguments as extraneous to the national culture. As the conservative daily *Svenska Dagbladet* put it, a debate on the metamorphosis of racism
in the context of the welfare state could not be a "Swedish debate."

An error of this kind demonstrates, more than any theoretical reasoning
can, why the repressed contents of Swedish collective memory have reemerged
as a topical theme.

Race and Politics: Sweden and the Refugees from the Third Reich

A recent anthology by the Swedish historians Svanberg and Tydén directly
addresses the type of questions we have just raised. It is one of the first
attempts to examine the issue of the impact of the Third Reich's racial perse-
cutions on public opinion and institutions.[17] Other recent research has broadened the scope of the investigation by focusing on related issues such as the
level of penetration of Nazi ideology within Swedish institutions, and the attitude of the latter towards its victims.[18] In spite of the centrality of the racial
refugee issue to the national debate in the 1930s, this subject has escaped critical reflection for over forty years.[19] What these new studies seem to have in
common is not so much a particular methodological slant but something
more profound: a decision not to run away from the embarrassing effect that
recounting the facts might have on a jealously guarded self-representation of
national identity. Rather than portraying the subject of contact with the Third
Reich as mere curiosity, drawing on the patterns and categories of self-representation of the times, this research examines the subject against the broader
framework of the ideological divide present in the rest of Europe. The subject
thus takes on a different, and newer, relevance and urgency for today's reader.

Approaching the question of wartime compromises in absolute terms
involves, of course, challenging the coherence of established representations.
It does not mean looking at history from a present-day perspective (anachronistic and instrumental), but rather with an awareness that things could have
gone differently. The sources that form the basis of studies like that of Svanberg and Tydén were in large part already known to specialists, but the reasons just mentioned are enough to counter the objections their reviewers
have often invoked—namely, that these authors have not discovered "anything new." It is not enough to acknowledge that Nazi attitudes were not a
"secret." The fact remains that the symbolic organization of the collective
conscience made them appear of little import, or blocked discussion of them.
It is said that the new "revisionist" version of history deforms reality. In many
respects the previous version did so too by systematically minimizing facts

that were part of public knowledge. That explains, at least in part, why well-known matters could suddenly appear as "news" and why they polarized public opinion to such an extent. It is, ultimately, not so much the presence and availability of facts as their processing into social awareness that matters. The fact that fifty years on, the racial issue could reemerge with such force confirms how much the mythical element in the transmission of social memory–linked as it is to emotions, and interacting with identity–not only deforms national history, but is the very condition of its interiorization.

The "Foreigner": A Juridical and Cultural Construct

It was the flow of refugees seeking to escape the Third Reich in the immediate aftermath of Adolf Hitler's rise to power, and the question of whether or not they should be the subject of special measures, that brought German racial persecution onto the Swedish domestic agenda. The collective memory still struggles with the fact that the official Swedish response was not only to allow no exception to the general principles of its immigration policy, but also to set up special, discriminatory barriers. The reason why Sweden is still uneasy with this element of its past is that the decisions taken at the time cannot be ascribed to any cynical orchestration, underhand maneuvering, or bureaucratic inertia. Instead they matured democratically, in line with accepted principles that would later be identified with the most progressive values. The news of the arrival in the country of a small number of Jewish intellectuals was sufficient to unleash, between 1934 and 1939, public demonstrations, outcries from professional group, and letters of protest in the daily press.

The explosion of the racial problem in Europe entailed a trend towards ideological "normalization" with totalitarian regimes that became particularly marked between 1940 and 1942. The scope of anti-Semitic persecution in Sweden is indicative of a situation where, in the face of the successes of Hitler, the assessment of the international situation was subordinated to what was called the "defense of the collective interest" at the economic level, and protection of Nordic values at the cultural and ideological level. What is striking to the modern reader who attempts to trace the sense and resonance of the legitimizing symbols and discourse employed at the time is the apparent refusal of politics to sway the bureaucratic logic of social utility.

In measuring Swedish reactions to this problem, we need to point to a contradiction. From the moment foreign correspondents began to file stories from Germany, quoting examples of measures that defined citizenship rights along racial lines, the reaction to the news was ambivalent. The prevailing view was one of consternation at what appeared to be the moral humiliation of a culturally close, civilized country. King Gustav V ventured to express his concern in a face-to-face meeting with both Hitler and Hindenburg in April 1933 over

the damage that the anti-Semitic laws would inflict on the international reputation of Germany. In that same year, support measures were introduced to
help the exiles from Germany, although the efforts of the workers' movement
were limited to the victims of political persecution, leaving all assistance for
racial refugees to voluntary or private organizations. But, at the same time,
there were growing fears about the danger of racial conflict in Swedish society
itself. In many cases the same commentators who were disgusted with the way
Germany was solving the "racial problem" decried the influx of refugees as a
serious threat to the social fabric of Sweden. In December 1933 both the liberal and the conservative press responded to a public appeal on behalf of intellectual immigration with a call for prudence. An attempt to muster mass
support for the initiative ended in fiasco. The 195 requests for visas in the year
of Adolf Hitler's rise to power were sufficient to cause *Svenska Dagbladet* to write
that Sweden was in the grips of "a large-scale Jewish invasion." [20]

The contradictions characterizing the Swedish reaction were not immediately evident, since the nature of the "threat" was couched in rational terms
and was, as such, hard to analyze critically. First of all, the refugees were seen
as a destabilizing element for the labor market, and thereafter as a social danger because of both their very presence and the risk of probable "contagion"
of racist feelings. In addition, there was fear of the biological "pollution" of
the Swedish stock, a concern already latent in the official immigration policy
of the time but one that came to be focused more and more on Jewish exiles.
It is in this context that the reaction takes on a more sinister, ideological
form, especially if we bear in mind that the Swedish eugenics movement–
unlike that in Germany–had not been informed by anti-Semitic ideas. Proof
of the implicit priority given to such concerns is best exemplified by the
apparent inability of the politicians of the time–and even more of the official
political "line"–to follow their instinctive moral reaction to the breach of law.
Most of the political parties seemed to regard the persecution issue as a German domestic problem, a conclusion facilitated by a widespread acknowl-
edgment that there was, in that country, a "Jewish problem," even if there
was no real analysis of what that problem was. The general desire not to
interfere with the "problem" was clear from the very first political debate on
the matter, following the ban in Germany on Jewish civil servants, artists, and
intellectuals taking part in German public life, and the boycott of Jewish busi-
nesses imposed in April 1933. When an attempt was made by a Communist
deputy to get the government to make an official statement on the chances of
certain well-known exiles being offered jobs in the public sector, the upper
house of Parliament voted that the proposal not even be brought to the attention of the Minister. Since the matter was deemed to be the "internal affair"
of a friendly country, any such statement would be inopportune.[21]

The opinions offered during the ensuing debate prefigure the kinds of
argument that would be invoked in the following years, when the cries for

help became increasingly urgent. Any attempt to address the problem of racial refugees from a non-administrative perspective was met with stiff resistance. Calls for legal rights to be enforced were dismissed as a form of political pressure, or else described as belonging to the realm of "sentiment" (i.e. "anti-German propaganda," "interference," etc.). To a certain extent, this attitude was corroborated by the institutional approach to the problem of immigration, which remained under the control of the State Board of Social Affairs (*Socialstyrelsen*). Emptied of all ethical content, the policy of accepting foreigners was assessed on the basis of "national interest" and depended on the shortfall of foreign workers in each sector of the economy. Such a procedure soon gave way to the notion that certain workers who did not share basic national values and virtues were per se undesirable. As the first refugees seeking refuge in Sweden soon found out, the existing legal framework left little or no room for considering the status of a foreigner beyond his or her productive use. When refugees did not meet the requirements for professional and social integration, they automatically became a "problem." The source of this approach can be traced on the one hand to the status of foreigners within Swedish jurisprudence, and on the other to the development of social science as embodied in the Functionalist movement.

Let us examine the first of these elements. A modern observer may easily underestimate the extent to which the letter and praxis of Swedish law on immigration were influenced by the imperative to defend imaginary "racial qualities" of the Swedish population. According to a line of thought dating back to the end of the nineteenth century, when the first signs of a migratory influx from Eastern Europe began to be perceived, a "foreigner" was, by definition, an unwelcome guest. The first laws regulating the free movement of people in Sweden included special discriminatory clauses against particular ethnic groups.[22] As the country was opened up to the internationalization of the labor movement, principles of selection were introduced. The democratization of social relationships led to other kinds of limitations on individual rights for social-hygienic reasons (e.g. the interdiction on marriage for epileptics). The distinction between suitable and unsuitable members of society claimed scientific legitimacy. As early as 1923, the State Board for Social Affairs included the defense of the "purity" of the Swedish race among its reasons for a clampdown on immigration.[23] Three years later, the first law restricting the legal status of foreigners was approved on these grounds, with no political movement raising any objections in principle.[24] The legislation included the following statement:

> The fact that our population is a highly homogeneous and uncontaminated race constitutes a value that it is hard to overestimate ... which is why it is of the greatest importance that control of the immigration of populations that cannot advantageously mix with ours be exercised.[25]

It is worth noting that this argument was put forward just as politicians and scientists were presenting the fall of the demographic curve as the greatest tragedy affecting the country. In order to understand how the humanitarianism behind the new measures to promote social welfare could coexist with such an exasperated sensitivity to "diversity" (embodied by immigrants taking advantage of national resources), we need to look at the body of evidence on the values underlying the transition, from traditional, parish-based systems of assisting unproductive members of the community, to the more rational system of social care. One of the implicit principles of the new system was a relationship between the distribution of social services and the contribution of the individual to the "well-being of the community." Here rights were seen not as a personal prerogative but as a function of an individual's contribution to the productive machinery. The survival of a limited and collectivist idea of freedom of movement and residence meant that the transition from an absolutist and locally self-regulated regime to a modern concept of citizenship could only deepen the rift between an increasing rationalization of social relationships and individualism. Symptomatic of this was the right of the authorities to order the expulsion from the country of any foreigners who became dependent, however many years after their arrival, on local parish assistance.[26] The procedure of obtaining a resident permit was also informed by the same rationale: the goal was the rapid introduction of the foreigner into the labor market, with priority given to the indigenous labor force. The backing implicitly given to this policy may be seen in the procedure prescribed for granting a work permit. It included prior consultation between trade unions/employers and the Foreign Ministry with a view to verifying whether there was a real lack of indigenous workers in a particular sector of the economy.

The consequences of the rapid growth of a scientific vision of man and society during the first decades of this century are ambivalent. While such a vision drew on the egalitarian utopianism of the political left in that it promoted the removal of hierarchies and privileges set by tradition, it also helped to reinforce those very prejudices by turning the difference into an objective and tangible fact. The political left integrated into its agenda the programmatic antidogmatism of "social engineering," premised its legitimacy on the absolute priority of the common good—seen as the welfare of a united *folk*–and ended by drawing close to the ideological precepts of the nationalists with whom it was in combat on the political front. The gradual extension of state regulation of the labor market, as reflected in the Social Democrats' policy of national solidarity and culminating in the agreement in Saltsjöbaden (1938), accentuated the social engineering aspects of the immigration policy of the Board of Social Affairs. After 1937 the latter took over the task of overseeing foreigners.

A typical feature of culturally determined imperatives is that they do not need to be articulated ideologically and can express themselves as pure reflexes. It is easy to see how the newspapers conscientiously monitored the process of consultation with professional organizations, making sure all the rules were respected in the name of defending the national interest. The power to veto immigration requests granted to professional and trade associations was not new in itself. However, during the 1930s the increasing participation of trade unions in the rational regulation of the labor market became part of the *folkhem* building process. Inherent in it were two ideological polarities: administrative rationality on the one hand and the feeling of national solidarity on the other. Swedish workers were thus called on to display loyalty to a particular kind of ethos, which often hindered acts of international solidarity. When, following the scandal provoked by the street pogrom of November 1939, an international medical association called for a symbolic act of solidarity from physicians all over the world, the women's association of Swedish doctors could not agree on a positive response to the initiative.

The Immigration of "Non-Aryans" and the Specificity of Discrimination

Between March 1938 and the spring of 1939, the mass exodus from Germany induced by the Nazi racial policy took on such dimensions as to bring it to the world's attention. At the end of 1938, news that the State Administration for Health had given its approval for the granting of resident permits to ten Jewish medical students expelled from German universities was enough to unleash the greatest xenophobic backlash in modern Swedish history.[27] The protest was grounded in purely corroborative arguments: to allow "foreigners" to fill places earmarked for young graduates was considered an attack on job security in Sweden's labor market. The student union at the University of Uppsala reacted to the news by drawing up a resolution. A plenary assembly of all university students was summoned on 17 February 1939. When it was over, few doubts remained about the reasons underlying the students' move: Jewish immigration was seen as an obvious threat to the national interest, and dissenting voices urging solidarity with the victims of Nazism over and above professional concerns were in a minority. The assembly ended by voting for a resolution that sharpened the polemical edge of the original text, removing even the vaguest references to a duty to help the victims of racial violence. The resolution called on the highest state authorities "not to endanger the future of academic youth by allowing foreign labor to get its hands on jobs that could be given to deserving Swedish men and women."

In the space of a few weeks, the other universities in the country adopted similar resolutions. The one approved by the student body of Lund University warned against "mixing our people with alien elements." The journal of one of the country's medical associations underlined the danger of "racial

contamination" from immigration.[28] Later, the outcries of the medical pro-
fession were dismissed as a "mistake" attributable to the defense of personal
egotistic interests, mere demonstrations of political insensitivity with no ideological relevance. Such a version of events, however, neglects the fact that
the protest (judging by the public reaction, or rather by its absence) reflected
the existence of a much broader hostility. It was soon to be followed by other
official statements, whose meaning went in substantially the same direction.[29]

We have been focusing on arguments that—in a part of Europe less
affected by regional, ethnical or religious fractures than others—helped to justify the widespread perception of the existence of a "racial problem." Our
aim is to find a plausible explanation for the inability to understand the deliberate and planned destruction of an entire ethnic group at the outbreak of
World War II. One might be tempted to ascribe Swedish society's receptive-
ness to the notion of racial "danger" to exogenous factors such as the attitude
of particular sectors of society which, following the example of other European nations, surrendered to the ideological pressure of totalitarian regimes.
But in fact the role played by Swedish Nazi movements (the only groups professing militant racism) remained marginal, even when the strategic appeal of
appeasement of the Third Reich and its Nazi worldview was at its highest.
Swedish attitudes, however rational, reveal ideological characteristics that
have more to do with a sense of belonging rather than rationality. The isola-
tion caused by the war brought them into sharper focus.

What were the chances of the young, rationalist elite seeing the line of
disengagement and negativism advocated by professional groups as an
infringement of their own principles? Was the general paralysis that affected
them caused by internal contradiction, or by a desire for a coherent *Weltanschauung*? True, adjustment to the self-regulatory mechanisms of the labor
market meant playing down their humanitarian vocation as well as the element of international solidarity. But even if the main initiatives to help the
persecuted grew from within the workers' movement, the goals of the
reformist movement were a continuation of the nonideological project of
national self-assertion. The social good and productivity were set up as the
only "objective" goals a modern social policy should aim for. All things considered, this suppression of conflicts that helped to bond the "folk" together,
in the sense of organic and self-sufficient solidarity, was in tune with the international policy of the Hansson government, where the line of disengagement
from major international conflicts prevailed as a guarantee of the party's commitment to the national interest.

This metamorphosis was not confined to mere rhetorical or political
strategy: it originated in a broader determination to sacrifice the notion of
individual dignity to a mythical quest for a community governed by rational
tools and modernity. If the rhetorical glorification of racial differences was the
stuff of the political right, biologism (or more exactly "the defense of the

numerical and qualitative" value of the folk stock) was a key element in the social policymaking of the ruling Social Democrats. It would lead, in 1934, to the unanimous parliamentary vote in favor of forced sterilization of individuals with inherited biological defects. Recent studies have tried to explain this move as a shift of motivation from purely eugenic considerations to social opportunism. Thus, for a group of experts associated with the Social Democratic project (with Alva and Gunnar Myrdal much to the fore), what spoke for the imposition of social control on the reproduction of the "feeble-minded" was not so much their biological inferiority as their manifest "untrustworthiness" as rational parents and educators.[30] Reformers saw the modernization of lifestyles as a test case for new forms of social loyalty. As stated in a contemporary state inquiry (inspired by the then alliance between socialist local government and Functionalist architects), housing reform policy must serve as "a tool ... for promoting change in a socially desirable direction with regard to people's life-styles and objectives." [31]

The Dream of Social Osmosis and the Philosophical Legitimization of Intolerance

In order to understand the way in which the racial question was treated in Swedish public discourse at the end of the 1930s, we have to remember that rarely, at least at an explicit level, was this question expressed in terms of principle. Its main function was to provide factual justification for instrumental arguments, inspired at times by diplomatic imperatives ("not to interfere in the internal affairs of a friendly country"), at times by the desire to maintain social harmony at home ("not to create a Jewish problem in Sweden"). Behind this position, however, it is possible to read a more broadly based concern: anxiety about damaging the social fabric, a desire to meet the demands of professional groups, to refound the community on the principle of self-identification and the idea of reciprocity between institutional objectives and individual aspirations. The legitimacy of every value judgement came to depend on this objectifying look that society was casting on itself. The Swedish perception of the great European conflicts of the 1930s shows—beyond the contingent problem of the attitude towards the persecuted—that, in an imaginary hierarchy of priorities, social loyalty preceded commitment to any principle. Such a tendency not only undermined moral resistance to regimes founded on terror but, at the intellectual level, it stood in the way of understanding their nature.

It is here that the logical discontinuity between the rhetoric of race and the explicit ideology of the new ruling class comes into focus. If cultural change can be measured by the metaphors informing it, we may ask whether the type of "pragmatic" anti-Semitism dominant in the Sweden of the 1930s does not express the conceptual essence of the '"sociologism" and hyper-rationalism of functionalist thought. Discrimination—usually based on ethnic criteria and disgraceful if justified by "irrational" arguments—is here legitimized on the basis of empirical "diversity" and executed without remorse in order to maintain an osmotic equilibrium within the community. The analogy may seem forced, but one should remember that the Swedish ruling elites used this latter line of reasoning to legitimate their position. Already in 1935, in a public speech, Hansson claimed that "defending society against useless conflicts" was an enterprise that would make the policies of Social Democracy "irresistible."[32] In 1936, the committee of inquiry set up to examine reform of the law concerning foreigners stated that humanitarian immigration of persecuted Jews should only be allowed on the condition that it did not entail "risks and inconveniences of various types."[33]

It is true that leading "social engineers" had distanced themselves from anti-Semitism, describing it as a form of "superstition" or as "an illness".[34] But the fact remains that their tendency to resort to "hygienic metaphors" to articulate a social ethics entailed two major deviations from the logic of democratic universalism. It subordinated the principle of self-determination and autonomy to a biologically determined "destiny"; meanwhile, the other it treated the efficiency of an individual in the social "machine" as the sole legitimate criterion of his or her worth. It allowed bureaucratic rationality to decide what elements in society were "inferior," "dangerous" to the common good, or "disloyal." Although this type of thinking diverged from traditional nationalist rhetoric, it showed an affinity with national-socialist discourse that justified the domination of one part of society by another on the basis of dichotomies such as cleanliness vs. dirt, health vs. sickness, and so on.

Leaving aside the fact that open hostility to refugees came from the conservative sector of politics and society, let us instead consider another fact: that shutting the door on refugees was justified as a means of defending the status quo. The racist and xenophobic nationalism of the right wing is less relevant here because of its continuity with the past. It was, instead, within those political circles where ethnic and cultural diversity did not immediately conjure up negative associations that the idea of the supreme importance of social peace was cultivated. Here it was decided to avoid addressing a "problem" that in other environments provoked bitter social conflicts. A step towards the convergence of the two types of "racism" came when the call for order was couched in biological terms. The very presence of particular ethnic groups on the national soil—quite independent of their real impact—had to be denounced as a danger to Swedish society. A sign of how this kind of argument cut across the political divide is to be found in the Social Democratic daily *Arbetet*, in an article of November 1938 that stated: "To welcome explosive personalities, whose political temperament was formed under other circumstances and who perhaps might become restless here, would be as unreasonable as the desire to increase the percentage of Jews in our population." [35]

Today, as then, these kinds of argument owe their force to the normative neutrality in which they are wrapped. Even if the goals of the Social Democrats were not identical with some form of aggressive racism, it seems incontrovertible that, in the context of the times, they accepted racism's central tenet that the coexistence of races represented, in itself, a problem. Thus, when one spoke of the need to "import" (the generalized use of this verb is already symptomatic) only individuals "with good social pedigrees," ethnic difference was given the form of rational and operative justification. [36]

We have already mentioned the existence of a common frame of reference that reconciled the practical philosophy of social reform with the demands of democracy and Realpolitik. It is now possible to broaden this perspective. The success of racial categorization and the subsequent receptivity of politicians and intellectuals to intellectual ideas from Germany shared a common ground, the only common cultural ground that could bring together movements of different inspirations.

This common ground was the "value-free" approach to social facts, which portrayed the production of ideas as the simple illusory projection of clear-cut interests, in both social and international policies. A scientific reading of social interest, freed from the categories of common sense, formed the ideological foundation of the reformist philosophy. Power relations seemed the only element worth taking into consideration, and the only legitimate foundation on which to ground the law. The most coherent development of the argument that moral abstraction should not be superimposed on the principle of reasons of state came from the school of philosophy that dominated the faculty of law in the 1930s–"the nihilism of values" [37] of Axel Hägerström.[38] Hägerström's theories were less innovative than representative of an epoch. Their importance lies in the influence they exercised on social reformers, especially the way in which they provided a powerful tool in the struggle against tradition and against the resistance of certain professional groups to the claims of scientific argument over social experience. The cornerstone of Hägerström's doctrine was the attempt, at the beginning of the century, to trace the fundamentals of Roman law to their religious origins, and thence to metaphysics and the realm of illusion.[39] The task ascribed to philosophy was to demystify a legal language that, due to the fossilization of linguistic constructs, was intrinsically inconsistent. The idea has its parallels in the work of the analytical school of Cambridge philosophers, though it does not seem that they directly influenced Hägerström. (This was hardly surprising, given the difference of emphasis and inspiration in the two movements.) The "nihilists" of Uppsala focused not so much on linguistic analysis as on its social effects, emphasizing the emancipatory result that could be achieved by distilling conventional jurisprudence–and politics–from metaphysics.

It was not "liberation" in a subjective sense that Hägerström and his followers sought. As champions of "law and order" and of ontological realism, they had no attachment to the principles of individual liberty. The dogmatic stamp of their thought distanced them from Anglo-Saxon empiricism and from the antimythology of Ernst Cassirer (who, closer to Kantianism, invoked the subject's cognitive faculty rather than any superindividual category of "interests"). Hägerström included the concept of individual self-determination under the category of "superstition"–almost turning it into the sociological projection of a totem. Since it was able to impose its will by force, society appeared to be more "real" than its component parts. In this spirit the philosopher's task was to suggest that society take on new responsibilities in those areas of activity that were still subject to irrational social resistance, such as the "right to property." The scientist's job was to pave the way for a rational reform of institutions that are immanent in every society and that express objective "interest." The law itself was considered no more than a projection of power relations, and the representations that legitimated it no more than a mask, a useful tool in the hands of politicians in their struggle to overcome particular interests.

It is well known that "social engineers" such as Gunnar Myrdal drew on "Hägerströmism" both as a source of inspiration and as a theoretical tool.[40] Their social criticism was permeated by the struggle against individualism, which was seen not only as an obstacle to the spread of science, but as a symbolic barrier between private and public space, preventing socially useful messages from being properly communicated. Above all, as it entered the common culture, Hägerströmism succeeded in providing a coherent paradigm for economists, reformers, and politicians of different hues, facilitating co-operation and greater understanding.

Karl Olivecrona, a disciple of Hägerström and a professor of law at Uppsala, was one of the leading exponents of this school of thought. At the outbreak of the war he joined the ranks of those Swedish scholars who vindicated the historical and moral legitimacy of Hitler's "new order." His case presents us with a striking example of theory and political practice coming together. A few months after the publication of his main work, tellingly entitled "Law as Fact,"[41] Olivecrona declared the accomplishments of the armies of the Third Reich to be a sure sign of the legitimacy of their political position. In 1940, when England found itself alone in the fight against the hegemonic aspirations of National Socialism in Europe, Olivecrona used the rhetorics of interclass conflict and social utility to sketch out a European "grand organism" in which the old nations would have to abandon all egoism and particularism:

> Just as we have seen that, to be able to exist in peace, individuals and social classes have to learn to renounce their own particular interests, so the single nations will have to come to a similar understanding for the European good. [42]

A year later, in his study "America and Europe," Olivecrona would look to Petain's France as a model. For him, overcoming the enduring hostilities between France and Germany in a "community of interests" represented the beginnings of a new European solidarity. The appeal of such arguments was not limited to those who were already sensitive to Nazi propaganda, or interested, for instrumental reasons, in finding a *modus vivendi* with the "new order." True, there were some dissenting voices, such as that of the historian and economist Eli Heckscher, who tried to take on Olivecrona. But the Social Democratic newspaper *Ny Tid* came out on the side of Olivecrona, defending him against Heckscher and describing the latter as a proponent of "doctrinairism."[43]

To depict the radicalism of the Swedish welfare state as paving the way for Nazism would be to oversimplify, if not to falsify, history. One might object that Hägerström, who was a supporter of Social Democracy and not of Nazism, did not draw any National Socialist conclusions from his own philosophical premises. It is possible to argue that, for the progressive "nihilists," attacks on cultural attitudes that took the law and social thought away from the control of reason were a continuation of the assault on the truly obscurantist use right-wing totalitarianisms had made of spiritualism. And spiritual notions, such as "the people's sense of justice," for example, undermined the certainty of law.

Paradoxically, nihilist rhetorical propensities marked by the search for "concreteness" (*saklighet*) ended by producing totally unexpected consequences. The identification of "legitimacy" with "collective interest" encouraged a renunciation of all positions of principle and justified pragmatic opportunism that had been dictated by "instinct" and "prudence."

Just before his death, Hägerström once again had an opportunity to apply his vision to actual events. In an interview of 1939, he noted that the conflict between the German and Czech nationalist groups in the Sudetenland had sprung from the fact that both parties claimed to speak in the name of "objective" justice. This, naturally, was impossible except for ingénues or impostors. What this abstraction did was to conceal the cynical use made of the principle of self-determination by Nazi propaganda. To urge a "compromise" based on power relations, within the context of the circumstances that had given rise to the Sudeten crisis, meant to grant legitimacy to the same order of "rationality" whose inadequacy would soon cost the Allies dearly.

A "Profile" without Ideology: Towards a Philosophical Interpretation of the Neutrality Stance

The influence of the philosophical mindset equating right with might (of which further ample testimony can be found in political thinkers less politically compromised than Olivecrona) is doubly interesting when one thinks of how it provided politicians with a reassuring argument that allowed them to escape the moral consequences of the war. When in the summer of 1940 Hitler, after having successfully established German rule on much of the European continent, proposed to the *Reichstag* a friendly cessation of hostilities with England, many politicians agreed, pressing for a greater effort at peace. Trusting in the doubtful rationality of a *pax hitleriana* was the logical consequence of having recognized, in principle, rationality immanent in the equilibrium sanctioned by the use of war and brute force. Can this reaction to the Nazi domination of Europe be seen as part of a more general canon of Swedish self-representation? Another exponent of Social Democracy, the editor-in-chief of the daily *Arbetet*, Allan Vougt, argued, after the occupation of Denmark and Norway, a line of appeasement that was not far from the "realism" of Olivecrona: "When it is said that Germany is predestined to occupy a dominant position in a united Europe, one is stating a truth which no reasonable man, here in Scandinavia, would contest."[44]

This point of view was not intended to aim at national cohesion: for Vougt, the destiny of democracy in a Europe dominated by Hitler was a theoretical problem that he chose to approach, writing: "we do not accept the ideology, but we accept the facts." The problem is that, though this "realist" approach was formulated in good faith, it involved the acceptance of crude falsifications, such as the anachronistic distinction between the legitimate will of the "German people" and that of the Nazi leaders. From this curiously pragmatic "optimism," the deformation of historical facts followed. "The German *Führer*," wrote Vougt, "says that he was forced to go to war. Opinions diverge on the truth of this affirmation." And further: "We have no reason to doubt the sincerity of German ambitions to construct a better Europe." As the title of the anthology of Vougt's wartime articles published in *Arbetet* suggests, the "Swedish Perspective" remained at the heart of his reflections.[45] That is why he was also a fervent supporter of the censorship of undesirable ideas and sentiments. He was far from being a marginal presence in the world of politics: the party sent him on an official mission to Denmark to find out how the Danish Social Democrats succeeded in maintaining power under German occupation. In his reports to the party, Vougt suggested emulating the Danish model, and called for a common stand by Scandinavian Social Democracy vis-à-vis the German "new order." [46] His calls for prudence on the part of the press and the man in the street transposed Hägerström's message into strategic terms. The best way of guaranteeing collective power is to submit principles to necessity. Swedish foreign policy depended on adjusting to geopolitical realities. While stressing Sweden's right to preserve its freedom of action in any situation so as to keep the country out of world war, Christian Günther, the Foreign Minister, also let it be known that Sweden would adapt to any change in the international balance of power, no matter what form it assumed. Flexibility was presented as a sign of strength rather than mere bowing to necessity. Holding fast to an abstract idea was a weakness that stood in the way of rational comprehension, as had occurred with Functionalism. In the autumn of 1941, while the German offensive in Russia was under way and after the Englebrecht Division had received authorization to cross Sweden, Günther summed up the situation as follows:

> We realize that a war, which affects the vital interests of European powers, must entail great changes for the entire world. Sweden has no way of exercising any significant influence on these changes. There is no doubt, however, that it will be profoundly touched by them. From now on, the main task of Swedish politics must be to build our country on the basis of tradition and Swedish worldview [*Svensk livssyn*] without, however, closing our eyes to the reality which surrounds us while recognizing the demands reality imposes on us.[47]

The philosophy expressed in this passage becomes meaningful only when one looks at the political choices it helped to inform. There is a paradox here: born out of a moral reaction to irrational doctrines in the Europe of dictators, the philosophy of extreme rationalism became extreme relativism, facilitating and justifying all manners of irrationalities. It would be wrong to explain away the pressures that led to submission by the impending threat of invasion. Rather, this statement reflects a particular reading of the basic guidelines of Swedish international policy that had been laid down before the outbreak of the war. It is worth remembering that, with the worsening of the political crisis in Europe, Sweden dissociated itself from the imposition of sanctions advocated by the League of Nations as a means of deterring the militarism of the totalitarian states. More profoundly, the failure of attempts to find an international consensus undermined the legitimacy of the supranational organizations that the Scandinavian countries had heretofore enthusiastically supported. By 1938, the government was under strong parliamentary pressure to withdraw Sweden from the League of Nations. Such a decision was justified by the "politicization" of the conflicts the organization was involved in and was completely independent of any evaluation of the crisis in progress or the search for political causes. "International harmony" was accepted as a state of fact, to be pursued flexibly, independently of any moral postulate. The philosophical refusal to admit the existence of an abstract criterion of supranational justice appears, then, not merely as an intellectual exercise but as the rationalization of a political practice, a "vocation" for mediating between conflicting interests. It was considered more worthwhile to renounce allegiance to any ideal or principle than to attempt to undermine national cohesion.

But the strength of a common culture cannot be measured solely in negative terms, by its power to dissuade morally. The success of Hägerström's nihilism is explained by the way in which it "liberated" social energy and inspired the transformation of Sweden towards a pacifist utopia. Here lies the difficulty, paralyzing the critical potential for a rational confrontation with Nazism. Further, the importance attributed to science and social thought also drew on the renewed significance, at the moral level, of "community" values. Advocates of philosophical nihilism were able to speak of the conciliation of two opposing mental universes–democracy and dictatorship–without deviating too much from an accepted "orthodoxy." Olivecrona integrated his vision of a coming European order in a national model based on the notions of "common good" and cooperation between classes. These attempts at using an entrenched rhetoric for one's own advantage remain symptomatic of a certain community of intention, as shown by the fact that the universities and the press continued to cultivate the idea of a military compromise between the warring powers. Neither Per Albin Hansson nor his closer collaborators can be accused of having sympathy for, or underestimating the ideological implications of, the Nazi regime. Still, it is revealing that Nazi sympathizers in Sweden never came to regard the country's democratic rulers as their outright enemies.

A good example in this regard is a volume published in 1941 by a group of Germanophile intellectuals of the Swedish-German Association, entitled *Germany at War.*[48] In spite of the openly propagandistic nature of the book, the vision of coexistence between two systems (the democratic and the authoritarian) based on respect for the two political traditions clearly shines through. Faith in the politics of neutrality and a pro-Hitlerian *Weltanschauung* seem to be reconciled in the work of the prestigious academic and literary critic Fredrik Böök ("The German Nature and the Swedish Solution"). The natural characteristics of every nation represent for Böök the ideal limit of all idealistic aspirations. The author claims, for example, to have tried to convince Hitler that he should refrain from anti-Semitism. He adds, however, that he gave up the attempt after coming to realize that the dictator's inflexible attitude of the dictator derived from his infinite love of the German people and his mystic participation in their suffering. The author vindicates the legitimacy of Swedish politics by arguing that, unlike in Germany, "democracy in Sweden is a household product." While German history seems to justify all the measures the chancellor took against "antinational" forces, in Sweden–Böök maintains–"the fact that the government is in the hands of the Social Democrats, is not an expression of folly and national decay, but rather a source of pride."

This brings us back to the other paradoxical condition of an ideology inspired by "reason": the role of moderation and the tacit understanding among all political parties not to take things to extremes. It is likely that this moderating stance saved Sweden from a radical confrontation between democracy and totalitarianism. It may also be an explanation of Sweden's inability to perceive the absolute character of the conflict on the continent, a conflict that opposed two irreconcilable views of law, national self-determination, democracy, and humanity. It is certainly telling that in 1944—when the horrors of Nazi domination were no longer a mystery to anybody—in reply to the question posed by a Gallup poll as to whether the war should cease with the unconditional surrender of one of the sides or with a "compromise", seventy one precent of Swedes either declared "I don't know" or supported compromise.

To interpret this spirit of tolerance from an epistemological point of view allows us to see it in its extreme consequences. When the coalition led by Hansson made Swedish "democratic" values a pillar of its neutrality policy, it sought to offset a concrete danger (invasion) with a rhetorical glorification of the "essence" of the nation, where the only given was the compactness of public opinion. A symbolical reference to national values was to reappear in the rhetorics of the prime minister, albeit in a disembodied and non-binding form. What was praised—through the new rhetorics emphasizing Swedish "democracy" and "way of life"—was nothing more than the National Soul. The metamorphosis of the antifascist heritage of the workers' movement—after embracing the Nation and adopting the political prudence that characterized the years just before the outbreak of war—reached its apogee during this time. The official memory of the years that followed would consider the success achieved in preserving national independence as a victory in itself, while attempts at an assessment of its moral cost would be interpreted as an intolerable breach of a secret code. A set of values that had once been central to the cohesion of the Swedish rural community had been transmuted into a complex ideological matrix with the potential to support—and manipulate—a mass society.

Notes

1. See Piero Colla, "La politica di sterilizzazione in Svezia 1934-1975. Dal consenso alla rimozione collettiva," *Rivista di storia contemporanea*, no. 3, 1994-1995.
2. It should be noted that the SAP (Socialdemokratiska Arbetarpartiet) was continuously in power, either on its own or in coalition, from 1932 until 1976.
3. The writer and journalist Maria-Pia Boëthius, the author of a best-seller focusing on the more troublesome records of wartime, *Heder och Samvete* (Stockholm: Norstedts, 1991) has recently witnessed how, as late as in 1989, her proposition to write on the role of Sweden in World War II was vetoed by the major publishing houses in the country ("M. Pia Boëthius om folkhemmets skuggsida," *Arena*, no. 5, 1997).
4. Virtually all the research that saw the light of day between the end of the 1960s and the beginning of the 1980s was part of a collective project, entitled "Sweden during the Second World War" (with Swedish initials, S.U.A.V.). This research was a state-promoted initiative, and it is revealing that the "classical" work on the foreign politics of Sweden during World War II was commissioned to be carried out by a former chief of the archives in the Foreign Ministry. See Wilhelm M. Carlgren, *Svensk utrikespolitik 1939-1945* (Stockholm: Allmänna

Förlaget 1973). As an example of a legitimizing and "justifying" historiography I can quote the popular monograph on the Social Democratic leader Per Albin Hansson by the historian Alf W. Johansson. See *Per Albin och kriget* (Stockholm: Tiden, 1983).

5. It is enough to compare the work of A. W. Johansson mentioned above with his more recent interventions (such as the essay "Neutralitet och modernitet," in *Horisonten klarnar* (Stockholm: Probus, 1995). The historian Gunnar Richardson decided to investigate one of the most burning issues of that problem with an essay centered on the informal relationships between Swedish and Nazi establishments between 1940 and 1942. See Gunnar Richardson, *Beundran och fruktan* (Stockholm: Carlsson, 1996). The same attraction to the guilt-loaded and the unsolved is revealed by large-scale works such as that by Ingvar Svanberg and Mattias Tydén on the Swedish attitude toward racial persecution, *Sverige och Förintelsen—debatt och dokument om Europas judar 1933-1945* (Stockholm: Arena, 1997), or by Sverker Oredsson on the attitude of the academic environment at Lund University, *Lunds universitet under andra världskriget* (Lund: Lunds universitetshistoriska sällskap, 1996).

6. This could be one of the reasons why the largest part of the bibliography available on this argument did not see the light of day till the years succeeding 1990.

7. Between 1940 and 1943 this traffic—euphemistically renamed "traffic of military on leave" (*permittenttrafiken*)—absorbed 10 percent of the capacity of the Swedish railways; recent historiography estimates that over two million German soldiers were allowed passage. The peak was reached when the permission was granted to the Germans to transport an entire division across Swedish territory during the invasion of the Soviet Union. After some commotion and argument among parliamentary groups, this request was also granted. The role of the king, Gustav V (who, according to the testimony of Prime Minister Hansson, threatened to abdicate if the German request was turned down), as well as that of the military hierarchy remains in part mysterious. The authorization was finally revoked in the autumn of 1943, following consistent pressure from the Allies. Cf. Sverker Oredsson, *Lunds universitet under andra världskriget* , 82; Kent Zetterberg, "Den tyska transiteringstrafiken genom Sverige 1940-1943," in Stig Ekman (ed.); *Stormaktstryck och småstatspolitik: aspekter på svensk politik under andra världskriget* (Stockholm: Liber, 1986); Stig Hadenius, Torbjörn Nilssons, and Gunnar Åselius (eds.), *Sveriges historia* (Stockholm: Bonnier, 1996).

8. A thesis defended by , among others, Stig Hadenius in *Sverige efter 1900* (Stockholm: Bonnier, 1967).

9. The most important of these, from the point of view of future developments, was the "decree on security"—adopted in 1938, and kept secret for ten years—which granted the new information service substantial discretionary powers.

10. At the outbreak of the war, the state authorities dug out a neglected paragraph from the 150-year-old constitutional law on freedom of speech, which repressed the dissemination of speeches containing biased statements towards foreign nations (as well as their "rulers, government or high civil servants"), holding good relationships with Sweden (paragraph 3: 8). Another paragraph widened this interdiction to information apt to provoke "misunderstandings" with foreign powers. The clause of "prohibition of transportation" (*transportförbud*) virtually served as a surrogate of a direct censorship providing sufficient to deter the media from direct criticism and reporting of war atrocities. The decisive step towards the suppression of freedom of speech was undertaken just after the German invasion of the USSR, when in order to neutralize communist agitation new norms were introduced authorizing the government to resort to preventive censorship in case of war or the "threat of war" (*Lag med vissa bestämmelser om tryckta skrifter vid krig eller krigsfara*, S. F. S. 1941:44). In spite of the neutral formulation of such dispositions, the policy of confiscations would soon turn out to be inspired by a unilateral strategy. Out of a total of 315 newspapers, books, and reviews confiscated from 1940 to 1945, 264 were accused of criticizing the Axis powers, 42 the Allies (the remainder were confiscated for other reasons). See Rolf Edberg, *Är skriften ej smädlig,* (Stockholm: Tiden, 1947). On the one-sidedness of the limitations of freedom of speech, cf. the testimony of the Social Democratic Minister of Foreign Affairs Ernst Wigforss. See Wigforsss, *Minnen* (Stockholm: Tiden, 1954), vol. III, 185).

11. *Svenska Institutet* is a state-funded institution responsible for promoting information on Sweden abroad. Its genesis is closely connected with the subject of this essay: the decision to set it up was made in 1943, on a proposal of a state inquiry launched to prepare the future development of cultural relationships with the West.

12. *Riksdagshandlingar,* 1996/1997, Protokoll, 119, 21 sq.

13. The relationship between identity and historical consciousness constitutes a thematic fulcrum of my research on contemporary Swedish history. For an analysis of the reform of the education system conducted from this point of view see Piero Colla, "Storia ed eredita culturale in eclisse nel sistema svedese di insegnamento," *Rivista di Storia contemporanea,* no. 4, 1993.

14. S. Bruchfeld and P. A. Levine (eds.), *Om detta må ni berätta ...* (Stockholm: Regeringkansliet, 1997). This text is now available in four different languages (Swedish, English, Finnish, and Spanish); many other translations are already scheduled.

15. 1876-1945, theologian and professor of religious history, liberal politician. He was editor-in-chief of the daily *Göteborgs Handels- och Sjöfarts-Tidning,* which, uniquely among the Swedish press, took a distinctly anti-Nazi slant from 1933.

16. Torvald Höjer, *Svenska Dagbladet och det andra världskriget* (Stockholm: Almqvist & Wicksell, 1969), 101-102. Analogous criticism of the attitude of Segerstedt is to be found in the memoirs of a later Prime Minister, Tage Erlander. See *Tage Erlander 1940-1949* (Stockholm: Tiden 1973).

17. One of the rarer precedents was that of a scholar of American descent, Steven Koblik, who dealt with the Swedish attitude towards the persecution of Jews before and during the war. Steven Koblik, *The Stones Cry Out* (New York: Holocaust Library, 1988).

18. See Ph.D. dissertation by Paul Levine, *From indifference to activism. Swedish diplomacy and the Holocaust 1938-1944* (Uppsala and Stockholm: Almqvist & Wicksell, 1996) and the above-mentioned work of Oredsson.

19. The only remarkable exception is a study by H. Lindberg, which provides a complete survey of Swedish policy towards refugees of all categories. See Hans Lindberg, *Svensk flyktingspolitik under internationellt tryck 1936-1941* (Stockholm: Allmänna Förlaget, 1973).

20. Lindberg, *Svensk flyktningspolitik,* op.cit.

21. *Riksdagshandlingar,* 1933, Protokoll, Första kammaren, 29, 10-16.

22. A general veto against gypsies entering would be kept in place until the 1950s (*Lag ang. förbud för vissa utlänningar att här vistas i riket,* no. 196, 1914).

23. Tomas Hammar, *Sverige åt svenskarna* (Dissertation, Stockholm University, 1964).

24. *Lag om utlännings rätt att här i riket vistas, Sveriges Författningssamling,* 1927, 33.

25. *Riksdagshandlingar,* 1927, Propositioner, 198, 32.

26. The studies that have been focused on the official reasons behind the expulsions, after 1914, show how rocky the juridical basis was, depending heavily on judgments of social conformity: accusations of supposed professional faults, illnesses, or alcohol abuse, if not–as an aggravating circumstance–an unsuitable racial background. Hammar, *Sverige åt svenskarna,* 343-344.

27. The approval indicated the possibility of completing their training in Sweden, in remote country zones lacking health infrastructures.

28. *Svenska Läkartidningen,* 1939, 510-512.

29. Six working associations addressed a petition to the government pointing out the danger "of contaminating the Scandinavian popular element, from the point of view of our racial policy"; the petition stressed also the danger Jewish emigration would constitute for both "business and civic ethics." Quoted in Svanberg and Tydén, *Sverige och Förintelsen,* 160; Lindberg, *Svensk flyktingspolitik under internationellt tryck,* 201-202.

30. The most recent and illuminating contributions on the theoretical genesis and implementation of eugenics in Sweden are Maija Runcis, *Steriliseringar i folkhemmet* (Stockholm: Ordfront, 1998) and Gunnar Broberg and Nils Roll-Hansen (eds.), *Eugenics and the Welfare State* (East Lansing,: Michigan State University Press, 1996).

31. Stockholm: SOU 1934: 14, 66.

32. "Sprängpunkten," in Per Albin Hansson, *Demokrati* (Stockholm: Tiden, 1935).

33. Stockholm: SOU 1936: 53, 56-57.

34. Alva Myrdal, "Antisemitism är sjukdom," *Aftontidningen,* 14 April 1943. Some examples of
     Gunnar Myrdal's stand against Nazi racial theories are included in the anthology of writings
     published for the centenary of his birth. See Alva Myrdal, *Vägvisare* (Stockholm: Norstedts,
     1998, 380-390). Some of these extracts show the kind of "social" racism to which we have
     already referred: "Jews get worse when they are maltreated. Our Jews [Swedish Jews,
     N.d.A.], who in fact are treated correctly, are in general decent people" (Ibid., 384).

35. *Arbetet,* 8 November, 1938.

36. Ibid.

37. From the Swedish neologism, *värdenihilismen,* which came to designate this school of
     thought.

38. 1869-1939. Professor of Practical Philosophy at the University of Uppsala from 1893 to
     1933.

39. See Axel Hägerström, *Der römische Obligationsbegriff im Lichte der allgemeinen römischen Rechts-
     anchauung,* Uppsala, 1927-1941.

40. A valuable reference on this topic is Staffan Källström, *Värdenihilism och vetenskap* (Göte-
     borg: Acta universitatis gothoburgensis, 1984).

41. Karl Olivecrona, *Law as Fact* (Copenhagen: Munksgaard, 1939).

42. Ibid.

43. See R. Lindström, *Ny Tid,* 8 July 1940.

44. Allan Vougt, *Ur svensk synvinkel* (Malmö: Aktiebolaget Framtidens Bokförlag, 1943), 25.

45. Ibid.

46. Report of the visit to Copenhagen, 15 to 17 July 1940, quoted in Alf W. Johansson, *Den
     nazistiska utmaningen* (Stockholm: Rabén Prisma), 188.

47. Christian Günther, speech at the *Riksdag* of 29 October 1941. See *Tal i en tung tid* (Stock-
     holm: Bonnier, 1945), 77-78.

48. See Sven Hedin, *Det kämpande Tyskland* (Malmö: Dagens böcker, 1941).

9

Crisis
The Road to Happiness?

Yvonne Hirdman

It seems as though we live with the feeling of an all-encompassing crisis without being able, however, to identify its causes clearly, unless we escape into easy, one-word pseudosolutions ("capitalism", "God has been forgotten" etc.).

(L. Kolakowski, *Modernity on Endless Trial*, London, 1990, 12.)

After World War I (1914–1918) the world was once again full of unresolved questions. There was the Housing Question, the Woman's Question, the Social Question—to name but a few of the more crucial ones. Casting the rationale of politics in the form of Questions or Problems to be resolved has been a traditional ploy not just to rehabilitate the political realm but to make it exciting. Posing a question or a problem holds the implicit promise of an answer or a solution. The post-Great War questions were the Enlightenment ones: What was to be done about the laboring class, about housing, the food supply, disease, education, women, the countryside? The answers proposed were Enlightenment answers, springing as they did from faith in the power of men (and men they were) rather than God.

Framing politics in terms of questions and problems was a modernist strategy. And the approaches to problem-solving were either conciliatory or Jacobin. The former demanded that everybody sit down and explore possible answers: arguing, disagreeing, and striking compromises. It assumed the existence of different political parties that were there to highlight different problems and different solutions. The latter, based on "The social and economic laws of society as I/we know them", insisted that the question had but one answer.[1]

Notes for this section begin on page 167.

There was yet a third possibility. It represented a combination of the two: a strategy of bargaining underlined by the conviction that there were in fact "correct" solutions to problems–correct, that is, according to science and social science. Problems became the domain of experts and expertise.

The specter of "crisis" that became manifest in 1929 went beyond "questions" and "problems," however. With its medical (and religious) connotations, "crisis" signified an acute condition. Acute conditions demand radical remedies. There was no time to sit down and dwell on alternative possibilities while "the boat was about to sink" or "the patient was about to die." It demanded taking urgent control, or putting trust in a commander, someone with "know-how."

Put like that, "problem" and "crisis" are not analogous concepts (though in the last years of the recent millennium the notion of crisis eclipsed almost everything else). The very shift from modernism to postmodernism, from national politics to a global economy and to *fin de siècle* gloom, has often been linked to the pervasiveness of "crisis" in public discourse.

As I shall argue, the key to understanding some of the most fundamental currents of Swedish Social Democratic policies in the 1930s was just this transformation of questions into "crises." Such transformations were not merely matters of perception; they provided rationales for expanding social welfare and for increasing social happiness. The rough outline of the mythical Swedish Success Saga in Three Acts offered below is an attempt to capture some of the main features of this transformation. Act One begins with a glance at 1930, 1932, and 1934 as important intermediate stages (timing is important in the construction of "crisis"). Act Two is the postwar program of the labor movement, in which the figure of "crisis" is established. A brief Act Three, which should be treated more as a loose reflection on future prospects, brings the so-called Social Democratic Crisis Group of the early 1980s on stage. Implicit is the question: Is "crisis" still a potent concept?

Act One

The Parliamentary Bill of 1930

In 1930, at the height of economic and political turmoil in the world, the Social Democrats–then the largest political party in Sweden–produced a legendary document. It was the so-called "crisis bill," designed to combat the acute economic slump and the unemployment associated with it. It turned upside down the economic wisdom of the 1920s, which held that to economize meant to save the state money. It proposed:

1. Instead of saving the Swedes should spend–spend even the money that did not belong to them–in order to get the proverbial wheels

rolling again and the smoke puffing from factory chimneys. This was Keynesianism in Swedish translation.

2. The state should be mobilized as an economic agent and expand its public economic involvement by, for example, building roads and supporting business enterprise.
3. The state should break with the older unemployment policy, and instead create jobs for the unemployed at salaries comparable to those in the open market.[2]

Election Propaganda in 1932

The two slogans used to advertise the program, *Work ourselves out of the Crisis!* and *Buy Swedish Goods!*, were also employed in the election propaganda of 1932. In short, people were told that something could be done; the crisis was not a catastrophe like an earthquake that one had to endure passively. If men (and again, they were men) trusted their own capacities, and if together they seized social control over the national economy, the capitalist disease would be cured.

But there was more to it than that. The point made by the Social Democrats was that this was not to be seen as a kind of temporary crisis policy, the type of "Band-Aid" used in World War I when the country also was in crisis, even if it was not at war. The new kind of crisis policy meant planning and state control in a much longer perspective.

When the Social Democrats won the election of 1932, Prime Minister Per Albin Hansson announced in his government statement:

> These events, harsh and trying for our country both morally and economically, have given rise to the question of social control over the management of the economic values of our society.[3]

This spelled out the ideological victory of the Social Democrats at a party congress a couple of months previously, where the idea was conceptually wrapped and introduced as "planned economy." At the congress the main architect of the Crisis Program and the man soon to be Minister of Finance, Ernst Wigforss, tried to convince the delegates that a planned economy was much more effective than socialism, which was, of course, the alternative solution. While drafting short and long term political measures that were implied by the notion of a planned economy, Wigforss chose the safe image of the "house" and its furnishings to persuade the left-wingers of the party to accept the new form of radicalism. It was a matter of simple common sense that without incentives for consumption—incitement to build houses, buy tables, beds, kitchen equipment, and so on—the economy would never recover.

Houses

It was no coincidence that Wigforss chose the image of the house to make the ideology of the New Economic Policy appealing. Nor was he the only one to use it. House and home had became synonymous with "modern life." In 1932, when the Social Democrats held their congress and subsequently won the election, only two years had passed since the great Stockholm Exhibition. Since then the exhibition has acquired mythological status, as an event that brought modernity, including modern architecture and design, to the Swedish capital and into Swedish politics.

The new program was a public success. All those white houses with flat roofs, furnished with steel chairs and occasional tables, were a delight to the Swedes. Functionalism became the word of the day, giving its name to clothes as well as to new dishes.[4] It was in the year of the exhibition and of the Crisis Bill that a certain political alchemy–transforming a problem into a crisis–was tried for the first time. Houses and crisis were lumped together in public discourse. There was a severe crisis in the housing situation, the argument went. The analysis was followed by a plea for action. Alf Johansson, economist, politician, a member of the young radicals who might be called the avant-garde of the Social Democrats or the social engineers of Swedish politics, wrote in 1930:

> There is nothing at all outlandish about the thought that a people and a culture can go to ruin because of their inability to solve the housing question. It is a question that concerns the essential preconditions of social life.[5]

The perspective of crisis was certainly there; disaster was close at hand. Not much happened, though. Two years later another attempt to provoke action by resorting to the concept of crisis was made by a leading social engineer, the economist Gunnar Myrdal. Among Myrdal's numerous crisis articles is one entitled "The Dilemma of Social Policy."[6] "Dilemma" carried more weight than "problem" or "question"–and was closer to "crisis." Again the "house" appeared as both a symbol and a concrete issue at the center of his argument. The main idea was to work out a proper *social prophylactics* (Myrdal's expression). If one was serious about preventing social misfortunes according to science and on the basis of facts, one practiced social prophylactics instead of just talking in the manner of liberal social reformers. According to Myrdal, "This new social policy ideology carries within itself strong radical and to some degree even revolutionary possibilities."

With the Housing Question as the primary example, Myrdal showed what had to be done–based on the best advice of economists, technicians, architects, family sociologists–in order to give the population proper lodgings at reasonable rents. The objective was to create the right conditions for a family, so that it could "function" as it should. This meant, for example, the expropriation of land and the erection of carefully planned housing based on the principles of (social) science.

Myrdal then linked *social prophylactics* to a planned economy, imbuing social and political reforms with a new, largely economic, meaning.

> A planned economy means exactly this: we are prepared to take measures thoroughly enough, in order to maximize their efficiency. A radical social policy is precisely the social policy of a planned economy.[7]

However, the effort to place the housing question on the political agenda as *the* issue for initiating a grand social program in dialectical harmony with a planned economy failed. Lodging policy was ultimately perceived as constituting a "problem" rather than a "crisis."[8] One reason for this failure may have been that the housing question was not as pressing as Myrdal made it out to be; it was very much a liberal question, too embedded in liberal politics and morality. Everybody could see for themselves that in spite of inadequate housing the situation in Sweden was surely better than in the previous decade. People really did not have to live in classrooms or gymnasiums as they had in the "years of crisis" during World War I.

Babies

The next attempt to construct a "crisis" was more successful. In the fall of 1934 Alva and Gunnar Myrdal published their famous *Crisis in the Population Question*. The argument was very much the same as in the Crisis Program. First, there was a dramatic depiction of the situation in graphs and percentages. The picture was very clear: Sweden as a nation was in danger. Figures showed the lowest level of childbirth in all of Europe. It was no longer merely a gloomy situation, or a troublesome political "question"; it was an acute, critical situation. Social prophylactics were brought forward again as the only sufficient remedy: without social reforms of a truly preventive nature, Swedes were on the verge of extinction as a people.[9]

Measures were taken quickly and with an astonishing political consensus. By the spring of 1935 a Population Commission had been established by the Minister of Social Affairs, Gustav Möller. It finished its work in 1938, by which time it had produced over twenty official government reports (*Statens offentliga utredningar–SOU*) on varying questions such as maternal and child care, family taxation, the creation of a state Institute for Public Health, nutrition, sexuality, the depopulation of the countryside, maternal insurance, maternity hospitals, kindergartens, housing loans, etc.[10] Even reforms that would guarantee women their place in the labor market were addressed.[11] In short, many neglected questions were finally faced up to at one go–and with long-term effects.

As was the case with economic policy, the crisis program involved grand social planning complementary to the planned economy. These two programs went together hand in glove–exactly as Myrdal had predicted in his 1932 article. Where houses had failed, babies succeeded. What were the reasons?

There are several possible explanations for the success of the Myrdals' appeal to crisis in the case of population and family policy. The population question was an older "question," related to the conservative discourse of Race, Nation, and Gender. In this discourse the perspective of crisis and catastrophe had been present since the late nineteenth century, but it had been brushed aside by both socialists and liberals, who saw it as a blessing that the number of children per family decreased.[12]

There are certainly different ways of looking at this "crisis" as constructed by the Myrdals. It could be seen as a response to an "objective" danger: Swedes *were* going to die out as a nation if no measures were taken. But the dramatic statistics might equally well have been procured as a tactical weapon to provoke fear and thus to decrease opposition to the Myrdals' broader, Social Democratic, political agenda. "True statistics" are of little help here as they are too much part of the realm of belief, possibility, "software."[13] If we look at notes made by Gunnar Myrdal during his lectures in the U.S. in 1938 we see that the second possibility might well have been the case.[14] In his notes Myrdal explicitly praised the genius of Malthus who succeeded in creating the population question as the "number one fact" to which everything else had to be adjusted. Did Myrdal want to be the Malthus of his time– Malthus in reverse, so to speak–predicting the social and economic catastrophe of underpopulation?[15]

It was both bold and ingenious to use a "conservative" theme and link it to modernity, socialism, and even feminism. It assured the success of the "crisis mentality" among left-wingers and Social Democrats, who had hitherto resisted the dark visions of national disaster. As members of the political party in power, they could now identify with the nation in quite a different way from before. The threat was identified as a real threat, and they felt responsible and compelled to take action. (It should be noted that the Communist Party rejected the warnings of underpopulation and stuck to the older rhetoric.)[16] The Social Democrats may have recognized the "crisis" as an overstated but ultimately effective way to create a fruitful climate for new social reforms, placating conservatives while enlisting the left to the cause of national solidarity.

Women, still as a group political outsiders, seemed to have been less moved by disastrously low birthrate figures.[17] Eventually, however, they too were persuaded, even if the number of babies they had to produce according to the grand Social Program designed by the Myrdals was as high as four. There were two reasons for their acquiescence. Firstly they were encouraged to see that the Program of Social Prophylactics was "their" program.[18] Secondly, the Myrdals succeeded in injecting a feminist dimension into various reforms. They did it through a subtle blackmail: If women were not treated better and allowed the opportunity both to be married and have children, and keep a job, then the best "human material" would not reproduce, as middle-class women would prefer work to having babies. A solution to the gender conflict seemed to have been provided at last.[19]

"Crisis" as a Positive Phenomenon

The concept of "crisis" enabled the Social Democratic government to initiate a program for a planned economy embracing larger portions of society than ever before. In the course of two years the notion of "crisis" became morally recharged. It no longer had negative connotations, as in the "crisis years of World War I." Now it was associated with things that were "progressive," "modern," and "good" for the Swedes.

The new demand was: More planning, more state intervention. The message was: A Bigger State is a Better State.[20]

Act Two

The Postwar Program of the Labor Movement

The years that followed further strengthened the positive, integrating aspect of crisis: for the Swedes, World War II was not a war (*krig*) but a crisis (*kris*). Although the Social Democrats ruled in a coalition government, they came out of those years stronger and more powerful than ever.

Ideas of a planned economy, or more accurately a planned society, were increasingly vindicated, it seemed. Thus, Gustav Möller, Minister of Social Affairs, asked the obvious question: Why must bad times and the threat of dictatorship be a precondition for orderly and systematic planning?[21] Why should one use efficient planning, even regulation, merely as measures to respond to crises and avert catastrophes? Why not use the same methods as measures to increase peace, welfare and social happiness? Uno Åhrén, an influential and politically active architect, argued: "Shouldn't the achievement of a planned, systematic organization of society be more possible in a democratic system, a system that is firmly anchored in elementary human rights?"[22]

In the so-called *Postwar Program of the Labor Movement*, this possibility was actively embraced. Referring explicitly to an expected, unavoidable crisis, the program, with its twenty-seven points, was intended to fend off chaos and promote social and economic progress:

> It is a primary objective of our Economic Policy to prevent a crisis and mass unemployment when the peace-time economy returns. ... The main task ahead of us is to co-ordinate economic activities into a planned economy so that the labor force and material assets are used continuously for efficient production. Such co-ordination should be orchestrated under the leadership of society and with the provision that individual interests be subordinated to socially desirable goals.[23]

The twenty-seven points were structured under three headings:

1. Full employment.
2. Fair distribution/consumption–higher standard of living.
3. Greater efficiency and more democracy in business (*näringslivet*), economic life, trade, and industry.

The third point was the truly utopian part of the program, and it was here that the Myrdalian ideas were most developed. The prominent element was a dialectic, intimate relationship between the economy and social policy, which were to empower one another.[24]

Vindication

This "Prophylactic Planned Economy" seemed to work in the thirty years that followed. There were ups and downs, but on the whole it seemed that the Social Democrats had found a formula for social happiness. The proof was rising annual GNP figures, increased salaries and consumption, a rising standard of living and housing, expanding education, low unemployment figures and a constant demand for labor. The labor market policy–the so-called Solidaristic Wage Policy developed by Gösta Rhen and Rudolf Meider–bore fruit. And when Prime Minister Tage Erlander spoke to the Trade Union Congress in 1961 of a new committee on the "Woman's Question" set up by the labor movement, he expressed his strong belief that everything was going in the right direction:

> Those who say that the deed is done and that all that remains is fine-tuning, are mistaken. There are still minor groups at a disadvantage, whose interests must be looked after if we want to be exponents of good, sound solidarity.[25]

The Wigforssian Effort

There is an interesting brief article, published in 1967 in the Social Democratic journal, *Tiden*, that highlights some of my points on the Swedish construction of crisis. The article was written by the master designer of the first Crisis Program, Ernst Wigforss. He referred to a crisis in the labor market, or rather in working life, in the context of ongoing and escalating technological changes and intensive rationalization. The main argument, put forward in an oblique way, went against the strong position of both the association of trade unions (LO) and the employers' federation (SAF), which prevented the state from intervening more energetically in legislation concerning wages.[26] When using the concept of crisis, however, Wigforss was explicit and precise:

> The crisis in the Labor Market is one of the factors that have been emphasized here *in order to revitalize Social Democratic policy and to activate a more explicit socialist line of action* [my emphasis].[27]

This attempt to curb the growing power and independence of the main actors in the labor market had little chance of success. The very "essence" of the so-called Swedish Model was a delicate balance of power in the triangular relationships between the State, Labor, and Capital, a balance that the state was not to upset.[28] From our perspective Wigforss' declaration represents a classical attempt to resort to the strategy of the "creation of crisis" as a prerequisite for state expansion.

Act Three

"The Red Years"

Wigforss's article had no effect on the situation, in spite of unrest in the labor market in the years to follow. Instead, in the "red years" between 1967 and 1976, radical, neo-Marxist ideas came into conflict with the reformist methods of social engineering. The concept of "crisis" used by reformist ideologists and social engineers was increasingly eclipsed by another mobilizing concept: that of equality.

As I see it, the ideological change within the Swedish labor movement was brought about in 1967 and 1968, not in the late 1970s, as is often claimed. A radicalization of ideology in a Marxist direction, one that privileged a renewed emphasis on power as a zero-sum game, undermined Myrdalian and Wigforssian conceptions of the role played by reformist social policy in the context of constant economic expansion. In this sense the new ideas on economy and social policy were far less sophisticated than those associated with the spirit of the reformist agreements struck in the 1930s. The balance of power between state, labor, and capital was now fatally undermined by a paradoxical policy that was simultaneously more capitalist, attempting to use the power of shareholding by setting up a system for transferring shares into the so-called wage earner funds, and more radical in the Marxist sense, in that this in effect over time would amount to nothing less than the gradual takeover of major firms by their workers.

Conversely, the old way of thinking was criticized, and Social Prophylactics was now seen as a expression of an unsavory class compromise, an unholy alliance between Capital and Labor. From this perspective, social engineering was seen as the opposite of socialist policy. This new way of thinking involved a dramatic shift. Under the banner of "Equality," state interventionist policy and expansion of the public sector became more conspicuous than ever before. It solved many a problem—not least in the realm of an expanding gender conflict. The incipient crisis in gender relations was resolved by transforming housewives into public sector employees, where they would continue to perform the traditional caring tasks—looking after children, take care of the sick and elderly—paradoxically retaining gender segregation even as women's work was transferred from the private to the public realm.[29] It should be noted, however, that while Alva Myrdal[30] (and others) saw the expansion of public consumption as being in line with economic development, other Social Democrats (such as Minister of Finance Gunnar Sträng as well as many trade unionists) perceived it as a policy that was pursued primarily for human and moral, rather than economic reasons.[31]

A new crisis emerged in the wake of the 1973 oil crisis, which had raised both fuel prices and unemployment to levels unseen in the postwar period. The emergency situation was confronted in the early years of the 1970s by the energetic use of a policy of expansion, especially in the public sector, and the return of the ideology of social engineering to the agenda: "To promote full employment in a future society, planning and a firmer rule are needed more than ever before," stated a leading Social Democrat in 1975. "Private enterprise will be able to provide jobs to a lesser degree than before."[32]

The Systemic Crisis and the Crisis Group

The Social Democrats lost power in 1976, and Sweden came under the rule of a coalition of liberal and conservative—so-called "bourgeois"—parties that endured until 1981. Their economic analysis was to a large extent a reversal of the ideas underpinning Social Democratic expansionist policy.[33] Their political vocabulary, too, was marked by an attempt to redefine the concept of crisis. The process started at a series of new political "happenings" created by SAF (the Employers' Federation) from 1979 onwards.[34]

The kernel of the crisis, it was argued, was precisely the outcome of "social prophylactics" combined with decades of energetic demands for equality, that is, the greatly expanded public sector. A new slogan was thus produced: there was a crisis in the political system—a systemic crisis—that must lead to a systemic change. "The volume and expansion of the public sector is simply our greatest social problem", said the head of SAF, Curt Nicolin, at one of these "happenings" in 1980.[35]

The economic crisis in turn provoked a political crisis for the Social Democrats, a party that now, after some forty uninterrupted years in government, found itself in opposition. They initiated a Crisis Group that wistfully dwelt on the legacy of their Golden Age: "In our debates on the crisis policy we might well be captives of our own glorious past," declared a party program, symptomatically entitled "Future for Sweden."[36]

The effects of this captivity were most acutely felt by those members of the Crisis Group who by and large shared the views of their political opponents. For them it was also a crisis of the system.[37] The long-suffering Swedish industry was compared to Atlas, bearing the burden of the public sector on his increasingly weak shoulders. There was uneasiness about the relations between the private and public sectors, and the memory of the good old days did not assuage it. Surely the public sector played an economic role as well—

if only as a consumer of the products of the industrial sector. But the public sector was ultimately the result of opportunities provided by economic growth and a surplus economy, which led almost immediately to the conclusion that in a situation of no growth and no surplus economy, that sector had become a burden.

The recipe that was concocted to overcome this crisis was expressed in two slogans. One was the familiar *"Work ourselves out of the Crisis!"* but invested with a completely new meaning. The intention was now to support the industrial sector not in terms of Keynesian-style deficit spending, but rather in terms of increased efficiency, a notion that differed little from what was suggested by the bourgeois parties and SAF. The second slogan– *"Save ourselves out of Crisis!"*–dovetailed with the first, the message being that what now mattered was saving rather than spending, and labor productivity rather than the expansion of the public sector.

This was a dramatically new political line, embarrassingly close to the demands of the bourgeois parties on the right. In order to support this new line of argument, the members of the Crisis Group tried to reread and reinterpret their own seminal texts. They quoted, for example, a passage from Wigforss's work in 1932 where he emphasized saving. But Wigforss' blessings they had not. What Wigforss had had in mind was not saving in the sense of not spending money, but saving in the sense of long-term planning.[38] Rather than dwelling on this elusive document, I want to highlight the Social Democrats' attempts to revise and twist their own history. What is important here is that crisis as redefined by the bourgeois parties—as a crisis of the system—marked a shift away from the constructive "positive crisis" of the Social Democrats toward what was once again a negative predicament linked to sacrifice and hardship. Why did the Social Democrats abandon a formula which seemed to work so well for so many for so long?

There are two possible answers. The capitulation might be understood as bowing to reality. Reality changed, new ways of tackling it were unavoidable. A crisis in fact did exist within the "system," rooted in the rapid and uncontrolled growth of the public sector, whose economy was parasitical on the state economy.[39] But the defeat could also be understood as a result of ideological shifts that began in the 1960s. The reason why so many Social Democrats adopted a right-wing interpretation of the crisis with such ease was related to the losses they had suffered in the late 1960s, when radical Marxism had staged a comeback, and with it an emphasis on the "real" economy and on the power balance between labor and capital. The social engineers lost some of their credibility during this time, not because of their methods per se, but because they were perceived as expressions of their reformist credo and their unorthodox (from a strict Marxist perspective) economic strategies.

Though the above explanation does not offer a full picture of the situation, it suggests one way in which to understand the confusions and loss of

self-confidence in the labor movement from the mid 1980s forward.⁴⁰ After
losing faith in the old, revitalizing power of crisis, Social Democrats found it
difficult to come up with any healing or energizing interpretation of an economic situation, in which the demand for industrial efficiency and growth
called for a weaker public sector. It was not the return of crisis as such, but the
return of a "negative crisis" which marked the (temporary) loss of confidence
of the Social Democrats in Sweden.

On Crisis and Democracy

The political potential of the concept of "crisis" lies, of course, in the fact that
it can be used to maximally mobilize: to put routine procedures aside, to
speed things up, to put concrete questions on the agenda. As I have argued
above, "crisis" in this sense could be seen as the opposite of a "problem" or
a "question" that one can afford to discuss, dwell on, invert, or postpone ad
infinitum. Did the "crisification" of a political question thus allow for more
radical solutions, that normal democratic procedures were put aside? In what
way did it affect the delicate balance of relations between the state and the
individual? In short, what has been the effect of the "crisis vocabulary" on the
model of Swedish democracy?

    We could say that the transformation of a "question" into a "crisis," pro-
moted by Myrdal in the 1930s, allowed politics to speed up. It harmonized
with modern forms of policymaking (social engineering); it enhanced the
role of expertise and science. By putting emphasis on efficiency and utility it
created a formula for strong political action.

    On the other hand, a less optimistic view of the potential of the social sci-
ences to diagnose problems and provide relevant solutions poses obvious
questions about the relationship between the world of experts and the world
of politicians. The danger of a "social engineering dictatorship" was avoided
not just because the *goal* of policies was "common happiness" (happiness and
democracy, of course, do not have to correlate). The real danger was never at
hand since the "crisis" was tackled within the framework of scrupulous, democratic routines which included official governmental investigations (SOU).
The SOU culture was further institutionalized during World War II and after.
If today there are increasing complaints about its practices, it is mainly
because its reports have deteriorated to the point where they have yielded
countless superficial, shallow documents of little import for policy making.

    It is worthwhile, I believe, to analyze the new situation in relation to the
growing use of the concept of crisis in its older, negative sense. Looking at the
world today (mainly through the lens of the media) one sees nothing but
crisis. As Reinhart Koselleck has noted, "problems" and "questions" seem to
belong to the past, "crisis" rules supreme. We live less and less in a world in
which we talk about "social questions." Most of the time, we talk about social

or economic "crises." We refer incessantly to a "crisis of democracy"—possibly because we have lost the ability to answers the "questions."

It may well be that the questions are increasingly unanswerable. Or it may be that the answers provoke ever new, unwanted, unintended questions to which there is no end. This conceptual change could be one reason why so many initiatives of "the modern project" have truly come to an end. Today they are replaced by non-ideas, non-visions, non-ideologies, and feelings of helplessness and disempowerment.

Or, less dramatically, the conceptual shift could be a manifestation of a shift in power from politics to economy, from the benches of parliament where questions were once discussed and crises resolved, to the more unpredictable financial market, where crises figure on every computer screen—and are largely beyond our control.

Notes

1. See Jacob L. Talmon, *The Origins of Totalitarian Democracy* (New York: Praeger, 1960); see also Talmon, *Political Messianism* (London: Secker & Warburg, 1960).
2. Whether this Swedish Keynesianism altered and ameliorated the economic situation or not, and whether things would have changed anyway, was a subject of debate among historians in the 1970s.
3. "För vårt land såväl moraliskt som ekonomiskt hårt påfrestade händelser ha aktualiserat frågan om en samhällelig kontroll över handhavandet av samhällets ekonomiska värden." See Yvonne Hirdman, *Vi bygger landet: Från Palm till Palme* (Stockholm: Tidens förlag, 1989).
4. See Yvonne Hirdman, *Den socialistiska hemmafrun och andra kvinnohistoier* (Stockholm: Carlssons, 1992).
5. "Utopia in the Home," an essay by Yvonne Hirdman, *International Journal of Political Economy, A Journal of Translations*, vol. 22, no. 2, 1992, 31. This is a translation of the key chapter of my book, *Att lägga livet tillrätta* (Stockholm: Carlssons, 1989).
6. Gunnar Myrdal, "Socialpolitikens dilemma," *Spectrum*, vol. 2, 1932.
7. Ibid. See also Yvonne Hirdman, "Social Planning under Rational Control: Social Engineering in Sweden in the 1930s and 1940s" in P. Kettunen and H. Eskola (eds.), *Models, Modernity and the Myrdals* (Helsingfors: Renvall Institutete Publications, 1998).
8. See also the initiative taken by Gunnar Myrdal and Uno Åhrén to create a special housing commission in late 1932; for the inside story, see Gunnar Myrdal, *Hur styrs landet?* (Stockholm: Rabén & Sjögren, 1982).
9. Allan Carlsson, "The Roles of Alva and Gunnar Myrdal in the Development of a Social Democratic Response to Europe's 'Population Crisis 1929–1938,'" unpublished dissertation, Ohio University, Athens, Ohio, 1978. See also Ann-Katrin Hatje, *Befolkningsfrågan och välfärden* (Stockholm: Allmänna förlaget, 1974); Ann-Sofie Kälvemark, *More Children of Better Quality?: Aspects of Swedish Population Policy in the 1930s* (Stockholm: Almqvist & Wicksell, 1980).
10. There were also other, parallel commissions working in the area of social policy. One of them was a housing commission (1932–35) headed by Uno Åhrén and Gunnar Myrdal. Other investigations dealt with delicate matters such as forced sterilization, abortion, contraceptives—sometimes in close cooperation with the population commission. On the topic

of forced sterilization, see Gunnar Broberg and Mattias Tydén, *Oönskade i folkhemmet: rashygien och sterilisering i Sverige* (Stockholm: Gidlund, 1991); Maija Runcis, *Steriliseringar i folkhemmet* (Stockholm: Ordfront, 1998).

11. Kvinnoarbetskommitén, *Betänkande angående gift kvinnas rätt till förvärvsarbete mm*, ("Report on the rights of married women to work").(Stockholm: SOU, 1938: 47)

12. For the Swedish debate see Elisabeth Elgán, *Genus och politik, en jämförelse mellan svensk och fransk abort och preventivmedelspolitik från sekelskiftet till andra världskriget* (Stockholm: Almquist & Wiksell International, 1994).

13. 1997 showed, for the first time since the beginning of population statistics in 1742, that the number of births was lower than the number of deaths. Still, when one newspaper (notably a Social Democratic paper) tried to talk about a "crisis in the population question," the effort did not seem to provoke any great unease (*Dagens Nyheter*, 3 January 1998). The roles were interestingly reversed: while Social Democratic papers attempted to revitalize the crisis perspective on the "question" (presented with quotation marks), the (neo)liberal paper *Dagens Nyheter* belittled the figures.

14. For an elaboration on this question see Hirdman, "Utopia in the Home," 41.

15. Gunnar Myrdal's lecture manuscript, "The population problem and social policy," Fall 1938, Alva Myrdal archive, vol. 9, *Arbetarrörelsens Arkiv*, Stockholm. Note how Myrdal continuously uses the term a "crisis of opinion."

16. Hatje, *Befolkningsfrågan och välfärden.*

17. Ibid., "Women" here should be read as "Social Democratic women."

18. See the open letter by Disa Wästberg, leader of the Social Democratic Women's league, to the members: "Isn't it our old program to give mothers and children the best possible care and conditions, to make life a little more sunny and safe for those with less means in the country?" September 1935, *Arbetarrörelsens Arkiv*, Stockholm.

19. Yvonne Hirdman, "Social Engineering and the Woman Question: Sweden in the Thirties," Wallace Clement and Rhionne Mahon (eds.), *Swedish Social Democracy: A Model in Transition* (Toronto: Canadian Scholars Press, 1994)

20. Yvonne Hirdman, *Magfrågan: Mat som mål och medel: Stockholm 1870-1920* (Stockholm: Raben & Sjögren, 1983).

21. Hirdman, "Utopia in the home," 70.

22. Uno Åhrén, *Arkitektur och demokrati* (Stockholm: Kooperativa förbundets bokförlag, 1942), 40f.

23. "Det är en första uppgift för vår ekonomiska politik att vid återgång till fredsekonomi förhindra kris och massarbetslöshet./.../ Den huvuduppgift som förestår, är att samordna den ekonomiska verksamheten till en planmässig hushållning, så att arbetskraft och materiella tillgångar stadigt utnyttjas för en effektiv produktion. En sådan samordning bör ske under samhällets ledning och med sådan inriktning, att enskilda interessen underordnas de mål, som i samhället eftersträvas." *Arbetarrörelsens efterkrigsprogram: Sammanfattning i 27 punkter* ("The Post-War Program of the Labor Movement," Stockholm, 1946).

24. Cf. interdependent key concepts of consumption–production, social needs–economic prosperity. Note that both Alva and Gunnar Myrdal were involved in this program.

25. "De som talar om att verket är fullbordat och att bara inputsen återstår misstar sig. Det finns alltjämt i detta land eftersatta minoriteter, vilkas intressen vi måste bevaka, om vi skall känna oss som bärare av en sund och riktig solidaritet." *Protokoll från Landsorganisationens ordinarie kongress,* 1961 (*The Trade Union Congress Reports*, 1961), 280.

26. "Det är i alla händelser en annan utveckling som främst ger anledning att bruka ord som kris. Det är utvecklingen av organsationerna till ett slags monopolister som gör att en arbetsmarknad i den gamla betydelsen knappast finns kvar inom vårt land. Då både företagen och anställda varit eniga om att hålla sina lönefrågor fria från statlig inblandning, har orsaken uppenbarligen varit, att akuta konflikter också av vidsträckt omfattning, av alla parter betraktas som uthärdliga." *Tiden,* 1967, no 4.

27. Ibid. "Krisläget på arbetsmarknaden har här tagits fram som en av de faktorer som kan föranleda en omprövning av socialdemokratins politik och aktualisera en mera markerad socialisitsk handlingslinje."

28. See Anders L. Johansson, *Tillväxt och klassamarbete: en studie av den svenska modellens uppkomst* (Stockholm: Tiden, 1989).
29. Yvonne Hirdman, "Women: from Possibilities to Problems. Gender Conflict in the Welfare State–the Swedish Model," research report no. 3, 1994, Arbetslivscentrum (The Swedish Center for Working Life).
30. Elected chairwoman for the "Equality Group" in 1967. See minutes from the SAP Congresses of 1967 and 1968.
31. See for example Sträng's speech at the LO congress in 1971.
32. "Full sysslesättning i ett framtida samhälle kräver större planmässighet och starkare styrmedel än förr. Den privata marknaden kommer ännu mindre än tidigare att kunna gatantera sysselsättningen." See also Peter Antman, "Vägen till systemskiftet" in Rolf Å. Gustafsson (ed.), *Köp och sälj, var god svälj?: vårdens nya ekonomistyrningssystem i ett arbetsmiljöperspektiv* (Stockholm: Arbetsmiljöfonden, 1994).
33. Sven-Erik Larsson, *Regera i koalition: den borgerliga trepartiregeringen 1976–1978 och kärnkraften* (Stockholm: Bonniers, 1986).
34. Sven Ove Hansson, *SAF i politiken: en dokumentation av näringslivets opinionsbildning* (Stockholm: Tiden, 1984).
35. "Den offentliga sektorns omfattning och tillväxt är helt enkelt vårt största samhällsproblem", Antman, "Vägen till systemskiftet."
36. *Framtid för Sverige. Förslag till handlingslinjer för att föra Sverige ur krisen* (SAP: Tiden, 1981).
37. Ibid., 36: "i den mån man skall tala om systemkriser är det en kris för sådana system som saknar förmåga att ställa om sin inriktning efter förändrade produktionsbetingelser."
38. Ibid.
39. This is the way the former Minister of Finance, Kjell Olof Feldt, must have experienced the situation. See Kjell-Olof Feldt, *Alla dessa dagar – i regeringen 1982-1990* (Stockholm: Norstedt, 1991).
40. The question invites further study, as well as a more extensive use of gender analysis.

10

The Crisis of Consensus in Postwar Sweden

GÖRAN ROSENBERG

Introduction

It is said that Swedes are a conflict-avoiding species. This of course is a generalization, but it is not without some empirical foundation. The Swedish ethnologist Åke Daun explicitly includes "conflict avoidance" among the traits of the "Swedish mentality,"[1] and recent studies of Swedish politics in the twentieth century have found that the element of conflict has been greatly exaggerated "and most particularly so if one looks at the contents of what the parties actually have proposed in parliament."[2]

Conflict avoidance is defined by Daun as "a tendency to avoid direct conflict with people with whom you deeply disagree." He continues: "Many Swedes typically avoid topics of conversation with a strong emotional charge and on which there are strongly diverging views. In conversations among people in the workplace or at a dinner party, Swedes will typically try to change the subject of conversation, come up with an evasive answer or even relinquish their own view on the matter, in order to avoid a deeper controversy."[3] Case studies in the 1980s by another Swedish ethnologist, Billy Ehn, detail the culture of conflict avoidance in a factory and a day-care center. In the factory, foreign workers "in a Swedish manner" avoid bringing up their conflicts and differences: "The striving for non-conflict is the rule." In the day-care center notions of conflict, aggression, and violence are almost nonexistent. Conflict avoidance is the norm in all relations between personnel and children, as well as between personnel and parents. Ehn concludes: "Conflict avoidance can perhaps be regarded as a form of Swedish 'self-understanding', a symbolic construction of one's own cultural identity.[4] In

1969 Susan Sontag characterized the Swedish culture of conflict avoidance as "little short of pathological" and the Swedish version of the generally admirable quality of reasonableness as "deeply defective, owing far too much to inhibition and anxiety and emotional dissociation."[5]

Any observation of this nature undoubtedly reflects a time-bound social and political context, and indeed cultural constructs are usually most clearly visible when they are about to crumble (the owl of Minerva flies at dusk). Nonetheless the signs of habitual conflict avoidance pop up in ever new forms and circumstances. One of them is the tendency in postwar Sweden to avoid having losers in public conflicts, or, rather, to arrange matters so that failure has few or no consequences for the persons involved. Swedish ministers and high public officials rarely resign or get sacked—even when defeat or failure is manifest. The differences in a conflict—if ever made public—are consciously played down, and a decorum of consensus is carefully nurtured. A rhetoric of common interests and understanding quickly disperses whatever gun smoke there may have been.

In December 1998 the Swedish Minister of Defense, Björn von Sydow, resoundingly lost an open conflict with Prime Minister Göran Persson regarding the size of the defense budget. The differences of opinion were clear-cut, the outcome of the struggle unambiguous. The defense appropriations publicly approved of by Mr. von Sydow were publicly retracted by the Finance and Prime ministers (making a difference of nine billion Swedish crowns over three years). In addition, the Swedish Chief of Staff, General Owe Wictorin, a former fighter pilot who quite extraordinarily voiced his dissatisfaction with the government's handling of the issue, was officially reprimanded.[6]

One would have expected that the two losers in such a grandiose public struggle would either offer their resignations or be discharged from their jobs. That, at least, is what regularly happens in other democracies, but rarely in Sweden, and evidently not in this case. Instead, the core issue of the conflict (what defense at what cost) was quickly and thoroughly muddled by a complicated budgetary maneuver involving short-term internal borrowing from existing military appropriations, thus converting funds for future expenditure into cash for immediate use. Any evaluation of the effects on actual defense programs was carefully postponed. Thus the double illusion could be created that the defense program was carried out as previously agreed—and that it was not. Each side of the conflict could claim victory, no-one had to concede defeat, and seemingly deep differences about goals could be reduced to a technical squabble about means. "What is true and false in this conflict is impossible to judge," complained a Social Democratic editorial.[7] Hard decisions about weapon procurements, the future of the draft system, and Sweden's defense needs were temporarily buried in technical seminars and negotiations as if the whole thing had only been a matter of different calculations or insufficient knowledge. It seemed as if both sides had been merely engaged in the common pursuit of the same rational goal.

But this conflict–about the future size and needs of Swedish defense–is, in fact, not a conflict between different means to achieve the same good but arguably a conflict between different goods–i.e., a conflict of values. One side, most explicitly Vänsterpartiet (the Left Party) and Miljöpartiet (the Greens), who provided the necessary parliamentary votes for the government's "reductionist" position, is ideologically convinced that disarmament makes for a better world. The other side, represented by the Minister of Defense (and the liberal-conservative opposition), believes that a strong military defense is a necessary public good. These two convictions are not easily reconcilable. In a newspaper article (and a speech in Riksdagen–the Swedish parliament) Mr. von Sydow made it perfectly clear that he saw no possibility of a defense policy based on cooperation with parties who basically wished to do away with military defense altogether.[8] A conflict of values and goals has no technical solution, no formula by which it can be converted into a conflict of means. Nevertheless, this was attempted. It led to yet another unresolved public conflict, to yet another public defeat with no personal consequences.

Swedish public figures might be pressed to resign if caught committing a "crime," such as using a government credit card for private expenses or vices,[9] or more seriously, abusing constitutional powers for private police operations.[10] Political failures or professional mismanagement, however, have rarely been a cause for dethronement. In the case of Inga-Britt Ahlenius, the director general of the Swedish National Audit Office, *Riksrevisionsverket*, whom the government tried to fire in September 1999, a very important and principled conflict between Ahlenius and the government concerning the constitutional independence of the auditing institution (Ahlenius arguing for more independence) was made into an issue of personal misbehavior on the part of Ahlenius. In a moment of pique she had made an unsubstantiated public allegation against the Minister of Finance, Bo Ringholm, for conspiring to lie in public. This came as a response to previous allegations by the Finance Minister that Ahlenius was only seeking to promote her own career.[11]

A Culture of Consensus—and Its Crisis

The notion of consensus, frequently attached to "the Swedish Model," is by no means unambiguously defined or interpreted. It may on the one hand indicate a genuine lack of conflict and broad agreement over existing values and goals. Such a notion of consensus will eventually approach the notion of conflict avoidance, since deeper conflicts of value will be regarded as anomalous and undesirable. A national mythology interacting with this particular notion of consensus might for instance develop the belief that public conflicts can and should be kept "within the family," that the nation in fact is a large family, a people's home. This notion of consensus implies the ultimate resolution of conflicts by rationalization rather than a never-ending compromise between inevitable differences of values and goals.

A very different notion of consensus implies the latter process; consensus as a temporary agreement based on acknowledged differences and on mutual forfeitures for the sake of peaceful coexistence. This is consensus as compromise rather than resolution. Both notions lead to a "common understanding," but they do so from very different points of departure, making for very different cultural and institutional constructs. The Swedish word for common understanding, *samförstånd*, tends to obfuscate the distinction between consensus and compromise. A spirit of common understanding, *samförstånds-anda*, is often expressed as a spirit of compromise, *kompromissanda*, while actually referring to a spirit of conflict avoidance or conflict absorption; agreement by rationalization rather than agreement by give and take.

Consensus is arguably the *modus operandi* of any democratic society under the rule of law, the peaceful *modus vivendi*, if one prefers, of incessantly conflicting opinions and values. But the assumptions behind the culture of consensus differ from society to society. A belief that conflicts are unavoidable and must be recognized will shape a society different from that shaped by the belief that conflicts are irrational and must be done away with. One society will develop a culture of compromise based on a value-laden, *political* conception of consensus, the other a culture of conflict avoidance based on a value-free, *institutional* conception of consensus. The former will regard consensus as the possible outcome of political deliberations, the latter as the necessary foundation of its political institutions. The Swedish culture of consensus is arguably institutional in character—as it is in a family.

The imagery of Sweden as a large family and a people's home is mostly associated with the ascent to power of the Social Democrats in the early 1930s. However, as Nina Witoszek has shown, a similar imagery can be traced to a specific Christian impulse within the Scandinavian national movements in the nineteenth century, movements that "require to be re-read through the prism of Christian values."[12] This unique Scandinavian version of the Christian Enlightenment, Witoszek argues, not only proved itself to be immune against the excesses of Romantic reaction, but also constituted the cultural setting for a national reconstruction imbued with the ideals of restrained reason and religious humanitarianism. At a time when "nineteenth-century Europe was romancing the North as a Gothic Utopia, the North was turning to the future—and to the South—in its search for Apollonian clarity and simplicity."[13] The Christian Enlightenment "inspired and constrained generations of Scandinavian writers and politicians both on the Left and on the Right," and the national images it created were assimilated and cultivated beyond the decline of Christian influence. A rationalism originally inspired and tempered by Christian values was incorporated into an explicitly secular model of self-representation. A largely religious imagery of "the family" as a source of community and consensus ("goodwill and cordiality, happy kindness and understanding") was assimilated into the national and social rhetoric of the times.

Out of this developed a particular Scandinavian–or at least Swedish– path to national construction and social modernization. And perhaps there also developed, as the sociologist Hans Zetterberg has remarked, a specific Swedish brand of rationality, distinct from its French, German, and British counterparts, "marked more by moderation than by logic driven to its final conclusion. Its key word is the (untranslatable) *lagom*, which means both 'reasonable' and 'middle-of the road.'"[14] This peculiar form of rationalism, writes Zetterberg, "permeates the content of radio and television programs and the editorial and opinion pages of the large newspapers. Political discourse often resembles seminars on economics, political science, and sociology. Political debate in Sweden deals primarily with technical questions."[15] Quoting Herbert Tingsten's characterization of the Swedish debate in the 1950s as being mainly about differences in economic and technical assumptions,[16] Zetterberg points out that a democratic debate of this nature "is a debate among rational experts, and the solutions proposed have the appearance of applied social science. Gone are the rabble-rousing, folksy, electioneering politicians; enter the technocrat with his [sic!] briefcase of statistics and research reports and his academic degree."[17]

This particular form of rationality might of course be attributed to a genuine, albeit extraordinary, confluence of values, in a nation characterized by a remarkable degree of continuity and homogeneity. But a more likely explanation is the existence of well-entrenched institutions culturally programmed to transform existing conflicts of value into conflicts of facts. Such institutions seem in any case to have preceded both the Social Democratic corporatist welfare state and the comparatively peaceful political and social transformations that took place during the Oscarian era of the nineteenth century.[18] Their seeds were sown by the forceful creation in the late sixteenth and early seventeenth centuries–during the reigns of Charles IX, Gustavus Adolphus, and Christina–of a strong and centralized state bureaucracy. The central power of the royal court in Stockholm needed to be consolidated after a protracted era of conflict between competing centers of power. Strong civil service departments, *ämbetsverk*, were created to run and control the affairs of state. A distinctive feature of these new departments was their collegiate leadership. Decisions were taken by a group of men, a collegium, not by single individuals, creating over time a specific culture of bureaucratic independence and self-importance. While these *kollegier* became efficient tools in the forging of a centralized Swedish state and undoubtedly strengthened the king's control of the country, they also restricted his autocratic prerogatives. Most royal initiatives henceforth had to be examined through the cool prism of an independent state bureaucracy, and to have their merits weighed against new standards of reason and rationality.[19] A language of matter-of-factness began to cloak and disarm potential conflicts between king and administration.

This specific culture of administrative independence and impartiality, *ämbetsmannakulturen*, was further strengthened in the early decades of the seventeenth century by a large influx of young, educated, and expediently ennobled commoners into the services of the rapidly expanding and incessantly warring Swedish state. Thus was created an extensive class of "lower" nobility, promoted on the basis of education and administrative skill rather than the traditional aristocratic virtues and prerogatives. In Sweden, unlike many other countries, no official positions could be sold or bought. This contributed to exceptional social mobility in Swedish society at the time, so that the step from yeoman to nobleman was not only feasible but sometimes quite rapid. Towards the end of the seventeenth century Sweden had five times more noblemen than during any year of the preceding century. This actual and potential social mobility created, as Eva Österberg has pointed out, a communicative link between separate strata of the Swedish population. The Swedish yeomen had not only formal representation in the assembly of estates (*ståndsriksdagen*, making them the *fourth* estate, *bondeståndet*), but also a real influence on the way rulers and ruled came to look upon each other.

The Swedish yeomen's estate was not as manipulated and subjugated by higher estates as has previously been assumed. In fact, it managed to develop an independent tradition of successful claims and demands that in time created a level of respect, trust, and dialogue between rulers and ruled. King Gustavus Adolphus came to value consultation and open debate "as a rational part of decision-making" and consciously strove for *concordia* in his policymaking, as did his successor, Queen Christina. This rhetoric of *concordia*, argues Österberg, was not just a tactical device, but the expression of a deeper view of "the common good" in which political negotiation came to be seen as a legitimate means to common and unified decisions. The mental universe of Swedish yeomen was thus formed in a specific sphere of "facts and representations," creating, among other elements, a preference for common solutions "in a *spirit of consensus*."[20]

In a recent critical discussion of the Swedish tradition of consensus, Leif Lewin takes his point of departure from the late nineteenth and early twentieth centuries, from the turbulent decades of democratic demands and labor organization that he defines as "the Oscarian legacy."[21] This legacy, Lewin maintains, perpetuates a strong aversion to conflict. The conservative elite of the Oscarian period regarded public discord as disturbing and unwarranted. It maintained that a government had to remain free of political "party considerations," that its task was "by way of compromise to even out remaining differences and reach decisions that are beneficial, not only to one single party but to the nation as a whole."[22] Decisions of the government should be based on "truth and justice," without a need "for that kind of arguments which are the mere expression of restrictive party discipline."[23] Lewin's main point is to show that the Oscarian legacy still permeates Swedish society, making for "a cooperative democracy" (*samarbetsdemokrati*) characterized by the ideals of "cooperation, consensus, compromise, to make odds even, to leave no one outside." This form of democracy, according to Lewin, is distinct from "majoritarian democracy" (*majoritetsdemokrati*), which is built on the idea of an acknowledged contradistinction between a government of the majority and an opposition of the minority.[24]

Irrespective of the terminology or the genealogy or the polemical intent of Lewin's analysis of Sweden's present-day "co-operative democracy," recent research seems to bear out the essence of his argument. The ideal of cooperation between classes and strata of Swedish society was not an invention of the Social Democrats in their effort to create a "people's home" in the 1930s. Rather, it came out of already existing institutions and arrangements founded on the basically conservative notion of a value-free, rational, "truth-seeking," class-transcending, corporatist, consensus-striving, national state. Emil Uddhammar has pointed to the practically uncontested decisions–by mostly conservative governments–to introduce progressive taxes on income and capital (1902 and 1910), to socialize the northern mine fields (1907), to implement the first public pension scheme (1913), to propose a new law for planning and construction (1917). These were all decisions that enhanced the prerogatives of the state and they were all taken by consensus.[25] Bo Rothstein has shown that the first and decisive steps towards the corporatist and interventionist state of the 1930s (associated with Social Democratic rule and symbolized by the "spirit of Saltsjöbaden" (*Saltsjöbadsandan*), were taken by a liberal government with the support of a conservative majority in the Riksdagen–initially against the votes of the Social Democrats. Rothstein concludes that "a collectivist view of democracy" was prevalent at the time among all major parties in Sweden.[26] Uddhammar also highlights the broad unity between the leading political economists of the right and the left, Gösta Bagge, Bertil Ohlin, and Gunnar Myrdal, with regard to the need for a Keynesian, demand-boosting policy of state expenditure, and the utility of public works as a means to combat unemployment.[27]

The government of national unity during the war years must naturally be regarded as an extraordinary arrangement for extreme conditions. However, as Alf W. Johansson has argued in analyzing the fundamental values underlying Sweden's war policy of neutrality and national unity, rigidity in pursuing these policies eventually went far beyond the demands of the situation. National unity became the pretext for detachment from outer events, for a value-free stance towards the outcome of war (expressed in March 1941 by Defense Minister Per-Edvin Sköld, who declared that Sweden could have no "interest in the victory of any of the belligerent countries").[28] Prime Minister Per Albin Hansson insisted to the very end on the non-ideological nature of Sweden's posture, failing to acknowledge that actions which during the war were defended "as skillful Realpolitik" were later perceived as "running errands for a tyrannical butcher."[29] Alf W. Johansson terms Swedish war policy "small-state realism," a policy that subordinated the ideological and moral considerations of the war to the overarching goal of keeping Sweden out of it. It is further documented that Per Albin Hansson was intent on retaining a government of national unity after the war, and that a similar arrangement was initially contemplated by Bertil Ohlin, the leader of the Liberal Party.[30] The potentially harsh social conflicts and confrontations of the 1930s and 1940s were thus moderated by a class-transcending spirit of reason and rationality, and successfully defused within an institutionalized system of central dealings and decision-making.

Hugh Heclo and Henrik Madsen find basically the same system at work when they explore Swedish politics in the 1980s: "To enter the world of Swedish politics and policy is to enter a small, ingrown realm of group decision-making, in which a professional class of politicians, administrators, and interest group functionaries must constantly expect to keep dealing with one another."[31] They quote approvingly another contemporary study[32] showing "Swedish politicians and administrators to be distinguished from their counterparts in other countries by the considerable emphasis they place on the social skills of getting along with others—not pushing advantages too far, encouraging the co-operation of others, avoiding outright confrontation, and not casting anyone in the role of permanent loser."[33] Heclo and Madsen eventually conclude that the apparent "coziness" of Swedish policymaking, a system of "principled pragmatism" based on a largely hegemonic (Social Democratic) perception of society, has grown out of "divisiveness, rather than monolithic power." It is a system "for absorbing internal dissent" and disciplining the diverse constituencies of the labor movement, as well as a system for stemming the growth of any effective opposition.[34]

A more or less consensus-based conception of Swedish society thus seems to have survived into the 1980s, still successfully appealing to the ideal of common reason and rationality to bolster a unified vision of the good society, or at least a vision that no political opposition could effectively manage to challenge. It was a system bent on absorbing internal dissent and disciplining potential adversaries into a sphere of tacit or formal agreement and consensus. This was largely achieved through a well-entrenched administrative culture imbued with the ideals of matter-of-factness (*saklighet*), objectivity, legal security (*rättssäkerhet*) and loyalty to established goals.[35] It created a state apparatus with a special knack for transforming conflicts of goal into conflicts of means. A particularly effective instrument for the neutralization of potential or actual conflicts of goal was the old institution of public commissions of inquiry and investigation, *Statens offentliga utredningar,* a traditional cornerstone of the Swedish system of governance, yearly producing tomes of facts, figures, and policy recommendations on every conceivable subject. This scholarly output, with its claims to objectivity, not only generated a widespread perception that political problems or conflicts could be solved or absorbed by rational inquiry and investigation, but it also generated a working political consensus among parliamentarians taking part in the public committees and subsequently within the political community as a whole. Open and formal opposition to the recommendations of a public committee was rare and mostly peripheral in character.[36] There was not, then, as in many other democracies, a common understanding based on compromise between open and acknowledged conflicts of value, i.e., different conceptions of good and evil, but a common understanding based on a hegemonic, "value-neutral" definition of the problems of society. Those who were privileged to formulate problems (*problemformuleringsprivilegiet,* to use the adroit expression of Swedish writer Lars Gustafsson) also decided which hidden value-premises had any validity, i.e., which kind of opposition was reasonable—and which was not.

To find signs of breakdown in the Swedish apparatus of consensus creation and conflict avoidance, the alleged rapid decline of the system of public committees of inquiry and investigation might be a good starting point. It has been convincingly demonstrated that the system has lost a great deal of authority and that the quality of committee reports has seriously deteriorated. The effectiveness of the system in creating a "rational" basis for common policy decisions has subsequently diminished. Since the early 1980s the committees have been working "within increasingly limited time frames while tending to have ever more binding ties with the Cabinet Office and the Ministries."[37] A system that for a long period successfully managed to use facts to absorb or disarm potential conflicts, that was fortified by a widespread belief that a thorough investigation would clear any political fog, has thus become a mere instrument for furnishing the government in power with a shallow mixture of facts, figures, and ready-made proposals. Or, as it was expressed by the recent public commission on administrative policy,[38] *Förvaltningspolitiska kommittén:* "The task [of the committees] has been redirected towards the compilation of already existing facts and their rapid transformation into [political] proposals."[39]

The tradition of creating common facts as a base for common policy has so permeated Swedish society that its current failure to deliver either common facts or consensus is arguably having detrimental effects on Sweden's overall ability to handle present-day political and social conflicts, many of them involving genuine clashes of goals and values. Institutions built for conflict avoidance are by definition not particularly effective in coping with conflicts that are unavoidable. The symptoms of a crisis in the Swedish system of political decision-making abound: decisions already made are retracted or reversed (defense policy, social security, taxes); decisions already made are found to be untenable or unfeasible (a new public pension system launched under a strained consensus has turned out to be so full of conflicting interests and complicated claims that the system as a whole could not be made to work on schedule); decisions by one government are now almost habitually reversed by the next (giving a new meaning to the Swedish word *återställare*[40]; binding commitments are unilaterally ignored (Sweden's obligation by treaty to join the European Monetary Union); important decisions are deferred to popular referenda or left to be "decided" by external pressures and developments (the future of nuclear power, the Swedish position vs. NATO, the substance of neutrality). A more profound and systematic manifestation of the demise of the traditional model of decision-making is an ongoing politicization of the state apparatus, substituting bureaucratic interpretation for political deliberation. "Today, civil servants handle the political production of ideology to a great extent," concludes a group of Swedish social scientists.[41] State programs and actions often appear to come out of a no-man's land of Swedish-European political, judicial, and administrative rule-making, blurring not only the distinction between state administration and political representation, but also the constitutional order of political and judicial responsibility.

There are, of course, specific and complex backgrounds to each and every case of disorganized or defective decision-making, but I would argue that what we essentially see at work is a system, deeply rooted in conflict avoidance, trying to cope in a world of open and unavoidable conflicts. What then happens is what often happens to individuals with a similar predisposition in a similar predicament: the defunct mechanisms of conflict avoidance give way to panicky and ill-conceived emergency reactions, often aggravating the conflict instead of tackling it.

The Anomalous Nature of Sweden's Conflicts

To what extent is the Swedish culture of consensus exceptional? And to what extent may Sweden's present-day problems be attributed to the demise of such an exceptional order of things? Clearly some of Sweden's difficulties in adjusting to a world of new and open conflicts of value are shared with other European welfare democracies. Economic globalization and political Europeanization are no easy challenges for any nation-state. I will nevertheless maintain that (1) the Swedish culture of consensus has been exceptional enough to have exceptional consequences, and that (2) as a consequence Sweden is having exceptional problems in dealing with open conflicts of value.

The first point I shall argue no further. I assume the existence of a particularly long and deep Swedish tradition of consensus to be satisfactorily established. It is also reasonably well established that the institutions of consensus began to show serious signs of weakness sometime during the late 1960s and early 1970s. This was mainly due to increased internal and external pressures on the political system, which created new, less avoidable conflicts of value. At the point where the exceptional competitive advantages of the undamaged Swedish postwar economy were about to be consummated, the fine print on the contract for national consensus began to show, demanding ever higher worker productivity, pressing for time measuring and piece wages, calling for an increasingly mobile labor force. All of these led not only to a sharp divergence of views on how to proceed with the modernization of Sweden, but to a divergence of values concerning the nature of the good society. A growing discrepancy between the increasing budgetary demands of the welfare state and the decreasing budgetary surpluses, simultaneously limited and strained the political space for consensus. Money could no longer function as the great mediator and absorber of conflicts. The appeal to *common* sense (traditionally and unquestioningly administered by the Social Democrats) made little sense to a growing number of Swedes. These were years when many experienced "a weakened instrumental relationship" and a failing loyalty to the "public systems." These were also the years when Gunnar Myrdal noted that Sweden had become a nation of *fifflare*, i.e., con-artists and cheats.[42]

The second point, however, needs some further elaboration. Few will deny that Sweden's political and social system has suffered from a considerable loss of efficiency and legitimacy during the last two decades. The "decline of the welfare state" is not a cliché. One can even argue that the decline has been quite rapid (plunging in merely two decades from number five to number fifteen in the OECD's league of GDP per head at purchasing-power parity),[43] and that the ability of Swedish society to adjust politically to changing social circumstances has proven especially weak. It is true that a period of strong-hand social democratic rule (1994-1998) managed to pull Sweden back from the brink of financial disaster (e.g., by regaining control over a galloping national debt), but this was mainly achieved by dodging painful long-term political decisions regarding the future nature of the welfare system, and by spending historically amassed political capital. The consequence was the growth of a strong *leftist* opposition to the Social Democratic Party (in the form of the Left Party, i.e., the former and reformed communists), expressing not only popular disappointment with the harsh measures taken to restore financial solvency, but also a nostalgic yearning for a lost Swedish *Sonderweg* in Europe and the world.

This anti-European welfare state nationalism (in both a Green and a Red version) is not the only exceptional feature of Sweden's post-consensus state of mind. Exceptional too is the apparent inability of existing institutions to break out of the stalemate in the decision-making process. Political positions in Sweden–regarding labor market reform, taxes, welfare arrangements, social security, etc.–remain rhetorically rigid and polarized. Confidence in politicians and political institutions seems to have declined more rapidly than in most other European countries. In 1986 51 percent of Swedes expressed confidence in parliament. In 1996, the number was down to 19 percent. The proportion of Swedes disagreeing with the statement that "parties are only interested in people's votes, not in their opinions" dropped from 51 percent in 1968 to 28 percent in 1994.[44]

I will argue here that some of these Swedish "shortcomings" may in part be the exceptional consequences of an exceptionally long and deep-rooted culture of conflict avoidance. There are reasons to think that political institutions bent on transforming conflicts of value into conflicts of fact might become a liability in an environment where conflicts of value are more clearly manifested, and thus harder to avoid or transform. I will further argue that such an inverse relationship between conflict avoidance and conflict resolution can be observed in the way in which some major conflicts of value in the postwar era have been handled–or rather, not handled–by Sweden's political institutions. My point is that these conflicts more often than not have developed in an *anomalous* manner, dramatically transgressing established institutions of conflict resolution. An anomalous event is capricious, unregulated, and inherently ad hoc. To demonstrate the anomalous nature of major Swedish conflicts is primarily to show that they could not be handled within the existing institutions of consensus, but perhaps also to raise the question of whether these institutions themselves pushed the conflicts into an *anomalous* state–and thereby lost control over them.

The Era of Affairs

During the early postwar period this runaway development of conflicts was mainly manifested in the sphere of foreign and defense policy and assumed the form of "scandals" or "affairs." These were the result of the strong pressures of consensus emanating from the war period and from the rapidly emerging liturgical character of Swedish neutrality. Neutrality not only remained the dominant feature of Swedish foreign policy after the war, but was transformed from a national necessity to a national "religion," satisfying among other things a need "to confer legitimacy and moral validity on the country's wartime policy."[45] In no other sphere of society were the pressures of consensus more intensely felt, and in no other sphere were the risks of anomalous conflicts larger.

One of these conflicts, the "Hjalmarson affair," erupted on 27 July 1959, when the Social Democratic government privately decided to exclude the

leader of the Conservative Party (*högerpartiet*), Jarl Hjalmarson, from participation in the Swedish UN delegation. This drastic measure was motivated by
the claim that Hjalmarson's strong public anti-Communist and anti-Soviet
statements had become a danger to Sweden's policy of neutrality and thereby
to its vital security interests. A proper signal had to be sent to the Soviets.
Hjalmarson was a long-time critic of what he regarded as a policy of appeasement towards the Soviet regime, especially in connection with the "Catalina
affair"[46] and the Korean War. He was also a proponent of alternative security
arrangements with Denmark and Norway, which made him the target of
severe attacks by Östen Undén, the Swedish Foreign Minister and the architect of Sweden's postwar doctrine of neutrality. Undén accused Hjalmarson
of conducting a "personally biased" campaign of defamation against "a
neighbor with whom we live in peace after all."[47] This latent conflict of values finally developed into an anomalous affair when Hjalmarson openly and
harshly criticized the upcoming state visit to Sweden of Soviet leader Nikita
Khrushchev, a visit which, in a speech on 17 July 1959, he deemed "an unfortunate and humiliating propaganda show, where we in words which do not
correspond to our feelings shall greet the representative of an inhuman political system and the prime organizer of war threats."[48] When two days later
the Soviet leader canceled his visit, citing "hostile campaigns," the Swedish
government (Östen Undén) apparently deemed it necessary to "strengthen
the credibility of Sweden's policy of neutrality in the eyes of the Soviets"[49] by
excluding Hjalmarson from the UN delegation and thus from the official
representation of Sweden's foreign and security policy.

Under established conditions of consensus, such a signal to the Soviets–
and hence the conflict seething beneath it–would have been kept under a
tight lid of secrecy and confidence; an informal deal would have been struck
between the parties whereby the outer appearance of unity would have been
preserved. This, in fact, was initially attempted. As revealed by Ulf Bjereld in
his extensive study of the affair, Hjalmarson was to be provided with a trivial excuse not to go to the UN session in New York. Or perhaps he could go
at a later date, when the link to the canceled state visit was no longer apparent. The pressure for a compromise was strong on both sides, not least among
conservative politicians and opinion makers. They favored a continued formal consensus in the sphere of foreign policy and basically supported the
cautious stance of the Social Democratic government.[50]

When the conflict ultimately became public, it immediately went out of
control, as had been feared by both Hjalmarson and Tage Erlander, the
Prime Minister. What could have remained a tacit, expedient agreement now
became an open conflict of values. In a public debate the government could
no longer offer trivial reasons for not including Hjalmarson in the UN delegation. Further, it refused to maintain the cover that presupposed continued
secrecy. The Hjalmarson affair developed into an inflamed exchange of accu-

sations and declamations, ripping apart the facade of a consensus of Swedish foreign policy—*against the will of the participants themselves.* The "ban" on Hjalmarson remained in force through 1960 and was lifted only in 1961, in the somewhat less conciliatory era of the Berlin Wall. Bjereld argues that the affair prompted a reformulation of the tenets of Swedish neutrality, paving the way for a new Swedish activism in international politics. This was to be a "third way" between the superpowers, leading to independent "moralist" positions on colonial and postcolonial conflicts, a high-pitched critique of U.S. policies in Vietnam, a tough stance against the apartheid regime in South Africa, and more generally hostility to "injustice and oppression" everywhere. Bjereld further argues that, from then on, conflicting opinions on Sweden's foreign policy could be openly voiced. The demand for consensus had reached "a dead end" and Sweden was moving from "a cautious concept of balancing between powers to the notions of world conscience and international solidarity, from demands of consensus and national consolidation to an open and free debate on foreign policy."[51] Bjereld actually regards the Hjalmarson affair as the "culmination of a decade-long conflict between the social democrats and the conservatives on how Sweden's foreign and security policy should be conducted."[52]

This, however, does not explain why new "affairs" continued to pop up regularly in the sphere of foreign and security policy. After the Hjalmarson affair came several others, based on similar accusations of not carrying the proper flag of neutrality, thus confirming the existence of some areas of conflict where the demands of consensus had not been slackened. Bjereld himself indicates that the Swedish policy of neutrality and nonalignment was never openly questioned during the 1960s or 1970s, either by the Conservatives (*moderaterna*) or the Liberals (*folkpartiet*), or by the opposition press. He could have added that the privilege of formulating what such a policy entailed—and what it did not—was still very much in the hands of a well-entrenched and consensus-craving elite. Underneath the seemingly more open debate on Sweden's new activist positions on faraway conflicts and high-flying global issues, the pressures for consensus on geopolitically more imminent and vital matters of policy were still unwavering. The institutions of consensus were thus maintained by, on the one hand, deflecting and absorbing genuine conflicts of value (regarding Sweden's role and position in the world) into a distant internationalist discourse, and, on the other hand, by keeping a continued tight rule on the closer-to-home tenets of neutrality and nonalignment.

Among the "anomalous" conflicts ensuing from this new *modus vivendi*, one could mention the Holmberg affair, the Bodström affair, the Ferm affair, and the Bildt affair, all creating a continuum of sorts, from the 1960s to the mid 1980s. They all developed around the interpretation of neutrality, they all involved moral castigation of persons and positions, and they were all the unintended and uncontrolled outcome of suppressed, but fundamental, conflicts regarding Sweden's national duties and commitments in the world.

The first Ferm affair (there was to be a second) broke out in December 1983 around the Swedish ambassador to the UN, Anders Ferm (a close friend and associate of Olof Palme), who had been caught pursuing a secret and highly personal channel to two prominent Soviet representatives in New York. Thereby, it was alleged, he had circumvented and undermined a Swedish note to Moscow delivered only a few days earlier, protesting the 1981 intrusion of a Soviet U-137 submarine into the waters of a major Swedish marine base, where it went aground. Ferm was said to have assured the Soviets that the Swedish note, based on the highly critical findings of a public commission on Soviet submarine activities in Swedish waters, *Ubåtsskyddskommissionen* (published in April 1983), had been beyond the Prime Minister's control, and should thus tacitly be disregarded. Fearing an embarrassing public debate on being under Soviet pressure, Prime Minister Olof Palme "chose" to make an appearance on prime-time Swedish television and attempted to defuse the affair by publicly reading from Ferm's letter to him on the meetings in New York. The letter seemed to alleviate the worst suspicions of a secret foreign policy and the debate tapered off. In May 1984, however, the daily *Expressen* managed to show that Mr. Palme had read only highlights, or rather lowlights, from the letter, and a second Ferm affair was suddenly on the loose. The Foreign Minister, Lennart Bodström, who had been left in the dark about the secret contacts, was said to be furious, but he did not have long to wait for his own scandal. At an "off the record" dinner with journalists, he questioned the findings of the submarine commission and raised doubts as to whether there really had been any Soviet intrusions into Swedish waters, other than the unfortunate U-137 trying to climb a rock outside Karlskrona.

This semi-submerged debate on the Soviet submarine threat also triggered one of several Bildt affairs during the 1980s. Carl Bildt, foreign policy spokesman of the Conservative party (later party chairman and prime minister), openly met with representatives of U.S. intelligence to discuss the findings of the submarine commission. Olof Palme, finding out about Bildt's U.S. journey, publicly branded him a security risk and a threat to Swedish foreign policy. Again, what could and should have been a debate acknowledging diverging values and ideals was forced into the cramped space of institutional consensus,[53] from where it could escape only as uncontrolled bursts of smear and defamation.[54]

This habit of resorting to "categorical statements about the requirements for upholding the credibility of the policy of neutrality" had already been authoritatively described and criticized in 1973, with the argument that since such requirements were impossible to know with any certainty, neutrality should be treated less as a dogma and more as an ordinary political issue where conflicts of goals were openly acknowledged.[55]

The Era of Flip-flops and Deadlocks

The pressures of institutional consensus are still affecting the debate on Sweden's neutrality and its position in Europe. The radical flip-flop in October 1990 on Sweden's membership in what was about to become the European Union, reversing decades of nay-saying into "an ambition to become a member of the European Community," was characterized by institutional decorum and a conspicuous avoidance of public debate. The proper occasion to have proposed such a radical policy change, and to have it debated, was the Social Democratic party congress in Stockholm in late September 1990, only six weeks before the actual flip-flop. Yet all debate on the issue was explicitly discouraged, most explicitly by the Minister of Foreign Trade, Anita Gradin, who argued that there was no need to debate EC membership before Sweden had concluded its negotiations with the EC on EEA, the European Economic Area.[56] Symptomatically, her intervention at the party congress effectively extinguished whatever sparks of debate there might have been. Thereafter not a single voice was raised for or against EC membership, nor a single question asked. The party congress only stated that the upcoming EEA Treaty "does not exclude future Swedish membership if this should prove possible and desirable."[57]

While by this time the party leadership and Prime Minister Ingvar Carlsson must have made up their minds on membership and been basically looking for the right moment and the proper formula, they carefully kept the process within a very small and informal circle of decision-makers, to avoid having party and public opinion backfire on them. The necessary consensus on such a radical departure from earlier positions and ideals would obviously have to be carefully manipulated. So far the arguments *against* membership had been explicitly political and strongly value-laden, referring as they did to Sweden's moral position in the world, its national ethos, its policy of neutrality. The *relevant* arguments *for* membership would have to be equally political and value-laden—substituting one view of Sweden's role in the world for another.

This, however, could not be openly declared by the party and state leadership since it would inevitably have created a deep and genuine conflict of values, particularly within the rank and file of the Social Democratic Party. The membership question was thus transformed from a political and value-laden issue to an economic and value-free one (jobs and welfare). It was made to coincide with a severe crisis in the balance of payments in October 1990. Foreign currency reserves were rapidly melting away, and there was an immediate demand for drastic and unpopular cuts in public spending. The genuine conflict of values anticipated with a decision on membership could thus be neutralized by (1) stating (somewhat prematurely) that the EC was not aiming at a common European defense policy (and therefore it would not

endanger Swedish neutrality) and (2) stating that EC membership would contribute to solving Sweden's economic problems. The second statement was
particularly remarkable, since the previous argument for joining the EEA
rather than the EC was that Sweden would thereby enjoy all the economic
benefits without paying any of the political costs. On Friday 26 October,
Sweden's formal declaration of its intent to become a member of the European Community was tucked away in a wide-ranging economic austerity
package, not quite literally as a footnote but certainly giving that impression,
considering the nature and importance of the matter. Subsequent inquiries
into the decision-making process all testify to the conscious efforts made to
absorb an apparent conflict of values and goals into a consensus-friendly conflict of means. EC membership was framed as simply a new and better way
toward economic growth and job creation. This also explains why the value
conflicts of EU membership were never allowed to play themselves out in the
Swedish referendum of 1994, and why a great many voters in Sweden were
made to believe that EC membership was indeed all about jobs, prices, and
growth, and not about a major political reorientation and a radical challenge
to the nation's self-image.

Just how powerful an urge for consensus still remained can be gauged
from the travails of Carl Bildt. In a memoir published in 1991,[58] Bildt claimed
that in 1987 he had already made up his mind on EC membership, but he
apparently forgot to tell his voters about it until the Spring of 1990. In the
meantime he had made public statements to the contrary. In July 1989 he still
publicly regarded neutrality as an obstacle to membership.[59] What would
have happened if he had dared to publicly voice his opinion in 1987? What
were the invisible pressures at work?

A deeply embedded institutional structure of national consensus can
probably not be dismantled without painful political sacrifices, and it therefore tends to remain in existence far beyond its political utility and democratic legitimacy. In the case of Sweden, the regime of consensus in the sphere
of foreign policy eventually had to involve a considerable amount of secret
diplomacy, closed-door negotiations, and political double standards, as well
as strong pressures for conformity. The extent of the political double standards practiced has recently been revealed by the release of new archive
material and reports. In 1994 the Public Commission on the Policy of Neutrality, *Neutralitetspolitik-kommissionen*, concluded that Prime Minister Tage
Erlander, in a speech to Riksdagen in 1959, had "consciously misrepre-
sented" important facts regarding Sweden's security policy, emphatically
denying that Sweden had ever taken part in "preparations or consultations"
regarding military cooperation with the West. The truth now seems to be that
there *was* secret planning of military coordination between Sweden and
NATO in the event of a war, including direct and close ties with U.S. military
agencies. In 1998 and 1999 Swedish radio and several leading newspapers

published detailed information on a number of fronts: on the planned use of Swedish airbases for Western security operations in the case of war, on secret plans (existing well into the 1980s) to evacuate the Swedish government to Britain in the case of war, on the fact that Sweden's ties to Western security planning were known to the Soviets (and that Sweden knew they were) and that therefore the only ones ultimately to be deceived by the official liturgy of neutrality were the Swedes themselves.

On the tight ship of neutrality, there appear to have been several decks to which most of the people, for the sake of their own good, were denied access, and where those who were let in had to conform to very strict rules of conduct and tacit limits of dissent. In hindsight one might even suspect that the "crime" of Jarl Hjalmarson in 1959 was not that he spoke without knowing the secret biases of Sweden's neutrality, but that he probably knew them all too well, and that he consciously wanted to tear open the veil of consensus on the nature and purpose of Sweden's policy of neutrality.

This veil of consensus, which for almost forty years blocked any real discussion on Sweden's neutrality, in my view also explains why no real discussion has yet taken place. "Neutrality," slightly reformulated, stubbornly remains a tenet of consensus in the political debate, devoid of all practical significance but enjoying a popular resonance that is hard to challenge. Under the institutional pressures of consensus, "neutrality" went from being a chosen position in Sweden's security and foreign policy to becoming a symbol of national identity and purpose. This symbolism is still strong enough to create a virtual political deadlock on issues where Sweden's identity is perceived to be at stake—and where genuine conflicts of value threaten to erupt. These conflicts involve Sweden's role in Europe (do we historically "belong" or not?), Sweden's membership in the EU (still not accepted by almost half the population), Sweden's participation in EMU (the Economic Monetary Union) (not yet supported by the very leaders who signed the Maastricht Treaty), Sweden's position vis-à-vis NATO and WEU (the Western European Union) (where political rhetoric and military practice remain far apart), and, more generally, Sweden's *Sonderweg* in world affairs, where the reflexes of neutralist activism have not yet been moderated by the realities of European collectivism. These are exactly the kinds of conflict purposefully avoided by the still entrenched institutions of consensus, which, not being designed to handle open and genuine conflicts of value, have created a *modus operandi* in Swedish politics where crucial policy choices and decisions are made to happen "by default," by the rule of "circumstances," by the "objectivity" of facts, rather than through open political conflict, deliberation, and choice. Sweden will decide to join the EMU when we *de facto* already have, and probably join NATO or a European defense order at the point when we are already fully militarily integrated.

Flip-flops, deadlocks, and the rule of "circumstances," and the conspicuous degree to which they characterize the current Swedish polity, are arguably the exceptional and debilitating effects of a long and exceptional rule of institutional consensus.

The Era of Battles

There have been a few significant instances in Sweden's postwar history where major conflicts of value could not be absorbed or suppressed by the traditional institutions of consensus. In these instances, the conflicts had to be dealt with outside the regular decision-making process, creating comparatively uncontrolled ad hoc "battles" (*strider*). The first was the battle on a public system of wage-related pensions, *ATP-striden,* in 1957, followed by battles on nuclear power and wage-earner funds in the 1970s and 1980s, and by the still raging battle on Europe in the 1990s. Some of these battles have led to popular referendums (an extra-ordinary institution in Swedish politics[60]). They have all featured frustrated political minorities trying to break out of the constraints of institutional consensus, and they have all contained elements of extraordinary drama and anomalous occurrences.

The battle on ATP (*allmän tilläggspension*) focused on the role of the state in organizing a supplementary wage-related pension scheme on top of an already existing but insufficient fixed-sum entitlement (*folkpension*). The apparent conflicts of value involved could not be contained at the negotiating tables of institutional consensus, and were soon formulated into three fiercely combative schemes. The Social Democrats and the Central Trade Union Organization (LO), argued for a mandatory collective system organized and guaranteed by the state. Their coalition partner in the government, the Peasants' Party (*bondeförbundet*) insisted on a wholly individual and voluntary system. The Liberals and the Conservatives, jointly with the Employers' Federation (SAF), proposed that a pension scheme should be worked out through central labor market negotiations.[61] This was a conflict that, in Bo Stråth's analysis of the campaign, pitted notions of "justice" and "security" against "personal unfreedom" and a "state quashing all initiative," a conflict about "important principles and visions."[62] It was a conflict where the strained routines of institutional consensus suddenly burst into a rare frenzy of value-laden attacks and counterattacks.

In her fascinating political diaries, Ulla Lindström, a Social Democratic minister at the time, is struck by the "un-Swedishness" of the parliamentary debate on 15 May 1957, when the terms of the upcoming referendum were discussed and voted on: "The flames of passions went high in a distinctly un-Swedish way. One could witness how Ohlin [the leader of *folkpartiet*] was unable to contain himself during Gunnar Hedlund's [leader of *bondeförbundet* and Minister for Domestic Affairs] intervention, and how arguments were thrown from pulpit to bench, as if in a shouting match between Per and Pål [figures of Swedish folklore] ... Hjalmarson [the leader of *högerpartiet*] on his part seemed half-choked from indignation during one of his 'rebuttals.'"[63] As the conflict escalated, the traditional mechanism of compromise and consensus broke down and the conflicting positions hardened rather than softened.[64] The political deadlock that ensued after the referendum, with the popular vote for the Social Democratic proposal but a parliamentary majority against it, led to extraordinary elections in June 1958, after which the parliamentary deadlock was nonetheless perpetuated. The battle on ATP lasted for three years and was finally decided in a dramatic parliamentary vote on 14 May 1959, with one single Liberal MP, the much castigated Ture Königson, breaking party ranks and thereby tipping the scales towards the Social Democrats.

I will not dwell on the reasons why the mechanisms of consensus did not hold firm in this instance.[65] It is enough to point out that when they finally gave way to a genuine conflict of values, the traditional institutions of consensus and conflict avoidance could neither handle nor control it. The course of the ensuing "battle" became far more antagonistic and unruly than would have been expected in the existing political culture, and the outcome was to a large extent decided by extra-institutional forces and events.

Ten years later another "battle" was fomenting: the battle on wage-earner funds (*löntagarfonder*). Although its outbreak can be dated to the mid 1970s, its roots may be traced to the dramatic upheavals in the Swedish labor market in the late 1960s, in particular the illegal miners' strike of December 1969. This led to increased agitation within the unions and the Social Democratic Party itself (not to mention the radical left), against the spirit of *Saltsjöbaden*, i.e., the symbol of institutional consensus. The consensus began to stand for the "selling out" of workers' interests to the benefit of capitalist profit. This was a period when the human costs of radical modernization and the growing pressures from foreign competition were being increasingly felt. It was a time too of increased use of piece rates and time measurement management, as well as pervasive demands for workers' mobility. [66] "Mobility for safety" (*Rörlighet för trygghet*) was actually adopted as the official policy of the LO, the central trade union, in a 1961 platform for economic policy described at the time as "the gospel of mobility."[67] A belief in radical modernization had by now become the core of institutional consensus in the sphere of economic development, backed by a stream of scientific and other authoritative reports testifying to its undisputed rationality.[68] What took place in the early years of the 1970s was, in fact, a breakdown of the authority and legitimacy of this seemingly value-free interpretation of rational economic action, and the beginnings of an open conflict of values regarding the nature and purpose of "the Swedish model."

What continues to puzzle students of the battle on wage-earner funds is the aggressive radicalism which it suddenly manifested. From being an issue well within the confines of institutional consensus—one actually pursued at the outset by the *folkpartiet* in an attempt to create a liberal link between Capital and Labor, with the Social Democrats and the LO as slightly indifferent but benevolent bystanders—it soon assumed all the characteristics of a Swedish *casus belli*. In 1975 Rudolf Meidner, a leading economist with the LO, proposed nothing less than a "thorough reformation of society" by making the trade unions owners of industrial capital through collective wage-earner funds: "We wish to deprive the old owners of capital of that power which comes with ownership. All experience shows that influence and control are not enough. Ownership plays a crucial role."[69] With bold value statements like this, Meidner and his co-writers set the tone for the battle to come.[70]

The system of institutional consensus had so far responded adequately to the challenge: a parliamentary commission, *Löntagarfondsutredningen*, stacked with representatives from every corner of the consensus apparatus, had been charged in January 1975 with the task of digging out "the facts" of the matter, smoothing out the differences and coming up with a broad consensus proposal on how to combine the "solidaristic wage policy" (whereby high earners forgo increases in favor of lower earners) with continued "high rates of capital formation." As usual, government directives were written with due conflict-avoiding finesse, and in fact in close collaboration between the Social Democratic government and the *Folkpartiet*. This time, however, it did not work. Hardened positions of value had already been allowed to crystallize outside the consensus system. Although the LO had been given a clear say in the formulation of the committee directives, it still continued to pursue its own separate line of inquiry. Meidner's report from 1975 was elevated from a mere "personal view" to the subject of a wide-ranging study campaign, and finally to the status of official document at the LO congress in September 1976. The LO leadership committed itself to its basic principle: the "democratization of ownership" through the transfer of industrial capital to collectively owned and controlled wage-earner funds. That this would also lead to a transfer of economic power—from an ever-smaller group of private capital owners to democratically-controlled institutions—was quite clearly stated.

This new position of the LO, reversing the existing consensus on the insignificance of ownership ("functional socialism"), or rather, on the benefits of a system where large private corporations worked closely together with a social democratic state, further emphasized the deep conflicts of value involved and thereby drastically narrowed future room for compromise and consensus. The rapidly evolving backyard shouting match between "Per and Pål" (LO and SAF) was soon making a lot more noise than the technical deliberations of the public committee, and political actors were pushed into positions they had not intended to take. The Social Democratic leadership in February 1978 made common cause with the LO and produced a report from which it later had to spend a lot of energy and political capital to extricate itself. SAF in the meantime developed a fierce anti-fund propaganda, using expressions like "trade union mafia," "a crime against human rights," "the demise of democracy," and "Sweden's grave." In the scholarly community the barricades went up as well, pitting one professor against another. Whatever rational "solutions" might have been concocted in the cool and secluded atmosphere of rational negotiations in a public committee or in the corridors of government and parliament, they were effectively undermined by the outbreak of an uncontrolled and "un-Swedish" public conflict of value.

The public commission on wage-earner funds dramatically failed to produce anything more than "a great number of expert studies and a meager final report" during six and a half years of work,[71] and eventually collapsed "with the kind of crash that had not been heard in the Swedish system of public commissions in several years."[72] The various members of the commission, according to its last chairman, Berndt Öhman, not only disagreed on how the given task should be interpreted, but also on what was actually to be investigated and what goals were to be achieved.[73] This was even more anomalous because the commission had been put together during a period of intensified consensus efforts in other areas of economic policy (symbolized by the consecutive deals at the castle of Haga outside Stockholm, between the Social Democrats and the Liberals), and because wage-earner funds were initially a liberal idea.[74] Berndt Öhman attempted in vain to infuse the conflict with a new rationality by trying to find an "objective" definition of democracy through a "matter-of-fact analysis" by a leading political scientist.[75] In the rising conflict about the scope and purpose of wage-earner funds, however, not only did the veil of common rationality rapidly disappear, but the actors were soon throwing the harshest invectives at one another and seriously questioning each other's motives. This eventually forced open a deep split within the labor movement itself, between political "realists" and trade union revolutionaries. The split is best conveyed by the self-derogatory rhyme scribbled on a piece of paper by Finance Minister Kjell-Olof Feldt during the final vote of the *Riksdagen* in December 1983 and picked up by an observant photographer's telescopic lens: "Löntagarfonder är ett jävla skit, men nu har vi baxat dom ända hit."[76]

In the early stages of the conflict a leading representative of the Employers' Federation, Erland Waldenström, could still characterize Rudolf Meidner's initial proposal as "interesting and thought-provoking," regardless of one's own "fundamental values,"[77] but the political climate for such conciliatory remarks and consensus-inviting overtures soon vanished. The public debate became increasingly emotional, and the spirit of confidence and consensus dissolved into an atmosphere of conspiracy and suspicion. Proponents of wage-earner funds were accused of planning a transfer of power that practically amounted to a coup d'état, drastically reducing the importance of democratic political institutions.[78] The wage-earner conflict culminated on 4 October 1983, with the first large-scale public rally of Swedish employers in recent history and an apparent breakdown in the corporatist apparatus of negotiation and consensus. Some of the active participants in the conflict later concluded that its diverging positions were truly irreconcilable, its ideological contradictions fundamental, and its scheme for consensus "stillborn."[79] Åsard still maintains that the system was never given a proper chance to prove itself, that conflicts of *value* (or, as Åsard prefers it, conflicts at the "systemic" level) were allowed to intensify beyond the point where they could be safely dealt with at the "reformistic" or "factual" level (*sakfrågenivån*), i.e., as conflicts of *means*. A system optimized for intimate face-to-face negotiations on *matters of fact* suddenly had to deal with a conflict where no such facts could be put in place. What originally seemed predestined to end in a grand compromise thus ended in "the toughest political confrontation of the postwar era." When a genuine conflict of value was eventually let out of control, even threatening the unity of the labor movement, the Swedish system simply fractured, exacerbating the conflict instead of contributing to its management. Bo Stråth concludes that the ultimate defeat of LO in the battle on wage-earner funds (the proposal finally voted on by Riksdagen in 1983 had little if anything in common with the visions of 1975 and 1978) would have lasting consequences for the organization, leaving "LO publicly disorientated and without a symbol."[80]

This disorientation and lack of a symbol would again become apparent ten years later in the conflict on EU membership, a "battle" that again demonstrated Sweden's difficulties in accepting and dealing with genuine conflicts of value. It left Swedish society with yet another political battle deadlocked by mutual resentment and suspicion. Instead of arriving at new symbols and positions evolved from an open conflict of values, obsolete positions were clung to in an increasingly futile (and inward-looking) attempt to restore the old terms of Social Democratic consensus. As Erik Ringmar has observed, the rhetorical battle over Swedish EU membership was not about whether to change Sweden's position and role in the world (and hence its self-perception) but about how to *preserve* the past: "The Swedes were in the end convinced to vote in favor since they believed that the membership would allow them to continue to be what they thought they had always been."[81]

I would argue that the continued symbolic value of "the Swedish Model" for important segments of the population (and for the corresponding institutional structure) has been a crucial and sometimes neglected factor in Sweden's comparative inability to tackle the societal and constitutional challenges of economic globalization and new technology. The difficulties in negotiating even minor labor market reforms, such as slightly liberalizing the terms of entry and exit, or modifying the wage structure (in order to tackle massive unemployment), seem to indicate that there is a high price to be paid for consensus lost. During state-sponsored central negotiations in the 1990s, recurrent attempts to revive consensus on wage formation and labor market regulations (starting in 1990 with the "Rehnberg commission") have gone practically nowhere.[82] The fact that during the same period countries like the Netherlands and Finland have managed to successfully retain and revive their political consensus seems to indicate that their systems have been less linked to a particular image of the nation, less imbued with a particular idea of the "good society," and more shaped by the pressing need to handle genuine conflicts of value (the Netherlands in particular being an openly multicultural society). The obvious result in any case is that these countries have been able to partially reinvent their social institutions and to negotiate new terms of a common understanding, while Sweden, so far, has not.

The Lesson of Nuclear Power

Perhaps the most instructive failure of Swedish institutions of consensus to absorb and suppress genuine conflicts of value concerns the use of nuclear power. An almost unanimous consensus during the 1950s and 1960s about the usefulness and urgency of nuclear power for energy production (complete with a local uranium supply and a uniquely Swedish reactor design based on heavy water) was ripped apart in the early 1970s by an emerging awareness of the short-term and long-term risks associated with the nuclear fuel cycle, and by new resentments and anxieties associated with increasingly complex, large-scale, and nontransparent technical systems. In 1973 the Center Party, led by the charismatic Thorbjörn Fälldin and guided by the renowned Swedish physicist and Nobel Laureate Hannes Alfvén, drastically reversed its position on nuclear power from an enthusiastic "Yes!" to a resounding "No!"

The controversy quickly permeated the Swedish political scene, where the Center Party and Mr. Fälldin had become instrumental in the opposition's efforts to put an end to almost half a century of continuous Social Democratic rule. They finally succeeded in 1976 when a non-socialist coalition of both pro- and antinuclear parties was formed, and huge efforts were immediately invested in trying to transform the dispute from a conflict of values into a controversy of facts—in which some ultimate fact would finally decide whether nuclear power was good or bad. Since this was obviously impossible, and since Mr. Fälldin had already stated that no government post would make him compromise with his own conscience, and since this to a great many people was a matter of conscience and not of fact, the first non-socialist majority government in Sweden's post-war history fell apart in 1978, while new nuclear reactors were still being constructed and charged with nuclear fuel. The ongoing attempts to find a factual formula that would disarm the conflict continued; new government commissions, new laws and regulations, all failed. The controversy on nuclear power was ultimately not about diverging facts but about diverging values. The way we produce our energy, its impact on the environment and society, and its uses and abuses can never be reduced to pure technical and economic calculations.

In March of 1980, in the wake of the accident at Three Mile Island, the nuclear issue was brought to a popular referendum—and again the genuine conflict of values involved was cunningly suppressed. Although three questions were eventually formulated, none of them openly argued *for* nuclear power. Instead, the Swedes were offered three choices on when and under what conditions to *end* the Swedish nuclear program. Those who in reality were in favor of an open-ended nuclear program (the Conservative Party and the organizations of Swedish industry) tactically concealed their true values in order to entice public opinion into supporting the existing nuclear program, and to better position themselves at the negotiating tables of institutional consensus. Swedish citizens who happened to believe that nuclear power was a collective good that ought to be sustained, further researched, and eventually expanded, were simply given no vote to cast. Not surprisingly, the referendum campaign became an exercise in Orwellian newspeak, where ending the nuclear program meant expanding it from six to twelve reactors, and where the "end" was subject to the "needs of employment and welfare," to the "lifetime" of existing reactors, and to the development of "alternative" sources of energy. This was also what the referendum eventually "decided."[83]

Sweden's nuclear controversy had thus been reduced to the gauging of welfare needs, the estimation of reactor lives, and the economic-scientific evaluation of energy alternatives. This implied that there existed a particular set of facts and measurements upon whose establishment disagreements would finally disappear and a rational energy policy reemerge under the old aegis of institutional consensus. The ensuing administrative lull, during which the issue practically disappeared from public debate (everybody being fed up with yet another committee report, fact or estimate), was dramatically interrupted by the disaster at Chernobyl in early 1986, which had a lasting environmental impact on a number of Swedish regions. Once again the value-based nature of the conflict became apparent, and demands for a beginning to the already decided abandonment of nuclear power became more pronounced.

I will not dwell on the ensuing political maneuvers to absorb and disarm the conflict; I shall only only point to the fact that the lines of battle again remained firmly drawn between contradictory sets of facts rather than between contradictory sets of values. Those who argued for a beginning of the end, i.e., a plan for decommissioning the first reactors, argued that the facts were on their side, that decommissioning would bring a boost to entrepreneurship, welfare, and employment. Those who were against argued that decommissioning amounted to an irrational destruction of capital, a recipe for unemployment, and a step back to the age of woodfire heating. This latter line of argument was pursued with particular vehemence by *Dagens Nyheter*, the liberal daily which in the campaign of 1980 had been a staunch proponent of rapid decommissioning (alternative 3), but which in the 1990s radically reversed its position. The debate became particularly heated in the spring of 1997 (seventeen years after the referendum), when the Social Democratic government with the support of the Center Party, declared its intention to close down the first nuclear reactor at Barsebäck. *Dagens Nyheter* basically argued that methods of energy production were a purely technical and economic matter, better decided by relevant experts than by ignorant and populist politicians. "One cannot vote on the physical and chemical properties of matter," stated one characteristic editorial (5 February 1997), implying that the decision to close Barsebäck was based on pure factual ignorance. A similar line of reasoning led Mats Svegfors, editor-in-chief of *Svenska Dagbladet*, to conclude (in a signed editorial) that Göran Persson, the Swedish Prime Minister, by his decision had come "to personify to the whole world the image of fully developed political stupidity" (21 January 1997). Another editorial in *Dagens Nyheter* (10 January 1997) again stressed the distinction between the factual basis of the anti-decommission position and the ideological bias of all others: "On one side there is a group which sees energy production as rather a philosophical or ideological matter, permeated by the idea that the use of nuclear energy is irreconcilable with a responsible human handling of our earthly heritage. On the other side there is a group which does not see nuclear energy as a great risk, but on the contrary believes that nuclear energy is preferable not only to fossil fuels but also to bio fuels."

The conspicuous fact that the editorial does not attach any "ideological" or "philosophical" values to the pro-nuclear position, assuming it to be purely factual in character, testifies to the entrenched mechanisms by which genuine conflicts of value tend to be transformed into never-ending disputes of facts. And, in this case, it also testifies to the dramatic failure of these mechanisms to even temporarily confront and resolve one of Sweden's most prolonged and painful postwar political conflicts. A recent pamphlet by two Swedish scholars attests to the continued influence of a tradition in which consensus is regarded as a matter of fact. The whole matter is very "simple and self-evident," they write. The only thing that needs to be debated is the future energy supply of Sweden in a global perspective. "In such a perspective the issue of nuclear power becomes a secondary one."[84] What they thereby seem to indicate is that "in such a perspective" the mushy values of the antinuclear stance will succumb to the hard facts of energy supply and demand, the treacherous play of politics will give way to the unambiguous recommendations of scientific experts, and the tradition of rational consensus will finally be restored.

Wars of History

Sweden's culture of consensus is a problematic one, not because it has been weakened and compromised in recent years, but because it remains a part of the Swedish national identity. A culture of consensus can be pragmatic, aiming at handling and resolving recurrent conflicts, and it can be ideological, aiming at doing away with conflicts as such. The current Swedish model of consensus has arguably been of the latter kind, decisively molded in the ideological fervor of the 1930s, when society was reconstructed as a People's Home based on a corporatist model of negotiations and rational (value-free) collective action. Swedish consensus was about finding the "right, factual solution to conflict, not about finding a temporary *modus vivendi* between conflicting values and interests. Few nations define themselves by their genius for consensus and rational action. Sweden to some extent did. The current crisis of consensus in Swedish society is thus less a crisis in the system of organized decision-making (which it undoubtedly also is) than it is a crisis in the national soul. Those who yearn for a return to the Swedish model yearn not only for a return to a previous order of encompassing collective action and decision-making and the "strong government" associated with it, but also for a lost sense of national purpose.

Swedish institutions of consensus cannot be easily replaced, which is why they are still standing, however debilitated and defunct. To devise new institutions and new modes of decision-making, taking into account the reality and the multitude of genuine conflicts of value, will demand no less than a redefinition of what Sweden "is all about." It will call for new historical "foundations" to take the place of *folkhemmet*, the now moribund core of Sweden's postwar identity and the Social Democratic hegemony associated with it. I believe that this process is already taking place in the sphere of Swedish historiography, where a number of "history wars" are now being waged. Long dominant versions of the origins of the Swedish model, of Sweden's social progress during the 1930s, of Sweden's policy of neutrality during the Second World War and the Cold War, have all been severely challenged. The clear-cut image of Sweden as a uniquely monocultural and hegemonic society with few or no real conflicts of value has been interestingly complicated by renewed inquiries into Sweden's hegemonistic policies towards ethnic minorities (*sami*, "tattare", gypsies) and its zealous policies of sterilization towards the "socially unfit."[85] In a similar way, the image of Sweden's policy of neutrality as morally unquestionable and meticulously implemented has been seriously undermined by findings of shady dealings during World War II, secret security arrangements during the Cold War and dubious double standards in the global business of arms trade.

I happen to believe that at the heart of these history wars lies one major conflict of value: between the still mighty appeal of a separate Swedish destiny based on a strong nation-state, wide-ranging state welfare, international neutralism, and institutional consensus, and the increasing push for a new and more "European" foundation based on concepts of subsidiarity, civil society, human rights, cultural pluralism, and conflict-handling. The idea of a Swedish separate destiny was once–and not too long ago–a uniquely powerful and successful one, and it is hard to see how this conflict can be resolved or even modestly handled without a major crisis in an institutional framework that still largely embodies that special destiny, i.e., operates under the assumption that conflicts of value can be transformed into conflicts of facts, and cannot therefore handle a conflict where deeply diverging values about the good society are pitted against each other. A tradition that does not allow for "irresolvable" conflicts of value, but assumes that one or the other side is not enlightened enough, will have difficulties in finding that precious *modus vivendi* in which conflicting values can communicate, coexist, and mutually evolve.

Like every modern pluralist society, what Sweden needs is not a tradition of institutional consensus but an institutionalized culture of conflict and diversity. Such a culture regards genuine conflicts of value as the most basic fact of modern life and society, and will thus endeavor to create institutions where such conflicts are recognized, confronted, and constitutionally regulated. In such a culture, social conflicts must not be shunned or avoided but must be seen instead as potential sources of human energy and creativity. The art of creating a decent society without resorting to high levels of cultural cohesion and political consensus is certainly a most difficult and challenging one. One could even say that if there were a *decent* way back to the era of *folkhemmet* it might have been preferable. Pluralism is always more complicated than homogeneity. But the way back to consensus and homogeneity from pluralism and diversity is most likely not a decent one at all, for it is prone to involve an all too familiar scenario of violence, exclusion, and coercion. A culture of conflict and diversity is perhaps a demanding way of life but–to paraphrase Churchill–all the others are probably worse.

The gist of this essay has been that some societies might have an easier transition to a culture of pluralism and diversity than others, and that Sweden will have greater difficulties than most. The main reason for this is the still existing link between Sweden's increasingly dysfunctional tradition of institutional consensus and Sweden's seemingly irreplaceable national mythology. The Swedish transition cannot be merely constitutional or organizational in nature; it will probably have to involve a painful break with past national beliefs and myths. This will not be made easier by the mental and cultural tradition of individual conflict avoidance that made Susan Sontag locate the early problems of the Swedish model not in its welfare institutions but in "a national temperament" going back to "centuries ago" and amounting to "a collective historical tradition of emotional disablement."[86]

If Susan Sontag is only half right, and I believe she is, then a transformation of Sweden's culture of consensus will have to involve a deep change in the way individual Swedes emotionally relate to a world where genuine conflict of value is an inescapable part of social life.

Notes

1. Åke Daun, *Svensk mentalitet, ett jämförande perspektiv* (Stockholm, 1989, third revised ed. 1998), 102 ff.
2. Emil Uddhammar, *Partierna och den stora staten, en analys av statsteorier och svensk politik under 1900-talet* (Stockholm: City University Press, 1993), 473.
3. Daun, *Svensk mentalitet*, 102.
4. Billy Ehn, *Ska vi leka tiger? Daghemsliv ur kulturell synvinkel* (Lund: Liber förlag, 1983), 145.
5. *Ramparts*, July 1969, 26.
6. This was perhaps the most remarkable case of military insubordination in the postwar era, and of political distrust in the military establishment. "I cannot recall such an open conflict between a minister and a chief-of-staff during the postwar era," stated professor Ulf Bjereld in *Göteborgs-Posten*, 6 December 1998.
7. *Arbetet Nyheterna*, 4 December 1998.
8. *Svenska Dagbladet*, 10 December 1998.
9. In the fall of 1995, Vice Prime Minister Mona Sahlin, a strong candidate at the time to succeed Ingvar Carlsson as leader of the Social Democratic party and Prime Minister, was forced to resign from the government when accusations to this effect were floated in the media. In the fall of 1998 she reentered the government, as did Björn Rosengren, the former chairman of TCO (the white-collar union), who had had to resign his job after being found visiting a strip-tease club in Stockholm.
10. In 1988, Minister of Justice Anna-Greta Leijon had to resign in the face of evidence that she had used her office in support of a private secret investigation into the murder of Olof Palme.
11. The "Ahlenius affair," involving among other things the publication of "private" letters between a top minister and a top civil servant and the playing of false phone messages in public, is an example of a principled conflict of value degenerating into an unprincipled and anomalous media scandal or "affair" due to the inability of existing institutions to handle such conflicts.
12. Nina Witoszek, "The Fugitives from Utopia," in Øystein Sørensen and Bo Stråth (eds.) *The Cultural Construction of Norden* (Oslo: Scandinavian University Press, 1997), 81.
13. Ibid., 85-86.
14. "The Rational Humanitarians," originally in *Daedalus*, vol. 113, no. 1, 1984, republished in Hans Zetterberg, *Selected Writings* (Stockholm: City University Press, 1997), 329
15. Ibid., 328.
16. Herbert Tingsten, *Demokratins problem* (Stockholm: Aldus/Bonnier, 1971).
17. Zetterberg, "The Rational Humanitarians," 328.
18. "Oscarian" refers to the period that coincided with the reign of Oscar II, 1872-1907.
19. See Nils Runeby's study, *Monarchia mixta: maktfördelningsdebatt i Sverige under den tidigare stormaktstiden* (Uppsala: Studia Historica Upsaliensia, 1962).
20. Eva Österberg, *Folk förr. Historiska essäer* (Atlantis, 1995), 192-194.
21. Leif Lewin, *Bråka inte! Om vår tids demokratisyn* (Stockholm: SNS, 1998).
22. Pontus Fahlbeck, *Engelsk parlamentarism contra svensk* (Stockholm: Gleerups, 1916), 45, 84, quoted in Lewin, *Bråka inte!*.
23. Lewin, *Bråka inte!*, 13, quoting Carl Hallendorff, "Parlamentarismen", *Svensk Tidskrift*, 1911.
24. Ibid., 14.
25. Uddhammar, *Partierna och den stora staten*, 432.
26. Bo Rothstein, *Den korporativa staten, intresseorganisationer och statsförvaltning i svensk politik* (Stockholm: Norstedts, 1992), 118-119. The "formative moment" (Rothstein) was the decision to put the power of the state in the hands of a private institution, the organization of farmers, legislating their right to intervene against unorganized milk producers, to control and regulate the milk market.
27. Uddhammar, *Partierna och den stora staten*, 432-433.
28. Alf W. Johansson *War Experience, Self Image and National Identity: The Second World War as Myth and History* (Stockholm: Gidlunds, 1997), 170.

29. Ibid., 172.
30. Sven-Erik Larsson, *Bertil Ohlin* (Atlantis, 1998), 182ff.
31. Heclo and Madsen, *Policy and Politics in Sweden: Principled Pragmatism* (Philadelphia: Temple University Press, 1987), 21.
32. Thomas Anton, *Administered Politics: Elite Political Cultures in Sweden* (Boston, 1980).
33. Heclo and Madsen, *Policy and Politics in Sweden*, 21.
34. Ibid., 324.
35. These ideals are enumerated in a recent public inquiry about administrative policies, "I medborgarens tjänst. En samlad förvaltningspolitik för staten," Förvaltningspolitiska kommissionen (Stockholm: SOU 1997: 57), 18.
36. Maktutredningen, *Demokrati och makt i Sverige* (Stockholm: Allmänna förlaget, 1990), 186 ff.; Jan Johansson, "Det statliga kommittéväsendet, kunskap, kontroll, konsensus", 1992; "Kommittéerna och bofinken. Kan en kommitté se ut hur som helst?", ESO rapport, Ds 1998, 57, 19 ff.
37. "Kommittéerna och bofinken," 98-99.
38. The difference between a commission and a committee is not fully clear, but the increased use of commissions instead of committees is probably another indication of the decreased status and authority of the public committees.
39. Stockholm: SOU 1997: 57, 99.
40. In popular language a drink you take in the morning to *restore* (*återställa*) yourself from effects of the drinks you had last night. In modern Swedish politics, the decision by a new power constellation to restore legislation to its *status ante*.
41. Bo Rothstein, Lena Sommestad and Lotta Westerhäll, "The Decline of the Strong State," Project description for the Bank of Sweden Tercentenary Foundation, reg. no. 1998-5125-01.
42. Lars Anell, "Världsordningen och välfärdsstatens kris", Sekretariatet för framtidsstudier, 1979. For further discussion of the end of the Swedish model, see Göran Rosenberg, *Medborgaren som försvann* (Stockholm: Brombergs, 1993), 34-36.
43. *The Economist*, 23 January 1999 (the issue contains a survey of Nordic countries).
44. *The Economist*, 17 July 1999, excerpting a comparative study by Robert Putnam, Susan Farr and Russell Dalton, *What Is Troubling the Trilateral Democracies?* (Princeton: Princeton University Press, 2000).
45. Johansson, 178.
46. On 13 June 1952 a Swedish military aircraft, a DC 3 with a crew of eight men, disappeared over the Baltic Sea. Three days later a smaller Catalina in search for survivors was shot down by Soviet Mig fighters, creating an acute crisis in Swedish-Soviet relations. In the 1990s, with material from Soviet archives, it has been confirmed that the DC 3 was shot down as well.
47. Östen Undén, 7 March 1956, quoted in Ulf Bjereld, *Hjalmarsonaffären, ett politiskt drama i tre akter* (Nerenius & Santerus, 1997), 11.
48. Quoted in Bjereld, *Hjalmarsonaffären*, 11.
49. Ibid., 114.
50. Ibid., 125ff.
51. Ibid., 149.
52. Ibid., 133.
53. In February 1985, following yet another round of anomalous accusations of endangering Sweden's security, running the errands of that or the other superpower, this author commented on the destructive pattern in foreign policy debate in an open article in *Expressen* (13 February 1985): "While there is a clear need to openly express different opinions about means and methods in Swedish foreign and security policy, there is at the same time a seemingly unavoidable logic which transforms every attempt at such a debate into a conflict of ultimate goals. The temptation to hit the means with the goals seems almost irresistible. The practical consequences are that the government in power is not only charged with representing the goals of Swedish foreign and security policy but is also maintaining a *de facto* monopoly on the formulation of its means."

54. Some scholars have argued that the Swedish Foreign Ministry, in responding to the diversification of the Swedish foreign policy agenda in the 1960s, concentrated on protecting its role as the ultimate authority on the tenets of neutrality: "By claiming to possess unique knowledge on the outer limits of this policy, the Foreign Ministry could successfully defend its position and carve out a role as 'gatekeeper' in Swedish foreign policy." Jakob Gustavsson, *The Politics of Foreign Policy Change, Explaining the Swedish Reorientation on EC Membership* (Lund: Lund University Press, 1998), 91.
55. Kjell Goldmann, "Trovärdighetskravet – onödigt och omöjligt?" *Internationella studier,* no 3, 1973, 97-101.
56. An arrangement that would allow for non-member EFTA-countries to join the inner market of the EC.
57. Congress protocols from September 18, 1990, quoted in Gustavsson, *The Politics of Foreign Policy Change,* 177.
58. Carl Bildt, *Hallänning, svensk, europé* (Stockholm: Bonniers 1991).
59. *Svenska Dagbladet,* 15 July 1989.
60. Only two "advisory" referendums had preceded the ATP referendum in 1957, one in 1922 on the banning of alcohol and one in 1955 on going from lefthand-side to righthand-side traffic. Neither of the results (no to alcohol, yes to righthand-side traffic) was heeded.
61. The fact that the more liberal proposal came from the generally corporatist Peasants' Party, while the ideologically more committed liberals proposed a more corporatist solution, perhaps testifies to the distorting effects of institutional consensus.
62. Bo Stråth, *Mellan två fonder. LO och den svenska modellen* (Atlas, 1998), 56-57, 67.
63. Ulla Lindström, *I regeringen. Ur min politiska dagbok 1954-1959* (Stockholm: Tiden, 1969), 155.
64. Stråth, *Mellan två fonder,* 59.
65. Stråth seems to regard the ATP battle as an attempt by the non-socialist opposition to wrest the "privilege of formulation" [of the tenets of consensus], from the Social Democrats. Their failure to do so in fact firmly established the Social Democratic values as the basis for continued consensus, while conflicting values, like the conservative ideal of small private ownership, were excluded. Stråth, *Mellan två fonder,* 64.
66. Rosenberg, *Medborgaren som försvann,* 20ff.
67. Stråth, *Mellan två fonder,* 75. The report was called *Samordnad näringspolitik,* "coordinated industrial policy," and was written by, among others, Rudolf Meidner, later the father of the wage-earner fund proposal of 1975, the *casus belli* of the ensuing "battle" on *löntagarfonder.*
68. Stråth, *Mellan två fonder,* 78.
69. Rudolf Meidner in the official organ of LO, *Fackföreningsrörelsen,* 1975, 19, 17.
70. Rudolf Meidner, Anna Hedborg, and Gunnar Fond, *Löntagarfonder* (Stockholm: Tiden, 1975).
71. Erik Åsard, *Kampen om löntagarfonderna. Fondutredningen från samtal till sammanbrott* (Stockholm: Norstedts, 1985), 19.
72. Ibid., 140.
73. Berndt Öhman, *Om löntagarfondsfrågan och fondutredningen,* Högskolan i Örebro, Skriftserie 26, 1983, 8.
74. The deals at Haga, *Hagauppgörelserna,* the first in the spring of 1974, came about as a consequence of the election results of 1973, when the two political "blocs" in parliament got 50 percent of the mandates each, and blocsplitting proposals had to be decided by ballot.
75. Stråth, *Mellan två fonder,* 162-163.
76. In free translation, "Wage-earner funds are a bloody bill, that we now have carried to the mill."
77. *Fackföreningsrörelsen,* 1975, 27, quoted in Åsard, *Kampen om Löntagarfonderna,* 1985, 103.
78. See, for instance, the pamhlet "Att taga över makten," written by three prominent opponents, Östen Bohlin, Assar Lindbeck, and Erik Anners, 19.
79. Åsard, *Kampen om löntagarfonderna,* 145.
80. Stråth, *Mellan två fonder,* 206.

81. Erik Ringmar, "Re-imagining Sweden, The Rhetorical Battle over EU-membership," *Scandinavian Journal of History*, vol. 23, 47.

82. The story of Sweden's failed corporatist negotiations is well told by Tommy Öberg, *Svenska Dagbladet*, 21 March 1999.

83. Two alternatives (1 and 2) proposing that Sweden at some point phase out the nuclear energy produced by a maximum of twelve reactors, jointly gained 57.8 percent of the vote. Number 3, proposing a rapid shutdown of the six reactors in use at the time, gained a vote of 38.7 percent.

84. Folke Johansson and Jörgen Westerståhl, *Kärnkraftsavvecklingen – ett politiskt haveri* (Stockholm: SNS, 1998), 30.

85. Among recent studies see Maija Runcis, *Steriliseringar i folkhemmet* (Stockholm: Ordfront, 1998); Gunnar Broberg & Mattias Tydén, *Oönskade i folkhemmet, rashygien och sterilisering i Sverige* (Stockholm: Gidlund, 1991); Ingvar Svanberg and Mattias Tydén, *Sverige och förintelsen, debatt och dokument om Europas judar 1933-1945* (Stockholm: Arena, 1997).

86. *Ramparts*, July 1969, 38.

11

Political Modernity's Critical Juncture in the Course of the French Revolution

ROBERT WOKLER

The remarks that follow trade upon the notion of profound discontinuity in crisis. To be at a critical juncture in one's life is to undergo, or confront the prospect of, momentous change, sometimes termed a climacteric. It is to experience, or to be at the threshold of, a medical, emotional, or professional transformation. In its military, clinical, or theological senses, as Reinhart Koselleck illustrates here, crises characteristically denote rites of passage by way of a decisive battle, a crucial enactment, a struggle of life and death, a last judgment. Nations and societies also undergo occasional crises, which in their most striking forms mark their disintegration or even their obliteration as communities. When a whole civilization suffers such a fate, a historical epoch may be said to have ended, on the analogy, in human history, of the greatest cataclysms of geological time.

This collection addresses images and perceptions of crisis with respect to the civic identities of two cultures, with profoundly disparate traditions but interconnected national histories, whose integration within the European Community has bound them together in a coalescence of divergent paths. By way of contrasts that nevertheless overlap, Sweden and Germany each encapsulate what might be termed Europe's legitimation crisis, its collective catharsis in pursuit of a communitarian goal approached along different routes and from different perspectives. Several authors focus on ways in which the Swedish and German models of modernity constitute alternative trajectories of the age of Enlightenment and its legacy, particularly with respect to eighteenth-century notions of instrumental reason as manifested in contemporary programs of social engineering and ideals of national identity in democratic states. My own main objective here will be to contextualize such notions of a project of modernity within the age of the Enlightenment itself, and with respect to the first great crisis of contemporary civilization which that project is alleged to have inspired, that is, the French Revolution.

When insurance companies pretend to their customers that they really have a soul, they sometimes claim that it is not their wish to make a drama out of a crisis. Historians almost always do just that, and those with talent often owe their success and their renown to that achievement. They make wonderful dramas out of crises. Leaving aside for a moment the towering significance of Koselleck's *Kritik und Krise*, dating from 1959, Let me note the popularity of works such as E. H. Carr's *The Twenty Years' Crisis*, produced, as it happens, two decades earlier, or Lawrence Stone's *The Crisis of the Aristocracy* of 1965, or, on a slightly more modest scale, George Mosse's *The Crisis of German Ideology* of the following year. For my purposes here in addressing the subject of the Enlightenment and modernity, perhaps the seminal work has been *La crise de la conscience européenne,* first published in 1935 by a man who, as only certain Frenchmen can, achieved immortality in his own lifetime by virtue of his membership of the Académie Française, that is, Paul Hazard. *La crise de la conscience européenne* is a work that is centrally addressed to the conceptual foundations of modernity in the light of the transfigurations of European philosophy, science, art, and other subjects in a concentrated period at the end of the seventeenth century and at the beginning of the eighteenth century, from around 1680 to 1715. It deals with the ferment of social thought that, according to Hazard, heralded the demise of an old order. It signals the collapse of a world of permanence and stability, speedily overturned by another in which change and movement are preferred instead. It marks the disintegration of the hegemony of Christian civilization and the rise in its place of skepticism, science, and the pursuit, not of eternal salvation, but of worldly happiness.[1] It defines the passage of the European mind from the age of classicism to the age of modernity within which, for the most part, we still reside.

Unfortunately, Hazard's thesis has failed to persuade a good many students of the same subject, who decline to trace the conceptual underpinnings of modernity to the end of the seventeenth century. In perhaps the most notable among postmodernist readings of the intellectual origins of our civilization, Michel Foucault has instead traced the epistemic break between *l'âge classique* and *l'âge moderne* to the end of the eighteenth century, and particularly to its last decade, when, as he claims in *Les mots et les choses*, the human sciences in their specifically modern form came to be invented. Around the pivotal year of 1795, he argues, biology, linguistics, and economics were transfigured from the investigation of outward signs into the deep structural study of underlying causes by which we currently recognize these disciplines and in the light of which we have come to treat them as genuinely scientific subjects for only the past two hundred years.[2] Even among commentators who have not been swayed by Foucault, the 1790s have gained a certain stature as a preeminent age of crisis of the European mind, in so far as that decade, dominated at least in French thought by the *idéologues*, is seen as having given rise to a new political culture, to new scientific institutions, and to the new vocabularies of modernity–including, for the first time in any European language, such initially French terms as *idéologie, science sociale, démocrate, révolutionnaire,* and *terroriste.*

To Koselleck and his associates in their production of the *Geschichtliche Grundbegriffe,* however much he has come to deplore the too-generalized significance of a word and concept largely manufactured by him, we owe what seems to me a richer and more plausible idea of the *Sattelzeit* of modernity than can be found in the work of either Hazard or Foucault. I make this claim partly because his period of the great transition to the modern world– that is, from roughly 1750 to 1850–encompasses around one hundred years rather than just thirty, as for Hazard, or ten, as for Foucault, but mainly because it embraces German intellectual history as well as French thought, because it addresses the social context of the transformation of the meanings of ideas in a manner overlooked by both Hazard and Foucault, and because it offers a more politicized interpretation of the foundations of modernity than can be found in their readings of philosophical and scientific texts, allowing, among other things, a far greater emphasis upon the contribution of the French Revolution.

I mean here to focus on certain developments within the French Revolution, but let me begin by noting that in passing from the crisis of modernity offered by Hazard to that provided by Foucault, we find ourselves squarely in the age of the European Enlightenment. Whether we take the Enlightenment to have been launched by Locke's *Essay Concerning Human Understanding* and completed by Condorcet's *Esquisse d'un tableau des progrès de l'esprit humain* or, alternatively, inaugurated by the Revocation of the Edict of Nantes in 1685 and completed by the *Déclaration des droits de l'homme* of 1789, our conception of the Enlightenment embraces just that century of the European mind that lies between Hazard and Foucault. It is by way of our perceptions of this intellectual movement and the French Revolution which it allegedly spawned that so many of our leading social theorists of the twentieth century have come to identify the most fundamental crises of modernity itself.

I intend to explain why I hold such claims to be fundamentally mistaken. Of course I can hardly deny that certain principles of the European Enlightenment inspired many of the ideals, as well as much of the symbolic language, of the French Revolutionaries in their denunciation of an aristocratic *ancien régime* and their republican embrace of the natural and civil rights of man. But I propose to show that in the political self-realization of its own project, if I may so describe it, the French Revolution broke away from its umbilical cord and—at the very moment of its inception, from which the age of modernity that we inhabit remains profoundly scarred—embarked on what Eric Santner, speaking of Freud with respect to Moses and the Jews, describes as the primal parricide of the collective birth of a new people. What I shall endeavor to illustrate is the manner in which the French Revolution, through its creation of the first genuinely modern nation-state in human history, actually killed the Enlightenment Project from whose loins it sprang.[3]

Readers of this collection hardly need reminding that seminal artists, writers, and scientists of virtually every epoch in modern civilization imagine that they are at a critical juncture of human history, at the threshold of a profoundly changed world that their undertakings herald or illuminate. With respect to the period from around 1750 to 1850, which Koselleck has offered to us as the *Sattelzeit* of modernity, we might note that it marks the first appearances in its modern form of the term *civilization* itself, and the first use in any form of the word *perfectibilité*, which would come to encapsulate the central meaning of so many eighteenth- and nineteenth-century theories of human progress. We might even note those two great monuments of human enterprise, outside the German-speaking world, that give form and substance to some of the most centrally dynamic forces of the period: at the end of it the Crystal Palace, which celebrated an age of industry and invention, and at the beginning the *Encyclopédie*, a kind of crystal palace of the human mind, celebrating similar industry and invention by way of the circulation of ideas among a public eager to consume them, newly enfranchised through the explosive spread of literacy in the course of the eighteenth century. Somewhere near the source of that *Sattelzeit* of modernity, we ought perhaps to place special emphasis upon the remarks made by Rousseau in 1762 in the text and a footnote of *Emile*: "We are approaching a state of crisis and the century of revolutions." "It is impossible that the great monarchies of Europe have long to survive."[4] Koselleck must somehow have asked Rousseau to write an introduction to his *Lexicon* more than two hundred years before it was published, since he could have hoped for nothing more appropriate than these lines.

As if to lend authority to modern social theorists who would come to attribute that state of crisis and the century of revolutions it inaugurated to the influence of his own doctrines, Rousseau also claims in his *Confessions* that the publication of his own *Lettre sur la musique française* in November 1753 had averted an imminent uprising against the state by provoking a popular insurrection against him alone: "The [Paris] *Parlement* had just been exiled," he reflects. "The fermentation was at its height. ... My work appeared; all at once every other dispute was forgotten ... and the sole uprising that occurred took place against me. So great was the reaction that the nation never recovered from it. Thus, whoever reads that my brochure may have prevented the outbreak of a revolution in the state will imagine himself in a dream. Nevertheless, that is exactly what happened."[5]

In commenting on the spark ignited by Rousseau's work on music, d'Alembert later claimed that it had grown into a conflagration fanned by other *philosophes* who had come to be perceived as members of a society covenanted to destroy Religion, Authority, Morality, and Music all at once.[6] Rousseau was at the head of a seditious party, in effect, for the first time in his life, regarded as a threat to the French nation. Ten years later, in drafting his *Neveu de Rameau*, Diderot remarked that the mid-eighteenth century revolution of French musical taste, known as the *Querelle des Bouffons* and encapsulated by Rousseau's work, comprised a leavening transplant that fermented an alternative culture;[7] while in 1807, just as the World-Spirit of modernity itself–that is, Napoleon Bonaparte–was laying siege to Jena, Hegel intercalated this very passage, as well as some others, drawn from Goethe's translation of the *Neveu de Rameau* long before Diderot's work ever appeared in French, within his own *Phänomenologie des Geistes*.[8] The very terms employed by Hegel as the rubric of the section of his *Phänomenologie* in which he incorporates Diderot's text, *Der sich entfremdete Geist*, had figured as Goethe's own translation from Diderot's *aliénation d'esprit*, invoked to characterize the condition of Rameau's nephew at the most dramatic moment of the dialogue in which he pantomimes the fresh ascendancy of Italian over French operatic arias. Here was the lacerated consciousness, the *zerissenes Bewußtsein*, of modernity itself.

By way of a crisis that embraced French music and politics together, an incendiary text by Rousseau thus appears to have illuminated a cultural revolution of the Enlightenment in the early 1750s that presaged the Revolution of 1789 allegedly inspired by the principles of his *Contrat social*. As Hegel himself plainly recognized, the owl of Minerva settles not only at dusk but sometimes in the twilight that precedes it. How else shall we explain that the expression, *Qu'ils mangent de la brioche*, never uttered by Marie Antoinette, can be found in Rousseau's *Confessions*?[9]

The political ideals embraced in the *Contrat social* would later earn for Rousseau his title of chief prophet or first legislator of a regenerated France, accorded to him, for instance, by Louis-Sébastien Mercier in his *Rousseau, considéré comme l'un des premiers auteurs de la Révolution of 1791*. Rousseau's portrayals in his *Contrat social* and elsewhere of an allegedly fraternal and collectivist past that mankind has lost–in effect, his images of Sparta or *Roma redivivus*–were also to give rise to the charge, made against him by Mme. de Staël and other liberals who followed her, that Rousseau "n'a rien découvert, mais il a tout enflammé,"[10] the passions, the senses, the Terror. To such critics of his philosophy, the liberty that French citizens managed to gain after 1789, insofar as they appear to have been inspired by him, might entail as well that they be put to death for refusing to obey the general will or, as Bonaparte imagined, the general's will. It would be claimed that in the course of the French Revolution, Rousseau's principles of *liberté*, *égalité*, and *fraternité* as allegedly realized in one nation, *une et indivisible*, came to be unsheathed as totalitarian violence, his ideals thus forming the springtide of modernity's, and especially the twentieth century's, cascading flood of barbarism committed in the name of public order and virtue.

That scenario seems to me altogether false, since neither Rousseauism nor whatever else might be taken to be the kernel of the Enlightenment Project ever triumphed in the course of the French Revolution. The invention of the nation-state, which marks the advent of modernity in its still currently predominant political form, cannot, to my mind, be traced either to Rousseau's philosophy or to the doctrines of his most illustrious contemporaries. As Hegel explains, again in his *Phänomenologie* in the abstract language he there employs, the real political crisis of the modern age began on 17 June 1789 with the establishment of the French National Assembly, plucked by cæsarean section from the womb of the Old Society. Setting aside Koselleck's *Sattelzeit* of one hundred years, and Hazard's *Crise de la conscience européenne* of thirty-five years, and Foucault's epistemic break of a decade or even just one year, I mean in the next section to concentrate upon the most fundamental crisis of the modern world, including our own age, from the moment of its explosive birth, or advent in a single day at the dawn of our creation—from which I suppose it follows that between 17 June 1789 and the Fall of the Bastille on 14 July, Western civilization, or the European mind, can have enjoyed only four weeks of innocence.

However much embraced by some of his admirers after 1789, in the course of the Enlightenment itself Rousseau's and other contemporary images of ancient republican Rome failed to overcome the predilection of most eighteenth-century *philosophes* for politically benign regimes of *enlightened absolutism* or even *enlightened despotism*, itself an expression that first appears in the late eighteenth century and may have been invented by Diderot.[11] Few of Rousseau's illustrious contemporaries, moreover, agreed with his contention that the citizens of ancient Sparta and Rome had enjoyed greater liberty than could be achieved in the commercial societies of the modern world. The *philosophes* of the eighteenth century were more characteristically attached to that ideal in terms of the liberty of conscience, the freedom of worship, and the freedom of contract and trade that had come from the North, as Montesquieu, anticipating the most famous thesis of Max Weber, made so plain in his *Esprit des lois*. Here, in complete contrast with Rousseau, he argued for the Germanic, and mainly Protestant, sources of freedom as against Mediterranean and Catholic despotism. Rousseau's ideals, we ought not to forget, would in many respects be better described as constituting an anti-Enlightenment, largely anti-progressive philosophy than as the vanguard of modern radicalism.

Other leading figures of the age of Enlightenment may have shared his admiration for the ebullient simplicity of Italian music as an alternative to the baroque and gothic decadence prevalent in France, but with respect to freedom, they drew more inspiration from modern Switzerland, Scotland, the Netherlands, and England than from classical Rome. The central idiom in which they articulated their attachment to liberty was couched in the language of toleration rather than of fraternity or solidarity, and while Rousseau's political principles may be deemed more communitarian than those of most *philosophes,* he was no less wedded to a belief in toleration than were Montesquieu, Voltaire, or Diderot. By and large, progressive thinkers of the eighteenth century believed that mankind's advance was best promoted by a multiplicity of religions, each practiced at home, rather than by the public celebration of one great civil religion that drew all subjects together.

The classic statement of their idea of freedom can be found in Voltaire's *Letters Concerning the English Nation,* where he remarks upon the peaceable assembly of the representatives of all mankind in the London Stock Exchange, each a follower of his church, but jointly, in their transactions with one another, professing the same religion, giving the name of "infidel" merely to those who go bankrupt. In such circumstances do Jews, Muslims, and Christians trust one another, and then, writes Voltaire, even Presbyterians are at ease with Anabaptists. Only in Scotland, where they are supreme, he observes—by way of rebuking Alasdair MacIntyre—do Presbyterians affect a solemn bearing, behave like pedants, and preach through their nose.[12]

Social and political thinkers of the Enlightenment were characteristically pluralists, specially sensitive, as was Montesquieu, to the local variety, specificity, and uniqueness of social institutions, customs, and mores. In what might be termed their deconstruction of the universalist pretensions of Christian dogmas by way of critical theory, they looked back to seventeenth-century England's Act of Toleration and its Declaration of Right rather than to the French Revolution's *Déclaration des droits de l'homme et du citoyen.* In the 1790s their followers imagined that if France had been able to enjoy a similar bloodless revolution around the same time as the Glorious Revolution of England, the minds of Frenchmen might have been changed without it having proved necessary to cut off their heads. In exculpating the *philosophes* of the Enlightenment from all blame for the Revolution that is said to have sprung from their doctrines, I do not just mean that they were reformers instead of revolutionaries, who indeed sought largely to avert a revolutionary crisis, which many of them perceived as imminent, rather than to promote it. I have in mind also the fact that virtually none of their constitutional schemes of reform came to be realized anywhere in the age of modernity that their ideas are said to have spawned. For unless it is the legal despotism of Le Mercier de la Rivière, not a single major scheme of government conceived by Enlightenment thinkers—not classical republicanism or its modern derivatives meant for large states, not enlightened monarchy, nor democracy, nor the reestablishment of the ancient constitution, nor the mixed constitution, nor the separation of powers–has come to prevail anywhere in the age of the nation-state sired by the French Revolution.

I should like next to elaborate this proposition specifically with respect to Rousseau's doctrine of republicanism, since, to my mind, if the Jacobin Terror and modern totalitarianism did not spring directly from any Enlightenment Project, neither are they features implicit in his political philosophy. As I have already implied, Rousseau was in many respects the revolutionaries' Moses, pointing the way to the promised land. After the fall of Robespierre in 1794, his remains were transferred from their grave at Ermenonville and brought to the Panthéon in Paris, where *le citoyen de Genève* could forever be acclaimed as a hero of the French nation that he loathed, and where every night he can be heard to cry out in pain on account of having to rest in eternal torment opposite the tomb of Voltaire. But allowing that the *Contrat social* would come to be esteemed as the holy writ of the French Revolution, fusing its Ten Commandments and its Sermon on the Mount in a blueprint for a new social order three decades before its actual Creation, Rousseau bears no responsibility for the establishment of the age of modernity on 17 June 1789.

On that day, the deputies of the Estates General, which had been convoked the previous autumn by King Louis XVI, resolved that they were no longer assembled at the monarch's behest but were rather agents of the national will (*le vœu national*), entrusted with the task of representing the sovereignty of the people of France. The three estates thereby constituted themselves as a single *Assemblée nationale*, bearing sole authority to interpret the people's general will. In this way political modernity came to be born, in France, through the establishment of a unicameral parliament corresponding to a unitary will and the creation of a unified state designed to give voice to an undifferentiated nation. Herein lay the establishment of the first genuinely modern state, in the sense in which it has become a nation-state, plucked from the womb of the *ancien régime* by its own offspring who, in transfiguring their delegated powers and hence their own identity, brought a new world into being. The United States of America, whose Constitution had been framed a fraction earlier, by contrast, never formed one nation and at first scarcely formed one state.

Since the motion that thus generated the National Assembly had been put, initially to the delegates of the Third Estate alone, by the abbé Sieyès, it may be said that Sieyès is the father of the nation-state, standing to the whole of political modernity as does God to his Creation. His incendiary tract, *Qu'est-ce que le tiers état?*, published in January 1789, not only prefigured much of the debate that was to lead to the establishment of the National Assembly and then its abolition of the vestiges of feudalism on 4 August 1789. In its first printing it also introduced the expression *la science sociale* to the history of social philosophy and the human sciences, thereby lending some support, of which Foucault was unaware, to his thesis in *Les mots et les choses* that the epistemic transformation of the classical into the modern age began around 1795. Striving perhaps even harder than God had done to ensure that his handiwork flourished, Sieyès set himself the task, after the nation-state had been born, of serving as its nursemaid and counselor as well. No one has contributed more to shaping the modern world's political discourse.

Hegel, who had witnessed modernity's birth and was to devote much of his life to portraying its childhood, came eventually to reflect upon Sieyès' paternity of modernity, as it were, in his *Über die englische Reformbill,* first published in the *Allgemeine preußische Staatzeitung* in 1831, where he observes that Sieyès managed to assemble from his own papers the constitution that France came to enjoy.[13] In the language he had employed earlier in his section on "Absolute Freedom and Terror'" in the *Phänomenologie,* he describes this birthday of modernity, in his fashion, as the undivided substance of absolute freedom ascending the throne of the world without there being any power able to resist it.

Space does not permit my retracing the events that were to generate the terror five years later, by way of the unfolding logic of the establishment of the National Assembly, so wonderfully described by Hegel in his own conceptual history of the philosophical and political foundations of the modern world. Let me provide the briefest possible sketch. In pursuit of the reasoning that had led to the formation of the National Assembly, it next followed from its members' debates of late August and early September 1789 that the King of France must be denied an absolute veto over its legislation, principally on the grounds that there could be no sovereign above the people's representatives. Both Robespierre and Sieyès argued forcefully in the same debates that the King could not even be permitted a suspensive veto, since the unity of the nation prohibited any executive constraint over its legislative will, while the King's particular will could not be elevated above the rest. They were of course perfectly right in their judgement, for the King, who was indeed granted a suspensive veto but at the same time denied thereby the right to represent the nation, was to find his office preserved in name only, cut off from the populace to which he might have appealed against the state. The people of France were thus able to see the fracture of their constitution that had been manufactured at its birth, and in a particularly striking way they came to recognize the weakness of the authority of their state. In the late summer of 1792, with the King in conflict with the Legislative Assembly that had succeeded the National Assembly in 1791, the nation in effect brought them down together, as Hegel recounts with perfect accuracy in his *Phänomenologie,* where he remarks that all social groups or classes that are the spiritual spheres into which the whole is articulated are abolished.

Around the time of its establishment along lines envisaged in Sieyès' plan, the National Assembly, seeking to make its identity clear, deliberated not only about the powers of the King but also about the powers of the people. Both in the spring of 1789 and again at the end of July, Sieyès argued successfully that the people of France must be denied any binding mandate, or *mandat impératif*, over their own delegates, since such a mandate would deprive the people's representatives of their freedom and would accordingly substitute the multifarious particular wills of scattered citizens for the collective will of the nation as a whole. The act of creation of the National Assembly that Sieyès had sponsored declared that the Assembly was one and indivisible. As the father of modernity insisted, if the general will was to speak with one voice in a unitary nation-state, it could no more be accountable to the people at large than to a king.

At the heart of Sieyès' conception of modernity lay an idea of representation that in his eyes was to constitute the most central feature of the French state. The modern age in its political form, or *l'ordre représentatif*, as he termed it, depended for its prosperity upon a system of state management that adopted the same principle of the division of labor as was necessary for a modern economy or commercial society. This system entailed that the people must entrust authority to their representatives rather than seek its exercise directly by themselves, their delegates articulating their interests on their behalf while they accordingly remain silent. As Sieyès knew perfectly well, nothing could have been further from Rousseau's republicanism than such notions of the representation of the people in a commercial society, in which the electors take no direct part in the political management of their own affairs.

Exactly contrary to Rousseau, Sieyès stood for both finance and representation at the same time, and it was owing to his genius in recognizing that the National Assembly could only be sovereign if it took the place of the people themselves that he introduced into Western political thought a scheme of the political division of labor. He thus transposed from the economy to the state a principle that Adam Smith had believed was actually in need of correction and control in the light of an ancient republican doctrine of public engagement and the active participation in the management of their own affairs by citizens themselves, rather than their representatives. Sieyès, by contrast, employed Smith's principle, which he supposed he had invented himself even earlier than the publication of *The Wealth of Nations*, to justify a distinction between active and passive citizens, whose separate identification for a brief period under the French Constitution of 1791 was to prove one of the crowning achievements of his career. By virtue of his doctrine of representation, it was plain to Sieyès that the people as well as the King must be barred from seeking control over the National Assembly, since any diminution of its authority from an external source would constitute a danger to the expression of the general will.

There could be no confusion in France between representation and democracy such as inspired Paine and others to imagine that the hybrid form of government established in America had nourished a classical principle of self-rule in a large state. For Sieyès, who sometimes spoke of direct democracy as a form of *démocratie brute*, it would be tragic for the first genuinely modern state in human history to make a retrograde step, hesitating between ancient and modern principles of government in the task of establishing a political system that was and must be without precedent. Democracy, he thought, was no more fit for modernity than was the mixed constitution that would issue from the preservation of a royal veto. No plebiscite or other vestige of direct democracy could be tolerated by the sole representative of the entire nation. Sovereignty thereby passed from the nation's multifarious fragments to the people's delegates constituted as one body, the populace ceasing to have any political identity except as articulated through its representatives, who by procuration had been granted authority to speak for the electorate as a whole.

While the conception of the modern state put forward by Sieyès thus required that both the King, on the one hand, and the people, on the other, should be marginalized from the government of France, the implementation of his plan did not proceed as smoothly as he might have hoped. The Jacobins, in particular, regarded Sieyès' distinction between active and passive citizenship as anathema. Opposing his principle of the indivisibility of the general will as articulated by the nation's representatives, they sought to return directly to the people, in their districts and through their communes, the indissoluble sovereignty of the whole nation that had been expropriated by their independently minded political delegates.

Yet the Jacobins' contradiction of Sieyès' logic of modernity was in a crucial sense illusory, since the nation they envisaged as comprised of all its people was to prove as monolithic as Sieyès' conception of a nation represented by the state. When they came to power within the Convention in the autumn of 1793, they behaved as Sieyès and his associates had done earlier, but in reverse–that is, they attempted to root out the people's enemies within the state, just as Sieyès had sought to silence the enemies of the state within the nation. In attempting to render the citizen population of France active so that the people's delegates could be accountable to and even decommissioned by their true sovereign, the Jacobins were obliged to cleanse the nation of its internal differences, closing the Catholic churches, for instance, and forcing the Commune of Paris, from which they had drawn so much of their own strength, to surrender its powers. Their immaculate conception of popular self-rule was not to be tainted by the people themselves. Universal freedom, by thus seeking to exist just for itself, in Hegelian parlance, effects the destruction of the actual organization of the world.

For the people to act as a collective grand jury of their government, they must also speak with one voice. Having supported the rights of primary assemblies against the state, the Jacobins came within the Convention to oppose assemblies that betrayed the nation. Pure democracy was to prove in practice as incompatible with Robespierre's populism as it was alien to Sieyès' notion of representative government. The Terror of the Jacobins was to follow directly from their idea of the sublime unity of the nation, which required a lofty purity of public spirit that made the vulgar purity of democracy seem an uncouth substitute for virtue. Popular sovereignty was not only to be given voice but actually created by the nation's genuine representatives. The greatest enemies of the people for whom they stood, and who had still to be manufactured in the image of what they might become, were all the fractious people cast in recalcitrant molds resistant to such change, who thereby stood in the way of the agents of the people of the future. As Hegel hence concludes by way of introducing a vegetable metaphor in the most trenchant lines of his section on "Absolute Freedom and Terror" in the *Phänomenologie*, in its abstract existence of unmediated pure negation, the sole work of freedom is therefore death, a death without inner significance, the coldest and meanest of deaths, like cutting off the head of a cabbage.[14] His reading of the French Revolution's descent, from the sublime idealism that infused its inception to the dreadful scourge of the Jacobin dictatorship, to my mind correctly describes the self-transfiguration of the first genuinely modern nation-state into the enemy of its own parent, ideologically the Enlightenment Project of freedom which gave rise to it, and politically the people from whose will it sprang. The French Revolutionary nation-state thus gave a practical embodiment, that is, made real, the primal patricide of modernity itself.

Let me attempt, briefly, to explain this claim. What was conceived by Sieyès and put into practice by both Sieyès and Robespierre was not a Rousseauist theory of popular sovereignty at all, but a Hobbesian theory of representation, which in the light of a political corruption of Smith's notion of the division of labor could be made to appear as if it were democracy itself–that is, the opposite of representation–so that since the late eighteenth century, but only since then, virtually every government in the world is said to be a *representative democracy*. The modern state, which since the French Revolution has of its essence been a *nation-state*, is unlike any form of political association ever conceived before. Hobbes had conceived a need for a unitary sovereign in his depiction of the artificial personality of the state, but he had not supposed that the multitude of subjects that authorized this power could be identified as having a collective character of its own. Joined together with his conception of the unity of the representer, as outlined in his *Leviathan*, the modern state since the French Revolution requires that the represented–that is, the people as a whole–be a moral person as well, national unity going hand in hand with the political unity of the state.

Sieyès never failed to oppose Rousseauist notions of republicanism in the National Assembly, because he recognized what he took to be the threat to the expression of the nation's general will that might be posed by the people.

It was of the essence of his plan that the nation in assembly spoke for all the people and must never be silenced by the people themselves. Over the past two hundred years the nation-state has characteristically achieved that end because it represents the people, standing before them not just as monarchs had done earlier, as the embodiment of their collective will, but rather by assuming their very identity, bearing the personality of the people themselves. While a small number of genuinely multinational states have in that period been established as well and continue to flourish, the majority of peoples everywhere now comprise nations which, by way of their representatives, are politically incorporated as states. All peoples that have identities form nation-states. What Sieyès did not foresee was that, in the age of modernity heralded by his political philosophy, a people might not survive except by constituting a nation-state. In the age of modernity, it has proved possible for the nation-state to become the enemy of the people.

To the Hobbesian theory of representation, the nation-state adds the dimension of the comprehensive unity of the people, the representer and represented together forming an indissoluble whole, the state now identical with the nation, the nation bonded to the state, each understood through the other. As Hannah Arendt rightly noted in her *Origins of Totalitarianism*, it has been a characteristic feature of the nation-state since the French Revolution that the rights of man and the rights of the citizen are the same.[15] By giving real substance and proper sanction to the various declarations of the rights of man within the framework of its own first constitutions, the French revolutionary nation-state invented by Sieyès joined the rights of man to the sovereignty of the nation.[16] It defined the rights of man in such a way that only the state could enforce them and only members of the nation could enjoy them. But so far from putting into practice the universal rights of man long advocated by proponents of cosmopolitan enlightenment, the modern nation-state was to ensure that henceforth only persons comprising nations that formed states could have rights. Since the French Revolution the history of modernity has characteristically been marked by the abuse of human rights on the part of nation-states, which alone have the authority to determine the scope of those rights and their validity.

Not only individuals but whole peoples that comprise nations without states have found themselves comprehensively shorn of their rights. At the heart of the Enlightenment Project, which its advocates perceived as putting an end to the age of privilege, was their recognition of the common humanity of all persons. For Kant, who in Königsberg came from practically nowhere and went nowhere else at all, to be enlightened meant to be intolerant of injustice everywhere, to pay indiscriminate respect to each individual, to be committed to universal justice, to be morally indifferent to difference. But in the age of the nation-state, it is otherwise. Thanks ultimately to the father of modernity, ours is the age of the passport, the permit, the right of entry to each state or right of exit from it that is enjoyed by citizens who bear its nationality alone. For persons who are not accredited as belonging to a nation-state in the world of modernity, there are few passports and still fewer visas. To be without a passport or visa in the modern world is to have no right of exit or entry anywhere, and to be without a right of exit or entry is to risk a rite of passage to the grave. That above all is the legacy bequeathed to us from the political inception of the modern age on 17 June 1789. It was then, it seems to me, that the metempsychosis of modernity began, when we started to manufacture Frankenstein's monster from Pygmalion's statue, and when whole peoples without states—above all the Jews—would be doomed if ever such a monster should rise up against them.

In his own contribution to this collection, Bernd Henningsen asks how we can avoid genocide in the future. How, indeed, could we in Europe have averted the ethnic cleansing of Bosnia and Kosovo? We might have required some courage, but I do not think the path we should have taken is obscure. Instead of acquiescing to Lord David Owen, we should have joined Voltaire and indeed all the *philosophes* of the age of Enlightenment who opposed the ethnic cleansing of their day, in the forms which it took by way of the Revocation of the Edict of Nantes and the Papal Bull *Unigenitus*. Since our faults lie in ourselves and not our stars, there is nothing in the history of human affairs, including the Holocaust, that was not preventable. Such is the burden of guilt that those who fail to act must always carry, and it is perhaps the chief lesson that we have still to learn from the *engagés volontaires* of the age of Enlightenment, the international brigade of the eighteenth-century republic of letters, who, unlike most of us, felt themselves charged with Voltaire's commitment to *écraser l'infâme*—to root out bigotry and to pursue it across all borders, since the moral boundaries of the modern nation-state are not impermeable.

By focusing upon the French Revolution as the critical juncture of modernity in its political form—that is, by making the establishment of the modern nation-state both necessary and possible—I have aimed in these remarks to exculpate the most central political doctrines of the age of Enlightenment from responsibility for such crimes against humanity as have been ascribed to their influence by social philosophers wrongly persuaded that the French Revolutionary nation-state was the practical realization of Enlightenment ideals. The *Sonderweg* of the so-called "Enlightenment Project,"[17] if that expression means anything at all, can only be established with reference to the theological doctrines and political institutions which it opposed, following the Revocation of the Edict of Nantes by King Louis XIV in 1685 and the events of around the same time leading to and surrounding the Glorious Revolution in England. Locke's, Spinoza's, and Bayle's writings on toleration and freedom of conscience, or, in France, Montesquieu's *Lettres persanes*, Diderot's *Supplément au voyage de Bougainville*, Rousseau's *Contrat social*, or Voltaire's *Traité sur la tolérance*, among so many other writings,

united *philosophes* of all denominations in common resistance to the unifor-
mitarian pretensions of dogmatic faiths, the persecution of heretics, and the
disenfranchisement of the civil rights of religious minorities. To the extent
that Enlightenment thinkers combated theological purification, their project
has regrettably had only scant success in our time, in the service of a benign
god that has largely failed.

My attempt here to portray the French Revolutionary nation-state as a
critical juncture unheralded by the doctrines of the Enlightenment alleged to
have inspired it carries implications as well for our perception of the national
cultures of both Germany and Sweden, which are at issue in this volume.
With respect to Germany, these remarks suggest, *pace* Daniel Goldhagen,
that many of Hitler's willing executioners could be found in the West as well
as in Central Europe, among persons convinced that only accredited citizens
of national communities that form states can have rights, secured and
enforced within circumscribed territories by locally sovereign powers. On
my reading of such matters, the Holocaust was made possible by the systematic indifference of Western governments and peoples to atrocities committed
abroad—in effect, by policies of appeasement whose origins in the age of the
modern nation-state I have sought to trace to the French Revolution—in addition, of course, to the official or voluntary perpetrators of such crimes.

With respect to Sweden my disengagement of the Enlightenment from
the French Revolution in these reflections might be thought to lend some
warrant to the thesis of the editors of *The Cultural Construction of Norden* that
the Scandinavian achievement of social democracy without violence points
to an Enlightenment Project uncontaminated by an aftermath of Terror,
embracing ideals that have nurtured the blossoming of a civilization fortu-
nately bereft of its barbarian sting. Whether the pastoral and Lutheran set-
tings for the Swedish experiment may be properly characterized as an
Enlightenment Project unskewed by revolution is a subject to which I cannot
here begin to do justice.[18] But that there may, and indeed must, be a Third
Way between Disneyland, on the one side, and Chernobyl, on the other, is a
tenet that in diverse formulations underpins much of the current ethos of the
European Community itself; and if the paths towards the promotion of social
welfare that have, at least until recently, predominated in Sweden were to
steer the fortunes of Europe as a whole, current descendants of the philosophies of Locke, Voltaire, Hume, Rousseau and Kant might at last have cause
to look upon our fractious continent and smile.[19]

Notes

1. See especially the preface to Hazard's work, published by Boivin.
2. See especially chs. 8 and 10 of Foucault's text, published by Gallimard.
3. Eric Santner, "Traumatic Revelations: Freud's Moses and the Origins of Anti-Semitism." Paper presented at the conference "Communities in Peril: The History and Memory of Crisis in Germany and Scandinavia," 3-5 Ocotber 1997, Instituto Europeo, Florence. See also Robert Wokler "The Enlightenment, the Nation-State and the Primal Patricide of Modernity" cited in n. 19 below.
4. Jean-Jacques Rousseau, *Emile*, livre III, in his *Œuvres complètes* (Paris: Gallimard, Bibliothèque de la Pléiade, 1959-95), IV.468.
5. Rousseau, *Confessions*, livre VIII, *Œuvres complètes*, I.384.
6. See d'Alembert's *De la liberté de la musique*, in Denise Launay (ed.), *La Querelle des Bouffons*, (Geneva: Minkoff, 1973), III.2210.
7. See Diderot's *Neveu de Rameau*, ed. Jean Fabre (Geneva: Librairie Droz, 1977), 81-82.
8. G. W. F. Hegel, *Phänomenologie des Geistes*, in his *Gesammelte Werke* (Hamburg: Felix Meiner, 1968-), IX.295-296.
9. See Rousseau, *Confessions*, livre VI, *Œuvres complètes*, I.269: "Je me rappellai le pis aller d'une grande Princesse à qui l'on disoit que les paysans n'avoient pas de pain, et qui répondit: qu'ils mangent de la brioche. J'achettai de la brioche."
10. Staël, Mme. Germaine de, *De la littérature considérée dans ses rapports avec les institutions sociales* (Paris: Maradon, 1800), II.33.
11. Diderot, *Observations sur le Nakaz*, in his *Political Writings*, ed. John Hope Mason and Robert Wokler (Cambridge: Cambridge University Press, 1992), 207-209.
12. See Voltaire's *Letters Concerning the English Nation* (London: C. Davis and A. Lyon, 1733), Letter VI ("On the Presbyterians"), 41-45.
13. See Hegel's *Politischen Schriften* (Frankfurt: Suhrkamp, 1966), 310. It must be noted that, in this passage of The English Reform Bill, Hegel refers not to Sieyès' role in establishing the National Assembly in 1789, but to his authorship of the constitution of the year VIII, which he drafted as provisional consul a decade later, following the bloodless *coup d'état* of the eighteenth Brumaire of Napoleon Bonaparte that marked the transition of France's revolutionary government from the *Directoire* to the *Consulat*. As First Consul, Bonaparte altered Sieyès' scheme to suit his own advantage and ambition.
14. Hegel, *Phänomenologie des Geistes*, 230-231.
15. Hannah Arendt, *The Origins of Totalitarianism* ([1951], 2nd ed., London: Allen and Unwin, 1958), 230-231. Arendt here comments on what she terms "the secret conflict between state and nation," arising with the very birth of the nation-state on account of its conjunction of the rights of man with the demand for national sovereignty.
16. The phrasing of the third article of the declaration of the rights of man and of the citizen, which begins, "Le principe de toute souveraineté réside essentiellement dans la Nation," is owed principally to Lafayette. For the fullest histories of the sources and drafting of the whole document, and of the deliberations leading to its endorsement by the *Assemblée nationale* on 26 July, 1789, see Stéphane Rials' commentary on *La Déclaration des droits de l'homme et du citoyen* (Paris: Hachette, 1988), and Marcel Gauchet's *La Révolution des droits de l'homme* (Paris: Gallimard, 1989).
17. This expression, so far as I know, first appeared in print in 1973 in Alasdair MacIntyre, *After Virtue*, where it forms the subject of three chapters.
18. See Øystein Sørensen and Bo Stråth (eds.), *The Cultural Construction of Norden* (Oslo: Scandinavian University Press, 1997), especially the introductory chapter by the editors, ch. 3 ("Fugitives from Utopia: Scandinavian Enlightenment Reconsidered") by Nina Witoszek, and ch. 4 ("The Swedish Construction of Nordic Identity") by Bernd Henningsen. I have addressed the question of an "Enlightenment Project" in Sweden in "Der bersondere Charakter der ländlichen Aufklärung des Nordens" in Henningsen (ed.) *Wahlverwandtschaft*, Band 9: "Das Projekt Norden," 2002, pp. 58-64.

19. This essay draws upon a number of my other publications, which embrace a fuller annotation of my sources than can be incorporated here. That material includes "Projecting the Enlightenment," in John Horton and Susan Mendus (eds.), *After MacIntyre* (Cambridge: Polity Press, 1994), 108-126; "The Enlightenment Project and its Critics," *Pozna Studies*, vol. 58, also published in Sven-Eric Liedman (ed.), *The Postmodernist Critique of the Project of Enlightenment*, 13-30; "The French Revolutionary Roots of Political Modernity in Hegel's Philosophy, or the Enlightenment at Dusk," *Bulletin of the Hegel Society of Great Britain*, vol. 35, 1997, 71-89; "Contextualizing Hegel's Phenomenology of the French Revolution and the Terror", *Political Theory* vol. 26, 1998, 33-55; "The Enlightenment and the French Revolutionary Birth Pangs of Modernity" in *Sociology of the Sciences Yearbook*, 20 (1996), reprt. in Johan Heilbron et al. (eds.), *The Rise of the Social Sciences and the Formation of Modernity*, (Dordrecht: Kluwer, 1998); "Ethnic cleansing and multiculturalism in the Enlightenment", in Ole Peter Grell and Roy Porter (eds.), and *Toleration in Enlightenment Europe* (Cambridge: Cambridge University Press, 1999), 69-85; and "The Enlightenment Project as Betrayed by Modernity," *History of European Ideas*, vol. 24, 1998, 301-313; "The Enlightenment, the Nation-State and the Primal Patricide of Modernity," in Norman Geras and Robert Wokler (eds.), *The Enlightenment and Modernity* (London: Macmillan, 2000), 161-183. I am grateful to Nina Witoszek and Lars Trägårdh for their forbearance in awaiting my completion of this text.

Bibliography

Abraham, David. *The Collapse of the Weimar Republic: Political Economy and Crisis,* Princeton: Princeton University Press. 1981.

Adlerbeth, Jacob. "Stiftelseurkunden jemte stadgarna för det göthiska förbundet." *Iduna,* vol. II, 1845.

Adorno, Theodor and Max Horkheimer. *Dialectic of Enlightenment.* London: Verso Classics, 1977.

_____ *Dialektik der Aufkläring.* Amsterdam: Queido, 1947.

Ahnlund, Nils. *Gustav Adolf den store.* Stockholm: Svenska kyrkans diakonistyrelses bokförlag, 1932.

Åhrén, Uno. *Arkitektur och demokrati,* Stockholm: Kooperativa förbundets bokförlag, 1942.

Alembert, Jean le Rond d'. *De la liberté de la musique.* In Launay, ed., *La Querelle des Bouffons,* 1973.

Aly, Götz. *'Final Solution': Nazi Population Policy and the Murder of the European Jews.* New York: Oxford University Press, 1999.

Aly, Götz and Susanne Heim. Vordenker der Vernichtung. Auschwitz und die Pläne für eine neue europäische Ordnung. Hamburg: Hoffman und Campe, 1991.

Anderson, Benedict. *Imagined Communities: Reflections on the Origin and Spread of Nationalism.* London: Verso, 1983.

Anell, Lars. *Världsordningen och välfärdsstatens kris.* Stockholm: Sekretariatet för framtidsstudier, Liber, 1979.

Antman, Peter. "Vägen till systemskiftet." in Gustafsson, ed., *Köp och sälj, var god svälj?,* 1994.

Anton, Thomas. *Administered Politics: Elite Political Cultures in Sweden,* Boston: Martinus Nijhoff, 1980.

Anzulovic, Brannimir. *Heavenly Serbia: From Myth to Genocide.* London: Hurst and Company, 1999.

Applegate, Celia. *A Nation of Provincials: The German Idea of Heimat.* Berkeley: University of California Press, 1990.

Arbetarrörelsens efterkrigsprogram: Sammanfattning i 27 punkter. (The Labor
    Movement's Post-War Program). Stockholm, 1944.
Arendt, Hannah. "A Reply." *The Review of Politics,* vol. 15, 1953, 83.
_____ *Crises of the Republic.* New York: Harcourt, Brace, Jovonaovich, 1972.
_____ *The Origins of Totalitarianism.* London: Allen and Unwin, 1958.
Åsard, Erik. *Kampen om löntagarfonderna: Fondutredningen från samtal till
    sammanbrott.* Stockholm: Norstedt, 1985.
Aschheim, Steven. "Nazism, Normalcy and the German *Sonderweg.*" In
    Aschheim, ed., *In Times of Crisis,* 2001.
Aschheim, Steven, ed. *Culture and Catastrophe: German and Jewish
    Confrontations with National Socialism and Other Crises.* London:
    Macmillan, 1996.
_____ *In Times of Crisis: Essays on European Culture, Germans and Jews.*
    Madison: University of Wisonsin Press, 2001.
Austerlitz, Friedrich. "Deutsche Demokratie." *Der Kampf,* August 1917.
Bagehot, Walter. *The English Constitution.* 1876; reprt. Brighton: Sussex
    Academic Press, 1997.
Baker, Keith Michael. *Inventing the French Revolution: Essays on French Political
    Culture in the Eighteenth Century.* Cambridge: Cambridge University
    Press, 1990.
_____ "Public Opinion as Political Invention." In Baker, *Inventing the French
    Revolution,* 1990.
Barclay, David, and E. D. Weitz, eds. *Between Reform and Revolution: Studies
    in the History of German Socialism and Communism from 1840 to 1990.*
    Oxford: Berghahn, 1998.
Barnouw, Dagmar. *Germany 1945. Views of War and Violence,* Bloomington
    and Indianaopolis: Indiana University Press, 1996.
Barth, Karl, *Der Römerbrief.* 1926; reprt. Zurich, Zollikon, 1954.
Bartov, Omer, ed. *The Holocaust: Origins, Implementation, Aftermath.* London:
    Routledge, 2000.
Bartov, Omer. *Murder in our Midst: The Holocaust Industrial Killing and
    Representation.* New York: Oxford University Press, 1996.
Baudrillard, Jean. *America.* London: Verso, 1986.
Bauer, Otto. *Nationalitätenfrage und Sozialdemokratie.* Vienna, 1907.
Bauer, Yehuda. *Rethinking the Holocaust.* New Haven: Yale University Press,
    2001.
Bauman, Zygmunt. *Modernity and Holocaust.* Cambridge: Polity, 1989.
_____ "On Crisis, Culture and the Crisis of Culture." MS presented at the
    conference, "Communities in Peril: The Memory and History of Crisis
    in Germany and Scandinavia," 2-5 October 1997, European University,
    Florence.
Becker, Carl Heinrich. *The Politico-Cultural Tasks of the Nation.* 1919.

Bell, Daniel. *Winding Passage: Essays and Sociological Journeys 1960-80.* New York: University Press of America, 1984.

Bengtsson, Jörgen. *Ge Norden en chans!* Alternativ till EG skriftserie, no. 1, 1993.

Bergman, Ingmar. *The Magic Lantern: An Autobiography by Ingmar Bergman.* London: Hamish Hamilton, 1987.

Bergstrand, N. *Analys av läroverkens målsättning 1898-1927,* Lund: 1972.

Berlin, Isaiah. *Vico and Herder: Two Studies in the History of Ideas.* London: Hogarth, 1976.

_____ *Against the Current: Essays in the History of Ideas.* Oxford: Clarendon, 1991.

_____ *The Magus of the North: J.G. Hamann and the Origins of Modern Irrationalism.* (Edited by Henry Hardy). London: J. Murray, 1993.

Bessette, Joseph M. *The Mild Voice of Reason: Deliberative Democracy and American National Government.* Chicago: University of Chicago Press, 1994.

Besson, Waldemar. *Die politische Terminologie des Präsidenten Franklin D. Roosevelt: Eine Studie über den Zusammenhang von Sprache und Politik.* Tübingen 1955.

Bildt, Carl, *Hallänning, svensk, europé.* Stockholm: Bonniers, 1991.

Bismarck, Otto von. *Gesammelte Werke.* Berlin, 1984.

Bjereld, Ulf. *Hjalmarsonaffären, ett politiskt drama i tre akter.* Stockholm: Nerenius & Santerus, 1997.

Björck, Staffan. *Heidenstam och sekelskiftets Sverige.* Stockholm: Natur och Kultur, 1946.

Blackbourn, David, and Geoff Eley. *The Peculiarities of German History: Bourgeois Society and Politics in Nineteenth-century Germany.* Oxford: Oxford University Press, 1984.

Bödeker, Hans Erich. "Journals and Public Opinion: The Politicization of the German Enlightenment in the Second Half of the Eighteenth Century." In Hellmuth, ed., *The Transformation of Political Culture,* 1990.

Boëthius, Maria-Pia. "M. Pia Boëthius om folkhemmets skuggsida," *Arena* no. 5, 1997.

Bogoslovskiy, Christina Staël von Holstein. *The Educational Crisis in Sweden in the Light of American Experience.* New York: Columbia University Press, 1932.

Bohme, Helmut. *The Foundations of the German Empire. Selected Documents.* Oxford: Oxford University Press, 1971.

Bottomore, Tom, and Patrick Goode. *Austro-Marxism.* Oxford: Clarendon Press, 1978.

Brandt, Peter and Herbert Ammon, eds. *Die Linke und die nationale Frage.* Hamburg: Rowohlt, 1981.

Breckman, Warren. "Diagnosing the 'German Misery': Radicalism and the Problem of National Character, 1830 to 1848." In Barclay and Weitz, *Between Reform and Revolution,* 1998.

Bredthauer, K. D., and A. Heinrich, eds. *Aus der Geschichte lernen/How to Learn from History,* Bonn: edition Blätter 2, Verleihung des Blaetter-Demokratiepreises, 1997.

Bremer, Fredrika. *Hemmen i den nya världen [Home in the New World],* 1851.

_____ *Hemmet,* 1837

_____ *Syskonliv,* Stockholm, 1848.

Brennan, Andrew, and Nina Witoszek, eds. *Worldviews: Community, Identity and the Natural World.* Cambridge: White Horse Press, 1998.

Broberg, Gunnar, and Mattias Tydén. "Eugenics in Sweden: Efficient Care." In Broberg and Roll-Hanson, *Eugenics and the Welfare State,* 1996.

_____ *Oönskade i folkhemmet: rashygien och sterilisering i Sverige.* Stockholm: Gidlund, 1991.

Broberg, Gunnar, and Nils Roll-Hansen, eds. *Eugenics and the Welfare State.* East Lansing: Michigan State University Press, 1996.

Bruchfeld, Stéphane, and Paul A. Levine. *Om detta må ni berätta,* Stockholm: Regeringkansliet, 1999.

Brunner, Otto, Werner Conze and Reinhardt Koselleck, eds. *Geschichtliche Grundbegriffe,* vol-8. Stuttgart: Klett-Cotta, 1972-1997.

Burckhardt, Jacob. *Weltgeschichtliche Betrachtungen.* Ed. Rudolf Stadelmann. Pfullingen, 1949.

Burleigh, Michael. *Ethics and Extermination: Reflections on Nazi Genocide.* Cambridge: Cambridge University Press, 1997.

Burleigh, Michael, and Wolfgang Wipperman. *The Racial State: Germany, 1933-45.* Cambridge: Cambridge University Press, 1991.

Buruma, Ian. *The Wages of Guilt. Memories of War in Germany and Japan.* New York: Farrar Strauss and Giroux, 1994.

Caenegem, Raoul Charles van. *An Historical Introduction to Western Constitutional Law.* Cambridge: Cambridge University Press, 1995.

Carlgren, Wilhelm. M. *Svensk utrikespolitik 1939-1945.* Stockholm: Allmänna förlaget, 1973.

Carlsson, Allan. "The Roles of Alva and Gunnar Myrdal in the Development of a Social Democratic Response to Europe's 'Population Crises 1929-1938.'" Unpublished dissertation, Ohio University, Athens, Ohio, 1978.

Carruthers, Bruce C. *City of Capital: Politics and Markets in the English Financial Revolution.* Princeton: Princeton University Press, 1996.

Chickering, Roger. *"We Men Who Feel Most German": A Cultural Study of the Pan-German League, 1886-1914.* Boston: Allen & Unwin, 1984.

Childs, Marquis. *Sweden: The Middle Way.* New Haven: Yale University Press, 1936.

_____ *Sweden: The Middle Way on Trial.* New Haven: Yale University Press, 1980.

Clement, Wallace, and Rhionne Mahon, eds. *Swedish Social Democracy. A Model in Transition.* Toronto: Canadian Scholars Press, 1994.

Cole, Margaret, and Charles Smith, eds. *Democratic Sweden: A Volume of Studies Prepared by Members of the New Fabian Research Bureau.* London: George Routledge & Sons, 1938.

Colla, Piero. "Storia ed eredita culturale in eclisse nel sistema svedese di insegnamento." *Rivista di Storia contemporanea,* no. 4, 1993.

_____ "La politica di sterilizzazione in Svezia 1934-1975. Dal consenso alla rimozione collettiva." *Rivista di storia contemporanea* no. 3, 1994-95.

Confino, Alon. "The Nation as a Local Metaphor: Heimat, National Memory and the German Empire, 1871-1918." *History and Memory,* vol. 5, no. 1, 1993.

_____ *The Nation as a Local Metaphor: Württemberg, Imperial Germany, and National memory, 1871-1918.* Chapel Hill: University of North Carolina Press, 1997.

Crew, David, ed. *Nazism and German Society, 1933-1945.* New York: Routledge, 1994.

Dahl, Gudrun. "Wildflowers, Nationalism and the Swedish Land." In Brennan and Witoszek, eds., *Worldviews,* 1998.

Daun, Åke. *Svensk mentalitet: ett jämförande perspektiv.* Stockholm: Rabén & Sjögren, 1989.

Davies, R.G., and J.H. Denton, eds. *The English Parliament in the Middle Ages.* Manchester: Manchester University Press, 1981.

de Molinari, Gustave. *L'Evolution economique du XIXe siecle: Theorie du Progrès.* Paris, 1880.

Dewandre, Nicole, and Jacques Lenoble, eds. *Projekt Europa. Postnationale Identität: Grundlage für eine europäische Demokratie.* Berlin: Schelsky & Jeep, 1994.

Diderot, Denis. *Neveu de Rameau.* Ed. Jean Fabre. Geneva: Librairie Droz, 1977.

_____ *Observations sur le Nakaz.* In Mason and Wokler, eds., *Political Writings,* 1977.

Dietz, Mary. "Patriotism" in Hall, Farr, and Hanson, eds., *Political Innovation and Conceptual Change,* 1989.

Dillard, Dudley. *Västeuropas och Förenta Staternas ekonomiska historia.* Lund: Liber, 1980.

Diner, Dan. *Beyond the Conceivable: Studies on Germany, Nazism and the Holocaust.* Berkeley: University of California Press, 2000.

Dish, Lisa Jane. *Hannah Arendt and the Limits of Philosophy.* Ithaca: Cornell University Press, 1996.

Dyzenhaus, David. *Legality and Legitimacy.* Oxford: Oxford University Press, 1999.

Edberg, Rolf. "Är skriften ej smädlig." *Tiden,* 1947.

Ehn, Billy. *Ska vi leka tiger? Daghemsliv ur kulturell synvinkel.* Lund: Liber, 1983.

Ekman,Stig, ed. *Stormaktstryck och småstatspolitik: aspekter på svensk politik under andra världskriget.* Stockholm: Liber, 1986.

Ekman, Stig and Nils Edling, eds. *War Experience, Self Image and National Identity, The Second World War as Myth and History.* Hedemora: Gidlunds, 1997.

Ekelund, Robert B. and Robert F. Hébert, eds. *A History of Economic Theory and Method.* New York: McGraw-Hill, 1997.

_____ "Mercantilism and the Dawn of Capitalism." In Ekelund and Hébert, *A History of Economic Theory and Method,* 1997.

Ekström, Tord, Gunnar Myrdal, and Roland Pålsson. *Vi och Västeuropa.* Stockholm: Rabén & Sjögren, 1962.

Eley, Geoff. *Reshaping the German Right: Radical Nationalism and Political Change after Bismarck.* New Haven: Yale University Press, 1980.

_____ *From Unification to Nazism: Reinterpreting the German Past,* London: Routledge, 1986.

Elgán, Elisabeth. *Genus och politik, en jämförelse mellan svensk och fransk abort och preventivmedelspolitik från sekelskiftet till andra världskriget.* Stockholm: Almquist & Wiksell International, 1994.

Elias, Norbert. *The Germans.* New York: Columbia University Press, 1996.

Engberg, Arthur. "Folkhemmet." *Social-Demokraten,* September 15, 1929.

_____ "Fosterlandskärleken." In Engberg, *Tal och skrifter,* 1945.

_____ *Tal och skrifter.* Stockholm: Tiden, 1945.

Engels, Friedrich. *The Peasant War in Germany.* New York: International Publishers, 1966.

Eriksson, Marianne. *Är EG en kvinnofälla?* Nej till EG Skriftserie no. 10, 1993.

Erlander, Tage. *Tage Erlander 1940-1949.* Stockholm: Tiden, 1973.

Ertman, Thomas. *Birth of the Leviathan: Building States and Regimes in Medieval and Early Modern Europe.* Cambridge: Cambridge University Press, 1997.

Evans, Richard. *Rereading German History 1800-1996.* London: Routledge, 1997.

Fahlbeck, Pontus. *Engelsk parlamentarism contra svensk.* Stockholm: Gleerups, 1916.

Feldt, Kjell Olof. *Alla dessa dagar - i regeringen 1982-1990.* Stockholm: Norstedt, 1991.

Fernández-Armesto, Felipe. *Millennium.* London: Bantam Press, 1995.

Feuchtwanger, Edgar J. *Prussia: Myth and Reality.* London: Oswald Wolff, 1970.

Fichte, Johann Gottlieb. *Addresses to the German Nation.* La Salle: Open Court Publishing Company, 1922.

Finer, Samuel Edward. *The History of Government from the Earliest Times: Vol. 2, The Intermediate Ages.* Oxford: Oxford University Press, 1997.

Fischer, Joschka. *Risiko Deutschland: Krise und Zukunft der deutschen Politik.* Cologne: Kiepenheuer & Witsch, 1994.

Fisher, Mark. *After the Wall: Germany, the Germans and the Burdens of History.* New York: Simon and Schuster, 1995.

Foucault, Michel. *Les mots et les choses: une archéologie des sciences humaines,* Bibliothèque des Sciences Humaines. Paris: Gallimard, 1966.

Friedländer, Saul. *Nazi Germany and the Jews: Vol. 1: The Years of Persecution, 1933-39.* London: Weidenfeld & Nicholson, 1997.

_____ "The Extermination of the Jews in Historiography: Fifty years later." In Bartov, *The Holocaust: Origins, Implementation, Aftermath,* 2000.

Funke, Hajo. *"Jetzt sind wir dran": Nationalismus im geeinten Deutschland.* Berlin: Aktion Sühnezeichen, 1991.

Gagliardo, John. *From Pariah to Patriot: the Changing Image of the German Peasant, 1770-1840.* Lexington: University Press of Kentucky, 1969.

Gallin, Alice. *Midwives to Nazism: University Professors in Weimar Germany 1925-1933.* Georgia: Macon Mercier University Press, 1986.

Gaunt, David, and Orvar Löfgren. *Myter om svensken.* Stockholm: Liber, 1984.

Gauchet, Marcel. *La Révolution des droits de l'homme.* Paris: Gallimard, 1989.

Gay, Peter. *Weimar Culture.* New York: Harper and Row, 1968.

Geijer, Erik Gustaf. *Samlade Skrifter,* vol. I. Stockholm, 1849-1855.

Gellner, Ernest. *Nations and Nationalism.* Oxford: Basil Blackwell, 1983.

_____ *Conditions of Liberty, Civil Society and its Rivals.* London: Hamish Hamilton, 1994.

Geras, Norman, and Robert Wokler, eds. *The Enlightenment and Modernity.* London: Macmillan, 1999.

Gerhardsson, Birgit, ed. *Ellen Key: 1849-1999: en minnesbok.* Linköping: Futurum, 1999.

Gerschenkron, Alexander. *Economic Backwardness in Historical Perspective.* Cambridge: Cambridge University Press, 1962.

_____ "The Advantages of Backwardness." In Gerschenkron, *Economic Backwardness in Historical Perspective,* 1962.

Glotz, Peter. *Der Irrweg des Nationalstaats.* Stuttgart, 1990.

Goldhagen, Daniel J. *Hitler's Willing Executioners: Ordinary Germans and the Holocaust.* New York: Knopf, 1996.

_____ "Modell Bundesrepublik." In Bredthauer and Heinrich, eds., *Aus der Geschichte lernen/How to Learn from History,* 1997.

_____ "Goldhagen und die Deutschen." *Psyche,* no. 6, 1997.

Goldmann, Kjell. "Trovärdighetskravet - onödigt och omöjligt?" *Internationella studier,* 1973.

Gopnik, Adam. "The Repressionists" *The New Yorker,* 14 July, 1997.

Grass, Günter. *Rede vom Verlust.* Göttingen: Steidl, 1992.

Gray, Richard T. and Sabine Wilke, eds. *German Unification and its Discontents: Documents from the Peaceful Revolution.* Seattle: University of Washington Press, 1996.

Greenfield, Liah. *Nationalism: Five Roads to Modernity.* Cambridge, Mass.: Harvard University Press, 1992.

Greider, Göran. "Jag tror på nationalstaten." *Kritiska Europafakta,* no. 26, 1993.

Grell, Ole Peter and Roy Porter, eds. *Toleration in Enlightenment Europe.* Cambridge: Cambridge University Press, 1999.

Groh, Dieter and Peter Brandt. *"Vaterlandslose Gesellen": Sozialdemokratie und Nation.* Munich: C.H. Beck, 1992.

Guerrier, Wladimir Iwanowitsch, ed. *Leibnez' Rußland betreffender Briefwechsel.* St. Petersburg and Leipzig, 1873.

Gunnarsson, Viviann and Marja Lemne. *Kommittéerna och bofinken: kan en kommitté se ut hur som helst?: rapport till Expertgruppen för studier i offentlig ekonomi (ESO).* Ds 1998:57. Stockholm: Fritzes, 1998.

Günther, Christian. *Tal i en tung tid.* Stockholm: Bonnier, 1945.

Gustafsson, Rolf, ed. *Köp och sälj, var god svälj? - vårdens nya ekonomistyrningssystem i ett arbetsmiljöperspektiv.* Stockholm: Arbetsmiljöfonden, 1994.

Gustavsson, Jakob. *The Politics of Foreign Policy Change, Explaining the Swedish Reorientation on EC Membership.* Lund: Lund University Press, 1998.

Gutmann, Amy and Dennis Thompson. *Democracy and Disagreement: Why Moral Conflict Cannot be Avoided in Politics, and What Should Be Done about it.* Cambridge, Mass.: Harvard University Press, 1996.

Habermas, Jürgen. "New Social Movements." In *Telos,* no. 49, 1981.

———— "Staatsbürgerschaft und nationale Identität: Überlegungen zur europäischen Zukunft" in Dewandre and Lenoble, eds., *Projekt Europa,* 1994.

Hadenius, Stig. *Sverige efter 1900.* Stockholm: Bonnier, 1967.

Hadenius, Stig, Torbjörn Nilsson, and Gunnar Åselius, eds. *Sveriges historia.* Stockholm: Bonnier, 1996.

Hafner, Sebastian. *The Rise and Fall of Prussia.* London: Weidenfeld and Nicholson, 1980; reprt. London: Orion Books, Phoenix Giant, 1988.

Hägerström, Axel. *Der römische Obligationsbegriff im Lichte der allgemeinen römischen Rechstanschauung.* Uppsala, 1927-1941.

Hall, Patrick. *The Social Construction of Nationalism: Sweden as Example.* Lund: Lund University Press, 1998.

Hall, Terence, James Farr, and Russel L. Hanson, eds. *Political Innovation and Conceptual Change.* Cambridge: Cambridge University Press, 1989.

Hallendorff, Carl. "Parlamentarismen." *Svensk Tidskrift,* 1911.

Hammar, Thomas. *Sverige åt svenskarna.* Dissertation, Stockholm University, 1964.

Hansen, Lene and Ole Wæver, eds. *European Integration and National Identity: The Challenge of the Nordic States.* London and New York: Routledge, 2002.

Hansson, Per Albin. *Demokrati.* Stockholm: Tiden, 1935.

_____ "Folk och klass." In *Tiden,* 1929.

_____ "Demokrati eller diktatur." In Per Albin Hansson, *Demokrati,* 1935.

_____ "Nordisk demokrati." In Per Albin Hansson, *Demokrati,*1935.

_____ "Land skall med lag byggas." In Per Albin Hansson, *Demokrati,* 1935.

_____ "Sprängpunkten." In Per Albin Hansson, *Demokrati,* 1935.

_____ "Tal till Sveriges flagga." In Per Albin Hansson, *Demokrati,* 1935.

_____ *Från Fram till folkhemmet. Per Albin Hansson som tidningsman och talare,* ed. Anna Lisa Berkling. Stockholm: Metodica Press, 1982.

Hansson, Sven Ove. *SAF i politiken. En dokumentation av näringslivets opinionsbildning.* Stockholm: Tiden, 1984.

Harrie, Ivar. *Tjugotalet in memoriam.* Stockholm: Hugo Gebers Förlag, 1938.

Harrington, Anne. "Metaphoric Connections: Holistic Science in the Shadow of the Third Reich." *Social Research,* vol. 62, no. 2, 1995.

Hatje, Ann-Katrin. *Befolkningsfrågan och välfärden.* Stockholm: Allmänna Förlaget, 1974.

Hazard, Paul. *La crise de la conscience européene.* Paris: Boivin, 1935-36.

Heclo, Hugh and Henrik Madsen. *Policy and Politics in Sweden: Principled Pragmatism.* Philadelphia, Temple University Press, 1987.

Hedin, Sven. *Det kämpande Tyskland.* Malmö: Dagens böcker, 1941.

Hegel, G.W.F. *Politischen Schriften.* Frankfurt: Suhrkamp, 1966.

_____ *Phänomenologie des Geistes.* In Hegel, *Gesammelte Werke.* Hamburg: Felix Meiner, 1968, IX. 295-296.

_____ *Philosophy of History.* Transl. J. Siberee, Vol. 32, London, 1878.

Heilbron, Johan et al., eds. *The Rise of the Social Sciences and the Formation of Modernity, Sociology of the Sciences Yearbook,* vol. 20, 1996. Dordrecht: Kluwer, 1998.

Hellmuth, Eckhart, ed. *The Transformation of Political Culture: England and Germany in the Late Eighteenth Century.* Oxford: Oxford University Press, 1990.

Henningsen, Bernd. "The Swedish Construction of Nordic Identity." In Sørensen and Stråth, eds., *The Cultural Construction of Norden,* 1997.

Henningsen, Bernd, Janine Klein et al., eds. *Tyskland og Skandinavia 1800-1914. Impulser og brytninger.* Deutsches Historische Museum, Nationalmuseum, Norsk Folkemuseum, 1998.

Herder, Johan Gottfried. *Reflections on the Philosophy of the History of Mankind.* Chicago: University of Chicago Press, 1968.

Herf, Jeffrey. *Reactionary Modernism: Technology, Culture and Politics in Weimar and the Third Reich.* Cambridge: Cambridge University Press, 1984.

Hillman, James. "Psychology, Self and Community." *Resurgence,* September/October 1994.

Hirdman, Yvonne. *Magfrågan. Mat som mål och medel Stockholm 1870-1920.* Stockholm: Rabén & Sjögren, 1983.

_____ *Vi bygger landet. Från Palm till Palme,* Stockholm: Tidens förlag, 1989.

_____ *Studier i svensk folkhemspolitik.* Stockholm: Carlssons, 1989.

_____ "Utopia in the Home," *International Journal of Political Economy, A Journal of Translations,* Vol. 22, No. 2, 1992.

_____ "Social Engineering and the Woman Question: Sweden in the thirties." In Clement and Mahon, eds., *Swedish Social Democracy,* 1994.

_____ "Women: from Possibilities to Problems: Gender Conflict in the Welfare State - the Swedish Model." Research Report No. 3. Arbetslivscentrum/The Swedish Center for Working Life, 1994.

_____ "Social Planning under Rational control: Social engineering in Sweden in the 1930s and 1940s," in Kettunen and Eskola, *Models, Modernity and the Myrdals,* 1998.

Hitler, Adolf. *Mein Kampf.* Transl. R. Manheim. London: Random House, Pimlico, 1992.

Höjer, Torvald T:son. *Svenska Dagbladet och det andra världskriget.* Stockholm: Almqvist & Wicksell, 1969.

Holt, J.C. "The Prehistory of Parliament" in Davies and Denton, eds. *The English Parliament in the Middle Ages,* 1981.

Horton, John and Susan Mendus, eds. *After MacIntyre.* Cambridge: Polity Press, 1994.

Huldt, Bo and Klaus-Richard Böhme, eds. *Horisonten klarnar.* Stockholm: Probus, 1995.

Huntford, Roland. *The New Totalitarians.* London: Allen Lane, The Penguin Press, 1971.

Iggers, Georg. *The German Conception of History: The National Tradition of Historical Thought from Herder to the Present.* Middletown, Conn.: Wesleyan University Press, 1968.

Jaspers, Karl. *Man in the Modern Age.* London: Routledge, 1951.

Jay, Martin. *The Dialectical Imagination.* Boston: Little, Brown and Co., 1973.

Jenkins, David. *Sweden: The Progress Machine.* London: Robert Hale, 1969.

Jensen, P.A. *Laesebog for folkskolen og Folkhjemmet.*1863.

Johannesson, Kurt. *Gotisk renässans: Johannes och Olaus Magnus som politiker och historiker.* Stockholm: Almqvist & Wiksell, 1982.

_____ *Heroer på offentlighetens scen: politiker och publicister i Sverige, 1809–1914*
(Stockholm: Tiden, 1987)

Johannsson, Alf W. *Per Albin och kriget.* Stockholm: Tiden, 1983.

_____ "Neutralitet och modernitet." In Huldt and Böhme, eds., *Horisonten
klarnar,* 1995.

_____ "Neutrality and Modernity." In Ekman and Edling, eds., *War
Experience, Self Image and National Identity, The Second World War as Myth
and History,* 1997.

_____ *Den nazistiska utmaningen.* Stockholm: Prisma, 2000.

Johansson, Anders L. *Tillväxt och klassamarbete - en studie av den svenska
modellens uppkomst.* Stockholm: Tiden, 1989.

Johansson, Folke, and Jörgen Westerståhl. *Kärnkraftsavvecklingen - ett politiskt
haveri.* Stockholm: SNS, 1998.

Johansson, Jan. *Det statliga kommittéväsendet: kunskap, kontroll, konsensus.*
Stockholm: Stockholm Univesity, 1992.

Källström, Staffan. *Värdenihilism och vetenskap.* Gothenbur: Acta Universitatis
Gothoburgensis, 1984.

Kälvemark, Ann-Sofie. *More Children of Better Quality? Aspects of Swedish
Population Policy in the 30s.* Stockholm: Almqvist & Wicksell, 1980.

Karacs, Imre. "Memoirs of an accidental mass murderer." *The Independent,*
13 August 1999.

Karlbom, Rolf. "Lång svensk folkstyrelsetradition," *Kritiska Europafakta,* no.
26. Gothenburg: Nej till EG, 1993.

Kedourie, Elie. *Nationalism.* London: Hutchinson, 1960.

Kelly, John Maurice. *A Short History of Western Legal Theory.* Oxford: Oxford
University Press, 1992.

Kermode, Frank. *The Sense of an Ending.* Oxford: Oxford University Press,
1967.

Kershaw, Ian. *The Hitler Myth: Image and Reality in the Third Reich.* Oxford:
Clarendon Press, 1987.

_____ *Hitler 1936-45: Nemesis.* London: Allan Lane, The Penguin Press,
2000.

Kettunen, Pauli and Hann Eskola, eds. *Models, Modernity and the Myrdals.*
Helsingfors: Renvall Institute Publications, 1998.

Key, Ellen. *Kärleken och äktenskapet: Livslinjer* (Stockholm: Albert Bonniers,
1911-1914

_____ *Folkbildningsarbetet: särskilt med hänsyn till skönhetssinnets odling. En
återblick och några framtidsönskningar* .Stockholm: Tiden, 1915.

Kjellén, Rudolf. *Politiska essayer.* Stockholm: Gebers, 1915.

Koblik, Steven. *Sweden's Development from Poverty to Affluence 1750-1970.*
Minneapolis: University of Minnesota Press, 1975.

_____ *The Stones Cry Out.* New York: Holocaust Library, 1988.

Koch, H. W. "Brandenburg-Prussia." In John Miller, ed. *Absolutism in Seventeenth Century Europe.* Basingstoke: Macmillan, 1990.

Kocka, Jürgen. "Assymmetrical Historical Comparison: The Case of the German *Sonderweg.*" *History and Theory,* vol. 38, February 1999.

_____ "German History before Hitler: The Debate about the German *Sonderweg.*" *Journal of Contemporary History,* vol. 23, 1988.

Kohler, Lotte and Hans Saner, eds. *Hannah Arendt/Karl Jaspers Correspondence, 1926-1969.* New York: Harcourt Brace Jovanovich, 1992.

Kohn, Hans. *The Mind of Germany.* New York: Harper and Row, 1960.

Kokk, Enn. "Världen, vi och Västeuropa." In Föreningen Laboremus, *Förändringens vind,* Stockholm: Rabén & Sjögren, 1962.

Kolakowski, Leszek. *"Fabula Mundi'* and Cleopatra's Nose." In Kolakowski, ed., *Modernity on Endless Trial,* 1990.

_____ *Modernity on Endless Trial.* Chicago: University of Chicago Press, 1990.

Koselleck, Reinhart. "Krise." In Brunner, Conze, and Koselleck, eds., *Geschichtliche Grundbegriffe,* 1982.

_____ *Futures Past: On the Semantics of Historical Time.* Cambridge, Mass.: MIT Press, 1985.

_____ *Critique and Crisis: Enlightenment and the Pathogenesis of Modern Society.* Oxford: Berg and Cambridge, Mass: MIT Press, 1988.

_____ "Volk." in Brunner, Conze, and Koselleck, eds., *Geschichtlische Grundbegriffe,* 1992.

Kramer, Jane. *The Politics of Memory. Looking for Germany in the New Germany.* New York: Random House, 1996.

Krieger, Leonard. *The German Idea of Freedom: History of a Political Tradition.* Chicago: University of Chicago Press, 1972.

Krokow, Graf von. *Preussen: Eine Bilanz.* Stuttgart: Deutsche Verlag-Anstalt, 1992.

Kushner, Tony. *The Holocaust and the Liberal Imagination. A Social and Cultural History.* Oxford and Cambridge, Mass.: Blackwell, 1994.

Kvinnoarbetskommitén. *Betänkande angående gift kvinnas rätt till förvärvsarbete* mm. [Report on the Right of Married Women to Work.] Stockholm: SOU 1938:47.

Lacoue-Labarthe, Philippe and Jean-Luc Nancy. "The Nazi Myth." *Critical Inquiry,* 1990.

Lagerlöf, Selma. *The Story of Gösta Berling.* Transl. Robert Bly. Karlstad: Karlstad Press, 1982.

Laqueur, Walter. *Young Germany: A History of the German Youth Movement,* New York: Basic Books, 1962.

Larsson, Sven-Erik. *Regera i koalition: den borgerliga trepartiregeringen 1976-1978 och kärnkraften.* Stockholm: Bonniers, 1986

_____ *Bertil Ohlin.* Stockholm: Atlantis, 1998.

Launay, Denise, ed. *La Querelle des Bouffons.* Geneva: Minkoff, 1973.

Lehnert, Detlef, and Klaus Meyerle, eds. *Politische Teilkulturen zwischen Integration und Polarisierung: zur politischen Kultur der Weimaren Republik.* Opladen: Westdeutscher, 1990.

Leibniz, Gottfried Wilhelm von. *Konzept eines Briefes an Schleiniz.* In Guerrier, ed., *Leibniz' Rußland betreffender Briefwechsel,* 1873.

Levine, Paul. *From Indifference to Activism. Swedish Diplomacy and the Holocaust 1938-1944.* Stockholm: Almqvist & Wicksell, 1996.

Lewin, Leif. *Bråka inte! Om vår tids demokratisyn.* Stockholm: SNS, 1998.

Liedman, Sven-Eric, ed. *The Postmodernist Critique of the Project of Enlightenment.* Amsterdam and Atlanta, Ga.: Rodopi, 1997.

Lieven, Anatol. "Qu'est-ce qui une Nation." *The National Interest,* no. 49, 1997.

Lindberg, Hans. *Svensk flyktingspolitik under internationellt tryck 1936-1941.* Stockholm: Allmänna förlaget, 1973.

Lindhagen, Jan, ed. *Bilden av Branting.* Stockholm: Tiden, 1975.

Lindström, Rickard. *Socialism, nation och stat.* Eskilstuna: Frihet, 1928.

Lindström, Ulla. *I regeringen. Ur min politiska dagbok 1954-1959.* Stockholm: Tiden, 1969.

Lipset, Martin. *Political Man.* London: Heinemann, 1983.

Lloyd, David. *Nationalism and Minor Literatures.* Berkeley: University of California Press, 1987.

Löfgren, Orvar. "Materializing the Nation in Sweden and America." *Ethnos* no. 3-4, 1993.

MacDonogh, Giles. *Prussia: The Perversion of an Idea.* London: Mandarin, 1994.

McGovern, William Montgomery. *From Luther to Hitler: the History of Fascist-Nazi Philosophy.* London: Harras & Co., 1946.

Machiavelli, Niccolo. *The Discourses of Niccolo Machiavelli.* Edited by Leslie J. Walker. London: Routledge, 1950.

MacIntyre, Alasdair. *Against the Self-Images of the Age: Essays on Ideology and Philosophy.* Notre Dame, Ind.: University of Notre Dame Press, 1971.

_____ *After Virtue.* Notre Dame, Ind.: University of Notre Dame Press, 1984.

Maktutredningen. *Demokrati och makt i Sverige.* Stockholm: Allmänna förlaget, 1990.

Mann, Golo. *The History of Germany since 1789.* London: Random House, Pimlico, 1996.

Mann, Thomas. *Thoughts in Wartime,* 1914.

Markusen, Erik, and David Kopf. *The Holocaust and Strategic Bombing. Genocide and Total War in the Twentieth Century.* Boulder: Westview, 1995.

Marx, Karl, and Friedrich Engels. *The Communist Manifesto.* New York: Appleton-Century-Crofts, 1955.

Mason, John Hope, and Robert Wokler, eds. *Political Writings.* Cambridge: Cambridge University Press, 1992.

Mathiopoulos, Margarita. *Das Ende der Bonner Republik.* Stuttgart: Deutsche Verlags-Anstalt, 1993.

Mayer, Jacob Peter. *Max Weber and German Politics.* London: Faber and Faber, 1944.

Mead, George. *Mind, Self and Society: From the Standpoint of a Social Behaviourist.* Chicago: Chicago University Press, 1964.

Meidner, Rudolf, AnnaHedborg, and Gunnar Fond. *Löntagarfonder.* Stockholm: Tiden, 1975.

Meinhold, Peter. *Geschichte der kirchlichen Historiographie.* Vol. 2. Freiburg; Alter, 1967.

Melberg, Arne. *Realitet och utopi.* Stockholm: Rabén & Sjögren, 1978.

Michalski, Krzysztof. *O kryzysie.* Rozmowy w Castle Gandolfo series, vol. II. Vienna: Instytut Nauk of Czlowieku; Warsaw: Respublica, 1985.

Micheletti, Michele. *Civil Society and State Relations in Sweden.* Aldershot: Avebury, 1995.

Mill, John Stuart. "Considerations on Representative Government." In Mill, *On Liberty and Other Essays,* 1991.

_____ *On Liberty and Other Essays.* Oxford: Oxford University Press, 1991.

Miller, John, ed. *Absolutism in Seventeenth Century Europe.* Basingstoke: Macmillan, 1990.

Millog, Michael. *Banal Nationalism.* London: Sage, 1995.

Milosz, Czeslaw. *Samlade dikter. 1931-1987.* Stockholm: Brombergs, 1988.

Moeller van den Bruck, Arthur. *Das dritte Reich.* Berlin, 1922; reprt. Hamburg: Hanseatische Verlagsanstalt, 1931.

Mohler, Armin. *Die konservative Revolution.* Darmstadt: Wissenschaftliche Buchgesellschaft, 1989.

Mommsen, Hans. "History and National Identity: The Case of Germany." *German Studies Review,* vol. 6, no. 1, 1983.

_____ "Die Realisierung des Utopischen." In Wippermann, ed., *Kontroversen um Hitler,* 1986.

Mommsen, Wolfgang. *Imperial Germany 1867-1918: Politics, Culture and Society in an Authoritarian State.* London: Arnold, 1995.

Montesquieu, Baron de. *De l'Ésprit des lois.* In his *Oeuvres complètes.* Paris: Seuil, 1964.

Mosse, George L. *The Nationalization of the Masses.* New York: Meridian Books, 1977.

_____ *The Crisis of German Ideology.* New York: Schocken, 1981.

_____ *German Jews Beyond Judaism.* Bloomington: Indiana University Press, 1985.

Myrdal, Alva. *Nation and Family: The Swedish Experiment in Democratic Family and Population Policy.* Stockholm, 1941; reprt. London: Kegan Paul, 1945.

_____ "Antisemitism är sjukdom." *Aftontidningen,* 14 April 1943.

Myrdal, Gunnar. "Socialpolitikens dilemma." Part II. *Spectrum,* 1932.

_____ "The population problem and social policy," Fall 1938, A.M. arkiv vol. 9, *Arbetarrörelsens Arkiv Stockholm 77.*

_____ *Hur styrs landet?* Stockholm: Raben & Sjögren, 1982.

_____ *Vägvisare.* Stockholm: Norstedts, 1998.

Nino, Carlos Santiago. *The Constitution of Deliberative Democracy.* New Haven: Yale University Press, 1996.

Norberg, Kathryn, and Philip T. Hoffman, eds. *Fiscal Crises, Liberty, and Representative Government, 1450-1789.* Stanford: Stanford University Press, 1994.

Nordström, Ludvig. *Lort-Sverige.* Stockholm: Kooperativa förbundets bokförlag, 1938.

North, Douglass C., and Robert Paul Thomas. *The Rise of the Western World: A New Economic History.* Cambridge: Cambridge University Press, 1973.

North, Douglass C., and Barry W. Weingast. "Constitutions and Commitment: The Evolution of Institutions Governing Public Choice in 17th Century England." *Journal of Economic History,* vol. 49, 1989.

North, Douglass C. *Institutions, Institutional Change and Economic Performance.* Cambridge: Cambridge University Press, 1990.

Oberndörfer, Dieter. *Der Wahn des Nationalen.* Freiburg: Herder, 1993.

Odhner, Clas Theodor. *Lärobok i fädnerslandets historia,* Stockholm: Nya tiden, 1902.

Offe, Claus. "New Social Movements: Challenging the Boundaries of Institutional Politics." In *Social Research,* vol. 52, no. 2, 1984.

Öhman, Berndt. *Om löntagarfondsfrågan och fondutredningen.* Högskolan i Örebro. Skriftserie 26, 1983.

Olivecrona, Karl. *Law as Fact.* Copenhagen: Munksgaard, 1939.

Oredsson, Sverker. *Lunds universitet under andra världskriget.* Lund: Lunds universitetshistoriska sällskap, 1996.

Orwell, George. *Nineteen Eighty-Four.* Harmondsworth: Penguin, 1989.

Österberg, Eva. *Mentalities and Other Realities: Essays in Medieval and Early Modern Scandinavian History.* Lund: University of Lund Press, 1991.

_____ *Folk förr: Historiska essäer.* Stockholm: Atlantis, 1995.

Oswald, Franz. "Integral and Instrumental Nationalism: National-Conservative Elite Discourse: The 'What's Right' Debate of 1994." *Debatte,* no. 2, 1995.

Paulston, Rolland G. *Educational Change in Sweden.* New York: Columbia University, Teachers College Press, 1968.

Paz, Octavio. "A Tradition against Itself." In Paz, *The Children of Mire,* 1974.

_____ *The Children of Mire: The Charles Eliot Norton Lectures, 1971-1972.* Cambridge: Harvard University Press, 1974.

Peukert, Detlev. *Inside Nazi Germany: Conformity, Opposition and Racism in Everyday Life.* New Haven: Yale University Press, 1987.

_____ *Max Weber's Diagnose der Moderne.* Göttingen: Vanderhoeck & Ruprecht, 1989.

_____ *The Weimar Republic: The Crisis of Classical Modernity.* London: Allen Lane, 1991.

_____ "The Genesis of the 'Final Solution' from the Spirit of Science." In Crew, *Nazism and German Society, 1933-45,* 1994.

Pflüger, Friedbert. *Deutschland driftet.* Düsseldorf: Econ, 1994.

Pois, Robert. *National Socialism and the Religion of Nature.* London: Croom Helm, 1986.

Polanyi, Karl. *The Great Transformation: The Political and Economic Origins of Our Time.* Boston: Beacon Press, 1957.

Pollock, Sheldon. "Deep Orientalism." MS, Collegium Budapest, 1998.

Pred, Allan. *Recognizing European Modernities: A Montage of the Present.* London: Routledge, 1995.

Prezzolini, Giuseppe. *Machiavelli anticristo.* Rome 1954; English transl., *Machiavelli,* New York: Farrar, Straus & Giroux, 1967.

Puhle, Hans-Jürgen, *Agrarische Interessenpolitik und preussischer Konservatismus im wilhelminischen Reich 1893-1914: Ein Beitrag zur Analyse des Nationalismus in Deutschland am Beispiel des Bundes der Landwirte und der Deutsch-Konservativen Partei.* Hannover: Verlag für Literatur und Zeitgeschehen, 1967.

Pulzer, Peter. *Germany 1870-1945. Politics, State Formation and War.* Oxford: Oxford University Press, 1997.

Putnam, Robert, Susan Farr, and, Russell Dalton. *What is troubling the Trilateral Democracies?* Princeton: Princeton University Press, 2000.

Raeff, Marc. *The Well-Ordered Police State: Social and Institutional Change through Law in the Germanies and Russia, 1600-1800.* New Haven: Yale University Press, 1983.

Rauschning, Hermann. *The Conservative Revolution.* New York: G. P. Putnam's sons, 1941.

Rials, Stéphane. *La Déclaration des droits de l'homme et du citoyen.* Paris: Hachette, 1988.

Richardson, Gunnar. *Beundran och frunktan.* Stockholm: Carlsson, 1996.

Ringer, Fritz. *The Decline of the German Mandarins.* Cambridge, Mass.: Harvard University Press, 1969.

Ringmar, Erik. *Identity, Interest & Action: A Cultural Explanation of Sweden's Intervention in the Thirty Years' War.* Cambridge: Cambridge University Press, 1996.

_____ "Nationalism: The Idiocy of Intimacy," *British Journal of Sociology,* no. 4, 1998.

_____ "Re-imagining Sweden, The Rhetorical Battle over EU-membership," *Scandinavian Journal of History,* vol. 23, 1998.

Roberts, Michael. *Gustavus Adolphus: A History of Sweden, 1611-1632.* Vol. 1-2. London: Longmans, Green & Co., 1953-58.

_____ *Essays in Swedish History.* London: Weidenfeld and Nicholson and Minneapolis: University of Minnesota Press, 1967.

_____ *The Swedish Imperial Experience: 1560-1718.* Cambridge: Cambridge University Press, 1979.

_____ *The Age of Liberty: Sweden, 1719-1772.* Cambridge, Cambridge University Press, 1986.

_____ "Swedish Liberty: in Principle and in Practice." In Roberts, *The Age of Liberty: Sweden, 1719-1772,* 1986.

Robertson, Ritchie. "From Naturalism to National Socialism." In Watanbe-O'Kelly, ed., *The Cambridge History of German Literature,* 1997.

Rokkan, Stein et al., eds. *Citizens, Parties, Elections.* Oslo: Scandinavia University Press, 1970.

Römer, Ruth. *Sprachwissenschaft und Rassenideologie im Deutschland.* Munich: Fink, 1985.

Rosenbaum, Ron. *Explaining Hitler.* New York: Random House and London: Macmillan, 1998.

Rosenberg, Göran. *Medborgaren som försvann.* Stockholm: Brombergs, 1993.

Roth, F., ed. *Schriften.* Berlin, 1823-43.

Rothstein, Bo. *Den korporativa staten, intresseorganisationer och statsförvaltning i svensk politik.* Stockholm: Norstedts, 1992.

Rousseau, Jean-Jacques. *Confessions.* Livre VI in Rousseau, *Œuvres complètes,* Bibliothèque de la Pléiade, Paris: Gallimard, 1959-95, I. 269.

_____ *Confessions.* Livre VIII in Rousseau, *Œuvres complètes,* Bibliothèque de la Pléiade, Paris: Gallimard, 1959-95, I. 384.

_____ *Emile.* Livre III in Rousseau, *Œuvres complètes,* Bibliothèque de la Pléiade Paris: Gallimard, 1959-95, IV. 468.

_____ *The Social Contract.* New York: Penguin, 1968.

Ruggie, John. "Territoriality and Beyond: Problematizing Modernity in International Relations," *International Organization,* vol. 47, no. 1, 1993.

Runcis, Maija. *Steriliseringar i folkhemmet.* Stockholm: Ordfront, 1998.

Runeby, Nils. Monarchia Mixta: *Maktfördelingsdebatt i Sverige under den tidigare stormaktstiden.* Uppsala: Studia Historica Upsaliensia, 1962.

Ruth, Arne. "The Second New Nation: The Mythology of Modern Sweden," *Daedalus,* vol. 113, no. 1, 1984.

Rydén, Värner. *Medborgarkunskap.* Stockholm: Nordstedt, 1923.

Ryner, Magnus. *Neoliberal Globalization and the Crisis of Swedish Social Democracy.* Working Paper SPS no. 98/4, Florence: European University Institute, 1998.

Samuel, Richard H. and R. Hinton Thomas. *Education and Society in Modern Germany.* London: Routledge and Kegan Paul, 1949.

Santner, Eric. "Traumatic Revelations: Freud's Moses and the Origins of Anti-Semetism." Paper presented at the conference "Communities in Peril: The History and Memory of Crisis in Germany and Scandinavia, 3-5 October, 1997, Instituto Europeo, Florence.

Schama, Simon. *"Der Holzweg:* The Track through the Woods." In Schama, *Landscape and Memory,* 1995.

_____ *Landscape and Memory,* London: Fontana, 1995.

Schiller, Friedrich. *Samtliche Werke.* 5 vol. Munich: C. Hanser, 1980-84.

Schmoller, Gustav. *Grundriss der allgemeinen Volkswirtschaftslehre.* 2 vol. Leipzig: Duncker & Humblot, 1900.

Schoeps, Julius H., ed. *Ein Volk von Mördern?: die Dokumentation zur Goldhagen-kontroverse an die Rolle der Deutschen in Holocaust.* Hamburg: Hoffman und Campe, 1996.

Scholem, Gershom. "Against the Myth of the German-Jewish Dialogue." In Scholem, *On Jews and Judaism in Crisis,* 1976.

_____ *On Jews and Judaism in Crisis: Selected Essays.* Ed. by Werner Dannhauser, New York: Schocken, 1976.

Schulze, Hagen. *The Course of German Nationalism: From Frederick the Great to Bismarck, 1773-1867.* Cambridge: Cambridge University Press, 1991.

_____ *States, Nations and Nationalism: From the Middle Ages to the Present.* Cambridge, Mass: Blackwell, 1996.

Schumpeter, Joseph A. *Capitalism, Socialism and Democracy.* New York: Harper Torchbooks, 1975.

Schwab, Raymond. *La Renaissance orientale.* Paris: Payot, 1950.

Schwilk, Heimo, and Ulrich Schacht, eds. *Die selbstbewusste Nation.* Frankfurt/M and Berlin: Ullstein, 1994.

Sen, Amartya. *Development as Freedom.* Oxford: Oxford University Press, 1999.

Sheehan, James. *German Liberalism in the Nineteenth Century.* Chicago: University of Chicago Press, 1978.

_____ "What is History? Reflections on the Role of the *Nation* in German History and Historiography." *Journal of Modern History,* vol. 53, March 1981.

Shirer, William. *The Rise and Fall of the Nazi Third Reich.* New York: Simon and Schuster, 1960.

Slagstad, Rune. *De Nasjonale strateger.* Oslo: Pax, 1999.

Sontheimer, Kurt. *Thomas Mann und die Deutschen.* München: Nymphenburger, 1961.

Sørensen, Øystein, and Bo Stråth, eds. *The Cultural Construction of Norden.* Oslo: Scandinavian University Press, 1997.

Sorokin, Pitrim. *The Crisis of our Age.* Oxford: Oneworld, 1992.

Spengler, Oswald. *Preussentum und Socialismus.* Munich: Beck, 1919.

Staël, Germaine de. *De la littérature considérée dans ses rapports avec les institutions sociales.* Paris: InfoMédia, 1998.

Steiner, George. *In Blackbeard's Castle: Some Notes Towards the Redefinition of Culture.* New Haven: Yale University Press, 1971.

Stern, Fritz. *The Failure of Illiberalism: Essays on the Political Culture of Modern Germany.* New York: Columbia University Press, 1992.

_____ *The Politics of Cultural Despair: A Study of the Rise of the "Germanic" Ideology.* Berkeley: University of California Press, 1961.

_____ "The Political Consequences of the Unpolitical German." In *History: A Meridian Periodical,* no. 3, 1960; reprt. in Stern, *The Failure of Illiberalism,* 1992.

Stråth, Bo. *Folkhemmet mot Europa.* Stockholm: Tiden, 1992.

_____ *Mellan två fonder. LO och den svenska modellen.* Stockholm: Atlas, 1998.

Stråth, Bo, ed. *Language and the Construction of Class Identities: The Struggle for Discursive Power in Social Organisation: Scandinavia and Germany after 1800.* Gothenburg: Gothenburg University, 1990.

Strindberg, August. *Gustaf Adolf.* Stockholm, 1889; reptr. Stockholm: Gernandt, 1900.

_____ *Svenska folket: i helg och söken, i krig och fred, hemma och ute eller Ett tusen år av svenska bildningens och sedernas historia.* 1882; reprt. Stockholm: Gidlunds förlag, 1974.

_____ "Svenska folket." In *Samlade skrifter,* vol 8, 1987.

_____ *Samlade skrifter.* Vol. 8. Stockholm: Bonniers, 1987.

Strindberg, Axel. *Bondenöd och stormaktsdröm: en historia om klasskamp i Sverige, 1630-1718.* Stockholm: Gidlunds, 1971.

Sundbärg, Gustav. *Det svenska folklynnet.* Stockholm, 1911.

Svanberg, Ingvar, and Mattias Tydén. *Sverige och förintelsen: debatt och dokument om Europas judar 1933-1945.* Stockholm: Arena, 1997.

Sveriges socialdemokratiska arbetarparti (SAP). *Framtid för Sverige: Förslag till handlingslinjer för att föra Sverige ur krisen.* Stockholm: Tiden, 1981.

Tallett, Frank. *War and Society in Early-Modern Europe, 1495-1715.* London: Routledge, 1992.

Talmon, J.L. *The Origins of Totalitarian Democracy.* New York: Praeger, 1960.

_____ *Political Messianism.* London: Secker & Warburg, 1960.

Thomasson, Richard F. *Sweden: Prototype of Modern Society.* New York: Random House

Tillich, Paul. *The Courage To Be.* New Haven: Yale University Press, 1952.

Tilton, Tim. *The Political Theory of Swedish Social Democracy.* Oxford: Clarendon Press, 1991.

Tingsten, Herbert. *Mitt liv: Mellan trettio och femtio.* Stockholm: Norstedt, 1962.

_____ *Demokratins problem.* Stockholm: Aldus/Bonnier, 1971.

Tocqueville, Alexis de. *The Old Régime and the French Revolution.* New York: Doubleday, 1955.

_____ *Democracy in America.* Indianapolis, Ind.: Hackett, 2000.

Todorov, Tzvetan. *Facing the Extreme. Moral Life in the Concentration Camps.* New York: Henry Holt, 1996.

Trägårdh, Lars. "Varieties of Völkisch Ideologies: Sweden and Germany 1848-1933." In Stråth, ed., *Language and the Construction of Class Identities,* 1990.

_____ "The Concept of the People and the Construction of Popular Culture in Germany and Sweden 1848-1933." Unpublished dissertation, University of California, Berkeley, 1993.

_____ "Statist Individualism: On the Culturality of the Nordic Welfare State." In Stråth and Sørensen, eds., *The Cultural Construction of Norden,* 1997.

_____ *Bemäktiga individerna: Om domstolarna, lagen och de individuella rättigheterna i Sverige.* SOU 1998:103. Stockholm: Fritzes, 1999.

_____ "Welfare State Nationalism: Sweden and the Spectre of 'Europe.'" In Hansen and Wæver, eds., *European Integration and National Identity,* 2002.

Uddhammar, Emil. *Partierna och den stora staten, en analys av statsteorier och svensk politik under 1900-talet.* Stockholm: City University Press, 1993.

Upton, Anthony F. "Sweden." In Miller, ed., *Absolutism in Seventeenth Century Europe,* 1990.

Vänsterpartiet. *Alternativ till Eu-medlemskap.* Stockholm, 1994.

_____ *Europeiska Unionen: Socialistiskt eller nyliberalt projekt?* Stockholm, 1994.

_____ *Frågor och svar om EU nr 2: Kvinnorna och EU.* Stockholm, 1994.

_____ *Program för en alternativ europapolitik.* Stockholm, 1994.

Voegelin, Eric. "The Origins of Totalitarianism." *The Review of Politics,* vol. 15, 1953.

Voltaire, François M. A. de. *Letters Concerning the English Nation.* London: C. Davis and A. Lyon, 1733.

Vonnegut, Kurt, Jr. *Slaughterhouse Five.* New York: Dell, 1969.

Vougt, Allan. *Ur svensk synvinkel.* Malmö: Aktiebolaget Framtidens Bokförlag, 1943.

Walker, Mack. *German Home Towns. Community, State and General Estate 1648-1871.* Ithaca: Cornell University Press, 1971.

Watanbe-O'Kelly, Helen, ed. *The Cambridge History of German Literature.*
 Cambridge: Cambridge University Press, 1997.

Wæver, Ole. "Identity, Integration and Security: Solving the Sovereignty
 Puzzle in EU Studies." *Journal of International Affairs,* vol. 48, no. 2,
 1995.

Wehler, Hans-Ulrich. *The German Empire, 1871-1918.* Leamington Spa,
 Warwickshire, UK and Dover, N.H.: Berg, 1985.

Weisz, Christoph. *Geschichtsauffassung und politisches Denken Münchener
 Historiker der Weimarer Zeit.* Berlin: Duncker und Humblot, 1970.

Werth, Christoph H. *Sozialismus und Nation. Die deutsche Ideologiediskussion
 zwischen 1916 und 1945.* Opladen: Westdeutscher Verlag, 1996.

Wigforss, Ernst. *Minnen.* Vol. III. Stockholm: Tiden, 1954

Williams, Emilio. *A Way of Life and Death: Three Centuries of Prussian-German
 Militarism. An Anthropological Approach.* Nashville: Vanderbilt University
 Press, 1986.

Wilson, Leslie A. *A Mythical Image: the Ideal of India in German Romanticism.*
 Durham, N.C.: Duke University Press, 1964.

Wippermann, Wolfgang, ed. *Kontroversen um Hitler.* Frankfurt/M:
 Suhrkamp, 1986.

Wippermann, Wolfgang. *Wessen Schuld: Vom Historikerstreit zur Goldhagen-
 Kontroverse,* Berlin: Elefanten, 1997.

Witoszek, Nina. "Stamsamhällets slut." In *Moderna Tider,* no. 108, 1999.

_____ "The Fugitives from Utopia: Scandinavian Enlightenment
 Reconsidered." In Sørensen and Stråth, *The Cultural Construction of
 Norden,* 1997.

Wittrock, Georg. "Gustaf Bondes politiska program." *Historisk Tidskrift,* 1913.

Wokler, Robert. "Projecting the Enlightenment." In Horton and Mendus,
 eds., *After MacIntyre,* 1994.

_____ "The Enlightenment and the French Revolutionary Birth Pangs of
 Modernity." In Heilbron et al., eds., *The Rise of the Social Sciences and the
 Formation of Modernity, Sociology of the Sciences Yearbook,* 20, 1996.

_____ "The Enlightenment Project and its Critics." *Pozna Studies* vol. 58,
 1997.

_____ "The French Revolutionary Roots of Political Modernity in Hegel's
 Philosophy, or the Enlightenment at Dusk," *Bulletin of the Hegel Society
 of Great Britain,* vol. 35, 1997.

_____ "The Enlightenment Project as Betrayed by Modernity." *History of
 European Ideas,* vol. 24, 1998.

_____ "Contextualizing Hegel's Phenomenology of the French Revolution
 and the Terror." *Political Theory,* vol. 26, 1998.

_____ "Ethnic Cleansing and Multiculturalism in the Enlightenment." In
 Grell and Porter, eds., *Toleration in Enlightenment Europe,* 1999.

_____ "The Enlightenment, the Nation-state and the Primal Patricide of Modernity." In Geras and Wokler, eds., *The Enlightenment and Modernity,* 1999.

Woods, Roger. *The Conservative Revolution in the Weimar Republic.* New York: St. Martin's Press, 1996.

Wyman, David. *The Abandonment of the Jews. America and the Holocaust, 1941-1945.* New York: Pantheon Books, 1984.

Zaremba, Maciej. *De rena och de andra.* Stockholm: Bokförlaget DN, 1999.

_____ "Skötesynden." *Moderna Tider,* May 1999.

Zetterberg, Hans. *Selected Writings.* Stockholm: City University Press, 1997.

Zetterberg, Kent "Den tyska transiteringstrafiken genom Sverige 1940-1943." In Stig Ekman, ed. *Stormaktstryck och småstatspolitik: aspekter på svensk politik under andra världskriget.* Stockholm: Liber, 1986.

Zittelmann, Rainer, Karlheinz Weißmann, and Michael Großheim, eds. *Westbindung: Chancen und Risiken für Deutschland.* Frankfurt/M and Berlin: Ullstein, 1992.

Index